Y0-DPI-693

By the same author

SUB-LIEUTENANT
NELSON'S CAPTAINS
ONE MAN'S MEAT
MURDER STORY *(play)*
TEN RILLINGTON PLACE
THE TRIAL OF STEPHEN WARD

Very Lovely People

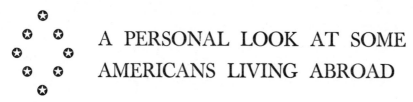

A PERSONAL LOOK AT SOME
AMERICANS LIVING ABROAD

by Ludovic Kennedy

SIMON AND SCHUSTER : NEW YORK

Published by Simon and Schuster
Rockefeller Center, 630 Fifth Avenue
New York, New York 10020

First printing

SBN 671-20205-7
Library of Congress Catalog Card Number: 71-84126
Designed by Irving Perkins
Manufactured in the United States of America
By H. Wolff Book Mfg. Co., Inc., New York

✪ TO THEM ALL

CONTENTS

7 Foreword

13 Prologue
NEW YORK : WASHINGTON

39 Part One LATIN AMERICA
COLOMBIA : BRAZIL : PARAGUAY

125 Part Two AFRICA
NIGERIA : LIBERIA

181 Part Three EUROPE
SCOTLAND : LONDON : PARIS : GERMANY

251 Part Four NEAR EAST AND MIDDLE EAST
ATHENS : ISTANBUL : JERUSALEM : SAUDI ARABIA : IRAN

359 Part Five FAR EAST
INDIA : THAILAND : VIETNAM : FORMOSA : JAPAN

 # FOREWORD

Mrs. Johnson and I are very happy to have you here, and we think you are all very lovely people.—PRESIDENT JOHNSON, *to White House visitors, January 1965*

THE IDEA for this book came to me when I was a reporter for the BBC's current affairs program "Panorama," between 1960 and 1963. Wherever I was sent in the world (and often it was to some very out-of-the-way places), there would invariably be a standard-bearer of Uncle Sam at the end of the trail: an AID man, a missionary, a salesman, a doctor, a bum. Two things struck me: first, how completely the Americans now filled the role once occupied by the British of the world's policemen, educators and bankers; and secondly, the extraordinary variety of those I met. It is unfortunate that the only Americans most non-Americans ever meet are GI's and tourists—the least representative, most boring and conformist of any country's ambassadors abroad. It is even more unfortunate, though perhaps inevitable, that they imagine all Americans are like that. I decided it would be fun, as a citizen of the country that had produced the old colonialists, to see how the new ones were doing and at the same time to show that not all Americans are the stereotypes so many think.

This book is the result. It is the distillation of some quarter of a

7

million words of notes, taken mostly on a world tour during 1965. A few of the events took place at a later date, and I have incorporated these into the narrative as they stand. Sometimes, and for obvious reasons, I have altered the names of people and places. The style of the book—visual descriptions followed by often quite long sequences of dialogue—unconsciously owes something to television practices with which I am familiar. I think, because of television, we are all much more receptive to dialogue in nonfiction writing than we were.

During the four years between my gathering material for the book and publication, the world's attitude toward America has perceptibly changed. In the early sixties America was what she had always been to many Europeans, a *nouveau riche* and somewhat naïve uncle surrounded by poor but better-bred relations who envied his wealth, resented his generosity and therefore continually belittled him. Now there is a healthier outlook. The Vietnam War and racial convulsions at home have shown America to be vulnerable and therefore human too; and those who formerly derided uncle now feel sympathy for him in his troubles and hope he will soon overcome them. It is the mood of the former rather than the latter time that is occasionally reflected in this book.

A very great many people have helped me in the preparation of the book, and I am grateful to them all, whether mentioned or not. Several big organizations kindly put their facilities at my disposal, in particular the U.S. State Department, the U.S. Sixth Fleet, the Agency for International Development, the Peace Corps, the Voice of America, the U.S. Army in Germany, MacV Command in Vietnam, Intercontinental Hotels, Hilton Hotels, Sikorsky Aircraft, the Arabian American Oil Company, the Coca-Cola Company, Careers Inc., and Pan American Airways. Countless individual Americans gave me generously of their time and thoughts. Mr. David Bruce, former American ambassador in London, and Lord Harlech, former British ambassador in Washington, did much to help pave the way. I owe a particular debt to Mr. Robin McEwen for reading the book in manuscript and making numerous suggestions which have improved it out of all recognition. I am also much obliged to Mr. Anthony Lewis, chief London correspondent of *The New York Times,* for the recommendations he made after reading the book in proof. Eileen O'Neill typed the manuscript with her customary zeal and accuracy, and both to her and to my wife I am indebted for many helpful comments. Lastly a cheer for my publishers, Mr. Hamish Hamilton in England and Mr. Peter Schwed in the United States, for having borne the long delay in delivery with such monumental patience.

LUDOVIC KENNEDY

My ardent desire is . . . to keep the United States free from political connection with every other country, to see them independent of all, and under the influence of none.—PRESIDENT WASHINGTON, *to Patrick Henry, October 9, 1795*

✪

Let every nation know, whether it wishes us well or ill, that we shall pay any price, bear any burden, meet any hardship, support any friend, oppose any foe, to assure the survival and the success of liberty.—PRESIDENT KENNEDY, *Inaugural Address, January 20, 1961*

✪

Prologue

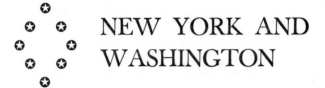 NEW YORK AND
WASHINGTON

It was Saturday morning in New York and Saturday afternoon in London; Saturday, January 30, 1965. I sat alone in the huge, empty dining room of the Yale Club, among the rows of bare wooden tables and chairs. The members had gone off for the weekend to Long Island and New Jersey, Texas and California, even Paris and Hawaii, leaving the place to me. Actually there were two of us there, myself in substance and, in the little box in the corner, David Brinkley in shadow. I was in his country and he in mine; but, while I was alone, he had half the world with him. For he was describing to his fellow Americans, direct from London, the last splendid journey of Sir Winston Churchill. He stood on a kind of raised platform in Fleet Street, and beneath him in the cold winter air the soldiers and sailors, statesmen and politicians rolled self-consciously by. I could see the steam from the horses' nostrils and hear the graveled bite of the moving feet; and it was still strange to think that one was seeing and hearing these things at the moment of their happening. The world had shrunk to a pinhead.

It had not been like that in Churchill's early days. Then there was no television or radio, and the telephone and motorcar were still in their infancy. People apart could communicate only by letter, and they often did so at prodigious length. Official letters were not only

15

written by hand but sometimes copied by hand too, for the typewriter was not yet in common use; and a reply to a letter sent to Australia in January would be lucky to reach London by May. To be sure, the train and steamship had speeded things up a bit, but in a hundred years the tempo of British daily life had hardly changed. On the throne there sat a lady of unmajestic proportions, whose regal manner and middle-class mind symbolized for her subjects the affluence and propriety of the age. Most, if not all, Britons had got the Queen they deserved. This spry and opinionated little matriarch was residual legatee of the largest property-grab organization the world had ever seen—a paradox on which future historians may ponder. The British Empire then encompassed a quarter of the globe, not only making the feats of Alexander and Xerxes shrivel in comparison, but enabling its possessors to boast, to the intense irritation of foreigners, that there was always some part of it on which the sun shone.

Every year thousands of dedicated young Englishmen, Scotsmen, Welshmen and Irishmen exchanged the comforts of home for a lifetime of service in faraway, romantic-sounding but often uncongenial places, to act as the Empire's protectors, administrators, bankers and developers. They went with a keen sense of adventure and mission, sure in their belief that the Queen and the Almighty together wanted them to bring enlightenment and salvation to those whom Rudyard Kipling, the Beowulf of the times, called lesser breeds without the law. They lived, many of them, in conditions that we would regard today as intolerable; and they and their wives and children suffered unflinchingly the scourges of sunstroke, typhus, cholera, yellow fever, gangrene, violence and, often, unexpected death. But it was suffering in, they believed, a good cause. They did what they had come to do, and on the whole they did it well. To many areas of darkness they brought order where there had been chaos, justice where there had been injustice, hygiene where there had been filth, and hope where there had been despair. They put an end to widow burning in India, cannibalism in Borneo, infanticide in Polynesia. They brought with them the idea of a loving God; they built roads and railways and hospitals and schools.

And yet, in many ways, their lives were a paradox. They extolled the virtues of parlimentary democracy but practiced instead a benevolent dictatorship. They told the natives they were there for the natives' own good, but whenever the latter showed they thought otherwise, they stamped on them with a quite surprising severity. Local leaders who propagated autonomy in their own affairs were known as "troublemakers" and were regarded as tiresome irrelevancies. "Those damned troublemakers are at it again. They're upsetting the natives, and it can't do any good." But in the end the troublemakers won through, as they had to, so that the political prisoners of the Empire became the political leaders of the Commonwealth: men like Nehru and Jinnah, Makarios, Kenyatta, Banda. The empire builders preach fair play, but exploited native labor ruthlessly; it was not to the indigenous that the first fruits of each newly developed country went, but to the hungry English manufacturers; and on these fruits England grew richer still. Native education, mostly the work of devoted missionaries, was encouraged so far but no further—too much learning would have been a dangerous thing. The colonists would have been incredulous and appalled had they been told, as the United Nations was recently told, that in terms of human potential they and the natives were equal; the only edge they had over them, and it was a big one, was two thousand years of Western civilization. "Johnny Native's a good enough fellow," they liked to say, "so long as you treat him right and see that he doesn't get too uppity. But you've got to tell him what to do. Leave him to his own devices and the poor chap doesn't know where he is." They genuinely believed that the native not only did not have but was innately incapable of ever having the ability for any post involving responsibility and decision. Any other belief would have threatened the entire fabric of the system to which they had devoted their lives.

Their social life was, as near as they could make it, a copy of the social life they had left in England. People who today criticize Americans abroad for living in enclaves and keeping up the American way of life either do not know or have forgotten that the old British imperialists practiced apartheid on a far grander and more elaborate scale. In many areas of administration, isolation was complete: there was the native quarter, the garrison quarter and the British resident's quarter; and between the first and the other two there was almost no communion at all. This was done less for reasons of security than of snobbery: in Victorian England one did not mix with those whom one regarded as one's social inferiors. Conversely, the Governors and proconsuls had no objection to hobnobbing with the princes and nabobs, whom many of them recognized as being a cut above them socially.

Within the British compounds the British way of life was faithfully carried on. In the bungalows that had been allotted to them the wives of majors and magistrates tried to provide their husbands with the familiar comforts of home. No matter what the heat or humidity, there was bacon and eggs for breakfast and roast beef on Sundays. Native dishes were shunned, less on grounds of taste than because no one knew where they had been, or who or what had gone into them. When the men were away the wives visited each other for tea and gossip, performed errands of mercy, did crochet work and petit point, read wholesome books, and sweated long hours in the sun with little packets of seeds—pansy and hollyhock and sweet william—to win from the stubborn soil the fragrance of an English garden. The men, as soon as they had a quorum, set up a club, manned by native servants but banned to native members, and here in the cool of the evening they sipped their Scotch and sodas, played billiards and snooker, and browsed through *Blackwoods Magazine* and old copies of *The Times*. Out of arid patches of scrub and rock they fashioned fields for golf and polo and cricket; and when they went out in the evening, they put on dinner jackets, as they might have done at home. The wig, the mace, the bat, the putter and porridge were some of the stranger legacies that Imperial Britain gave to an innocent and credulous world. In many places they are still to be found. In blazing India, for instance, almost as much porridge is eaten as in the whole of the British Isles.

At the top of this social pyramid was the viceroy or governor, regent of the Queen, and thus, in the eyes of those set under him, aglow a little with the magical mystique of monarchy. These latter-day proconsuls lived in style in miniature palaces, their paths eased by myrmidons of servants capped in turban or fez. When the Governor of Bombay drove from Government House to open the Poona races, he was escorted by two hundred Sikh outriders, all over six feet tall and caparisoned in scarlet and black. Many governors came from the great English country houses, and they simply carried on, if rather more formally, the sort of life they had lived at home. They made and received official calls innumerable; they shot and hunted and fished; they gave luncheon parties and dinner parties and balls; and on balmy tropical afternoons there would be china tea and cucumber sandwiches on the lawn. To be summoned to hospitality at Government House was the greatest treat that any colonial family could have. Many a young subaltern or district officer's wife waited anxiously for the rich, gilt-embossed invitation card; and, oh, the heartache when it failed to come or one's neighbor was asked to a more exclusive function than oneself.

The lower down the colonial social scale, the less satisfactory the relations between rulers and ruled. Little men whose authority over others in England had amounted to perhaps one ill-paid maid suddenly found themselves men of power. Often, out of ignorance and insecurity, they abused this power abominably and, as the saying went, treated the natives like dirt. But the governors set an example which those who wished could follow. They wore their authority lightly, with practiced ease; there was, after all, not much to choose between the tenants and servants of an empire and the tenants and servants of one's estate. They radiated self-confidence and well-being. As gentlemen they had been brought up always to keep their tempers and never to show their feelings about anything; and they did this so successfully that many foreigners wondered, and still do wonder, whether they *had* any feelings about anything. They never deliberately gave offense, and so it was impossible for anyone, even those who wanted to, to take offense against them. They were not perplexed, as some Americans are, by self-doubt; it never occurred to them to question the morality of the system they served. Had they done so, they would have been of little use in their jobs. "Wider still and wider," they sang on ceremonial occasions, "shall thy bounds be set." They thought not only that British imperial rule was the best system of government in the world, but that the world would be a much happier and more efficient place if it were run entirely by Englishmen. Then things would get done.

With some modifications, this Empire had remained in being for most of Churchill's adult life. Indeed, as late as 1940, in one of his most famous speeches, he could refer to the possibility of the Empire and Commonwealth lasting a thousand years. Even he could hardly have foreseen then that the Empire would be dead within his lifetime and the Commonwealth, a thin shadow of it, would soon wither too. The manner of its going had been typically British; like all the social revolutions with which we have had anything to do, it had been for the most part bloodless. We had seen the wind change direction early enough to set in motion the apparatus for relinquishing power. In one country after another elderly men in knee breeches and plumed hats watched the Union Jack come down, heard "God Save the King" played for the last time, and sadly packed their bags. They had gone out in state, in slow stately ships; now, in the twinkling of an eye, among film directors and advertising men and tourists, they were jet-propelled rudely home. Those who had given their lives to what they believed to be a great cause came back from the warm plains of India and Africa to the chill shires and windy towns of Britain, to an alien world of TV personalities and pop music and the credit squeeze, to a country that had already turned its back on them and their problems. The ease with which they absorbed themselves into modern British society says much for their adaptability and courage; but then it might be said these were the qualities which had made them good colonists in the first place. Thus, the twilight of the Empire coincided with the twilight of the life of its greatest leader. Through a glass darkly the old boy saw it all and understood it all, even if he didn't approve of it; for he, more than most, knew that the current of history is never still.

With our going we had created a vacuum, of men and money and skills. Had anyone come forward to fill this vacuum? Yes, the Americans had, those who had once been part of the British Empire themselves but had long since contracted out; who, when the Empire had been at its zenith, had stayed inside Fortress America and preached the virtues of sturdy isolationism. Imperceptibly, almost apologetically at first, later with increasing enthusiasm and sense of purpose, they had begun to spread themselves across the globe. Today, as any seasoned traveler knows, there is no corner of a foreign field that is not in part American; no mountain however high, jungle however deep, desert however wide, that there is not a GI, Peace Corps volunteer or missionary somewhere nearby. The world, often against its will, is going American, shopping in shiny supermarkets, wearing sweat shirts and jeans, eating hamburgers and ice cream, drinking Coca-Cola. These are the new gentlemen-adventurers of the day, imperialists without an empire, colonists without a colony, the self-appointed, sometimes reluctant, often abused, servants and masters of half the world. How were they making out? What were they doing? What did other people think of what they were doing? Soon I would see for myself.

The funeral cortege rumbled eastward, and the camera tilted up to show the great west front of St. Paul's, the sanctuary of Nelson, Wellington and other English heroes. The gun carriage neared the steps, and at the top the Queen awaited the arrival of her dead leader. David Brinkley said:

"And so the body of Sir Winston Churchill is taken to St. Paul's

Cathedral, whose onetime dean, the poet John Donne, wrote these words: 'No man is an island, entire of itself. Any man's death diminishes me, because I am involved in mankind. Therefore never send to know for whom the bell tolls. It tolls for thee.' "

The coffin was borne up the steps, the picture faded. It was an epitaph and, I hoped, an augury.

✪

BUT BEFORE I left, I thought I might see a few people whose knowledge or ideas might be useful to me. They lived mostly in tall skyscrapers, in offices of carpet and glass, with stunning views over the city. They were kind and welcoming, but seemed rather baffled at what I was proposing to do. "A Britisher writing about Americans? Well, what's the idea behind that?" Some said, jokingly, "Don't be too hard on us, will you?"

My first visit was to the new Pan Am Building, which rises like a headstone over the airy tomb of Grand Central station. My appointment was with Mr. Balas, the food and beverage manager of the Intercontinental group of hotels, with which Pan American Airways is associated. They had started, I was told, about the same time as Pan Am, with the object of providing American businessmen who couldn't stand Latin-American food, temperament or climate, with a congenial operating base in the Southern Hemisphere. Now there were hotels in twenty-nine countries, catering to more than a million guests a year, of whom at least 25 percent were American citizens. Mr. Balas, a cheerful, brisk man, said:

"Traveling is now a way of life, and we have to satisfy the demands of those who do it. No, we don't have a typical American menu any more. We used to have, but that was in the days when people got worried about getting diseases from the local food. Our customers don't seem to want so much American food now. They don't want French food either, because they find it too rich. Some of the local dishes in India and Africa are getting popular, though they're normally so hot we have to modify them. Chinese food is getting popular too. But I guess the standard type of food we have in most places now is the English type—roasts and grills and so on. They're *really* popular. That's a funny thing when you come to think of it," Mr. Balas said, "because many people say the English can't cook." He said this with such a winning smile that it was impossible to take arms against him.

"We buy our food," said Mr. Balas, "all over. We purchase beef from Australia, Ireland, Scotland. Vegetables we get locally wherever possible. In many places we have our own vegetable farms. Or sometimes we'll ask local farmers for specifications, and if they can oblige, we'll order their whole crop. We have frozen stuff only when there's no alternative. Another thing, we have our own filtering system in every hotel, so all our tap water is drinkable. In some *very* hot places we have ice water straight from the tap. Yes, we try and give our people the same kind of comforts they expect at home." As Mr. Balas was showing me to the door, he said, "You know what the secret of jet travel is today? It's not food or drink. It's taking it easy the day after you arrive. That way, you don't get sick. Nice to have met you."

★

Up Riverside Drive, on the west side of Manhattan, stands a large, austere stone building, which in another country might be mistaken for a hotel or a hospital or even a police headquarters. In fact it is the Interchurch Center, the clearinghouse and coordinating body for the work of America's many religious organizations. It employs 2,200 people, and much of their work is concerned with foreign missions. I had been told that there were some thirty-five thousand American missionaries living and working abroad, sponsored by nearly five hundred different agencies. In addition to the more orthodox agencies, these included the Air Mail from God Mission, Back to the Bible Mission, Door to Life Mission, Go-Ye Fellowship Inc., Harvesters International, Pillar of Fire Mission, Pocket Testament League, Self-Help Inc., and Things to Come Inc. I was making inquiries about missionary work in South America, the first area I was visiting; and a helpful man told me that an interdenominational meeting on that very subject was just starting, and I would be very welcome if I cared to come.

There were about a dozen people at the meeting, half a dozen in dog collars. One young minister with ginger hair was puffing at a huge cigar, which, to British eyes, gave him an air of slight rakishness. Another had a small Bible in front of him, and he glanced at it occasionally as though to quell rising doubts. There were two women, one a large middle-aged lady in a green hat, the other a secretary. They were all very friendly and relaxed, and they swapped ecclesiastical jokes. When the meeting was ready to begin, the secretary put a tape recorder on a spare chair and switched it on. She picked up the microphone and said, "Testing. One, two, three, four, five," and played it back. Then, in turn, we were asked to say who we were. Some people found this very shy-making, and tried to overcome their embarrassment by being funny; they weren't funny at all, but the others, especially those whose turn was to come, gave little forced laughs to put them at their ease.

The object of the meeting was to allow the assorted Baptists, Presbyterians, et cetera, present, to hear a report from Father Vermilion, a Roman Catholic priest, on an interdenominational conference on Latin-American missions that had just taken place in Chicago. Father Vermilion was a dark, smooth, energetic man with lots of black fur on his hands, especially the backs of his fingers. Aware that he was a stranger in a foreign land, that his audience's route to God was not his route, he determined to impress by the power of his personality. "First," he said, "I know you would all like to join with me in an expression of regret that Mr. Kantor, that fine young preacher, cannot be with us today. I was visiting with him last week, and he was telling me he was looking forward to this little gathering and meeting with you. Unfortunately, we heard only yesterday that he had been stricken with hepatitis." Somehow Father Vermilion made this sound like the plague, and there were murmurs of sympathy all round. "As many of you know," Father Vermilion went on, "Mr. Kantor—or Harry, as his friends know him—is a true witness in Christ [pause], a man respected by his Church [pause], by his family [pause], and by his community [pause], the kind of man who, in his own humble way, has helped to make America great. I'm sure we all wish him a speedy recovery." The audience nodded approval, and Father Vermilion passed to the Chicago conference. "At Chicago," he said, "we set the guidelines [pause], guidelines for the future [pause], guidelines for what I believe will be exciting and challenging work for Christ in the mission fields of Latin America." He raised one hairy hand upward. "At Chicago one of the first things we did was to establish joint workshops [pause], workshops on almost every aspect of Latin-American field work. I am happy to tell you that those workshops are in session right now [pause], and I don't doubt that they're having some real, down-to-earth discussions."

I didn't doubt it either. I could see them all at it, crowds of earnest and dedicated young men, pontificating away at each other for hours, grabbing hold of some minor point and worrying it to death, spending weeks and perhaps months reaching conclusions that a few informed, intelligent men could arrive at in a matter of days. The growth of the workshop in American life has always seemed to me an extension of Parkinson's Law—that work expands not only according to the number of people available to do it, but in proportion to the amount of money available to support it. In America there are many political, cultural and religious organizations that have more money than they know what to do with; for them, workshops and people to put into workshops are the answer.

Some of Father Vermilion's more histrionic moments were punctured by late arrivals. When Father Hooter showed up, the only chair left was the one supporting the tape recorder. The recorder was put on the table, Father Hooter sat down, and someone said gravely, "Man has taken the place of the machine." The meeting was full of jokes like that, and the machine recorded them all. When Father Vermilion was through, which took quite a time, the meeting was open for comments. Most people rang tinkling variations on the theme of church unity. One minister spoke of the difficulties for missionaries of what he called "professional orientation," and Father Vermilion said that one of the workshops was taking care of that. The lady in the green hat said, "What we have to teach the people of Latin America is citizenship responsibility. We have to help them to strive toward a better life." She said this more than once. No one seemed inclined to question whether the Latin Americans *wanted* citizenship responsibility or a better life, or indeed, what was meant by "better." Father Vermilion, as you might expect, had the last word. "What we have to do," he said, clenching two hairy fists to the side of his head as though he had earache, "is open the minds of these people to Christ [pause]. That is the task before us."

The tape recorder was switched off, the meeting ended. Now some secretary would have to spend a day transcribing it all, including the jokes, and then another day typing, copying and circulating it. But who was going to wade through it all, and what possible benefit would they gain from it? It had been a jolly, friendly meeting, nice ecumenically too, at which not a memorable word had been said. Lucky Mr. Kantor, I thought, to be stricken with hepatitis.

✪

DOWN ON West Fortieth Street, in an area which is not on any tourist's map and is not likely to be, are the offices of the National Association for the Advancement of Colored People. I had an appointment with Dr. Mansell, the Secretary, at eleven o'clock, but he wasn't there. So I spent a profitable fifteen minutes outside the elevator looking at a huge plaque on which were inscribed the names of those who had given the NAACP five hundred dollars or more; people like Lena Horne and Alan Paton, whom you'd expect, and the Aga Khan, whom you wouldn't, not to mention the Moles, the Minks, and the Chums, and the Hands of Love and Benevolence.

Dr. Mansell came out of the elevator and took me to his office. It was a modest, homey place; there were the usual posters and certificates on the wall, and a photograph of two ducks deep in conversation. I asked Dr. Mansell about Negro representation in government and private institutions abroad, but he couldn't get more than a couple of sentences out before being interrupted. "I'd say there'd been a substantial improvement in Negro representation in the last ten years, but—oh, excuse me, will you?" A colored secretary came in, wearing glasses and a purple blouse. "Ben Whitehorn is on the line, Dr. Mansell. Will you take it?" Dr. Mansell said, "Okay, Miss Jones. Excuse me, will you? Hullo, Ben?" I read the posters and certificates and looked at the ducks. "Okay, Ben, I'll see you. . . . Well, as I was saying, Mr. Kennedy, the position's better than it used to be, but there are still too many organizations which only have *token* Negro representation. Of course, one of the difficulties is that there are so few Negroes educationally prepared for high executive positions. But that's something we're looking into. Another of our problems is that so many foreigners have a totally false impression of—yes, Jim, what is it?" A tall shambling Negro stood in the doorway. "All right if I go down to the drugstore for fifteen minutes?" Dr. Mansell said, "Okay, Jim." Jim said, "Betty'll be around," and Dr. Mansell said, "Okay, okay. . . . Yes, Mr. Kennedy, we get foreigners coming here or writing to us here and saying, 'Well how about all these Negro lynchings in the streets of New York?' So we have to lean over backward to help them get the record straight. 'You mean you don't *have* any lynchings in New York? The Negro's treated pretty good then? So what's all the fuss about?' Well, then we have to start at the beginning, and tell them what *is* wrong, but we've upset their beliefs and they're not so interested." I told Dr. Mansell that I had just read two articles by American Negroes on the question of affinity with African Negroes. One article said that there was a sense of affinity, the other that there wasn't. Dr. Mansell said, "Well, certainly there's *some*. After all, we're branches of the same tree. But perhaps not as much as some American Negroes would like to think. There is an interesting problem though, and that is—oh, pardon me." A buzzer sounded on Dr. Mansell's desk and he picked up a telephone. He spoke for a few moments and then waited for someone else to come on the line. While he was waiting, a very old, bent, white man shuffled through the office, in one door and out the other. He looked about a hundred. Dr. Mansell whispered to me, "That's our President. He's a great old guy." He finished his conversation and said, "Yes, it's the problem of Negro representation in diplomatic posts in Africa. *We* want the Africans to see as many American Negroes in these posts as possible, because they're a living refutation of all the propaganda that's been put out about Negro underprivilege, and we have to do what we can, in a responsible way, to point out where it is. Then, the Africans on their part don't want to be made to feel that Africa is becoming a sort of repository for Negro diplomats. After all, the Israelis wouldn't be too pleased if we staffed our embassy in Tel Aviv with nothing but Jews. It's a tricky problem, you see, a question of balance. But if you're going to Africa, Mr. Kennedy, as I understood you to say, then you'll be able to assess the situation and come to some judgment on it yourself. Excuse me."

The girl with the purple blouse was at the door again. Her mouth was already open, but I beat her by a short breath, thanked Dr. Mansell for letting me see him, and left. Waiting for the elevator, I noted that other five-hundred-dollar subscribers to the NAACP were the Grand Lodge of Louisiana, the International Hod Carriers Association, and the Paragon Girls Club.

✪

Mr. Herbert Bonner, of *Reader's Digest,* had an office in one of the new skyscrapers, halfway to the cumulus. It was a corner office, so we could see over most of New York. Mr. Bonner was a smallish, middle-aged man, very friendly and outgoing and articulate. He said that he had previously worked with Hilton Hotels, and that they and Intercontinental Hotels were having a tremendous impact on the countries where they were established. "The people see these hotels as symbols of American power and wealth, and believe they will bring in American businessmen and money."

Reader's Digest overseas, said Mr. Bonner, sold ten million copies in thirteen languages in more than a hundred countries. They employed a foreign staff of over five thousand, of whom, astonishingly, only four were American citizens. (Time and again in my researches into American enterprises abroad, I was told of the tiny proportion of American-born staff.) "For those of us who work in *Reader's Digest,*" said Mr. Bonner, "it's a kind of religion. Yes, I know what the cynics say. They say that *Digest* articles are only about good people doing good things, that everything's too pat, that it's an untrue reflection of life as it is. Well, maybe that's true. What we're trying to do is not show life as it *is* so much as life as it *can* be, to create hope in people's minds instead of despair. And whether the cynics like it or not, it's proved to be a very successful formula."

Was there any guiding philosophy behind the magazine? Mr. Bonner said, "No, I wouldn't say so. We're pro-Christian and anti-Communist, but we're not alone in that. The only dictum we have is that articles should be of universal and lasting interest, expressed in the simplest possible language." Mr. Bonner said that there were thirty-two articles in each issue, of which sixteen were original commissions by *Digest* editors, and sixteen were taken from other magazines. Of the second sixteen, eight were originally commissioned by the other magazines and eight first planted in the other magazines by *Reader's Digest,* and then digested back, or regurgitated, for the *Digest.* Incestuous cannibalism, I thought, could hardly go any further.

I asked Mr. Bonner how he had become so interested in the *Digest.* He said:

"I read it as a child, and it affected me deeply. I wonder how many others, perhaps without knowing it, got their sense of decency and justice and fair play originally from the *Digest*. I feel that the individual in the world right now is fighting a losing battle, and the *Digest* helps him to believe that his cause is not lost. That's why we have so many articles about personal achievement, to show what the individual can do *in spite* of all the difficulties in his path. Mr. Kennedy, *Digest* is not for intellectual people. It's not for sophisticates. It aims to make complex issues articulate, and if at times the articles appear a little superficial, at least the reader's been given some idea of the subject instead of none. If he's really interested in it, he can go to his local library and read some more.

"In a way," said Mr. Bonner, "it's a sort of mass education. It's a force for good. That's why those of us who work in it believe in it so much."

✪

"FOR MANY of us who work in Coca-Cola," said Mr. Preston Stephens, the sales manager, "it's gotten to be almost a religion." I had expected the Coca-Cola offices to be at the top of the grandest skyscraper of them all. In fact they were in quite an old-fashioned building up on Madison Avenue, and the offices themselves were rather dingy, like those of an old, established law firm that feels no need to keep up with the times. Mr. Stephens was a Southerner with one of those rich, pumpkin-pie accents at which Britishers never cease to marvel. With him was Mr. Laurence Gardiner, the public-relations manager, who had been kindness itself ever since I arrived in New York, sending me books about Coca-Cola and books not about Coca-Cola, and Coca-Cola itself and offers of tickets to the theater. Many public-relations men are brisk, slick creatures with smooth suits and shiny shoes and gray ties, flowers in their buttonholes, and an ever-ready line of patter. Mr. Gardiner was none of these. He dressed, one felt, to please himself, and he had a creased kindly face which somehow made him sad, as though the very thought of serving an empire so vast weighed heavily on his mind.

"The basic facts about Coca-Cola," said Mr. Gardiner, "are that eighty million bottles are sold a day,* and that there are two thousand bottling plants in one hundred thirty countries. But the Coca-Cola

* Now 100 million bottles (1969).

organization doesn't own any of these. All we own are the regional and area offices, and of course the concentrate, which, as I daresay you know, is a very closely guarded secret. Many of our competitors have tried to reproduce it themselves, and all have failed. We do everything on a franchise basis. Less than one percent of our employees abroad are Americans."

"If I might just explain the franchise," said Mr. Stephens, "when Coca-Cola goes into a new area we invite bids for the franchise. You've no idea of the competition there is to get it, and of course we make the closest possible investigation into the credentials of those who apply. Happily, a Coca-Cola franchise is so valuable that it inevitably attracts the best type of businessman. People are knocking at the door for our franchises all the time."

"There is no place in the world," said Mr. Gardiner, "where Coca-Cola has been rejected, though in some countries we've had to wait a little longer to get in than in others. That's because local industries, like the wine trade in France and the beer companies in Denmark, have worked to keep us out. They thought—wrongly, as it proved and as we said—that we would be taking business away from them. We got into Turkey just the other day. Portugal and Greece are still holding out on us, but we'll get in there too in time."

How did Coca-Cola set about opening up new areas? How did they persuade people who had never set eyes on it before to start drinking the stuff?

"Our slogan," said Mr. Stephens, "is 'Within an arm's length of desire.'" It sounded to me a better slogan for a brothel. "First, we do a survey—what we call a walking survey. We send along a team of men on foot, and they count—yes actually count—the number of houses in the new area, who lives in them, and what their Coca-Cola potential is likely to be. When we've done that, we don't start selling right away. We give out free samples—cases of them. We do this on what we call a repetition basis; that is, we go on giving it away until the people have developed a real taste for it. Then we send in a group of salesmen, specially schooled in courtesy and decent dealing, to take firm orders. By that time, of course, we have a ready-made market." Mr. Stephens sounded like a drug pusher describing how to hook junkies. "Of course, we throw a lot of money away with the free samples," he said, "but we reckon to get it all back in the end."

Mr. Gardiner said, "Where are you going on your travels?"

"South America first, and then Africa."

"We have some very interesting franchises in Africa, and we're getting a lot of cooperation from the local chieftains. In one place the Emir of Kano has the bottling rights. In some of the remoter villages the bottler has to take a movie with him and show it on the schoolhouse wall. It's about the only practical way of selling the stuff. Are you going to Nigeria?"

"Yes."

"We have a regional office there and a bottling plant. Our manager there is Mr. Alex Parissis, a very go-ahead man. I'll write and tell him you're coming."

✪

MR. WALTER B. WRISTON, president of the First National City Bank of New York, worked in an office that Coca-Cola might have coveted. I came out of the elevator to find myself in a vast carpeted room, in which perhaps a hundred people sat typing or writing at little desks, spaced out in neat orderly ranks, like rows of spring potatoes. A cool, pretty secretary led me to one end of the room, where there was a table and magazines and smart chairs. "Mr. Wriston is engaged right now," she said, "but if you'll kindly wait here, he'll see you in just a few minutes." She was, like most American secretaries, poised, efficient, friendly, and totally impersonal; I knew she didn't give a damn whether I lived or died. Presently some men came out of Mr. Wriston's office, and I went in.

Mr. Wriston not only was tall, dark, handsome and impeccably dressed, but radiated such intellectual vigor and inner confidence that I felt quite overawed by his presence. "Sit down, Mr. Kennedy," he said, motioning me to a chair, "and tell me what I can do for you." He gave the impression of a tremendously occupied man who had nevertheless found it possible to set aside twenty minutes of his valuable time and, during this twenty minutes, would give me his undivided attention. Most busy and successful men manage to do this. But my trouble was that I had come unbriefed, and I suddenly felt an aching need, as perhaps Mr. Wriston did, for a neat list of pointed questions.

I outlined in a general way what I was proposing to do, and Mr. Wriston said, "I trust you are not going to write another *Ugly*

American? That was an *extremely* inaccurate book." He was the first of many hundreds of Americans to ask me the same question. This book has made more of an impression on more Americans than I would have thought possible. Whether the stories in it are true, or even typical, thousands of Americans believe they are; for them, Messrs. Burdick and Lederer have unlocked dark cupboards in their minds, and pulled out and rattled skeletons of which they are most afraid. No, I said, I was going off without prejudice of any kind; I would simply report what I saw.

"During the last twenty years," said Mr. Wriston, "there has been a complete revolution in the role of the American abroad. Before then, the American who went abroad didn't know the language of the country, didn't want to know it, kept to his own people, and to all intents and purposes was *dead*. Well, that's all changed." He pointed through the door to the rows of desks stretching away beyond one's vision. "Last year alone two thousand hours of foreign languages were taught on this floor. In addition another five thousand hours of languages were taught to our people abroad. I would no more dream of sending one of our men abroad without his learning the language of the country he was going to than I would of flying to the moon." He added, "The kind of people we are now sending abroad are a quite different type of people from those who want to work here in the States. They have a real desire to serve not only the bank, but their country as well. They are extremely high-class and dedicated people. I am proud of them all."

He sounded like a general talking about his troops. I asked about the extent of the bank's activities overseas. He said, "We have the largest overseas business of any bank in the United States, but we don't want to reveal the breakdown, so we don't publish the figures. What I *can* tell you is that we employ more than eight thousand people in one hundred sixteen offices in forty countries. Less than four per cent of these are American citizens. Our objectives are threefold: to help exports and imports, to finance local industry, and to bring American technology to banking methods."

I asked Mr. Wriston how American banking technology differed from other banking technology; and he said, "We believe in the theory of cash flow. Most banks will loan money against visible assets. What we do is loan money against invisible assets. If a man wants a big overdraft, has good prospects but few visible assets, we investigate his position in depth, grant him a loan if we get a good report on him, then set up a situation for him whereby he can repay the loan and become solvent."

I said, wasn't that what most banks did? Mr. Wriston said, "Not anything like to the same degree. In Britain, now, you still have the greatest liquid-money market in the world. But your banks are slower in responding to financial needs than we are. We make six hundred thousand loans a year in the city of New York alone. We have a million people go out of debt every year. We have practically driven the United States Post Office out of the savings business. Why, we even make loans to college students who we know can't pay for six months." Mr. Wriston got up and led me to the door. "What we do, Mr. Kennedy," he said, "is give service."

With Mr. Wriston in charge, I didn't for a moment doubt it. It was what he had given me for twenty minutes.

✪

WHEN IT was time to leave for Washington, it was snowing hard, and the airport had closed down. So I took the train. Penn Station was rebuilding, and the redcap who took my bags along with those of a lady from Buffalo said that we would have quite a walk. We had a half-mile marathon; up ramps, down ramps, into elevators, out of elevators, round pillars (sometimes *into* pillars), through tunnels, out of tunnels, all over. Sometimes the redcap told us to go one way while he went another; he said we would meet up, and we did, though *how* we did was a mystery. When we reached the train, the lady from Buffalo asked how much she should give the redcap. My feeling, in view of all the exercise we'd had, was that he ought to give us something; but I said, how about a dollar? The redcap said, "Five pieces at a quarter a piece is one dollar and twenty-five cents. Thank you, ma'am." I had three cases and gave him a dollar; he didn't give me any change.

The train to Washington was pretty crowded. I went along to the club car and found myself next to a delightfully tight man of about fifty with sandy hair and a Hitler mustache. "My name's Pitman," he said, "and I'm in adult education. I arrange workshops and seminars and things all over the country. Christ, how I hate it. This is Mother." Mrs. Pitman was a large spreading blonde. She was holding a newspaper and a pencil, and she said, "Barnyard fowl. Eight letters." Mr. Pitman said, "Mother's produced three daughters. They're all married and have children. Christ, are they prolific!" He sipped at his drink. "Mother and I are on our way home. We went to New York last night to see *Hello Dolly*. Isn't that a great show? Isn't that something?" I said I had found it so boring I had come out halfway through. "Oh, we didn't find it boring at *all*," said Mr. Pitman, "did we Mother?" Mrs. Pitman said, without looking up, "It was lovely, just perfectly lovely." Mr. Pitman said, "Oh, we both thought it was just *great*."

Mr. Pitman looked around and noticed a man in a blue suit who had sat down beside us. "This man looks like Faulkner," said Mr. Pitman. The man looked embarrassed. "My *God*," said Mr. Pitman, "he *is* Faulkner."

Mrs. Pitman said, "Honey, Mr. Faulkner's dead; you know that"; and to me, "What's 'Alcoholic refreshment' in five letters?" I said, "Scotch?" and Mrs. Pitman said, "No, that's six."

Mr. Pitman said, "Do you know where this man's going? He's going to Hickory, North Carolina, to get better. Do you know how many people are in Hickory? Forty-eight. That's right, forty-eight. Christ, there's nothing else to *do* in Hickory but get better. He can't miss." His mind went off at a tangent, and he said, "Our eldest girl married a young Jewish boy. He hasn't got a thing. But he's a real doll."

Mrs. Pitman said, "*E, F,* blank. Salamander."

"What do you mean, *E, F,* blank, salamander?" said Mr. Pitman, and the man who looked like Faulkner said, "I think it's *eft,* which is a kind of newt."

"Well, my, aren't you clever?" said Mrs. Pitman. Mr. Pitman said, "Noot? Who said anything about a noot? You're crazy. I'm going to wee-wee."

He got up and lumbered off down the corridor. Mrs. Pitman put down her pencil and said, "I love Gordon, though his mother was a nut. We have three beautiful children. My second daughter's blind— did he tell you? She's just the loveliest creature in the world. Both her sisters are pregnant right now, and boy, are they jealous of her figure! My youngest is a joy, too. She's been borrowing the car Tuesday nights. She wouldn't say where she was going for a long time, and then last week we finally got it out of her. She's been going to give extra coaching to some of the backward colored kids. Now that the schools are integrated, the backward ones can't keep up unless they have extra coaching. Isn't that just wonderful?"

Mr. Pitman came back, and Mrs. Pitman said, "Honey, that was a real good idea you had there"; and she got up and teetered down the train. Mr. Pitman yawned and said, "Oh, boy!" He looked as though he had sobered up a bit. He said to me, "You know, you were right about that *Hello Dolly* thing. I thought it was a load of horseshit." I said, "Why didn't you say so?" He said, "Well you can't, can you? Not in public. Not about a big hit like that. Besides, it would have upset Mother."

✪

WASHINGTON AFTER New York is like Edinburgh after Glasgow, Delhi after Bombay, Ottawa after Toronto. These cool colonnaded capitals march at their own tempo, giving space to talk, time to think, room to breathe.

And, for me, everywhere there was the presence of Kennedy. He had been dead now for over a year, amoldering in his grave at Arlington across the river, but still his ghost lingered. He had made this city his own, as a king does, so that it was hard to believe that it no longer belonged to him. More than some, I had been unable to bring myself to accept his death. Only the week before in New York, his sister-in-law Lee Radziwill had taken me to a small dinner party given by Mrs. Kennedy in her apartment. It was an unexpected pleasure and honor, but through the evening I felt pierced by the pain of his absence, at times overwhelmed with despair.

I had seen him first at the Democratic National Convention at Los Angeles in 1960, which I was covering for television for the BBC. As an ardent Adlai Stevenson supporter, I had found it difficult to shift my allegiance; besides, American political intellectuals in the European mold are rare. But from the time of his acceptance speech right through to election night, I had watched his progress with growing admiration and excitement. During the election I spent a week on Nixon's campaign train, and had to listen to perhaps six or eight of his speeches a day. They did not wear well. They were repetitive. They revealed an undistinguished mind. Kennedy's speeches, on the other hand, seemed to grow in stature and statesmanship as the campaign wore on. Indeed, during his brief political life the man seemed to go on growing and developing every day. He had many qualities: style and authority and dignity and wit; youth and breeding; but above all, perhaps, perception, and with perception, understanding. Those unique, restless eyes took in everything; there was, one felt, no facet of American life, however recondite or sleazy or obscure, that escaped him. Whether history will consider him a great or even a good President, it is too early to tell; but he certainly had that elemental quality which the great men of history have always had, an amalgam of courage and compassion, wisdom and humility, stubbornness and flexibility. And above all of love. It was love that these men inspired in others, that enabled them to take others by the hand and lead them where they wanted. And the apogee of this love was manifest in their deaths. Kennedy at his death was mourned as Nelson and Lincoln had been before him, as Churchill was to be after him. I could go now unerringly, as thousands of others could, to the exact spot where I first heard the news; to the stretch of highway near Greenford, Middlesex, where on the car radio I heard that he was dead. Of whom else can this be said? Though I was alone, I said aloud: "Oh, no!" It was as though a beloved brother had gone, not a stranger one had met once.

Not that our meeting is one I am ever likely to forget. It was in June 1961, and he and his wife were briefly in London after meetings with Khrushchev in Vienna and de Gaulle in Paris. They were to leave the Radziwills' house in Buckingham Place shortly after 8 P.M. to drive round the corner to have dinner with the Queen. At that time of evening the BBC current-affairs program *Panorama* was on the air, and as one of the commentators I was asked to wait in the street until the President appeared, and then put a couple of questions to him. This was a big operation to mount for perhaps only a couple of minutes' screen time, and we had no idea whether the President would be agreeable; but if he was, it would be the only television interview given by him in Britain.

I got down to Buckingham Place at about 6 P.M., and soon after, a number of guests began streaming out of the Radziwills' house. They had been to the christening of the Radziwills' baby, to whom the President had become godfather. While Stas Radziwill, whom I know, was saying goodbye to the last of the guests, he caught sight of me and invited me over. I explained why I was there. He asked if the President was aware of our plans, and I said I thought not yet, although the BBC had been in touch with the White House press office all day. "Then," said Stas, "you had better come in and ask the President yourself."

He opened the door of the house and led me in. I suppose, if I had thought about it, I had expected the President to be in some upstairs room, dictating perhaps, conferring with advisers, in some way *busy*. What I had not expected was to find him, as I did, in the entrance hall to the house, squatting on a little stool or small chair and reading what appeared to be the cricket scores in the *Evening Standard*. On the other side of the fireplace sat his wife, deeply beautiful, on another small chair, reading a different section of the same paper.

Stas said, "Jack, I'd like you to meet a friend of mine, Ludovic Kennedy. The BBC want him to ask a question of you on the way to dinner." The President put down the *Evening Standard,* got up and shook hands. I had an extraordinary urge to bow, but checked myself. He looked at me with those searching eyes and then he said, "I'm sorry, I didn't quite catch your name." I said, "It's the same as yours, sir, but my Christian name is Ludovic." Now remember that this man had just had two grueling days with Khrushchev in Vienna, another full day with de Gaulle in Paris, and a session with Macmillan in London; in addition, as we learned afterward, he was in great pain with his back, and as soon as he arrived back in the States the next day he had to have treatment and be put on crutches. Finally, he had no prior knowledge of my coming, and so could not have been briefed. "Oh, yes," he said, as though the computer in his brain had clicked audibly, "didn't you write a very interesting book about some murders in—I think it was Notting Hill—and where they hanged the wrong man? And wasn't there a piece about it in *The New Yorker* a couple of years back?" I had, and there was. But I was too stunned by such a feat of memory to do more than nod, and go on nodding, like some absurd puppet. Stas brought me a glass of champagne, which helped, and then I asked the President if it would be all right if I were to buttonhole him on the pavement, and he said it would be, and then I went upstairs and telephoned the office and told them that the thing was on.

And this, according to the official transcript of that evening's *Panorama* tape, was how it ended.

DIMBLEBY *(beside monitor in studio)*: And looking at another scene in London S.W.1 out of the corner of my eye, it seems to me the President is about to leave the house at any moment, so we go now, in fact we've gone, to join President Kennedy's namesake, Ludovic Kennedy, in Buckingham Place.

KENNEDY: And here outside the house of Prince and Princess Radziwill in 4, Buckingham Place, we're all waiting for the President and Jackie Kennedy to come out of the house and get into their cars to go to the dinner party at Buckingham Palace. Just about thirty seconds ago, the American Ambassador Mr. David Bruce and his wife came into the house, and a second or two after them, Mrs. Sargent Shriver, who is the President's sister. It's a fairly small crowd here, they've been here most of the day I gather, a small crowd but a vociferous one. I don't know if you can hear them shouting as they have been for some time now, "We want Jack" and "We want Jackie." And about an hour ago the President came to the door with his wife and waved to them—a gesture which they seemed to like very much.

I said it was a small crowd—it's so small in fact that it seems to be dominated by the police who are standing the whole of the length of the street. You can see them in their uniforms and the motorcycle police in the far distance, ready to start up and lead off the cavalcade to Buckingham Palace, which, of course, is only about forty seconds away from here by car. . . .

I had a word with the President earlier . . . (*cheering*) . . . I think he's coming out now . . . (*cheering*) . . . Mr. President, how do you feel about your reception in England after this very short visit?

PRESIDENT: We've had a great trip here . . . In addition we've successfully baptised a godchild, and I had a chance to talk to the Prime Minister, so those twenty-four hours were very useful.

KENNEDY: Do you feel that, because this meeting with Mr. Khrushchev was one in which Mr. Macmillan didn't take part, the influence of this country in world affairs is very much less than it was?

PRESIDENT: Oh, no, this wasn't intended to be a summit meeting. Mr. Macmillan himself, the Prime Minister, has seen Mr. Khrushchev on several occasions, but I bear responsibilities as President of the United States, and I thought it important to have an exchange of views with Mr. Khrushchev, and also to make clear our position, and after that conversation I was particularly anxious to see the Prime Minister. This was not a summit meeting, but it was an opportunity to make a more precise judgement on our future course.

KENNEDY: It's been a very short stay. I hope you'll come back, sir.

PRESIDENT: Well, I'm delighted. I appreciate that very much indeed. . . .

KENNEDY: The President and Mrs. Kennedy are now in the leading cars, the motor bikes have revved up, just in front of me there is Mrs. Bruce, the Ambassador's wife . . . there is Prince Radziwill and Princess Radziwill, there's Mrs. Shriver in front (*cheering*). . . . The crowd are streaming forward here to get as close to the President's car as they can, and the police are having quite a job to hold them back. . . . And there they go now . . . they're just leading off, through the lines of the motorcycle police, and they'll turn right there to go into Buckingham Gate and round to Buckingham Palace. And so to the last two hours of President Kennedy's very short visit to this country . . . and with those pictures I return you now to Richard Dimbleby in the *Panorama* studio.

How exciting and important it all seemed at the time. How flat and stale it seems now, with all the principal actors dead or retired. And yet, on the public level, I would think that the image of John F. Kennedy abroad did more for America than any other American since Franklin Roosevelt. And, on a personal level, I may be forgiven for having found Washington so empty without him.

Part One

LATIN AMERICA

COLOMBIA
BRAZIL
PARAGUAY

To FLY from New York's Kennedy International Airport to Caracas International Airport is to be moved, in a matter of hours, not only from winter to summer but from the twentieth century to the nineteenth, from the familiar and congenial to the alien and bizarre. The Pan Am building at Kennedy Airport is like some futuristic dream palace, all glass and light and revolving stairways and self-opening doors and nice waterproof tunnels to take one straight to the aircraft instead of those windy buses; and there inside the warm womb of the Boeing are, as there should be, sexy Pan Am hostesses in cool gray uniforms, with dry martinis and lukewarm lunches to soothe one through the stratosphere at half the speed of sound.

But Caracas Airport isn't like that at all. It is not so much typical of the Latin-American world as a parody of it; and if you are an American and arriving for the first time, you are in, whizz-bang, and without any kind of warning, for your first dose of what their psychologists call culture shock. It is night by now, and they spill you out into a dimly lighted bare hall which looks like a reception center for Arab refugees. Here you are shuffled into booths, where small, greasy laughing men peer at your passport and tease you with Venezuelan technicalities. You smile and nod uncomprehendingly—what else can you do?—and then you go to a larger hall with filthy, peeling pale-green walls. There are a lot of pillars in this room and a lot of smells too, customs counters in the middle, and behind them a conveyor belt bringing in the luggage. This conveyor belt is not like the one in New York, which puts your luggage to one side until you want to collect it; this one spews the luggage out like so much vomit, and then sends it reeling and skidding across the room. There were more of these unshaven men hanging around this conveyor belt, and when I saw my luggage come hurtling across the floor I waved my ticket and shouted at some of them to fetch it. But they just looked up and smiled and went away, and had a pee, I daresay, and came back. Then they exchanged cigarettes and jokes and occasionally, when they felt like it, they would pick out a case at random and take it over to the counter. I said to an American next to me, "How long does this go on?" He replied, "You never can tell. Could be five minutes. Could be fifty. Anyways, there's nothing we can do about it." He seemed an old Caracas hand.

In about fifteen minutes my case was brought to the counter. The customs man stuck a big green label on it marked "Revidado," and stamped it several times in purple ink. Then I fought my way through about a hundred Venezuelans who were milling round the entrance door, and looked for a taxi. A small fat man with awful teeth said "Caracas?" and took my bag. Inside the taxi I found two middle-aged Australian sisters who had also been on the flight. They were having a holiday. "What did you think of America?" I said. They looked at each other, wondering who was going to speak first. Then one said, "Well, it's not the same as home, is it?" The other nodded. So, they'd been having culture shock too.

We left the sea and drove through the warm rain into the mountains and down the other side. Presently great neon signs appeared saying mad things like GORDON'S GINEBRE and KLIM, and then we were in Caracas. It was raining hard now, so one couldn't see much. Presently we came to a huge hotel set in its own grounds with the word TAMANACO shining on top of it. I went into a cool lobby, where one sign said "Men's Shop" and another "Coffee Shop." A smart bellboy took my bags. To register, I borrowed a pen from the Venezuelan clerk, and when I thanked him he said "You're welcome, sir." I was back, before I had arrived. Near the elevator, in pots, was a great mass of mountain greenery, and a man in shirt sleeves was polishing the leaves with a damp cloth. In my room I found a little ticket which said NO MOLESTE, and I stuck it on the handle of the door.

✪

NEXT MORNING I shared a taxi to the airport with a Mr. Russell, an American whose job was to go round Latin America servicing aircraft engines which had been made in the United States. On the way out of Caracas we passed the site of an American exhibition which had been opened the day before. Mr. Russell said there had been an account of the opening in the morning's paper, and offense had been taken because champagne had been served to some but not others. "When I read that," said Mr. Russell, "I said to myself, There we go, blundering again." I said, "Do you think Americans abroad do a lot of blundering?" Mr. Russell said, "Yes, I'm sorry to say, I do. I've done quite a lot of research on this thing, and when I'm abroad I make a point of talking to foreigners, not always sticking with Mr. Hilton. The trouble is that we're taking on a role we never envisaged, which we were never prepared for. It's a question of relationships really. I think we're awfully immature in our relationships with foreigners. We expect them to be the same as us, and we're upset when we find they aren't. We don't seem to be able to get across to them. How *do* you make yourself understood?" I said, "What do you think the answer is?" Mr. Russell said, "Education, I guess. I'm on the education board of our local community, and I go a lot for education. But it's a long process. We've been isolated too long." We arrived at the airport. Mr. Russell said, "A lot of my friends think I'm a bit of a nut."

✪

BOGOTÁ, THE capital of Colombia, is eight thousand feet up, and for the first few days there the rarefied air is apt to catch at the throat. It must be one of the noisiest capitals in the world. Canned music blares out from almost every other shop. Car drivers honk their horns for the sheer joy of it. Ancient, squat buses, painted yellow and blue and marked, unbelievably, PARIS, go roaring down the streets like demented chargers; in the country, I was told, they sometimes leap over cliffs and are never seen again. At intersections policemen with whistles, perched on little circular, canopied platforms, try desperately to control them. To add to the din, the day is rarely free from the noise of exploding firecrackers, the children's favorite game.

Nor is there much evidence of what the lady at the Interchurch Center called "citizenship responsibility." A few baby skyscrapers have gone up in the middle of the town, but otherwise things are much as they were. The pavements are pock-marked with holes, hazards for the preoccupied and the stoned. In the country, kidnaping and holding for ransom have become almost a national sport; in the town burglary is so rife that many householders put treble locks on their doors. Paper blows about like autumn leaves. There are public incinerators for burning it, but the wind takes its share. Near one incinerator I found some cows knee deep in the stuff, taking their evening meal.

The Peace Corps offices were in an unprepossessing building at the back of the main street. Up one flight of stairs was a door on which was a notice in red ink: "If you need something from the warehouse, please don't knock on door, but ask Mr. Roar for the key." On the next flight another notice said, "Out-of-Town Volunteers. Please sign in when you're in town, in case we may need to get in touch with you. Thank you." I went up a third flight and came to a door marked "Representante Cuerpo de Paz."

The "Representante," or Director, of the Peace Corps in Colombia at this time was Chris Sheldon. He was an impressive man. He had a big, strong head and very blue eyes and looked a little like Marlon Brando and a little like the British naturalist Peter Scott. I'd been told that he had a doctorate in Spanish literature and a degree in Divinity; that he used to take boys on training cruises through the Pacific and on one of them the ship sank and he lost his wife. I gave him my letter of introduction from Washington, and he read it through a couple of times and nodded his head and said they were just going to have a monthly meeting of regional leaders, and why didn't I sit in on it.

✪

THERE WERE about fifteen of them at the meeting, most in their early twenties, most in jeans and shirts, a few smoking pipes or cigarettes, no one chewing gum. Chris Sheldon asked them in turn to report on their various areas. He was always nicely in control, breezy and to the

point, but among some of the volunteers I noticed a kind of earnestness, a formality of language, which was surprising. "Well, what's
happening in the north?" said Mr. Sheldon, and the man from the
north said, "We're not making much progress with the experimental
farm." Mr. Sheldon said, "I don't like experimental farms. I don't
like the experimental farm theory. You've got to have the people on
their own land growing their own stuff. One *must* get involved with
the people." He asked another volunteer about this area and the man
said, "We're having more trouble with that priest I was telling you
about. He's going around telling everyone the Peace Corps is anti-
Christian. He says the *campesinos* are disturbed about losing their
voice and that the Peace Corps have put them up to it." Mr. Sheldon
said, "Sounds like a real trouble shooter." The volunteer said, "I
don't think I mentioned Elliot Le Vien's tree-planting project. We
think it might be a help to have the priest in on this." Mr. Sheldon
said, "How's he going to be in on it? You going to get him to plant a
tree or something?" The volunteer said, "Well, the idea was to do a
diplomatic job—get him with us rather than against us." Mr. Sheldon
said, "I don't think you'll make much headway with that guy. He's
gone too far." Someone said, "I wonder if the bishop is aware of the
situation." Mr. Sheldon said, "That's it! Does the bishop know, or is
he doing it on his own? These bishops are pretty autonomous." The
leader said, "I could fix an appointment with the bishop"; and Mr.
Sheldon said, "Good, that's agreed. We'll see what happens with the
bishop."

They ranged over other areas and other problems. One volunteer
said, "We tried rerouting a river which was tearing out a cornfield.
We didn't have the tools to do a proper job, so then the local army
got to hear about it and they moved in. Well, they tore up everything, and now there's no cornfield at all." Another fair-haired young
volunteer said, "We feel the need for a concrete-type project in our
area." No one took him up on this. They talked about the Food for
Work program whereby villagers are given food for specific community jobs, like enlarging a road or laying a pipe. Mr. Sheldon said, "I
don't like this Food for Work stuff. It's too much like charity. My
belief is when you stop the food the work gets stopped. Our community relationship ought to have developed beyond that kind of
thing."

Finally they discussed an area where several volunteers were having to be pulled out because of civil unrest. The leader of the area

said, "They've done a great job there, Chris. They're real sad to be going, and so are the local people. But this gang who killed this army guy have balled it all up. There's kidnaping going on all the time." Mr. Sheldon said, "It's a government decision. If I had my way I'd put them right back in there."

After the meeting, Mr. Sheldon said to the fair-haired young man who had asked for a concrete-type project in his area, "Dave, when are you going back to Cunday?" Dave said, "Tomorrow morning, early." Mr. Sheldon said, "This is Mr. Kennedy, a British writer. He wants to have firsthand experience of what the Peace Corps are doing. You like to take him with you?"

"Sure," said Dave, "be glad to."

✪

IT WAS still dark when Dave came for me in a Willys Jeep at five the next morning. He was wearing a khaki-colored cotton shirt and trousers and, considering the hour, looked remarkably spruce. He has sandy hair and a fresh complexion and seemed about twenty-five—as good an example as you could find of integrated, healthy, American youth. We had a cup of tea and an orange and then set off through empty Bogotá. It was a relief not to see any of those mad buses. "I hate this place," said Dave. "It's a big, ugly dirty city. I'm glad we're getting out." Cunday, where we were going, was about a hundred miles to the south; there we would look up a couple of girl volunteers for whom Dave, as regional leader, was responsible.

We cleared the town and came out onto a big, flat plain, with fields on either side and the road like a long pale ribbon. There was very little traffic. As it grew light I noticed several advertising signs, among them one for "Bretana," a fruit drink; this sign had a picture of a London bobby directing traffic. What was the connection? Perhaps dependability, the idea that Bretana, like the London bobby, didn't let you down. A little later we passed a sign that said "Sun Valley Farm," and Dave said this was an American private-enterprise venture aimed at raising vegetables. We saw some of the vegetables growing near the road. They looked out of place, yet impressive, in this arid landscape, a visible symbol of American capital and technology.

Dave said, "Ask me anything you want to know." I said as a start I would like to know about him, where he came from and what had brought him into the Peace Corps. His home was in Philadelphia, but his mother had died when he was twelve and he had been brought up by an aunt. "My father's a leather cutter. He lives in a hotel in Philadelphia by himself. He cuts ladies' handbags. He's an alcoholic. It's a deliberate choice. He likes it that way." Dave had four brothers, a Catholic priest, a sales engineer, a manager of a Food Fair store, and the youngest a sophomore in college. He himself had worked his way through a Jesuit college in Philadelphia and then gone on to Georgetown Graduate School in Washington, where he had studied international politics. He had stayed on in Washington after this, working first at the National Council of Catholic Men and then at the National Liturgical Conference. "Then I felt I wanted to do something. I had a friend in the Peace Corps in Washington, a young psychiatrist, and he first got me interested. I said I didn't want to go into it just like that, I'd wait until something came along that really interested me. So when this educational-TV thing came up, I put in for that. I did ask myself, do I want to put in all that investment in time? But then I thought about it and what it could do for me and for the future. I thought, well that's going to be a good investment. And everything that's happened since then has proved me right. I feel I've really achieved something worthwhile."

After being accepted he was sent on the usual four-month training course, and given intensive instruction in Spanish. "They were five of us in our group and we used to speak Spanish five hours a day. Gee, that was something!" He and his group arrived in Bogotá, ready to conquer the world, but the TV sets hadn't arrived, and no one knew when they would be arriving. "We got so frustrated. There were eighty percent of us in Bogotá at that time, which is the most depressing city in the world, and nothing to do. We got to calling the Colombians 'Japs.' That just shows how frustrated we were. The word 'Jap' has a special meaning for my generation of Americans. We were brought up to regard them as rotten, sneaky treacherous little bastards. Of course we were referring to the Colombian officials, not the campesinos, and in any case, it wasn't all their fault." When the sets arrived they ran into more difficulties because no one had thought to tell the teachers they were coming, and the first the teachers knew of it was when they found them installed. Dave was sent down to Tolima province to supervise installing sets there. "We didn't make the same mistake again. We made contacts with all the teachers and told them what was happening."

After this Dave was promoted to regional leader for Tolima, the position he now held. His flock consisted of twenty-eight volunteers, eleven in the educational-TV program, six agricultural and nutrition advisers, three in community development, three in health education (it was two of these we were going to see), three English teachers, and two cooperative volunteers to advise on bookkeeping and loan savings. He kept in touch with them regularly, driving between eight hundred and a thousand miles a week. I asked if he ever had to discipline them, and he said, "Sometimes. For instance, volunteers aren't supposed to go outside the province for any day which is not part of their vacation. Well, of course, they do. I know they do, and they know I know. I can't really *do* much about it, but it makes relationships kind of difficult. Then, sometimes you find volunteers just aren't doing anything. So I have to go and see them and sort out their problems. Very often their problem is that they don't have a problem."

We had left the plain now and began descending a steep ravine, with the rock face on one side and lightly wooded valleys on the other. At some corners there were little shrines of the Virgin set back from the road, with candles burning around her, and also one or two disused car headlamps. Dave said it was the custom for drivers to get out and light candles to the Virgin when the mood took them; some put down car headlamps instead of candles, in the belief they would last longer. At some hairpin bends there were little white crosses stuck in the roadside. "That's for those who didn't make the corner," said Dave. "As you've probably noticed, they drive like maniacs here."

I asked Dave where he lived, and he said in Ibagué, the capital of Tolima, in the house of a Colombian businessman. "That's quite an interesting story. This guy's father won two hundred thousand dollars in a lottery some thirty years ago, so he sent his son to England for his education, to Lawrence College, Birmingham, I guess. He has two sons and a retarded daughter. I share a room with one of the sons. I want to tell you a funny thing about this retarded daughter. When I heard I was going to this house, they told me that there was an *enfermada* living there. I thought that meant a nurse, and I said, 'Boy, that's great.' So after I'd been living there a bit I said, 'Where's the nurse?' And they said there isn't a nurse, there's only this retarded daughter. The food there's really great."

We went on down this ravine and after about an hour leveled out.

It was very hot now; Dave said that in the last twelve miles we had dropped from eight thousand to four hundred feet. There was thick vegetation on either side, bananas, coffee, sugar cane, as well as wheat, potatoes and onions. We passed peasants wearing blankets and straw hats, and at intervals Coca-Cola signs winked from the foliage.

I said to Dave, "How do the Peace Corps get along as regards money?" and he said, "In theory, it's not too bad; in practice, we're nearly always broke." He was paid 1,500 pesos, or about $115, a month. Out of this, 450 pesos went to his landlord for board and lodging and another 300 on incidental expenses when traveling. He put 300 pesos into the bank each month, and the Peace Corps also put another 75 dollars into his home bank against the day of his release. ("I pay ten bucks from that to help my younger brother at college.") This left him 500 pesos, or about a dollar, a day for out-of-pocket expenses. "The last few days before my pay check I'm always broke. We all are. But we get by, I guess."

Outside a place called Melgar, we were held up by a detachment of the Colombian Army who happened to be marching by. They were going into Melgar in single file, a column on either side of the road. They were very little men, like Cambodians or Vietnamese, and the big packs they carried on their shoulders looked much too big for them. They had tin hats and short, brutish weapons. The two rear men seemed to be enveloped in huge transmission sets.

As we watched them go by Dave said, "There was a time here, after the civil war, when everybody just hated soldiers. They represented tyranny and oppression. Then they started a plan to bring them in on reclamation schemes, building bridges and damming rivers and running courses for teen-agers. It's helped to change their image a lot."

We headed out of Melgar and turned off down a dirt road, very dusty and uneven, and with thick foliage on either side. The sun was well up now, and it was a glorious, blue day. Ahead of us was a range of hills, all smoky in the haze, and Dave said that Cunday, where we were going, lay on the other side.

I had been with Dave now about four hours. He seemed to me an enormously likeable fellow, relaxed and cheerful, energetic and perceptive, ready to take on whatever fate threw up at him, whether it was the company of a British writer, the intractability of Colombian officials, or the problems of his own volunteers. But from time to time he had a curious habit of breaking the flow of his natural talk by shifting suddenly into officialese. Once, when talking about the future of the Peace Corps, he said he thought its main work would be in "a structure-type project related to education." What he meant was American teachers teaching foreign teachers how to prepare and carry out educational programs. Another time, he spoke of the need for volunteers to meet monthly for "a group dynamic conference." He just meant a conference. Again, the purpose of the conference was to establish "a built-in evaluation system," and this meant that those taking part should compare notes. It was as though the uttering of such high-sounding and meaningless phrases somehow gave him solace. This was the same territory as "culture shock," but it was surprising to find it in one so natural and unassuming.

We climbed up into the hills. There was hardly any traffic on the road, just the occasional bus, which came tearing round the corners in a parcel of dust, so that we had to swing over sharply to avoid it. God, it was beautiful up there! There were marvelous yellow flowers in bloom which Dave said were called *copa de oro* ("cup of gold"), and trees like Scottish rowans with bright-red berries, and scarlet poinsettias and big blue butterflies, the size of a man's hand. When we got to the top, we stopped and got out to let the engine cool. Below us, on the other side, was a huge green valley, about ten miles long, empty except for a few cattle, lush, untouched, utterly unspoiled; and beyond and above, the great purple chain of the Andes. There was a sweet smell of wet vegetation and a low susurration of crickets. The air was so still you could hear a small sound a mile away. I looked down at the valley and said to Dave, "If this were the U.S., there'd be an observation tower where we're standing, and a rest room and a Coca-Cola bar and a knickknack shop." Dave said, "Yes, and in twenty years' time there probably will be."

We came into Cunday. It was a small town of about 2,500 people, built in the classical Spanish tradition round a square. The square was as every *New Yorker* drawing has pictured a Latin-American square for the last thirty years. There was a statue of Simon Bolivar in the middle, and a fringe of cool trees under which a few people were talking or sleeping. In the square were a church, a hotel, and a large building marked *"Telecom—Larga Distancia."* Dave said this was the post office and housed Cunday's only telephone. But it was unreliable, and they did a lot of their communicating by telegram; you could send a short telegram for as little as eighteen cents. Next to the post office was the jail, and through the open doors I could see the bars of the cells and the prisoners, like inmates of a zoo, chattering to people on the other side. Dave said it was quite a friendly jail, and prisoners' friends and relatives could drop by to have a word with them more or less when they felt like it.

We drove through Cunday and out to a settlement called La Victoria, where Dave said the girl volunteers we were going to see would be. La Victoria consisted of perhaps a dozen newly built little houses, each with its own garden, standing on a hill. Dave said this was part of a government resettlement scheme; with the breaking up of large haciendas, peasants who had formerly worked on them as laborers had each been given a house and ten acres of land. They were nice-looking little houses, but hemmed in by coils of ugly barbed wire to keep the wild animals out of the gardens.

We entered one of the houses, which, Dave said, the two girls used as an office. We found one of them in. Her name was Susan. She was a short, soft-spoken girl, wearing a white blouse, skirt and sandals, her hair was combed tightly back on her head, and she had a rather muddy complexion. The only furniture in the room was a table and a couple of chairs. On one of the chairs sat a fifteen-year-old girl, knitting. Susan said, "I'm teaching her how to knit. I learned to knit here myself." On the walls were about twenty seed packets marked "Radish," "Collards," "Swiss Chard," "Tomatoes," "Cabbage," et cetera, and the name of the maker, W. Atlee Burpee. Susan said that W. Atlee Burpee had given seeds to the Peace Corps as a present, and volunteers tried to persuade the peasants to grow them in their gardens; the idea was to provide an alternative to the habitual and debilitating yucca root. Dave asked where Karen, the other girl, was, and Susan said that she had gone up to a hamlet in the mountains called Caymito, to see about the new school.

We hadn't been in this room long when a very old woman came in with a very small boy. The boy looked about four. The old woman was dressed in black and the boy had round, sad, dark eyes. He had been having terrible stomach pains, and Susan had sent them into Cunday to see the dentist, because she thought his teeth were all rotten. So the old woman and the little boy had walked all the way to Cunday, which took them over an hour, and when they got there they found that one of the two dentists was away and the other was too busy to see them. So they had walked back. Here they were, and what were they to do now? I looked at the little boy and his sad, still face. It was impossible to tell whether he was in pain or not. In a way he looked as though he had lived with pain so long he had become deadened to it. Susan told them there was nothing to do but walk back to Cunday another day. The old woman nodded as though that was all she expected, and the two shuffled out. Susan said, "That's the kind of problem we have every day. It used to break my heart when I first came here. So little you can do."

Dave went off to see someone, and I sat down and talked with Susan. She had been born and raised in Iowa, but later her father, who was a teacher, had moved the family to California. They lived in a place called Escondido, near San Diego. "I joined the Peace Corps because I've always wanted to learn a foreign language really well, and live in another country and get to know it."

After their four-month training course, she and Karen had been posted to Cunday as public-health volunteers. "The government had just set up a public-health scheme here, and we were going to work through that. But at the last election the vote here was so solidly anti-government that the government got annoyed and withdrew it. So we've just had to do what we could on our own."

They had been in Cunday eighteen months and were due to leave in another six. "The first month or two was so strange and different. Although I majored in Spanish at college, I still couldn't understand very much. We spent the first two weeks just visiting people—the mayor, the colonel, the priest and so on. We stayed the first week in the colonel's house, but he charged us so much we couldn't afford it and had to move out. After that we lived in the hospital for a time. That was a real eye-opener. There was *nothing* in there, but *nothing!* One man was brought in who'd been run down by a car, and he had lost the skin off his legs. There wasn't any anaesthetic there, and we heard this guy screaming and yelling in the operating theater while the doctor sewed back his skin without anaesthetic. We could have done so much in that hospital, but the woman in charge didn't trust us, and wouldn't let us stay."

Since then they had been doing every sort of work. "We teach English twice a week in the high school. We give health classes for the smallest children. We teach handicrafts, home gardening, prenatal care, dieting, knitting, games, and anything else we can. But you have to be terribly patient with yourself and everybody else. When volunteers first arrive they think they're going to conquer the world, and they're just *hit* by frustration. You're up against centuries of prejudice and ignorance. There's a new Colombian doctor in the town.

He's from Bogotá, and when he got here, he told us all the things he
was going to do. We just laughed. We'd been through it all ourselves.

"When I'd been here a few weeks I thought it would be a good idea
to form the wives in La Victoria into a group, so that we could have
weekly meetings and I could tell them about health things—a sort of
Mothers' Club. It didn't work too well, even from the start; women
here aren't used to any kind of group activity; they feel their place is
in the home. But what finally killed it was electing a president and a
secretary. Those who didn't get elected were so jealous they refused
to speak to the others. They just wouldn't share what we could give
them. After that they wanted me to visit them individually in their
homes."

"What's the commonest problem they have?"

"Birth control, I guess. They all want it so much. They start off by
asking about your own family, and when I say I have only one sister,
they say, well how did your parents manage that? Married women
here have children every year. Six months out of every year they can't
bend down to do up their shoelaces. It's always been like that, and
until a little time ago they thought it always would be. Now they've
heard about the pill, they're desperate to get it."

"Can they?"

"Some of them are just beginning to. But it hasn't been easy. The
Church was against it to start with, though the priest here is very
reasonable. Then it costs money, and they say they can't afford it,
though actually it works out cheaper than another pregnancy. The
pills cost about eighteen pesos a month, or just over two hundred
pesos a year. A baby costs forty pesos to deliver and about another
thirty for alcohol to relieve the pain. They have babies here without
any anaesthetic. Then to feed a baby, even on the little they give
them, costs about thirty-five pesos a month. So, from an economic
point of view, the pill's cheaper. But they don't have the foresight to
see that. Even the few who start on the pill mostly aren't cute enough
to appreciate that you have to take it every day. So when they've
missed a day or two and gotten pregnant again, they say, oh, the pill's
no use, and throw the rest away."

A tiny boy appeared at the door, wearing a black hat. He was even
smaller and sadder than the first boy. He said something to Susan in
Spanish and Susan said, "He says his mother wants to see me. Why
don't you come too? It's quite an interesting family."

We followed the tiny boy up the road and came to the entrance to his house. There was a beautiful garden in the front, flowers round the side and lettuce and other vegetables in the middle, the first fruits of Mr. W. Atlee Burpee. The garden reminded me of the back gardens of suburban houses that you see from the train in England. "This family has made real progress with growing things," said Susan. "They're about the only ones who have." The gardens on either side were almost derelict.

An old bent woman in black came out of the door, and greeted Susan. She looked about sixty. She was followed by several shy, tattered children. She chatted with Susan for a few minutes and then we went into the house. We passed one room which had a minimum of furniture, four or five chairs and a table, but the walls were whitewashed and it looked quite clean. We went on into the kitchen. There was a dog and a couple of hens in there, and the old woman shooed them out. The only furniture in here was a sink and a stove; on top of the stove was an ancient black pot. The floor was filthy with animals' excrement, and crawling about in this was a little baby girl. She had nothing on but a little shirt, so that her lower half was stained with muck. She was playing with a tin bowl in which were congealed scraps of rice. She looked at us gravely as we came in, and, still looking at us, urinated. Round her neck was a string of beads. Susan said these were pods of garlic and were supposed to be a charm against worms. In La Victoria most of the small children had worms.

Susan and the old woman had a long conversation, and then we left. On the way out Susan said, "Did you take a close look at that woman?"

"Yes," I said. "I suppose that was the little boy's grandmother?"

"No," said Susan, "that was the little boy's mother, and the little girl's mother, too. You want to know how old she is?" We walked a couple of steps. "She's thirty-nine. She's had twenty children, and ten of them have died. Her eldest daughter is twenty-two, and she's had six children already. It's like rabbits, isn't it? Now you can see why they're so desperate to know about birth control."

"What did she want?"

"The government give these people three hundred pesos a month to keep them going until their first crops come in. She went into Cunday this morning to collect this month's money, but there was some mistake and it hadn't come in. So she wanted me to lend her some."

"And did you?"

"Yes. Karen and I have already lent her eight hundred pesos."

"Should you do that?"

"We're not supposed to. But what can you do? If I hadn't, none of those children would be eating tomorrow. I lent fifty pesos for that other little boy's medicine yesterday, and another twenty pesos for a little girl who was undernourished. These people have *nothing*. I shall be home in six months' time, and I should hate to think I'd left behind people I could have helped and didn't. No, we're not supposed to, but what can you do?"

★

DAVE TOOK us to lunch at the hotel in the square. On the way he nodded to people he knew, and once or twice men came up to exchange civilities or ask a question. Striding along the street in his khaki shirt and trousers, he was an impressive figure. He reminded me of someone or something I had seen somewhere before, but I couldn't recall what.

In the dining room of the hotel there were two tables set, one for the manager and his family and one for us. When the manager heard I was British he said, "When Churchill passed away, my daughter cried." For lunch we had small bananas, soup, mutton and rice, and a piece of fudge. All through lunch a record player was blaring out Beethoven's *Emperor Concerto,* so there wasn't much talk.

After lunch Susan went back to La Victoria, and Dave and I went up to Caymito to look for Karen. We drove up one mountain, down the other side and up another. It was wild, wooded country, broken by little plots of coffee bushes and sugar cane, palms and bananas. Occasionally we passed peasants in wide hats astride small mules, like pictures from a travelogue. There were more of those lovely trees with red berries, and great splurging red flowers called Man's Life, and frail purple Primavera. There were more of the big, blue butterflies too; they had yellow circles on their wings so that when one settled on a bush, it looked as if a huge eye was staring at you.

Twenty miles from Cunday we came to a village called San Pablo, just a long sloping street with a few houses and shops. Dave said that Caymito was a mile further on, but there was no road and we would have to walk. The path to Caymito led uphill into the woods. It was cool up there, among the tall trees. Parts of the path were covered with paving stones, old and worn as though from the beginning of time. An old woman came down the path, and when she was a few steps away she stood aside and said, *"Pido permisso, señor?"* Dave muttered something and the woman smiled and went on. "What did she say?" I asked; and Dave said, "She was asking permission to pass. That's the sort of status women have around here."

As we went along Dave told me that a girls' school in Greensboro, North Carolina, had collected a thousand dollars for the building of a school at Caymito. The money had been sent some time ago to the bank at Cunday, but there had been a muddle over the name, so that when the representative from Caymito had gone to fetch it, he was turned away. This had happened twice, and now there was no money left to order new materials, and building at the school had stopped. The villagers were very disheartened, especially as the Colombian teacher for the school had arrived a few days before and was ready to start work. Dave had sorted out the muddle at the bank, and we would take the representative in to Cunday in the morning and see that he got the money. Karen was here to put new heart into the villagers and tell them that the school would soon be completed.

After half an hour we reached Caymito, twenty cottages spread out over perhaps a square mile. A boy came out of one of the cottages to take us to the house of the government coffee agent, where we were to spend the night. He led us uphill, through a wood and a grove of coffee bushes. The agent's house was half hidden among trees at the hilltop. It had a stunning view, over the top of the wood we had just been through, and then clean across a great valley to the Andes. The agent's wife took us to a terrace where mounds of coffee beans had been drying in the sun. On the wall was a plaster head of the Virgin. We sat down on the terrace and the agent's wife brought us coffee. This had a marvelous smoky taste, like the smell of a woodfire on an autumn morning. It was the best coffee I ever had.

Dave said, "There's one piece of information you ought to have for your book. In the Peace Corps in Colombia there's a new V.D. case every week. That's not a guess, that's a statistic." I said, "I was going to ask you about sex." Dave said, "It's quite simple really. The Peace Corps men don't do it with Colombian girls, because the girls are too heavily protected. They don't do it with Peace Corps girls, because there aren't enough of them around in the first place, and anyway most of the girls reckon they didn't come here for that. So that leaves the brothels, which is where the V.D. comes in."

"How about yourself?" I said.

"I'm lucky, I guess. I'm engaged to be married to a Peace Corps volunteer right here in Colombia. The Bishop of Tolima is going to marry us in three months."

At this moment there was a sudden cry of "Hi!" I looked over the edge of the terrace and saw coming up the path a tall, mannish-looking girl, with spectacles and short-cropped hair; she was not unlike Katharine Hepburn. "Hi, Karen!" shouted Dave. She came up the steps to the terrace and said, "Big deal. The soldiers are starting at the school tomorrow. I've been to six cottages and I'll do the others in the morning. They said they'd get me a horse." She expelled a lungful of air and sat down.

Karen was twenty-three and came from Costa Mesa, in California, near Los Angeles. She had majored in Spanish at school, and one reason she had for joining the Peace Corps was to gain practice in using the language. Another was that she had spent vacations helping to reconstruct churches and schools, and this sort of thing appealed to her. She seemed a natural do-gooder. Like Susan, Karen wore sandals and a simple skirt and blouse. Like many Americans, she had the greatest difficulty in stopping talking.

"You just can't believe how time goes," she said. "After the first month, it seemed as though I'd been here all my life."

"Tell me about the first month."

"Oh, it wasn't too bad. I guess the only *really* bad bit was the first twenty minutes after the truck had left us and gone away, and I felt, here I am in this itty-bitty tropical village, a tremendous long ways from anywhere. But that *soon* went. The village gave us a tremendous welcome. The first night we were there two girls came over with a parcheesi board, and for the next two months we played nothing but parcheesi. Did Sue tell you about lodging with the colonel? He gave us a bill for three hundred fifty pesos each after two weeks. The hospital was much better, only eighty pesos a week. Oh, they were nice, those people, the mayor and the priest and the doctor and even the colonel. They made us so *welcome!*"

"Did you feel very frustrated when you first started?"

"No, not really. All our training taught us not to expect too much. We knew pretty well what we were up against. All the same, the ignorance is just frightening. Do you know, when the mothers are pregnant, they won't drink milk, because they think that will make the babies too fat and give them painful deliveries. So we put on a film we have that shows what a terrible time a thin undernourished woman has in delivering a baby, but what a comparatively easy time a well-nourished, healthy woman has. I've been with them sometimes when they're delivering, and it's real painful. Do you know, some of them cut the cord with a broken plate. And then they wonder why they get septicemia. You know what these poor little babies get for food? Sugar cane and water. That goes on until they have some teeth, and then they're given a whole potato or a yucca root to chew. No wonder the doctor says the whole town is suffering from anemia, that they all have fifteen percent less oxygen in their blood than they ought to have." Suddenly she leaned toward Dave and said: "Remember seeing Patty the other day, and what we said?" Before Dave could answer she said, "This is a friend of ours in the Peace Corps who's having a baby. Her husband's a volunteer too. Well, this may sound silly to you, but I had *forgotten,* yes actually *forgotten,* what it was like being with a woman who was *glad* she was going to have a baby."

One moment while Karen was talking, it was light, the next so dark I was unable to see my notebook. We got up and went into a cool, dark room. The agent's wife brought us a paraffin lamp and put it on the table. Above the lamp was a picture of the faithful going to heaven and the wicked going to hell. The wicked had the best of the deal: wearing comfortable lounge suits, and smiling cheerfully, they looked as though they had just drawn the lucky numbers for some splendid orgy. The faithful looked dreadfully glum; they were dressed in Roman robes and looked like an amateur dramatic group about to perform *Julius Caesar.*

Dave said, "Do you agree with Sue, Karen, that the whole of a volunteer's two years should be spent in his country of assignment, and the four-month training period counted as extra?"

"But of course, Dave. *Absolutely!* I think we're all sold on that. The way it is now, with only twenty months abroad, it doesn't give you time to acclimatize properly or anything. One of the things you need more time for is to profit from your mistakes. And you know that Sue and I have made plenty. There was that Mothers' Club idea at La Victoria for a start. Then there was the Laubach method of learning to read and write. Sounded fine in theory, but in practice it just didn't work out at all. Then there were mistakes which weren't of our making—like my teaching the prisoners literacy in jail."

"Why didn't that work out?"

"Because the turnover's so quick. The minor cases aren't there for more than a week or two, and the serious ones, like rape and murder and assault with machetes, they get transferred to the state prison. So I didn't have time to work on them."

"Do you agree with Susan," I said, "that what the women want most from you is information about birth control?"

"Yes and no," said Karen. "It's certainly one of the things they want to talk about most, but to me the important thing is that they want to come and talk at all. And they do. They look on us as quite different from their own people. Very often they don't want anything *from us* at all. They just want us to listen while they sit there and let off steam. That makes them feel a lot better. I'd say in that respect we were doing a good job."

"Do they think of you as being superior to them?"

"Not so much superior, as different. Of course, we are better educated obviously, but I don't think they judge us on that. They recognize that our customs and habits are different from theirs, and they respect us for it, as we respect them for theirs. For example, we go to market with our own baskets and wash our own clothes, and I've heard mothers saying to girls of our age, 'You see those two ladies do that, so there's no reason why you shouldn't.' We've had men in our house talking till quite late. They accept it. They know we're freer, but that we also have more discipline. Sure, I've had proposals—marriage *and* otherwise—but I've never ever *encouraged* anyone, because if I did, I'd at once lose their respect."

Did she really mean *their* respect, I wondered, or her own? But before the point could be explored further, the agent's wife, followed by two mongrel dogs, came in with supper. Karen went off to wash, and while she was away Dave said, "As you can see, for Sue and Karen the Peace Corps is just tailor-made." Supper consisted of soup with an egg in it, fried bananas and yucca, and a strange fish. Most of it was inedible; but happily the problem of disposing of it without hurting the feelings of the agent's wife was resolved by the two dogs.

Picking at the fish's head, I said, "Is there anything that either of you really miss?"

"Yes," said Karen immediately, "green salads."

Dave thought a bit and said, "I don't believe I miss anything unless it's a glass of good, cold water. But I do know this. I don't believe I could live here without a strong contact with magazines and that sort of thing. And at least once a month I feel the need to visit Girardot or Bogotá or some other town."

Karen said, "I don't feel the need for that kind of thing at all."

We pushed away our empty plates, and the two mongrels smacked their chops and rolled on the floor. The agent's wife came in with more of the smoky coffee.

Karen said, "Dave, shall I tell about Christmas Day?" Dave said, "Sure." Karen said, "It was the most wonderful thing. We didn't do much our first Christmas, but this year we decided to give gifts. We made a hundred and two gifts. We knew how to choose them. We worked it all out. We made potholders with names embroidered on them, and colored milk cans and papier-mâché dolls. In a way these were two-pronged gifts—the idea was to show them what they could do themselves. It was the same with the kids. We gave them books and hobbyhorses and knitting needles, so that was two-pronged too. Then on Christmas Day we planned to have a feast. We got people to donate what they could, and we got five scrawny chickens and some chocolate and popcorn—they grow popcorn like mad here—and we made star cookies and *campadinos* and we got the kids all frosting graham crackers. You don't know what graham crackers are? Oh, but I thought everyone knew that.

"Well, nine days beforehand we put up a manger scene in the school and we built a thatched roof over it. We had just about everything in that manger, toy buffaloes and bulls and airplanes and dolls and a Volkswagen and even little houses. And then we taught them carols and we recorded some of theirs from the religious radio program, and we learned them all, and on Christmas Day we sang them together. We sang all the carols and then we ate the chickens and chocolate and cookies. Oh, it was fun! There was enough for everybody, but I don't know how. They kept the breast and the wishbones and brought them to us afterward; they kept them especially for Sue and me. Some families didn't come, because they were fighting families, so we took our gifts to them on Christmas Eve, and that was the saddest thing of all. They had no decorations, no gifts, no nothing. It was just too sad. Then, after the party was over, we all went into town together and attended midnight Mass."

"Are you a Catholic?"

"No, nor's Sue, but it didn't seem to matter. They're funny about religion here. One time a woman stopped me in the street and said

she was worried about my soul, and did I pray? So I said, 'Well . . .'
and she took me right into the church and sat me down and made me
say 'Our Father.' They're really superstitious, you know. We've had
people come to our house to ask for mustard seed to catch witches.
And they believe that if you visit a cemetery, you must change your
clothes and take a bath, because the cold air from the dead bodies can
infect your children. And they think the best cure for tuberculosis is
the boiled beard of a black goat."

We sat talking round the table until the paraffin lamp was quite
low and the wicked and the faithful had merged into a single blur.
Karen spoke of the difficulties she and Sue had teaching, as none of
the schools where they taught had textbooks or maps. But the children were wonderfully receptive to new ideas and had welcomed proposals for a basketball court (organized games were unknown) and a
school garden. For her and Sue there was no clear dividing line between work and leisure, for they never knew when they might be
needed. In the evening they read, talked, knitted, and played the guitar. "We take it in turns for one of us to be available so that the other
can write letters and rest." The most difficult problem they had was
checking themselves from forcing an idea on to the community, instead of dropping hints and letting the people come up with it themselves. "If they don't come up with the idea, we try and sneak it in,
and then when they do come up with it later, we compliment them
on having thought of it."

I said, "On the whole, do you think the people in Cunday are glad
you came to live among them?"

She said, "Let me tell you what happened when President Kennedy died. A *campesino* came running up one day and said, 'The
President's dead.' Sue and I thought he was talking about their president, so we weren't too worried. But when we got home and heard
the news on the radio, we were awfully upset. Well, the rest of that
day we had people dropping by all the time, to see if we were all
right, and give us their condolences. And then, in the evening, so we
wouldn't be on our own, they took us out walking and visiting their
homes. You've no idea of the number of homes where there were
pictures of Jack and Jackie. It's funny, Johnson's done more for Latin
America than Kennedy ever did, but it's Kennedy they remember.
Oh, they were wonderful that night."

Suddenly she said, "You know what I want to do when I get back to
the States? I've taken pictures of all the people I've gotten to know

here—you know, the poor people in La Victoria and so on—and I'm going to show them to everybody I meet in the States, and I'm going to say to them, 'These people aren't animals, *these are my friends.*'"

Her eyes shone with a splendid passion. I said, "And when you do that, your friends will nod and smile and say they understand, but they won't really, because they won't have had the experience themselves."

She said nothing. The lamp went out. We sat there in the dark, not speaking. The only sound was the dogs breathing. Karen said, "I do think this, though, I think we've made a lot of friends for the United States. Most of them in Cunday had never met any Americans before, and they thought we were all pretty 'ugly,' I guess. A few of them had seen some of those awful tourists in the city. I think they know now that there are some Americans who are just ordinary people like themselves."

"And what do you think will happen in Cunday when you and Sue have gone?"

She was a long time answering. "That's what worries me," she said. "Will they just drop back into their old ways? Will they forget all the things we've tried to teach them? I don't know. But I'd settle for very little. If there was just *one* family that went on growing vegetables, just *one* mother that kept boiling water, that'll have made it worth while. It'll have been a start, at least, and perhaps later someone else will come by and take it on from there."

✪

NEXT DAY we left Karen still doing the rounds while Dave and I returned to Cunday with one of the villagers who was to collect the money from the bank. In the afternoon Dave had some business to do, and I went back with Susan to the little house that she and Karen shared. The place was sparsely furnished: a bed, a chair, and a dressing table in each of the two bedrooms; some canvas chairs and a bookcase of paperbacks in the living room; bare floors everywhere. In Susan's bedroom was a basket which she said she was weaving to a local pattern. The books were a present from the Peace Corps, part of the two hundred volumes of ancient and modern classics that they give to every volunteer.

Susan asked if I would like to see her diary and notebook. The first entry for La Victoria went as follows:

About 100 People

20 men
18 women
7 older girls
7 older boys
16 niños
14 niñas
15 babies

After this there were pages of diary entries and I read some at random:

Administered Incaparina to the undernourished children. Crisanto and Maria Dolores eat dirt. Handed out posters. Husband beat little boy severely and the military came and took him to jail. Cut hair of Amelia, who has infected area on head from rolling in dirt. Elbia Romero pregnant again.

September 29th. Torres family house still a horrible mess. Bathroom foulsmelling. Virginia realizes the place is a mess but doesn't care. She hates La Victoria and wants to get away to Cunday. The Seche family have planted lettuce and tomatoes. Teresa hasn't got a jug to boil water. Sinia inclined to be left-handed. Father punishes her, try to convince him to let her alone. Teresa causes problems between Elvira and another woman by sharing confidences.

Further on in the diary were drawings that Sue and Karen had made, copied from magazines, of how to make a simple shower, dresses, boxes for pepper and salt, and practical hints on gardening. Then, at the end of the book was a set of typed directives from the Peace Corps. Some of these made sensible reading.

The Group Approach to Introducing New Ideas.

You are working in an area where you want to bring about a change to improve conditions for the people. You want to educate the villagers in new ways. You can't do it. Villagers must decide to improve or change their ways of doing things themselves. You *can* stimulate their thinking in a direction that a change *might* be desirable. You can help them to know that change is possible. Only the villagers can bring about change in their behavior.

And again:

Our role is not to tell people what to do, but to create the idea that something can be done if they want it. This approach means putting ourselves on the same level as the village people in being able to sit with them and ask their ideas about particular problems—not standing over them and handing down dictums from superior positions.

This was good stuff, but there were places in the instructions where one was suddenly brought up short. "Group discussion," said the pamphlet suddenly, "is an activity related to a problem." I read this three times and found it as meaningless after the third reading as after the first. Again, "We will be the resource person to their program." And at the end, the humdinger of them all: "Specific problem + Motivation of people concerned × Various ways of learning through activity = Education Program." Or, put another way: find out what the problem is and then try and solve it. Now I knew where Dave had picked up his fancy phrases.

I said to Susan, "Looking back after your eighteen months here, what would you say?"

"I'd say it had been the most wonderful experience I've ever had. It's taught me so much. We get people down here from Bogotá and they ask us where we come from. And when we say San Diego and Los Angeles, they say, how can you stand it? And we say we haven't had a boring moment since we arrived. Another thing the Peace Corps has done is to have a lot of American parents go into out-of-the-way places to see their kids. When they find the conditions we're living in, they're shocked. But when they get home they think about it, and in that way it's helped to enlarge their experience too. What they don't realize is that you can be perfectly happy without all the comforts of home. When you go on vacation, you look forward to the cold water and the shower and the car and the icebox, yet when you get there, you realize how happy you were in Cunday. Once, for fun, my mother sent me a packet of flowered toilet paper. I sent it to a friend in the Peace Corps in Guatemala, and he wrote back and said, 'That's clinched it. Now I'm *never* going back to the States.' "

And what of the future?

"I don't know. I'd like to stay on here. I feel I could really do something, and I wouldn't make the same mistakes again—like the Mothers' Club and starting the gardening scheme without a good follow-through. But I have to go back to the States for a year to get my teaching credentials. After that, I think I'd like to go on doing the same sort of work I've been doing here, in the war-on-poverty program maybe, or with the Mexican immigrants in Southern California or in one of the Indian reservations. I wrote to Enos Poor Bear the other day—he's the head of a reservation at Pine Ridge, South Dakota. They're starting a project there on literacy and health. I think I'd like that."

It was time to meet Dave, who was going to take me into Girardot, a nearby town, to catch a taxi back to Bogotá. We went into the sunshine and strolled toward the square. Dave was standing outside the telegraph office, talking to a small, old man. With his tall, slim figure, blond hair and khaki dress, he was as distinctive as a cornflower in a field of poppies. Even at that distance it was clear that he was once again dishing out encouragement and advice. Suddenly I realized what it was about Dave that I had experienced before, something that had struck a chord in my memory but which I had been unable to recall. He was the living embodiment of the old British District Officer, of all those young men who went out from England in the nineteenth and early twentieth centuries, to serve the native peoples in the plains and jungles of the world—to resolve their disputes, activate their minds, minister to their health. The jobs they were doing were almost identical; the only differences were those of time and birth—they had been British civil servants, these were American volunteers. *Plus ça change, plus c'est la même chose.*

○

WE DROVE out of Cunday the way we had come, up into the green mountains where the butterflies flew and the Primavera grew and the cups-of-gold flouted their profusion at the roadside, over the ridge of the great virgin valley and down the other side. As we came into Girardot, I said to Dave, "What are you going to do when your time's up?"

"I function well as a functionalist," he said. I felt that he was trying out the phrase to hear how it sounded. "I'd like to go into politics, but that takes a lot of money, which I haven't got. I think I'll go to business or law school for a while and try to earn some dough. After that it'll be the public-service field. I think I shall probably do a dozen different jobs in public service before I'm fifty-five. I guess I'm just waiting for another Kennedy to come along."

He drove me to the central taxi station, and we got out and shook hands. "Well, let me know how the book goes," he said, "I've really enjoyed meeting you." I thanked him for his company, and watched his tall figure go sloping down the street.

I shared a taxi to Bogotá with an old man, an old woman and a young man. Once, during the journey, I said to them: "What do you think of the Americans?" The old man said to the old woman, "He wants to know what we think of the Americans!" They thought about it for a bit, and then the old woman said, "We have never met any Americans." The old man nodded and then the young man said, smiling, "The Americans are very *rich,* yes."

They all laughed at this. The richness of Americans was always a good joke. In the dark we came up onto the cool plain; ahead were the twinkling lights of Bogotá.

✪

I WENT to two parties before I left Bogotá. At the first I met a pretty redheaded English teacher, from Manchester, I think. Her name was Margie and she was about twenty-three. She had spent a year or so teaching at a small town in the provinces called Medellin and had got to know the local Peace Corps people quite well. I told her about my two days with the Peace Corps in Cunday, and she said:

"I'll tell you a funny thing about those Peace Corps boys. There were five or six of them stationed in the country round about, and a couple of Peace Corps girls, and another English girl, who was teaching there, and she and I shared a flat. We were all about the same age, and none of us had any money, and the American community down there didn't want to know the Peace Corps anyway, so we used to get together a lot. Every so often the boys would drive in from the country and come to the flat and plunk themselves down and say, 'My God, an armchair,' and 'My God, a green salad.' Well, that was fine. We liked to see them; it was company for us. They used to sit around talking about religion and politics and the United States till two or three in the morning. But what do you think they did then? Went off to the local brothel. Didn't make any secret of it either. Told us they were going and went. Why, even after parties and things, when we'd all been together, they'd ask the taxi to drop them off there on the way home. Well, I was quite offended, I don't mind telling you. I mean, I'm not unattractive, am I? No, be honest. Am I?"

"No," I said. She wasn't.

"No! But did they ever make a pass? Never. *Never.* I couldn't understand it, so one evening when I was out with this boy and had had a few drinks, I asked him point-blank, why don't you ever make a pass? And you know what he said? It was sad really. He said, if I made a pass and you didn't want it, you'd throw me out and then I wouldn't be able to come here again, and you're the only European girl I know. Well, what could I say to that? Then there was this other boy, and he used to hold my hand and say, Margie you don't mind my holding your hand, do you? And then he'd kiss me, you know, really kiss me, slobber all over me, and get himself all excited and me as well. But that's as far as he'd go. After a bit he'd calm down and light a cigarette and have a cup of coffee, and that was that. I went to bed, and I suppose he went to the brothel. God, it was so *humiliating.* After all, I'm normal and healthy just like anyone else.

"There was *one* boy who did make a pass, you know, a real one. Well, I rejected him because it was the first time. You know, just to see if he was serious. Well, you've never seen anyone so hurt. He was like a dog that's going to be hit. He carried on as though he'd done something *terrible.* I never saw him alone after that, only in parties. It was as though he'd done something to be *ashamed* of."

"It wouldn't have been like that with an English boy, would it?"

She giggled. "Not most I've met. But these Peace Corps boys take it all so seriously. They think that if a pass is rejected it means they aren't loved any more, aren't wanted. So long as they don't try, they'll never know. Christ, why have some people got to be so *complicated?*"

❂

I WENT also to a dinner party given by an Englishman and his wife. There were about eight of us there, including a Colombian diplomat, a European ambassador and his wife, and a German air hostess.

The Colombian diplomat said, "A lot of people come here and

read the notices on the walls 'Go Home, Yanks,' and think we're very anti-American. But it isn't so. There's no great anti-American feeling here at all. Not like Mexico, where they depend on them for the tourist trade. In Mexico they really dislike them. But here we do not dislike them, because we do not depend on them. The U.S. investment here is quite small. Oil is about the only thing they have a big stake in, and we have control of exploiting it. Eventually we shall own all our own oil.

"We did expect there might be a little trouble with the Peace Corps, but it has turned out very well. The Peace Corps has been good for Colombia and good for the volunteers. It has made them grow up in a way they never could have done in the States."

The European ambassador said, "The last American ambassador here was very popular. He used to go to Colombian dances dressed up in Colombian clothes and be photographed dancing and carrying on with the local people. The English community here thought it was very shocking—'infra dig,' they called it, 'beneath one's dignity.' Well, I'm not saying I would wish to do it myself, but the Colombians loved it. It showed them that whatever else the ambassador might be, he wasn't stuffy; and English diplomats, as I daresay you know, are rather stuffy. All the same the American embassy here is ridiculously overstaffed. I have seven officers in my embassy. They have over two hundred. What do they all find to do?"

His wife said, "They are not good mixers. They keep themselves to themselves."

The Colombian said, "So do the Colombians, and so do the Europeans. We are all inclined to keep ourselves to ourselves. We prefer it that way."

The ambassador said, "When Europeans or people of European stock are together, like tonight, we can relax and be ourselves. But put an American in the middle of us, and at once we are *aware* of each other. They're always telling each other to relax. 'Why don't you sit down and relax?' they say. But in fact they don't know how to."

The Colombian said, "Europeans say, 'I was talking to so-and-so the other day.' Americans say, 'I was talking *with* so-and-so the other day.' But they don't talk *with* you at all, they talk *at* you. They don't make conversation, only statements."

The Englishman said, "It's the same when they're courting. In Europe a man and a girl *know* when they're attracted to each other, and part of the fun is not saying anything, but exchanging looks and smiles and touches. But Americans have to say right out, 'Gee, you're nice, honey. I *like* you.' And they must analyze things. Jesus, how they analyze things."

And the air hostess said, "In planes they are very nice, very polite. The Latin Americans say *'tu'* instead of *'vous'* and make passes at you. The Americans are happy to just talk and drink and give you those silly little cards which one always throws away."

✪

THEY GAVE us a free packet of coffee at the Bogotá airport, to boost the trade, and then I boarded a K.L.M. plane for Caracas. When we were in our seats the captain told us on the loudspeaker that he was very glad to have us aboard. He had the good old Dutch name of McKenzie.

On my right there were three small nuns. They were the saddest nuns I ever saw. One of them, who looked about twenty, was openly weeping. They had with them a little plastic box in which lay a single mauve orchid. They kept passing this box from one to the other and fondling it as though it were a holy relic. They crossed themselves as the plane took off, and again before lunch. Two of the nuns had Coca-Cola with their lunch. I do not think they can have been used to the stuff, for later one of them surprised herself as much as me by giving a loud belch. She put her hand quickly to her mouth, the sort of useless gesture people make in such circumstances, closing the stable door after the horse has gone. After lunch the nun who had been weeping did a very strange thing. She collected all the unopened salt and pepper packets, sugar packets and dehydrated-cream packets from the trays and put them inside the plastic box, along with the mauve orchid. I've sometimes wondered where they all ended up.

✪

WE LANDED at Rio with the sunrise and drove into the already bustling town, down wide Botafogo, through the Pasmado tunnel, and round to Copacabana Beach. It was just like the pictures, the long, curving biscuity bay fringed by matching houses, all bleached and sugary, as delicate as papier-mâché, as liquid as sand. Behind were the hills, green and wooded, and out in the bay the green islands and gray rocks, and the soft, gray sea. The roads were full of Simcas and Volkswagens, and on the sidewalks were men in shirts and light suits, and brown bosomy girls in trim summer dresses. I checked in at the Copacabana Hotel and got a room for six dollars a night; it was the best value for money on all my long tour. The beach outside the hotel was maggot-thick with people, a chocolate soufflé of Cariocas, lying about, standing up, playing ball or mostly just milling around. It was surprising to see so many on the beach so early in the morning. The concierge said they were mostly from the *favelas,* the terrible shanty slums up in the hills above the town; and they were there because they had nothing else to do. I have seen slum people in London and Chicago and Moscow and Milan, but none as merry and clean and healthy as these; but then they had what the others would always lack: sunshine and sand and the healing sea.

I came to Brazil because it was here, in a country almost as big as America, yet supporting less than half of America's population, that the United States government was directing one of its most ambitious efforts. Already it had poured more than a billion dollars into the tottering economy, and if much of it had found its way into the pockets of venal politicians or been absorbed by the galloping inflation, it had at least served to keep the idea of capitalism alive. The American AID program (through the Alliance for Progress) was now investing more money in Brazil than in any other country in the world except Vietnam.

But the AID program was mostly a question of high finance and investment, of the setting up of industrial plants and the purchasing of farm equipment and the building of highways; and what I wanted to know was what, if anything, the individual American businessman was doing. Here, a hundred years ago, British businessmen, following the British flag, had a business monopoly. Now this was over. Americans—businessmen and tourists alike—traditionally have eschewed Latin America; frequent revolutions, doubtful food and sanitation, and unpredictable and unreliable people have combined to make it a poor place either to do business or to have fun in. But now, with all the Stateside frontiers crossed, and a great virgin territory on their doorstep ripe for exploitation, how far had this traditional attitude changed?

✪

I CALLED up the American embassy, and was put through to the press officer, Mr. Jack Wyant. Mr. Wyant said, "Hullo there! So you finally made it." I said, "Yes, how did you know?" Mr. Wyant said, "Oh, the State Department can be quite efficient when it wants to. We had a telegram about you. You're the guy who's writing another *Ugly American?*" I said, "Well, not quite." Mr. Wyant said, "A lot of people don't know that the 'Ugly American' was the good American."

Mr. Wyant said he would come and collect me for lunch, and he arrived soon after. He was a good-looking young man, energetic and friendly and full of jokes. He spoke perfect Portuguese. He told me that his parents had been missionaries in São Paulo, and he had been brought up here. He asked whether I wanted a full lunch or a light one, and when I said a light one, he took me to a place called "Bob's," in the center of town. Bob's was a big American-style snack bar. It served sandwiches and hamburgers and ham and eggs and orange juice and ice cream. It was very full. Some people were sitting on stools at two long counters, and others, behind them, were eating their food standing up. We got a couple of seats at the counter and ordered ham and eggs.

"Well," said Jack Wyant, "what's your schedule? Do you want to see the ambassador? Call me Jack."

"If he has time," I said and Jack said, "He doesn't, but I'll see what I can fix." The ham and eggs came, and Jack said, "Been here before?" I said I hadn't, and Jack said, "This is a great country. When you've been here a little longer, you'll find that the girls here look at men in the way that men look at girls in other countries. They kind of undress you. It's quite an experience till you get used to it. And even when you have. And I'll tell you another thing. There are no flat-chested women in this country.

"Seriously, though, Brazil is now really on the map. To give you an idea, there are over forty resident foreign correspondents assigned here. Back in the forties there were about three, and the rest of the work was done by stringers. That's how important it's become."

"And the Americans?"

"We're here in a big way. I remember my father saying that when he first came to São Paulo forty years ago, the only other American there was a fellow missionary of his. Now the town is full of them."

"How many Americans are there in Brazil?"

"It's hard to say. Quite a few take out Brazilian nationality to avoid the tax on foreigners, and then they just disappear into the economy, and we don't hear of them again. But I guess about forty thousand. That takes in most everyone—diplomatic, consular, Peace Corps, Alliance for Progress, military, missionaries (there's a hell of a lot of them), businessmen—"

"It's the businessmen I'm interested in," I said.

"Sears Roebuck is an interesting story," said Jack. "Back in 1948 they imported pretty well everything they sold. Now over ninety percent of what they sell is made on the premises. In that way they've avoided the foreign-exchange problem, helped the Brazilian economy *and* made a lot of dough."

"It wasn't the big firms I was thinking of," I said, "but the individual who's trying to start something on his own. Do you know any of those?"

Jack said, "Yes, I do." He thought for a moment. "Come to think of it you couldn't do better than start right here."

"Here?"

"Sure. Bob's."

✪

"Bob" was Bob Falkenburg, whose name was already known to me as a former Wimbledon tennis star, as well as the brother of the celebrated Jinx. More surprising, he was now, according to Jack Wyant, owner of a small chain of lunch counters in Rio. I got in touch with him on the telephone, and he said he would take me round.

He came for me at the Copacabana in a green Volkswagen. He was a big, long, handsome man—about six foot two, I should say—with darkish hair and a very healthy complexion. He was wearing a freshly laundered pair of light-blue jeans and a white shirt with "R.F." embroidered on the pocket. He had hands like a weight lifter's, which explained his success at tennis. He told me he was thirty-nine years old.

I got into the car and we drove off. Mr. Falkenburg said that he owned six lunch counters, a factory and a laundromat, and that we would visit them all: he visited them all, himself, he said, every day. His father had been an electrical engineer at Boulder Dam, he said, and he had started playing family tennis at ten, and competitive tennis at sixteen. At the end of the war and in the years immediately after, he had won several major championships including the U. S. Junior and the Wimbledon singles and doubles. "The only one I didn't win was the U.S. singles, and the reason for that was that I was playing Kramer and nobody ever beat Kramer." He spoke with the softest of drawls and there was a nice catch in his voice when he laughed. In 1946 he was playing in Rio in the South American championships when he met the girl whom he subsequently married. At this time he was studying engineering at the University of Southern California, but in order to support himself and his wife, he chucked this in and got a job as manager of a Los Angeles movie house. "I humped cases up and down, and issued tickets, and did about everything. I was a janitor in a tuxedo, and I worked sixteen, seventeen hours a day. After a time I said, this is silly, and I quit."

In 1949 he retired from big-time tennis and thought out what he was going to do. In California a friend had interested him in an idea for making ice cream on a franchise basis. This idea had stuck in his mind, because when he was in Brazil, in 1946, he couldn't get any ice cream worth eating. "Kibon ice cream, which was started by Kent Lutey, was okay, but there weren't many places you could get it. After tennis my friends used to take me off for a cool drink, and all they could produce was chocolate and water. So I said, My God, is that the best they can do? Why can't they make a proper milk shake? So I decided there was a need for ice cream in Rio, and I would come here and start making it. At that time I didn't know the first thing about ice cream. I didn't even know what went into it."

At this moment we arrived at the largest of the lunch counters, where they made the ice cream and orange juice for the whole chain. The ice-cream–making machine was like a sort of huge stainless-steel vat, and through little windows you could see the ice cream churning about inside. Near the machine were stacks of white bags. They looked like cement bags, but Mr. Falkenburg said they contained powdered milk. This had to be pasteurized to kill the bacteria and then homogenized to break up the fatty particles. In a matter of seconds it went from 175 to 35 degrees Fahrenheit, and this quick transition from hot to cold killed everything. For a man who had only just finished telling me of a time when he didn't know what ice cream was made of, I found his performance impressive.

Mr. Falkenburg took me into his deep-freeze, which was full of cheeses and hamburger meat and dressing for hamburgers and scores of bags of powdered milk. Then he showed me his mayonnaise mixers and potato peelers and hamburger flatteners and shapers. "I make almost everything on the premises," Mr. Falkenburg said, "because then I have everything under my own control. Bread's one of the few things I don't make. I thought about it, but the bakery that serves us does us very well, and buying in bulk from them is more economical." He showed me a huge machine for making orange juice. "I don't own that either," he said. "I'd like to, but the firm that makes it only lets it out on lease. I pay three thousand dollars a year for it." I asked why the machine wasn't operating, and Mr. Falkenburg said that he made all his orange juice at night, so that it would reach the lunch counters early in the morning. "My orange juice is absolutely fresh. You don't get fresh orange juice even in the States." He looked at the machine lovingly and said, "This machine consumes two hundred boxes of oranges a night." He patted it as though it were some dear but voracious pet.

Mr. Falkenburg had a word with his manager and looked at some papers, and then we went off to the next place.

I said, "You were telling me how you got started?" and Mr. Falkenburg said: "Yes, well, I thought at first it would be quite a simple business. I assumed that this friend of mine I was telling you about who makes ice cream in the States would let me have the franchise for selling it here. I would arrange the lease of premises and he would send me the powdered ice cream in bulk, plus cups and napkins, et cetera. All I would have to do was add the water and refrigeration and sell the stuff. But that all fell through. Because of Brazil's foreign-exchange problems, I couldn't get the necessary import license.

"Well, I wasn't going to give up the idea because of that, so I said to myself, I'll just have to make the ice cream myself. As I was telling you, I didn't know the first thing about it. So I got myself a little book on how to make ice cream, and I studied it, and when I was through studying it, I started making it. I'd set aside ten thousand dollars of my own for the franchise deal, but that wasn't enough for the capital costs of making it, so I borrowed another five thousand dollars from my wife's uncle. That was the limit of my borrowing.

"I set up my first shop just behind the Copacabana, and when it was just about ready, there was a critical power shortage. I couldn't get any power, and without power I didn't have any refrigeration. I didn't know what to do. So I went along to see the president of the power company. He had an office like you see in the movies. So I told him my problem, that I was running out of dough and that if I didn't get power I'd have to give up and go back to the States. Well, luckily he had seen me play tennis, so he called in his engineers and asked for a report. And they said, well, it was very sad and they were very sorry, but if they gave me power they would overload the plant. So the president waited until they had finished and then he just looked at them and said, 'Listen. You give him power.'

"So I got the power the next day, and a few days after that I opened the shop. It was pretty hard to begin with. I had just my wife and a boy to help me, and we were working eighteen hours a day, making the ice cream, serving it, and cleaning up afterward. We had a cigar box instead of a cash register. Some people didn't pay, but I just went ahead anyway, because I wanted to get the thing moving. After a few weeks I didn't know whether I was coming or going. But by the second month I had started to show a profit."

We paid a succession of flying visits to the rest of Bob's lunch counters. It was near midday now, and they were filling up with customers. The men behind the counters looked very smart in their clean white uniforms—the word "Bob's" in green script was embroidered over their breast pockets, and they wore white forage caps with a green border. "Cleanliness," said Mr. Falkenberg, "is very important, especially in this climate. I don't mind being robbed, but I can't afford complaints." I was amazed at the speed with which the men took and served the orders. Mr. Falkenberg said, "They have to be fast because a lot of these people don't have too much time for lunch. I train the manager, and the manager trains the men. They work flat out at that speed for eight hours a day. You won't find anything to compare with that in the States."

"There's one staple ingredient of any American's diet," I said, "which I notice you don't sell. Coffee."

Mr. Falkenburg said, "Well, this is a coffee-making and coffee-drinking country. This town is full of places where people stop off for coffee all day long. But it's not American-style coffee. They don't like our way of drinking coffee. They like it black, in very small cups.

Now, I could sell that here if I wanted, but with everyone else doing it, what would be the point? I'd get a whole string of people wanting coffee only, and the hot dogs and hamburgers wouldn't get sold. It wouldn't be economical."

We drove out to Mr. Falkenburg's factory, which was some distance away on the road to the airport. I said, "What amazes me, if I may say so without offense, is your effrontery or courage, or whatever you like to call it, in thinking you could get this thing off the ground in the first place. After all, at that time you weren't as familiar with the language as you are now, you've admitted you didn't know the first thing about ice cream, and you were in a country whose laws and customs were quite different from the United States." Mr. Falkenburg said, "Looking back on it, I'd agree with you. But at the time I wanted to do this thing so much—I guess to prove myself right as much as anything—that I just wasn't going to let anything stand in my way. I did have one good break, though. After I'd spent weeks of frustration going through all the regular channels to get a permit issued or a license fixed, I met a man who said, 'Why don't you get a *despachante?*' Now, literally that means dispatcher, but in fact he's an intermediary. He knows just where to go and whom to see to get things done, and what you do is take him out and give him some coffee and slip him something, and tell him what it is you want, and away he goes and the thing usually gets done. You have to do it their way here. If you try doing it your way, you'll go crazy."

The factory looked much like any boring old factory anywhere. It was full of machinery for making machines for making ice cream and other things. One of the machines was for making cups. Mr. Falkenburg said that previously he used to buy the cups, but he couldn't get the kind he wanted. He showed me an old French printing press that he had picked up somewhere and which he used for printing "Bob's" on the cups.

Then we went to the new canteen for his eighty workers. "It used to be a musty, beat-up sort of place. Now each man will have his own locker." I said, "What will they have to eat? Hamburgers and ice-cream?" and he said, "No. Rice and beans."

I asked what the workers were like, and Mr. Falkenburg said, "They vary. On the whole the Brazilians are a very easygoing, happy people. They just adore life. So long as they can get a good square meal and somewhere to sleep, they're happy. But that's not much use to me. When a man comes to me asking for a job, the first thing I say to him is, Why do you want it? If he says because he has a family to support, the chances are I won't take him. But if he says because he wants to make money, then he's the man I'm looking for.

"The Portuguese are the best. If I had a choice I'd employ nothing but Portuguese. But under the law, two thirds of my employees have to be Brazilians. It's a tricky situation, really, because the Brazilians look down on the Portuguese. They equate them with priests. So I have the Brazilians here, and the Portuguese mostly at the lunch counters. They're really good workers, as you saw for yourself. Their idea is to make a lot of money, save it, and then go back to Portugal as a big-shot. Well, that suits me."

We left the factory for the laundromat. This was a modest establishment on two floors, with men at washing machines on one floor and women ironing in the basement. "The laundromat," said Mr. Falkenburg, as we walked round, "is really a logical extension of everything that has gone before. About four years ago I found that I had over a hundred employees' uniforms to wash each week. So I started the laundromat for that purpose. Then I expanded it, so that now for every one order within the firm there are six outside.

"This whole laundromat idea is only just beginning to catch on. Ninety percent of the middle classes here used to have maids, and the maids used to do their laundry for them. So after we got started, the maids began coming round here. In those days we used to let customers work the machines themselves, but the maids didn't understand them and they got broken. So now our own people work them. The customers bring us their washing and we weigh it and then charge according to weight. It works out at around twelve cents a pound. The girls check over each garment before it goes into the machine, and make a note if anything is torn. A lot of people have a suspicious nature and like putting the blame on others, and this way we can always tell whether we made the tear or it was there in the first place."

On the way out of the laundromat I said, had he any plans for opening lunch counters elsewhere in Brazil, say São Paulo or Brasilia? "A lot of people have suggested it," said Mr. Falkenburg, "and I've even had offers. But I'm not keen about that. I like to be where I can see what goes on. I like to be able to check in every day and see that everybody is happy. If I had a place I couldn't visit more than once every two weeks or so, there might be all sorts of trouble going on." He spat out of the window into the Avenida Princesa Isabel.

"Anyway, I don't like these local flights too much. They're like taxis, they just warm up and take off. I don't mind international flights, but that's something else. Anyway, I'm not that ambitious."

We turned into the Avenida Atlantica, and I said, "After fifteen years, what would you say your business is now worth?" Mr. Falkenburg said, "I don't care to discuss the business side. I've got nothing to hide, but I don't believe in making a point of showing it. But I'll tell you this. Six months ago, when the inflation was really bad, if someone had offered a hundred thousand dollars for it, I'd have grabbed it. Now I wouldn't accept a million.

"Anyway, the money side doesn't interest me that much. The sense of achievement I find much more satisfying. My demands are modest. I take out enough for my family to enjoy a good standard of living, make a trip to Europe occasionally, play a couple of golf tournaments. All the rest I plow right back."

As we arrived at the Copacabana Mr. Falkenburg said, "You know, there's no secret about my business. People often write to me and say, what can I do in Brazil? And I write back and say, well the first thing is come here, which most of them aren't prepared to do. But once you're here the opportunities are terrific. All you've got to do is choose something that isn't being done, and do it. That's all there is to it."

✪

At the hotel I went up to the big reading and writing room on the first floor. The only other occupants were three American businessmen gossiping in a corner. Most of the talking was being done by a gloomy man in glasses. "Listen," he said, "did I tell you about the telegraph poles? It's unbelievable. There were these telegraph poles, see, way out in the boondocks, and they'd fixed the insulators so the conductors wouldn't reach. So I said, well we've got to clear that somehow, because of this great overhanging branch. They'd put the pole up right under this overhanging branch. You wouldn't believe it was true unless you saw it for yourself. So then they went away to get a ladder to clear the branch. It took them half an hour to get the ladder, and when they got it, it wouldn't reach by three feet. They hadn't measured it. Now how can you do business with people like that? There's only one word for them. Pathetic; Absolutely pathetic!"

✪

THAT EVENING Jack Wyant came on the telephone. "Well, I've fixed the ambassador for you. Lunch on Saturday. How will that suit?"

"Fine. How did you manage it?"

"Well, I just suggested it on my own, and he said, 'Do you think he'll be satisfied with that?' So I said I thought you would, and all you really wanted was to take a critical look at him to see how he comported himself. So he's promised to be on his best behavior. How did you get on with Bob Falkenburg?"

"Very well. I had a very interesting day."

"I thought you would. Did he tell you that he is amateur golfing champion of Brazil?"

"No."

"He's a very modest guy. Aren't we all? I have another name that I think will interest you."

"Yes."

"Charles A. Cabell III. Sounds promising, doesn't it? He's president of a thing called Brazil SafariTours. Organizes trips and excursions and so on. Not yet thirty and I'm told is going places. Hold on, and I'll give you his address."

✪

A DAY or two later Mr. Charles A. Cabell III lunched with me at the Copacabana Hotel.

Before this I had paid a call at his imposing offices high up in the Edificio Avenida Central, a baby skyscraper in the middle of what the Americans call downtown Rio. Mr. Cabell was out, but his secretary showed me his room, which had a stunning view of the Sugar Loaf Mountain, and gave me a sheaf of pamphlets about the organization. These covered almost every activity that the eager traveler in Brazil was likely to pursue. There were tours in and round the city to places like Santos ("the coffee port of the world") and Forest Gardens ("for those who are lovers of botanical beauty, the gardens and Orchidorium are a must"); to places farther afield like Brasilia ("the city of the 21st century"), Recife ("the Venice of Brazil") and Belem ("the gateway to the Amazon"). In Rio itself you could choose from two nightclub tours, RO11 or RO12 ("this tour, although less luxurious than RO11, nevertheless will thrill the tourist who wishes to be a part of Rio by night but with economy in mind"), and in the daytime go spearfishing, skin diving or sailing "in breathtaking Guanabara Bay." Mr. Cabell had something for every pocket. At one end of his bill of fare a Macumba tour was offered for only $15.75. This was described as "an authentic Macumba ceremony which very few have ever seen. You will be an eyewitness to a genuine Macumba—right in the *'favelas'* at its point of origination. This is an original tour offered exclusively by Brazil Safaritours through special arrangements with the Macumba High Priest." This idea of the customer being a privileged spectator at some obscure native religious rite is at the heart of much of American holiday advertising. At the other end of the scale was a sixty-day safari in the jungle for four hunters accompanied by two "white hunters," or guides, at an inclusive fee of $14,280. "Our white hunters," said the brochure, "have many years' experience leading safaris here in Brazil. They are all multi-lingual and will give your clients a hearty welcome in English, Italian, French, Spanish, Portuguese, German, Russian, Hungarian or Hebrew." There was an impressive list of things to shoot (goat, pig, dog, otter, sloth, ocelot, jaguar, et cetera) and among the services provided were "a comfortable tent with bathroom, washroom, dining-room tent, bedding, linen, table and chairs, gunbearers, waiters, personal servants, cooks, skinners, pilots, first-aid kits and snake-bite outfit." Here again, the importance of softening the idea of the dangerous and unknown with (a) friendliness (that hearty Hebrew welcome), (b) hygiene, and (c) comfort, was typically American. Yet these were the people who, not so long ago, were laughing at the notion of the Englishman dining in the jungle in his dinner jacket.

Mr. Charles A. Cabell III and I sat at a little table by the side of the Copacabana pool and ate hamburgers, melon and apple pie. He could hardly have made more of a contrast to Mr. Falkenburg. Mr. Falkenburg was tall and wiry and had dark, dryish hair parted on the left, Mr. Cabell was square and stocky and had fair brilliantined hair parted on the right. He had let his hair grow long too, so that although he wore dark glasses and smoked cigars, he looked more like a German or a Swede than an American. Unlike most American businessmen, he had a very healthy complexion. Above his right lip was a quite noticeable scar. He said he was twenty-seven years old.

I asked him how he had started, and he said that he had been born in a little town in West Virginia where there were just seventy-five people—fifty whites and twenty-five Negroes. "The hills there are so close that you can stand on the side of one and throw a rock over to the other." His father was vice-president of a coal company, and a keen hunter. "In our house we could sit on the porch and shoot squirrels, and skin them and have them for dinner." While at Christ Church Episcopal School he applied for a place at Yale, but Yale turned him down and he was accepted by the University of Miami. He stayed at Miami five years and got two degrees, in management and marketing. "While I was there I made a deal with my father. He paid for my studies, and I looked out for my spending money." This sort of deal is commonplace in American life, yet in England, where studying is regarded as a full-time occupation, it is almost unknown. After graduation, his father had wanted him to join one of his businesses. "But I said no. I wanted to get away from the country-club, vegetable kind of life, and see how I could make out on my own."

The waiter brought the hamburgers, and a very small girl with a harelip and wearing a bucket hat and a crucifix sidled up to Mr. Cabell and stared at him long and hard. "It was at Miami," said Mr. Cabell, "that I decided to come to South America. I had some friends there who knew Rio well and I was at their house on and off all the time I was there. I met a lot of Brazilians with them, and I thought, Maybe there's a real opportunity down in Brazil. So I read everything I could about the place. I did a tremendous amount of research. And I thought, I'll go down there and get a job and take a look around."

The small girl with the harelip continued staring, bemused by Mr. Cabell's eloquence. She was a tremendously unattractive child. "Well, it took me twenty-six flying hours to get here," he went on, "and it was raining when I arrived, so it wasn't love at first sight. I had about eight hundred dollars and a return air ticket. One thing I'd neglected to learn was the language, so I decided to make my English pay off. I spent a few days reading about jewels and jewelry, and then I applied for a job as a salesman at a jeweler's called Stern's. And I got the job—a hundred dollars a month plus commission. Well, I hadn't been there long when I realized that they knew absolutely nothing about business methods as we know them. So I gave them a few ideas like arranging the tables and having Muzak and separate booths for the customers, and they did what I suggested. Here was I, only twenty-two years old, and they were doing what I said.

"When I saw they were interested in my ideas, I suggested going out and doing a market survey of why people were buying or were not buying their jewelry at Stern's. They agreed to that, so I went out and I interviewed a ten percent sample of American society here— about three hundred people, and I asked those of them that didn't like Stern's to say *why* they didn't. And most of them said he was too Jewish and aggressive. So I made a thirty-page report and I suggested that Stern should switch over from aggressive advertising to institutional advertising. Institutional advertising is having a slogan like 'Diamonds are Quality. H. Stern has quality diamonds.' It's what you might call *Tiffany's* advertising, instead of *salesman* advertising. Anyway, he accepted everything I said, got a press agent to help him change his business image and started giving money away to charity and letting people know he was doing it. And it paid off."

While I was pondering on the simplicities of American business methods Mr. Cabell said, "During this market-research period, I took two weeks off to go hunting. I think I told you I grew up with hunting. I went off to a place called Goiânia which is the last frontier town before the Mato Grosso. I wandered round the hotels and whorehouses and bars. Matter of fact, I *stayed* in one of the whorehouses. It turned out to be cheaper than the hotel. I met a Brazilian Indian up there, a young kid who was raised by missionaries and spoke perfect English. At this time I wasn't speaking any Portuguese at all. We bought a canoe for three dollars and loaded it up with guns and canned food and a case of whisky. We took a couple of hammocks to sleep in, because in the nonrainy season there it doesn't rain *at all*. Then we set out down this river and stopped off at various outposts and hired horses and shot whatever we could. In one place we collected about twenty dogs to hunt jaguar. These dogs were all mongrels—we just picked them up as we went along. When you hunt a jaguar, you follow it for maybe two days. It's the hardest animal to hunt in the world. And by the time you catch up with it, you reckon to have lost maybe four or five dogs.

"When I got back to Rio, I reckoned I'd had a ball. And I'd done it on my own. So I made out a big report on this trip, because I figured that nobody knew a thing about it. I was down to four hundred dollars by this time, so I bought a secondhand Olivetti portable and I hired a part-time girl, and I had her type out a thousand letters to foreign hunters. I got this list of hunters from another safari firm. This whole deal started on my dining-room table."

At this point a small man in a dark suit, whom I recognized as being in a position of authority in the hotel, came up to Mr. Cabell and said, "Good afternoon, Charles, and how are you?"

Mr. Cabell said, "How about that single room you promised for the Carnival? Is that still on?"

"Our wish," said the man, "is always to help you, Charles. We are positive. We are nothing if we are not positive."

He melted away, and Mr. Cabell said, "That man is the biggest ass in Rio. Let's see, where was I?"

"Writing a thousand letters on the dining-room table."

"Yes. Well, all that took a little time, naturally. Meanwhile, I began getting interested in the idea of nightclub tours—anything to start making money. I looked into it and I found there was no nightclub deal in Rio. So I got in touch with the directors of the cruise lines and I worked out what I thought was a good tour at a fair price. And they accepted it. And I and my secretary used to go along on these tours to see that everything was okay. Did I tell you about her?"

"Who?"

"My secretary?"

"No."

"She started this whole thing with me, and she's still with me now. She's only twenty and she speaks and writes six languages. Her father's one of the big doctors here. She's had a ball."

The waiter brought us coffee. "Of course, I told Mr. Stern what I was doing, and he said, 'There's a conflict of interests here'—which there was. So I left. But we have remained good friends."

Mr. Cabell took out a cigar. "Well, after we had got the nightclub deal organized, I was able to go ahead with the safari idea. Out of those thousand letters we wrote, I got firm replies from two hunters who said they wanted to come. At this time we were barely able to make ends meet. We bought our first safari equipment with the money from the first deposit of the first hunter. I had no idea what to charge. I had nothing previous to go on. I just hit on a figure that was a little below the prices they were charging in Africa. It was a flip-of-the-coin deal really, one of the most unprofessional things I've ever done. At this time I was spending half the day on the beach and half working. When I heard that the first hunter was definitely coming, I flew up to Goiânia a week ahead and set up the whole idea with this Indian kid I was telling you about. And that's how the safari trips started."

He lit the cigar and puffed a few times. "The next thing that happened was that Varig Airlines started tourist flights, so we talked to the man at Varig and asked if we could take them deep-sea fishing. And that began to work out too, and the guy at Varig liked the way we operated and so on, gave a fair deal and didn't charge too much, so he said, would we like to take on a whole tour? So I looked into it and found the existing tours were too expensive, and I said yes. Then with the experience I got from that, I started setting up these incentive tours, you know, where big firms gave special holidays for employees who do very well. And I guess that was about the turning point."

"You began making money?"

"No. For the whole of the first two years we didn't make money at all. But we weren't losing it either. I used to take out seven or eight hundred dollars a month for living expenses, and every cent above that went right back into the business. It still does. But we needed to expand. It was about this time that I moved into that office you saw yesterday in the Edificio Avenida Central. I always wanted a spectacular office, though I had to pay a little bit of premium to get it. Besides, they're the only fully air-conditioned offices in town. When we moved in, there was just myself, the secretary, and an office boy. Now I employ forty people, half of them full time. Next month we'll be taking over another two offices on the same floor."

"So you're making money now?"

"We're making it and putting it back in, like I said. We're increasing the value of the business all the time. I could sell out for fifty thousand dollars any time I wanted, but I wouldn't. I want to see it continue to grow. Next year we shall be handling ten percent of all the American tourists who'll come here—that'll be about eight thousand tourists. We shall have a turnover next year of around a million dollars." *

"And you enjoy it?"

"You bet I enjoy it. I enjoy making money and I enjoy the business. Once you start making money, you want to see if you can make some more. Just to show yourself you can. Just to satisfy yourself. Every day I see all my employees leaving the office, I say to myself, they're all dependent on me, if it wasn't for me, they wouldn't be

---

* Mr. Cabell informs me that today (1969) his firm, now called Brasil Safaris and Tours, employs over two hundred people and last year handled twenty-seven thousand tourists, or approximately seventy per cent of all American bookings.

here. That's a helluva responsibility. Naturally I want to see them happy. Who wouldn't? Then I want to build this thing into the best thing of its kind in South America. Already the leading agents in Europe and the U.S. are recognizing me as the leading agent here. That's a tremendous satisfaction."

"What would you say was the secret of your success?"

"Figuring out all the problems and then deciding how to overcome them. Before you propose any kind of a deal to anyone, you've first of all got to convince yourself about it. If you can't convince yourself, you won't convince anyone else. It's mainly a question of good planning, good timing, and good execution."

"How about your private life?" I said.

"I don't have much. I have this apartment along the beach here, but I'm not often in it. I get up at six every morning and have a swim. I go to the office about eight, and I leave around seven or seven-thirty in the evening. I eat late as a rule, and I don't usually get to bed before midnight. I can do with about four hours' sleep a night."

"You're not married?"

"I'm not against it, but I just haven't had time to think about it. I've been too busy. I guess I'll get around to it before long."

"Do you ever feel you would like to go back to the States?"

"Never. I have no intention whatever of leaving this country. It's a great place. Forty percent of it is still unexplored. They need a great motivating force here to open it up. America is losing out on this country. The States are full of people earning five to six hundred dollars a month and working nine to five each day. They're up to their ears in debt and haven't got enough balls to get off their asses. They're just not prepared to go and slum it out in a country like this and eat what the poor people eat. It's not ready-made for them. If you want to succeed in a place like this, you have to go out and make it yourself."

Like Bob Falkenburg, I thought. Their stories were variations on the same theme: originality, single-mindedness, drive. The pool was filling up now with early afternoon bathers, and I noticed the child with the harelip and bucket hat creeping gingerly into the shallow end.

Mr. Cabell got up to go, and I asked him a question that had been in the front of my mind ever since we sat down. "That scar on your lip," I said, "did you get that hunting?"

Mr. Cabell smiled. "No," he said, "I got that in a fight over a girl."

He drifted away, and when he had gone, a long, thin, elderly American lady came up to me and said, "Excuse my asking, but the name of that young man who was with you doesn't by any chance happen to be Scobie, does it?"

"No," I said. "Why?"

"He reminds me so much of a very dear suitor I had thirty or forty years ago."

I tried to figure it out, but it was beyond me. "No," I said, "that wasn't Scobie, that was Cabell. Mr. Charles A. Cabell," I added, "the Third."

✪

I HAD asked Mr. Cabell if any tours of his were in Rio, and he said only one, the Association of New York Cattlemen. They were leaving for home the next afternoon, but in the morning they were going up the Sugar Loaf mountain peak to look at the view and the statue of Christ the Redeemer. I would be welcome to join them if I cared to.

They were staying at the Copacabana, and we assembled in the lobby at eight-thirty in the morning. There were about thirty or forty cattlemen, and they wore little badges which said "GOODWILL AMBASSADOR U.S.A. PEOPLE TO PEOPLE." I wondered whose benefit this was for, and what kind of reaction was expected, and whether a real goodwill ambassador would ever wish to emphasize that he was one. The cattlemen were all shapes and sizes. They mostly wore shirts and slacks; some had golfing caps and some straw hats and some no hats at all. A few had brought their wives and most their cameras. The party's guide was a handsome young man of nineteen called Byron, and I remembered what Mr. Cabell had said about him. "I found him up the Amazon. He speaks nine languages, and I give him the cream of the tours. It's a hell of a responsibility for a kid of his age, but I pay him well and he's up to it." Byron introduced me to the cattlemen's leader, a Professor Vazey, who shook me warmly by the hand and said he was real glad to have me go along with them. "We represent all types of cattle breeders," he said, "big ones, little ones, pedigree, regular. We think that's pretty nice."

We all got into a bus to go to the cable-car station. When everyone had taken his seat, Byron got up at the front and said, "Was the service any better for breakfast this morning?" They chorused that it was, and the man next to me whispered, "Yesterday it was just lousy." As we drove through Rio the cattlemen kept peering out the windows, as though fearful of missing something important.

At the cable-car station there was a train already waiting. It had a roof but no windows. The compartments consisted of simple wooden benches facing each other. Some of these were already occupied by local people who lived up the mountain and had been down in Rio shopping at the market. We all piled in and sat down seven or eight to a bench. It was a bit of a squeeze. Presently a little bell rang and the train moved off, or rather up. One of the wives said, a bit late, "Let's go!" and another, "Where are the life preservers?" They were all determined to enjoy themselves. Opposite me a dark Carioca combed wet hair flamboyantly.

We stopped at two stations, and then, at the third, which was quite large and called "Silvestre," we waited for the train coming down the mountain. Most of the locals got off here, which gave us rather more room. We climbed slowly through cool jungly trees and admired at the side of the track a profusion of pretty pink flowers, shaped like four-leaf clover. Then, suddenly, we were above the tree line, suspended in space, clinging to the mountainside like flies to a curtain, all Rio beneath us. "Hold your hat," shouted one of the cattlemen, "here we go!" They were great jokers, these cattlemen, and never tired of wisecracks about the precariousness of our position. "Glad I checked up on my life insurance before I took this trip," said another man ponderously, and those round him giggled. Some leaned over the edge of the compartment and peered down. Beyond the track the ground fell sheer away, so that we looked down on treetops a hundred feet high. "Long ways down there," murmured one man, and his friend said, "I never saw such tall trees." They all snapped away with their cameras, and another man took out a huge map and said to his wife, "Honey, do you want to orientate yourself?"

Presently we reached the station at the top. Byron told us that it was a five-minute walk to the platform at the summit, and that we must be back at the station in twenty minutes. The cattlemen piled out of the train and set off up the steps like a sort of ragged army. As they went they exchanged questions like "How ya coming?" and "How's tricks, Charlie?" and answers like "Okay, Ed," and "Pretty good, I guess." It was a long pull up the steps and when we reached the top some joker said, "Twenty minutes up. Time to go back."

It was misty on the platform but the view was impressive. You could see the whole biscuity coastline, Leblon, Ipanema, Copaca-bana, Botafogo, Flamengo, and the local airport beyond. Nearer, on the green hills beneath us, which looked like so many ant-heaps, sprawled the cancerous *favelas*. And behind us stood the reason for our visit, the monstrous white Christ, feet together and arms out-stretched, weighing 1,450 tons, and with an arm span of over ninety feet. From below it had looked quite attractive, even moving, but here, close to, it was gross and overpowering, like Battersea Power Station or the Eiffel Tower, a feat not of art but of engineering. The cattlemen didn't pay much attention either to Christ or the view. Tourists everywhere have a knack of diminishing everything they see, and these were no exception. They bought postcards and drank Coca-Cola, photographed each other, and generally milled around. I heard one man say, "That was a pretty good breakfast this morning"; and another, "We took the radiator cap off, and the water just poured out everywhere." Two wives ate fresh pineapple at a stall, and one said, "Why can't we get fresh pineapple in the States?" After ten minutes we drifted down the steps again and met a sad-looking cattleman sit-ting on a bench at the bottom. "I never made it," he said. "I'm glad I didn't. What was it like up there?" A voice in the crowd said, "Oh, you didn't miss a thing."

Back at the station Byron told us that the bus which had collected us at the hotel that morning had also been climbing the mountain, and would pick us up at another station a little way down the line. I think the party was glad of this, finding going downhill in the cable car a good deal more unnerving than going up.

When we were all in the bus and Byron had counted us like sheep, Professor Vazey came and sat beside me. I asked him what he was professor of, and he said Animal Husbandry at Cornell. He added that all together there were thirty-five professors of animal husbandry at Cornell. I looked at him sharply to see if he was drunk or joking, not believing there were that many professors of Animal Husbandry in the world. I said I had never thought of New York as being a cattle state. "And you'd be right," said Professor Vazey, "because it's *not* primarily a cattle state, not numberwise, not percentagewise. It's more a *dairy* state." I wondered whether to tell Professor Vazey that he had missed the point and that I hadn't thought of it as a dairy state either.

"Let me wise you up on our little group," said Professor Vazey. He pointed down the bus. "That man is an undertaker, but he keeps a few cattle on the side. That one in the check shirt is a poultry farmer, and he also keeps some cattle on the side. This man just in front of us is one of the biggest cattle owners in America. That guy over there in the golfing cap . . ." Locustlike, Professor Vazey left no cattleman untouched, and by the time he had finished, we had reached the bottom of the mountain.

"You seem a very varied group," I said.

"We're what you might call a selected group," said Professor Vazey. "We're pretty choosey who we have. We don't just put an ad in the papers. Basically, this is not a sightseeing holiday. We tell people, if you just want to go sightseeing, you've picked the wrong trip."

"What kind of trip is it?"

"Basically, it is to get to know our counterparts and their families in Latin America, visit their ranches and see how they're doing. Of course, we do a little sightseeing as well, it would be silly not to, but that's not the object of the trip."

"How much time have you spent in Brazil getting to know your counterparts?"

"Well now, I should think one day or maybe two. Of course we would like to have had more, but we have only three weeks for the whole tour, and that takes in three other countries besides Brazil. So, with the sightseeing and all, we can't spend as much time with everyone as we would like. Now, yesterday we had a very interesting day. We went visiting at a ranch in the morning and the university in the afternoon. That was a *delightful* day."

"You don't find it too rushed?"

"Oh no, we don't find it rushed at all. We just love to meet people and for them to see what we're like, and it's nice for us too, because everybody has been so friendly. We wear these little goodwill-people-to-people badges, as you see, and everybody think's that's pretty nice."

"Does this goodwill-people-to-people idea work in reverse?"

"How do you mean?"

"Well, do Latin-American cattlemen and their families go on goodwill trips to the States?"

Professor Vazey thought deeply. "Well, now," he said, "if they do, I don't recall it. I don't recall any Latin-American cattlemen doing a thing of that kind." He was struck by the novelty of the idea. "Now that you mention it," he said, "I sure do hope they will, because I sure would like them to come and visit with us."

Professor Vazey then told me about the various strains in cattle which he said he knew would interest me, and when he was through with that, we arrived back at the hotel. I went up to my room to make a couple of telephone calls, and when I came down, the cattlemen were getting ready to leave for the airport. Near the cashier's desk there was a bit of a commotion going on. I edged round toward it, and saw one of the cattlemen waving his arms about and shouting. "How do you get out of this place?" he bawled. "You ask these people to give you a bill and they won't *give* it you." He lowered his head like one of his own bulls and glared around him. "I'm going to forget about the whole thing and get out of this goddam place. I wish I was back in the United States."

The desk staff of the Copacabana stood silent, appalled. Even among the cattlemen and their wives I detected a certain simmering unease. Two American ladies staying in the hotel appeared beside me, and one said, "Excuse us, but who is that gentleman?"

I couldn't resist it. "That, madam," I said, "is a good-will ambassador U.S.A."

✪

I SPENT a lot of time in Rio wandering around, buttonholing people, posing questions about Americans.

At the British embassy I asked a charming senior diplomat if he knew of any Britishers like Charles Cabell or Bob Falkenburg who were running one-man shows, starting their businesses from scratch. He thought hard and said he didn't. There were no brave young men here from Leeds or Glasgow or Devon setting up pubs or teahouses or fish-and-chips shops. Rio was not going British, but American. The hamburgers and ice cream, laundromats and bowling alleys spoke for themselves. They were here because the Cariocas wanted them; but they only knew they wanted them because people like Cabell and Falkenburg had given them the opportunity of finding out.

Mr. Callado, editor of one of Rio's leading papers, said to me, "You have no idea of the colossal influence of America on the young people here. I know many older Brazilians who are quite worried about it.

They think the Americans are going to take our personality away. It's in the cities, mainly. The further you get away from the cities the less American influence there is. But in the cities it is very strong. It takes all forms—jazz music, clothes, literature. They read Hemingway and Fitzgerald, and Mailer and Bellow. When they want to say something anti-American, they quote American writers who are rebels themselves. That is how American they have become.

"Or you take a place like Bob's. You have to have something very good at home to prevent the young people going to Bob's. One hates it oneself. One wants to sit down for lunch and take one's time. But they love it. It's good and it's cheap; and when they get in there they feel they are in the movies."

And what of the Americans themselves? The British diplomat said, "They have a vast embassy here which is unnecessary and ostentatious. In the economics department they have five men doing the job I'm doing. They're simply pouring money into the place. They fixed the revolution, and now they're paying for it. In diplomacy they're a hundred years behind us, but learning fast. By and large, the people they've got here are a first-class crowd. Normally I find Americans oppressive, but here they're simply splendid, and I've never been able to say that before."

Mr. Callado said, "Before the war, they were just like the British, only louder. They kept themselves to themselves, and visited their own clubs, and went home regularly for holidays. But now it is different. Now they have learned the language. They are good mixers now." He paused and smiled. "We don't really like them any better," he said, "but we need them."

Mr. Lengyel, a reporter on Mr. Callado's paper, who looked a little like Danny Kaye, said, "One thing they're very bad at here is public relations."

"In what way?"

"This is the four-hundredth anniversary of the Rio Carnival, and for us it is a very big occasion. But they are not sending us anyone we want. Whom do we want? Ideally, we would like a football team, but they don't have any football teams. Right. Whom else do we want? Sinatra. The American government should get hold of Sinatra and if necessary pay him ten million dollars to come. They are spending far more than that here on AID and wheat and that kind of thing, but that makes no impression on the common people. Sinatra would. If they sent Sinatra here, Rio would go mad."

"Perhaps Sinatra is doing other things," I said, "or perhaps he doesn't want to come."

"Never mind. They should pay him enough money to *make* him want to come."

✪

LUNCH AT the American embassy was a very private affair; just the ambassador, Lincoln Gordon; his wife; Jack Wyant; and me. We sat at a small table in a very large room and ate asparagus, cutlets and chocolate pudding. The ambassador was a tiny, twinkly man who had been a Rhodes Scholar at Oxford and was well spoken of by almost everyone in Rio. I had hoped we might talk of Brazil and Brazilian politics, but the ambassador seemed more interested in England and English books and plays.

After lunch the ambassador and Jack had to go off to an appointment, so I spent the afternoon with Mrs. Gordon, who had a brown crinkled face like a walnut and sounded so New England she might have passed for British. She loved Brazil, she said, and so far had visited twenty of its twenty-two provinces. "I just adore their churches. To me the Portuguese style is much more attractive than the Spanish. There's a baroque church in Recife which I think is the loveliest church in the world." We spoke about the coming four hundredth anniversary of the Rio Festival, and she said that not as many or as varied American artists were coming as they would have liked. "Lincoln didn't get the information about what was wanted soon enough." I told her what Mr. Lengyel had said, and she laughed. "Oh, everyone always wants Sinatra. *Everyone.*"

I mentioned the size of the embassy staff, which everyone had commented on, and she said, "Oh, we have *far* too many people. It's a question of specialists. We have to have specialists in everything. It's not enough to have an agricultural specialist. We have to have a whole lot of specialists who specialize in different departments of agriculture." She said that when she was in London and had been taken in a group to Buckingham Palace to meet the Queen, the wife of the American ambassador there had whispered to them, "All keep very close together. Disguise the fact that we're the biggest group here."

One of her jobs was to see that newly arrived wives of embassy staff were properly oriented and instructed in the dos and don'ts of Brazilian society. "I suppose this is the American touch," she said. "One must organize everybody. But, goddammit, it works." What sort of dos and don'ts, I asked? "Well, what to do in a car accident, for instance. Not to run away—which is what the Brazilians do. What to wear at a wedding or a funeral. Women don't wear hats here, so we tell the wives where you can rent a hat for the day. Then we organize monthly lectures by Brazilians, and that way they learn about the country."

Much of her free time and that of other embassy wives was spent in working for voluntary organizations. "You'll hardly believe this, but I get requests from twenty-four hundred voluntary organizations a year. In Rio alone there are eight hundred and eighty-seven of them. Many of the embassy wives had had no previous experience of voluntary work, and frankly I found this astonishing." Some wives now went up to the *favelas* to teach the children to play games. "It's a curious thing, but children here aren't taught to play games at all. Of course they get very excited and argue and scream, but they do learn." She told me how she had raised money to pay for a social worker at an orphanage. "There was an international fair here, and I decided I wouldn't have anything sent in from the States, so I got a local man to make book matches, white with red and blue stripes and tiny stars in the center. The profit on these was enough not only to pay for the social worker but for the man who had made the matches to buy himself a new cow as well. Believe it or not, the old one had been destroyed by bats."

Just before I left, Mrs. Gordon said: "I wish you success with the book. By the way, what are you going to call it?"

"*Very Lovely People,*" I said.

There was a tiny pause, and Mrs. Gordon said, "I imagine the interpretation of that would be in the pejorative sense?"

"There isn't meant to be a particular interpretation," I said. "The interpretation can be what anyone cares to make of it. It's just a phrase that Americans use and Britishers don't use."

"Of course, you realize," said Mrs. Gordon, "that it's a phrase that many Americans don't use either. It's only *certain* Americans that use it. Lincoln and I would never *dream* of using it."

She said this not the least bit snobbishly or patronizingly. But, then, she was not a snobbish or patronizing person. Indeed she, and the ambassador, were both very lovely people.

✪

AFTERWARD JACK took me to his apartment to meet his wife. She was a soft, sleepy blonde, with blue, blue eyes and full lips, as pretty and natural as could be. (On the way there Jack had said, "She comes from Seattle and has U.S.A. written all over her. You couldn't mistake her nationality a mile away.") She went off to organize drinks and presently a large colored woman came in with tumblers and a tray of ice. Jack offered me a cigar, which I declined. "Brazilian cigars," he said, "are marvelous. If only the Brazilians were a little more aggressive and imaginative with their merchandising, they could do a lot with their cigars." I thought, perhaps another Cabell or Falkenburg will come along, and they will.

Mrs. Wyant brought in the drinks, and Jack said, "We entertain here every weekend. We have about a dozen people along, but never more than one or two Americans or people like yourself. They're mostly Brazilian newspaper people. We get our girl in there to put on a special Brazilian lunch, and she gives *feijoada*, which is a mixture of black beans and about nineteen different cuts of meat, and *batida*, which is a drink made of lemon, honey, alcohol and sugar cane. She comes from the north, so she makes the best *feijoada* in the world. So when the guests come, they know they're not going to have to worry about the *feijoada*. It's a gimmick, if you like, but it works."

We had a couple of drinks and Jack said, "You mustn't get the idea that the Americans are the only large group of foreigners here. They're the most noticeable, certainly, but that's another thing. Rio is full of Portuguese, which you wouldn't know about if you didn't speak the language. Then there's a crowd of Sephardic Jews from the Middle East. They generally start off by pushing carts, and the Brazilians call them Turks. Then they open a store and the Brazilians call them Syrians. When they get a stage further and own a business, they're called higher-class Syrians. And finally, when they have a home in the mountains and own a boat, they're Lebanese. No, they're not resented as some Americans are, because they've become integrated into the society."

"The unsuccessful Americans," said Jack, "are mostly those who come here on their own. After a time they find they can't take it, so they just go back to the States. But one or two stay on, hoping for better times."

"Do you know any?"

Jack said, "Yes, I do. I know one pair who aren't half a mile from here."

✪

Their names were Homer and Arnold and they worked in a one-horse garage down a side street in Botafogo. The garage was long and narrow and gloomy, and it specialized, so a sign in English said, in wheel alignment and brake adjustment. There were photographs on the walls of racing cars and boxers. Homer and Arnold were the only people there. They were two sad, bald, paunchy middle-aged men who had grown old before their time. Their faces were lined and their hands yellow with car grease. Homer, who wore a stained white coat, said his real name was Winkelstump.

I said to Arnold, "How did you come here?" and Arnold said, "I came here in my mother's belly. I was conceived in Brazil and born in Ireland. My father was born in Glasgow and my mother in Newmarket. When I was eight I went to school in Ireland, and after that in Wales. I've been around."

"Yes."

"My father died when I was twenty-one. He had the first Ford garage here in Rio. I sold the business, and with the money I got from it I started up this place. I ran it for five years and then I was broke. I was too young, too stupid, and I had a sharp partner. Then Homer came along and bought the lease off me."

"And then what did you do?"

"I did a lot of things. For a time I worked with a gangster."

"What did he do?"

Homer said, "He drank. The two of them used to get drunk together."

Arnold said, "He operated in processed meat, for one thing. So I became a butcher. I didn't even know how to cut the damned stuff. Then later Homer took me on here again, as an *empregado*."

"What's that?"

"That's an employee. I told you, I used to run the joint."

I asked Homer where he came from, and he said, "Chicago. And I wish I was back there right now."

Arnold said, "You mean you wish you'd never left."

"That's right," said Homer. "I wish I'd never left."

"Why did you?"

"Because I have a brother here who's an executive in Lojas Americana—that's the big chain store—and he told me there were lots of opportunities for good mechanics here, and to come on down. That was a bad, sad day."

"Why?"

"Why? Because in Chicago I was earning around one hundred thirty-five bucks a week, saving nearly half. I had my own house and my own car. I got home at five and I had supper. At seven I had a shower, and then I'd say to the wife, 'What's it to be tonight? Visit friends or see a movie?' I don't make one hundred thirty-five bucks here."

"Like hell you don't!" said Arnold.

"I make around seventy at the present rate of exchange, and I don't save a cent. The more the dollar goes up, the less I get. Last year the cost of living rose by ninety percent. That's inflation for you. With one week's pay in the States, I could buy a TV set. Here it would cost me about nine months' pay."

Arnold said, "I'm getting kicked out of my apartment. The rent was six thousand cruzeiros in 1957, and now the man wants a hundred twenty thousand. It consists of a bedroom, living room, kitchen and bathroom, and you can put small before all of them."

Homer said, "I don't see much of my family except at work. I have a daughter of sixteen who helps my wife in the office here, and a boy of thirteen. The boy's at school and school fees are high. We never go to a show. I don't have the money and I don't have the time. I get up at five and by the end of the day I'm so goddam tired I go to bed."

Arnold said, "Why don't we go have a drink?"

We went across the road to a tiny, sad bar and had a round of drinks. The drinks were sticky and small and rather sour. There were a few workmen in there and Arnold and Homer exchanged greetings. Homer said, "Do you understand Portuguese?" I said no, and Homer said, "I understand it, but I don't speak it too well. It's a hell of a language."

I said, "What are you going to do?"

Homer said, "What the hell can we do? You tell me."

"Go back to the States?" I said. "Listen," said Homer. "I have a lot of equipment here. I paid good dollars to bring it in from the States. Now they've put a ban on foreign imports, so when any of that equipment wears out or breaks down, I have to improvise the spare parts. If I sold all that equipment tomorrow, do you know what I'd get?"

"No."

"I wouldn't get enough to buy two hamburgers. Not with the exchange the way it is. So there's no going back to the States. Besides, I'm fifty-five. What would I do? Where would I go? Who'd want me?"

We had another round of drinks and Homer said, "We're not able to make a decent living here, and we can't raise the dough to get out. We're *stuck*. Right?"

"Right," said Arnold.

"And you want to know the worst thing?" said Homer.

"Yes."

"The worst thing is the social thing. The average American who works here is an executive, and he moves at an executive level. But the American mechanic here isn't on any kind of level. The American executive doesn't want to know you. Oh, he comes into the garage and has his car serviced and his brakes adjusted, and he's very nice and friendly, but socially he doesn't want to have anything to do with you. Because he thinks you haven't made the grade like he has, see? Now, where the Brazilians are concerned, I have one or two very good friends. But even these relationships aren't too easy. I'm not what the average Brazilian expects an American to be. I'm not an executive. On the other hand, I have had a better education than he has. So he can't place me, see? I don't fit into any established category. The thing is just about fouled up everyways."

"Have another drink?" I said.

"No, thanks," said Homer. "Time we was getting back." He swallowed his drink and pushed the glass across the counter. "Don't misunderstand us," he said, "we're not bellyaching, and we don't dislike Brazil. It's not a bad country. In many ways it's a good country. It's just that we have certain problems, and until this goddam inflation gets outside itself, we'll go on having them. Well, so long, mister."

They shuffled out of the bar, stained and weary, and walked heavily across the street. They reminded me, in their slow gait and resigned manner, of mariners you sometimes see in seaport towns who have just learned that their ship has sailed without them. The garage swallowed them up.

✪

BEFORE LEAVING Rio I thought I should see someone connected with
the vast AID program, whose investment here was second only to that
in Vietnam. At the AID office they bandied a number of names
about. When they mentioned Kent Lutey my ears pricked up: this
was the man who Bob Falkenburg said had started Kibon ice cream in
Rio; and ever since, I had noticed the yellow Kibon carts plying their
trade about the streets. Now Kent Lutey was back in Rio as a director
of AID.

The Luteys lived high up in a big Copacabana apartment block,
and their sitting-room windows embraced the bay. It was a big, spacious room, full of light and colors and beautiful, delicate things.
There were Chinese scrolls and a Chinese teak screen and green
plants in tubs, and a charming ornamental bird resting among carna-
tions on a mahogany coffee table. There was a red Chinese tapestry
and a pre-Ming stupa, cast in bronze and dipped in gold. And there
was an exquisite Japanese screen, which Mr. Lutey said was four hundred years old and had been given by the Japanese to an American
general at the end of the war in gratitude for the good behavior of his
troops. It was a collector's room, that of a man whose success in a
lifetime of business had enabled him to gratify his tastes.

Kent Lutey was a quiet, gentle man in his early sixties who bore
some resemblance to the late General George C. Marshall. His wife
gave us dinner, and afterward we put our coffee cups on the mahogany coffee table, round the ornamental bird. The beat of the surf
came to us through the open windows. I felt content and replete, and
that all I wanted was to listen to the whispering sea and look at the
beautiful things around me and hear from this cultured man how and
where he had found them.

"Tell me about AID," I said, "and Kibon, and this room and
everything."

"One thing really followed another," he said. "Where would you
like me to begin?"

"At the beginning," I said.

So he did. As a young man in 1926 he had gone out to China as a
representative of an American egg firm. The firm specialized in dried
and frozen eggs. Later he and a partner bought the business and ex-

panded it to include other foods including ice cream. "Teaching the Chinese to eat ice cream was a bit of a trick, because the Chinese think that anything cold is death. The reason for that is that at that time the only fertilizer they used there was human fertilizer, so that you had to cook everything to make it safe." For the next few years the business continued to expand and it was then that he collected many of his Chinese art treasures. "In 1937 the Japs arrived and destroyed the plant. I stayed on to help rebuild it, but by 1939 I'd come to the conclusion that a conflict between us and the Japs was inevitable, so I left.

"Well, by this time I'd had some experience in seeing how successful American business methods could be abroad, so I came on down to Latin America with two handbags and a modest sum for capital investment."

"What do you call a modest sum?"

"A hundred thousand dollars."

I thought, but did not say, that ideas of modesty differed.

"I went to Argentina first, but I didn't like the regime. So then I came here and started a dried-egg business. It went along all right, but it wasn't really paying the rent. So I looked around again and saw the possibilities in the ice-cream market. There was ice cream of a sort here, but it was only really a milk sherbet, with about thirty percent sugar and very, very sweet. Everyone said to me, if you're going to make ice cream here, you've got to make it sweet. Well, as a food man I knew that was wrong, because sweetness cloys—you just don't come back for more. I went to a lot of parties then, and I'd notice that the tables were all loaded with sweet things, but that after the guests had gone, there were almost as many sweet things left as when the party started. So then I began making exhaustive food analyses of what the Brazilians ate and drank, and I found out that the most popular beverage in Brazil was not a sweet drink but *beer*. Now, beer isn't sweet. Well that put me on the right track, which was that everybody I had spoken to was wrong, and that Brazilians didn't have to have sweet things at all.

"I decided to make ice cream to U.S. standards, which was about half the sugar content of Brazilian ice cream. I gambled on being able to get my raw materials from abroad until such time as I could get them locally. In those days there weren't these import restrictions. It took me seven years. I got most of my raw materials from the United States and the Argentine. I had one or two Brazilians come in with me and we set up a small factory and made the stuff and offered it to the shops. But the shops all said, 'You're asking five cruzeiros a liter, and our stuff sells at one cruzeiro a liter. Why should we buy yours? Of course, it's better, but in the hot weather people will buy anything.'

"So here I was with a product I believed in but couldn't sell. I decided I had no choice but to go out and sell it on the streets. So I got carts and hawkers and made some beautiful selling containers, and we loaded up the carts and sent the hawkers off. Now, these hawkers were supposed to come back to the factory when they'd sold out and load up with more. But a lot of them didn't show up. They were on a commission basis—which all my Brazilian friends had advised me against—and with the commission they got from selling the first load, they were able to take it easy for a day or two.

"In the end, the thing paid off. When the hawkers finally showed up, I told them if they wanted the job back, their names could go at the bottom of the list and they'd have to wait a week or maybe a month to get their carts back. After that, they worked all week.

"From then on we didn't look back. When the hawkers became a success, the shops found they couldn't sell their poor products any more, and we started selling to them. Then I took on one or two Brazilian directors, and that paid off too. We opened up centers in other parts of the country. The thing just grew and grew and grew. We branched out into other fields, like chocolate and breakfast foods, and finally in 1960 I sold out my controlling interest to General Foods and was able to retire."

"What did you sell your interest for?"

He smiled again. "That is a secret between me and General Foods."

"This name Kibon," I said, "what is the origin of that?"

"One night at the casino I heard Carmen Miranda singing a song called 'Chicaboom.' I liked that name, so I got an advertising agency to arrange a contest for a trade name and mention that something like 'Chicaboom' was what we were looking for. Well, about four hundred names came in and I didn't like them at all. Then, right down among the also-rans, I spotted this name 'Kibon' and it hit me and that was it. 'Kibon' is slang for '*Que Bom!*' which means 'How good! How wonderful!' My Brazilian colleagues were dead against it; they thought it didn't have any prestige, it was too vulgar. But it must have stuck with them, because about two months later they said it didn't sound so bad after all, and they agreed to it and it became one of the successes of the company."

"It sounds a long way from there to becoming an administrator of AID," I said.

"After I sold out to General Foods I stayed on here for a while, but my health wasn't any too good, and I became increasingly depressed by the regime. So I took my family back to the States and we settled down in a house in Bronxville, which is in Westchester County, in New York State. I stayed there a couple of years and then along came the revolution and they wrote to me out of the blue from Washington saying would I help administer the AID program. By this time my health had improved, and I had the kindest feelings toward this country and its people for all they had given me, so it seemed the most natural thing in the world to accept."

"What exactly do you do in AID?"

"I set up loans for projects that we think are going to help the economy of Brazil. We get many more requests for loans than we can meet, and we have to examine them very carefully. We give money toward basic things. Factories that will sell stuff to other factories, capital for housing projects, money for cooperatives. We don't just lend money to build houses. We say, 'You form a savings and loan society, or a cooperative society, our money will help to get you started and your monthly payments will carry you on.' We don't give any of this money direct, it's all done through Brazilian institutions."

"What's your biggest problem?"

"Inflation. Inflation has made it difficult to get credit for new machinery and fertilizers for agriculture. At times we've been able to do no more than keep the economy afloat. If they could really get a hold on inflation, the country would really go ahead.

"This country," said Kent Lutey, "in terms of growth potential, has the biggest future of any country in the world, including the United States."

I walked home through an empty Rio. The cars had gone from the streets, the tarts from the sidewalks, the Macumba worshipers from the beach. Deserted Rio symbolized deserted Brazil, a country, as people never tired of telling me, almost as big as America but with less than half its population. But slowly things were changing. The old Brazilian machine, inasmuch as it had ever existed, was worn out, rusted, useless. Now a new one had taken its place, huge and bright and shining, American designed and built, for the use of Brazilian operatives. All sorts of people, from the President of the United States to Lutey and Gordon and Wyant and, yes, even Falkenburg and Cabell, were seeing that its nuts were tightly screwed and its sump kept filled with oil. It was already beginning to hum with power, a machine geared to keep running day and night, year after year; like the strong Atlantic which even now, in the cool Cariocan night, was continuing its measured assault on Copacabana's sands.

✪

PARAGUAY, AS I think John Gunther once pointed out, is Ruritania. Of all Latin-American countries, it is perhaps the most isolated, the least known. The easiest way of getting there from Buenos Aires is by air; but those with time on their hands may travel in the thousand-ton *Ciudad da Paraná,* three days and a thousand miles up the rolling river, with hostesses and Muzak to while away the hours; or, if they are gluttons for punishment, by the non-air-conditioned, still-woodburning State Railway. The tracks were laid down by the British in 1859, and the sleeping cars, built in 1901, are still in use today.

Fewer than two million people live in Paraguay, an area larger than Italy. Another half million are exiles in Argentina, some for political reasons, more, like the Irish in England, to seek work they cannot find at home. Europeans first came to Paraguay in 1537, soldiers of His Most Catholic Majesty of Spain, and on the banks of the river they set up their capital of Nuestra Señora Santa María de la Asunción, now a rose-red city of 300,000 people. With sword and crucifix they subdued the Guarani Indians, whose lands they had appropriated; but the invaders did not crush the natives as they did elsewhere in South America, or make them second-class citizens of the new society they had made. Instead they married them, so that today there is no native-born Paraguayan without at least some drops of Indian blood. And it was the Guarani language, not the Spanish, that prevailed; everybody, or almost everybody, in Paraguay speaks Guarani; about half can speak Spanish as well; no one, or almost no one, speaks Spanish alone.

Westward, across the Paraguay river from Asunción, is the green ocean of the Chaco, the fearful swamp in which Paraguay fought her last bloody war with Bolivia, and now one of the last great natural bird sanctuaries of the world. And to the north and east stretch away the rolling acres of grassland where graze the poor cattle which, when canned or squeezed into Oxo, are the country's principal export. But always in Paraguay nine tenths of what you see is the sky. It is like the sky nowhere else; at night it bubbles with stars, and by day, like a great, blue, tranquil sea, it harbors fleets of tiny milk-white clouds, of astonishing variety and beauty.

✪

A FEW miles up the Paraguay river from Asunción is an island, about a mile long and half a mile wide, thick with trees and other vegetation. It is called Indian Island because a tribe of four hundred Maca Indians live there. They came originally from the northwest of Paraguay, having been befriended by a White Russian general who fought for Paraguay in the Chaco war. After the war he bought the island as a sanctuary for them to live in. The general was a devout Christian and, some say, believed himself to be the Second Coming; his mother, he told the tribe, was the Virgin Mary. This did not prevent him from encouraging tourists from Asunción to come and gape at them, and charging a fee every time anybody landed. In 1938 the general died. But he told the tribe that he would continue to watch over them, and that one day, like his predecessor, he would rise from the dead and come and see how they were doing.

When a motorboat approaches the island today, a group of Indian women of all ages gather at the water's edge and hurriedly shed their blouses, like strippers who have arrived late for their act. As one lands, the first words one hears, from a long-haired brave, are "Cinquenta guaranis," almost the only Spanish he knows. We pay up, the brave gives a signal to the women, and they start a little listless shuffle. As a dance it is nothing, as a strip tease execrable. True, the younger girls have small, firm, horizontal breasts, but those of the majority hang like spaniels' ears. Movement of any kind does not improve them.

After the dance we walk down a track in the center of the island, passing little groups of Indians cooking with pots, picking fleas from each other's hair, lying prostrate in small huts. Some of the women are naked and when they see us they quickly cover up. But they will uncover for photographs at a hundred guarani a session. Presently we come to a sandy clearing, where perhaps fifty more Indians are waiting. Here sits an elderly Indian with corks sewn into the lobes of his ears. This is the Third Chief. The First Chief is drunk and the Second Chief asleep. A bargain is struck with the Third Chief, and we then watch and photograph a dance which is only marginally less gloomy than the first. Someone wants to photograph the Third Chief, but is told that it will cost him another hundred guarani.

After this, all, particularly the Indians, have had enough, and the tourists troop back to the beach. The tourists think they have had a good afternoon and have seen everything on the island worth seeing. What they have not seen are Marvin and Delores Cole.

❂

A LITTLE way beyond the clearing, between the track and the river, stands a wooden cottage. Here live Marvin Cole, his wife, Delores, and their five children: Timothy Gene, thirteen; Carol Dee, eleven; Marva Lee, nine; Jerry, six; and Loren, one. The Coles are missionaries who are giving their lives to the Macas. They built the house themselves, with the help of Maca labor. It cost five hundred dollars.

The house consists of one big room and one small. The parents sleep in the small room, and they all live, work and eat in the big room. Here are four bunks and four little desks and chairs for the eldest children, and a pen for the baby to sleep in by night and play in by day. There's a kerosene-fired cooker and an icebox, and on crates all over the room the essentials of a missionary's life: transistor, two-way radio, sewing machine, tape recorder. On one wall is a big red cloth of lakes and mountains in the state of Washington, and there are two bookshelves full of religious, educational, and children's books. On the rafters under the roof religious slogans have been pinned up: "The Lord has risen indeed," "Thou shalt not covet," "Remember the sabbath day, to keep it holy."

Marvin and Delores Cole are in their early thirties. He is a lean, fair, spectacled young man with something of the student still about him. She is not unlike him, with a rather small mouth and bright, candid eyes. He is wearing a shirt and trousers, she a blouse and skirt. To look at, there is nothing remarkable about them. They have the sort of faces that you pass in the main streets of America a hundred times a day. What is remarkable is that they are here at all.

I spent a day with the Coles, and took with me an American friend with the unusual name of Pooh Kuhn, whom I had met in Washington. She was in her late twenties, a long, gangling girl, very gay and companionable and with an abiding curiosity about foreign parts. She took long, springy strides when she walked, so that her heels seldom seemed to touch the ground.

Pooh Kuhn and I sat round the Coles' table and listened to their story. One or two Indians had followed us up the track and now, with flat, expressionless faces, they gazed at us through the window. The elder Cole boy, Timothy, hobbled about on crutches, the others wandered in and out, and the baby played in its pen. Outside, on an orange tree, a cock sat and crowed.

The Coles both came from Tacoma, in the state of Washington, and they first met when he was sixteen and she fourteen, as members of the same Pentecostal Church, the Assembly of God. He had worked his way through high school in the dry-goods business and later in a dime store, where she worked too. When he was twenty and she eighteen they married. By this time he knew that he wanted to go into the ministry, and had already enrolled in a Bible college. While there he decided he wanted to do missionary work, and when he talked it over with his wife he found that she had reached the same conclusion. "We felt from the Scriptures that we had a personal obligation to share what we had ourselves. In the Scriptures you find what man's condition was before he met God, and how he changed after. This is the root of man's problems."

Marvin graduated from Bible college and Delores had her first baby. Then they went to a mission training school in the Mendocino Forest, in California. "This was to expose us to some of the conditions we were likely to meet with in the field. Better to come to terms with them at home than meet them overseas and have to come to terms with them later." Here they learned languages, linguistics, medicine and religious teaching. "We all did manual labor and we also belonged to the Hot Shot group, which was for putting out forest fires."

Their training over, they took a two-month course in basic Spanish and came to Paraguay in 1954, under the sponsorship of the nondenominational New Tribes Mission.

For the first few years they worked in various parts of the country, both with Indians and with Paraguayans. One of Marvin's greatest difficulties was communicating with Indians who knew no language but their own. So he arranged to return to the States to take a course at the Wycliffe School of Linguistics, which specializes in unwritten languages. But in Asunción "I was with my elder boy getting off a streetcar when he fell and the car went over his left leg, and he had to have it amputated. So that put an end to the summer school, and I spent the rest of that year getting my boy rehabilitated." But he was able to take the course at Wycliffe later.

During these years, and in widely different places, Delores continued to have babies. On their return to Paraguay they spent two years at mission headquarters in Asunción, and then went to a place on the Bolivian border to work among the Ava tribe, who spoke only ancient Guarani. "We were getting along real nicely there when we came down one time to Asunción to check up on things, and the Indian Society asked us if we would come and look after these people here. At that time the Indians were getting drunk all the time and going over to Asunción and making a nuisance of themselves. The Catholics and one or two other missionary groups had been asked, but they'd refused. So Delores and I talked it over and we figured it was God's will. That was three years ago, and we've been here ever since."

During this conversation, Marvin and Delores had had to break off at intervals to see Indians at the door. I asked what they wanted, and Marvin said, "One or two want a bar of soap or medicine or things like that, but many of them have come to say goodbye. There's a whole bunch of them leaving tomorrow for a hunting trip in the Chaco. They'll be away four or five months."

"What do they hunt with?"

"Bows and arrows, and shotguns."

Delores said, "That last one that came, his wife has T.B. real bad. She's had five babies in the last five years and lost every one of them because of breast abscesses."

I said, "All these ten years you've been working here in Paraguay—who pays you?"

Marvin looked at Delores and smiled. "No one. We live on charity. On what people send us."

"How does that work out?"

"We've had the shelf cleaned out more than once, but it's not a thing that worries us. We know that God is looking after us. He's never let us down yet. It's a funny thing about God. He's always surprising you. Often you think He's going to act one way, and then He acts another." I said nothing, and Marvin said, "For us, God isn't remote and intangible. He is a close personal friend."

Delores said, "Tell them about some of our trips back home."

Marvin said, "Oh, man! We go home about once every five years. Before we go, we never know if we're going to have enough money to make the trip, and when we're there we don't know if we'll have enough to get back. But somehow God finds it for us.

"I recall the time we went to the Mission Camp. We figured we had just enough to get there. The day we left I opened a letter and found twenty dollars inside. On the way to the camp the back tire blew and it cost twenty dollars less twenty cents to get another one. I figured God had allowed for that back tire.

"Then, the first time we came to Paraguay, we took the train to Florida. We had the two elder children then, and stopped off near Miami to stay with an Air Force captain whom we had known at Tacoma, who belonged to our Church and was really interested in this work we were doing. When I went to the travel bureau, I found we were still two hundred dollars short on passage money. So there we were, four thousand miles from home and with no visible means of support. It was an embarrassing situation, because we couldn't disguise it though our friends were sympathetic. But we said, what are we worrying about? Did God send us all the way down here just to make fools of us?

"Well, after two weeks the Air Force captain gave us the two hundred dollars and he didn't do it just to get rid of us. He told us afterward that the two weeks we had been in his house had been of real value to him, that we had helped him spiritually. At the time we thought we were being a burden to him, but I know now that God deliberately placed us in the house to be of service. That's what I mean when I say you think God is doing one thing and then find He's doing another. God," said Marvin, "is real clever."

"Tell them about the last time we went home," said Delores.

"Oh, man!" said Marvin. "We needed a thousand dollars for the trip, and we only had two hundred. We'd made all our plans and we needed the money in three weeks. But we didn't worry, we just left it to God. We arrived at Miami with no car, five children, eighty dollars left and four thousand miles to go. We went to a mission receiving home for the night, and Mr. Wegler, who's the director there, had a '55 Plymouth which some other missionary had left on his way to Peru. He said we could have it for two hundred twenty dollars and pay him the money within two months. We spent the first night in a motel, but after that we slept in the Plymouth, and we arrived at my sister's house in northern California with half a tank of gasoline and a dollar in our pockets. She gave us fifteen dollars and her husband gave us twenty, and that just got us through to Tacoma. That was God's will again. God always thinks up something."

"Haven't you ever wondered," I said, "if there might be a time when God would let you down?" I had slipped into Marvin's vernacular almost without knowing it. He had made God so personal that I half expected Him to appear at the window and hear Marvin say, "Hi, God! Come on in!"

"Basically," said Marvin, "I believe that God meant what He said in the Scriptures, especially Matthew 6, about taking care of us if we do His work. But I wouldn't be truthful if I didn't say there have been times when we felt some uneasiness—though when we didn't have the money to do a thing, we've known that it was because God didn't want us to do it. We haven't been able to see it at the time, but afterward we've said '*Wow!* Wasn't it lucky we didn't have the money for that? God really knows what is best for us.' "

It was a great philosophy, I thought; it covered every eventuality. Whatever you did, you couldn't go wrong.

"When you first came here," I said, "did you just show up, or what happened?"

"I came over with one of the members of the Indian Society in Asunción. They'd arranged a meeting with the chiefs. I told the Indian Society I wouldn't go unless all the chiefs wanted me. The first thing I saw when we landed on the island were two drunks leaning on a gate and two others slugging it out on the riverbank. Well, we had this meeting with the chiefs and all agreed they wanted me, except one chief. So I went back to Asunción and made that my headquarters and visited the island regularly with medicines. I just kept on visiting. And I decided to get the folks back home to make this a matter of prayer, because God answers prayers. And soon after this I got word that the chief who had held out had had a dream in which he saw himself and me walking through the village together, and that everything was okay and I was to come on over. Since then he's been one of our strongest supporters.

"So we started building the house, and everything was in except the windows when I had a car accident. I was driving through a little country town about forty miles from Asunción when a woman rushed out of a dead end with a great basket of vegetables on her head. There wasn't a thing I could do. She hit her head on the curb and died within about two minutes, I guess. I was put into a stinking Paraguayan jail with flies all over the place and sewage running down the corridor. They thought that, being an American, I was rich, and they were really going to get me. I had liberty at night, but I had to spend each day in jail. In the end I was brought to trial and completely acquitted.

"Soon after, we moved in. I bought a little furniture, I made some of the rest, and the Indians made those little desks for the children from wood in the Chaco." He turned to his wife. "Remember that first night?" She nodded. "We had to undress in the dark."

"Why?"

"Because there were about forty pairs of eyes staring at us through the windows. They've no sense of privacy, see. And they'd never seen so many beds before."

"Why don't you have curtains?"

"Because they'd be suspicious of what we were doing behind them."

I said, "When you'd finally settled in, what was the first thing you did?"

"The first thing was to learn the language, because until I'd done that I didn't really have communication with them at all. I remember our first day here, the chief came and visited. But I couldn't speak any Maca and he couldn't speak any Guarani, so after we'd exchanged greetings we just sat and stared at each other."

Marvin explained how he applied the technique of linguistics he had learned at Wycliffe. This consisted of phonetics, which was hearing the language correctly and annotating it with written symbols; phonemics, summing up the phonetics, discarding what was not essential and making an alphabet; morphology, which was grammar and sentences; and syntax. One great difficulty, he said, was that what sounded as one thing to him sounded as something else to the Maca. "For instance, when I say *r*, they hear *l*. I have three *k* sounds, but they only have one. For a long time I was puzzled by the word *Maynol. Maynol* means 'Do you have?' and whenever I said '*Maynol*,' they used to reply, '*Maynol*'—which didn't make sense. In the end I discovered that what they were saying was not '*Maynol*' but '*May-nol*' —just a little bit longer—and this meant, 'I still have' or 'There still is.' Another difficulty was their vocabulary, which is completely geared to their way of life. There are many English words for which there is no equivalent in Maca, but they have many words for which we have no equivalent. For instance we have the one word 'Firefly,' but they have words to describe every different *type* of firefly—every plant, every insect, every leaf, many of which, to our eyes, look the same."

"Tell about the hymn you mistranslated," said Delores.

"Oh, man!" said Marvin, "that was real good. I've translated a number of hymns into Maca and they come and sing them every evening. You'll hear them later. Well, I had meant to translate into Maca the line 'I am following Jesus,' but I made a mistake with the symbol, and much later I discovered that what they were singing was, 'I am running away from Jesus, and he can't catch me.' "

Along with the language, said Marvin, he had continued work on the medical side. "These people were in real bad shape. They were riddled with T.B.—they still are, and their nutrition is so poor they'll catch any infection that's going. They drink out of the same pot, spit on the ground, and then the kids sit and play in it. When I'm with them and they're drinking *terere,* which is a kind of tea, they'll offer me the communal pot, and often I don't know whether to refuse and offend them or take it and risk getting T.B. Sometimes I get away with it by saying I have a cold and I don't want to pass it on to them. This they understand; this is a greater gesture of friendship than accepting the tea.

"They have absolutely no idea of hygiene. When they urinate, the women stand and the men squat—it kind of throws you—and they wipe themselves with grass or weeds or anything. Some go over to Asunción and get meat which has been T.B.-rejected by the factory, and they'll bring it back and cook it. One family was always getting ailments, so I checked on where they were getting their water and found it was from a stagnant pool, so I told them to draw it from the river, and after that they got a little better.

"Our worst problem has been the witch doctors. When we first came here, the sick wouldn't come to the house at all. They were afraid the witch doctors would cast a spell on them. When I'd begun to win their confidence, they'd come at night, when they thought the witch doctors wouldn't see them. One night a child was brought to me. It was very sick, and soon after it got here, it died. I thought there might be real trouble then. But another child died the next day not in the house, and so that was all right. They're real fearful of these witch doctors. They think they eat children's flesh like we eat cow's meat. About three weeks back, there was a big outbreak of measles and whooping cough and other things, and nine of the tribe died. One of the children had a dream about the witch doctor, so the tribe decided he must be responsible. They had a conference about it. They all drank this stuff which they make from the cassava root, and when they were drunk, they decided to kill him. They make all important decisions when they're drunk. When it was dawn, they took him out and executed him and buried his body near the river. They thought he was casting spells on them, but he was just a harmless old man with trachoma."

"What happened?" I said. "Did the police come?"

Marvin laughed. "The Paraguayans have washed their hands of this place. They don't want to know anything that goes on here. Here it's the law of the jungle.

"This witchcraft," said Marvin, "makes them very reluctant to give blood. They'll give me sputum and stools to send down to Asunción for analysis at the Baptist hospital, but they don't like giving blood. They think that once you give your blood to someone, that person is then in a position to cast spells on you. Once I found two or three children almost dead from hookworm. I got them over to Asunción, and the Baptist hospital took them in. One of them had T.B. as well as hookworm, and another was so thin the doctor couldn't find any flesh to put the needle in. More times than not he was hitting the thigh bone. Well, it was essential that these kids have a blood transfusion from their fathers, and I thought, Oh dear, here's trouble. But it was okay. The fathers saw their blood going into the bottle and then from the bottle into their children, so they didn't worry."

I said, "Haven't you ever worried that you and your children might pick up some of these diseases?"

"We keep a pretty good eye on things," said Marvin. "We all take tests from time to time, the B.C.G. test for T.B., the sputum test and so on, and we spray the house. All the same, we do have venchucas in the house. They're little bugs about an inch long, and when they're infected, they bite you at night and give you incurable heart disease. We've found them on the floor loaded with blood, so we presume we've been bitten. So far, though, we've got by."

All this time Indian faces continued to stare at us through the windows, and Indian bodies continued arriving at the door. One, a tall hairless man like Yul Brynner, wanted his shotgun fixed. Another had been bitten on the foot by a piranha, the vicious fish that inhabit South American rivers and attack any living thing. An old woman wanted treatment for a carbuncle on her finger ("that's a real ugly finger," said Marvin); and another brought a little bead handbag to sell. "She wants money for it," said Carol Dee, bringing it into the room, and Marvin said, "Tell her I don't want it, honey."

Several others had come for pills, and Marvin said, "Sometimes the children won't take their pills, so the parents come to me and say, 'The boy won't take his pill, what do I do?' So I say to them, 'Well, you're bigger than he is, aren't you? You make him take it. If he doesn't, he'll die.' See, they don't discipline their children at all. I believe in using the rod occasionally, and I find it works pretty well. When I do that, I hear the Indians outside saying 'Man, they're killing them in there.' See, they have the same word for 'beat' and 'kill.' "

Delores, who was over at the cooker, said why didn't Pooh and I take a little walk while she fixed supper? So Pooh and I went down the track, and Pooh said, "My God, don't they make you feel so *unworthy?* I feel I ought to go and join the Peace Corps right away, only I know I'm not the right type." We passed by the little groups of Indians sleeping and cooking and weaving, and Pooh said they looked like the tableaux of Indian life in the American Museum of Natural History. In one group a small girl was clutching a fat, flaxen-haired American doll.

When we got back, the table was laid. Marvin put his hands together and looked at his plate. "Thank you, O Lord," he said, "for looking over us today and guarding us, and for providing this food. And let us thank you also for sending along these two people, and please bless them and direct them in whatever they have chosen to do, and thank you also, Lord, for the day that has been."

For supper we had spaghetti and beans and meat balls, a salad of carrots and avocado, and iced lemonade in plastic mugs.

"How much," I said, "have you tried to teach them Christianity?"

"Well, the first thing I had to do," said Marvin, "when I'd gotten to know the language, was give them a little simple education. See, these people are real savages. They haven't been taught to use their minds or anything. They hunt and fish and cook, and that's about it. When they're not doing that, they get drunk and they dance. They go out and collect this wild honey and let it ferment and then make a brew of it. Some of these dances are real primitive. When a girl is having her first menstruation, the women will form a circle and dance round her in honor of the event. These dances start off harmless enough, but in the early hours of the morning they get real drunk and wild and start fighting. I've seen a man get so drunk he slugged his own mother. They don't seem to have any affection for each other in the way we do, though there's an awful lot of promiscuity. For them, marriage consists simply of an agreement for the man to go and live in the woman's house, and the most I've ever seen in the way of affection is a husband lying on his wife's lap while she picked fleas from his hair.

"When we started education, we had to begin at the bottom. We had three classes, about thirty aged six to thirteen, another thirty teenagers, and a class of ten teen-age girls. I started off showing them the *National Geographic* magazine with pictures of animals, and underneath I'd write the word phonetically in their language. Sometimes they'd look at the pictures the wrong way round. See, they have no idea of depth or proportion. But after a time they got to like it. It was a new experience for them, and soon they were hounding me for education all day long.

"I took it stage by stage. I started teaching simple arithmetic, and I found there were some who could learn real quick, adding three columns, four columns, division, multiplication. There are two fellows just now I'm starting fractions with. One of the best students dropped out one day. So I went to her dad and he said, 'She's getting married soon. Is it right for a woman who's getting married to go to school?' So I said, 'These belts the women make and sell in Asunción for two hundred G's, what'll happen when they can't sell them for two hundred G's?' He said, 'They'll sell for a hundred and fifty'; and I said, 'Yes, because your daughter can't count between one hundred fifty and two hundred. If she could, she'd sell them for one hundred ninety G's.' Well, he saw the point of that. Next day she was back at school."

"How about your own children?" I said. "What do they do for education?"

"Delores takes care of that. Don't you, dear?"

Delores said, "Each time we've gone home, I've put the children into school to see how they are with their grade levels, and they've done just beautifully."

"We teach them the Bible daily," said Marvin. "We tell them it's not just another book, but the living word of God, and full of promise."

"What do you tell the Indians about God?"

"First I used to teach them just morals. Then I started telling them Bible stories and they took a real liking to that. Teaching them about God has been more difficult. See, many of the older ones still believe the Russian general is God. When a storm hits here, they say it's because the general is mad with somebody. There are a lot of snakes in the island, and they say, 'We didn't have that many snakes in the general's day, he used to keep them away.' They talk a lot about God when they're drunk, God this and God that. I say to them, 'You got God at the end of your tongues but not in your hearts. If you ease up on all this drinking and dancing, you'll find that you won't be deprived of anything but lifted to a better plane of life. God gives you better things instead.' I tell them God is the Father, he's greater than the general or the witch doctors or anyone."

Two of the children came in with fish they had caught in the creek. One was a piranha fish and still alive. Somebody put a stick between its jaws and, dying, the fish snapped at it with cruel teeth. "They're real nasty," said Marvin. "Sometimes a wounded animal tries to swim the river, and before you know what's happened, there's nothing left but bones."

Another child said, "Dad, there's a woman at the door who says she has stomach pains real bad."

"Give her some of those antacid pills," said Marvin, "and tell her if she's not better by the morning I'll see her then."

He went over to the shortwave radio and switched it on. There was a lot of crackling, and then we heard a man at mission headquarters in Asunción talking to the field stations. He was talking in a conversational way, finding the words as he went along, but the crackling made him almost inaudible. Once, when it cleared, I heard him say, "We've got a real good school now for the mission children, right opposite the old embassy building. We're going to have to pay thirty thousand G's for it. . . ." The crackling smothered his voice. Later, missionaries from other stations came in with their news, and Marvin tried to say something himself. But the interference was too bad and he switched off. "I guess the atmospherics aren't too good tonight," he said, "but it's a great way of keeping in touch and hearing what everyone's doing."

"How often do you go into Asunción?" I said.

"About every two or three weeks. We go for stores. Some things I get here, like fish and eggs, and others I buy from the Indians—sweet potatoes and squash and guavas and so on. But you can't always rely on them."

"Do the Indians have much money?"

"They have a little. They get a few G's from the tourists, and then the women make little belts and bags like the one you saw, and go over and sell them in Asunción. But they've no idea of thrift. When they have a little money, they'll buy a transistor radio for eight hundred G's. So I rib them. I say, 'That's great. You'll keep it for two or three months and then it'll wear out, and you'll throw it away. But if you'd spent the money on a new machete and a new cook pot and several other things, that would have lasted you years.' They could make more money if they wanted to, but they're lazy."

It was dark now, and the sounds of insects came to us from outside. Delores lit the lamp and put it on the table. Then she took the toys out of the baby's pen, and put down a mattress and got the baby ready for sleep. It was a good baby. It hadn't cried once all the time we had been there. The other children busied themselves with books and drawings. I wondered if any of them was old enough to consider the oddness of their upbringing, whether they were glad it was different from other children or whether they longed for a more conventional childhood in the good old U.S.A. They seemed a remarkably well-integrated family.

Presently there was a sound of voices outside, and Marvin said it was time for the evening sing-song. We went out onto the veranda, where some forty Indians between about five and fifty were chatting together and swatting at the flies. The men had very long hair, and Marvin said that the Russian general had told them long hair was a sign of manhood. At one end of the veranda was a blackboard with a drawing of two trees and, beneath it, three candles and a group of houses. Marvin said that this was where he gave the lessons, and that the candles and houses represented the Heavenly City.

The Indians took their places on rows of benches, the little ones at the front. First they sang a hymn, then Marvin told a story in Maca about Jesus. The language was very odd—a series of glottal grunts, like a pig surprised. I remembered Marvin saying the sounds were so unnatural that at first they made his stomach muscles ache. But he was a compelling speaker. His free hand pointed and soared and dived, and the audience, continuing to swat at flies, looked at him transfixed. Afterward I asked him what he had been saying, and he said, "Where there is Christ, there is good, where there is not Christ, nothing is good. God is more powerful than the Devil." When he had finished he gave a blessing. The Indians put their hands together and leaned forward reverently. It was rather touching. They sang a final hymn, broke into smiles and giggles, and vanished into the night.

"Why don't we go see if there are any crocs?" said one of the children, and we all went down to the water's edge. It was a clear night, and on the surface of the slow, brown river were reflected the lights from a village on the other side. "Crocs are real good to eat," said Marvin, "especially the tails." Timothy, on his crutches, said, "I speared one this afternoon, but I have the rifle now." He shone a powerful torch up and down the creek. It had a long beam, seventy or eighty feet. "You won't see the crocodile," said Marvin, "because its body is under water. What you want to look for is its eye. It's red, like a coal." Timothy weaved the torch about some more, and then, on the far side of the creek, the beam picked up what looked like a small red light. Timothy raised the rifle, but by the time he had trained it the eye had gone. We swept the creek a few more times, but there was nothing. "I guess they've all gone to bed," said Marvin.

We walked back to the house and found that the boatman who had brought us over in the morning was waiting to take us back. He had a friend with him. The friend had a lantern, and they were both carrying rifles. "Why the guns?" I said to Marvin. "Oh, they're real scared," he said, "I'm surprised they've dared come this far." I said, "Would the Indians attack them?" and Marvin said, "Only if they were drunk. When they're drunk there's no telling what they won't do."

Delores gave us a nightcap of lemonade, and I said, "What's going to happen here eventually?" Marvin said, "Eventually they're all going to have to leave. The mortality rate's going down and one day the island won't be able to support them all. It's very low ground, see, and there's only so much of it that's tillable. Besides, the Indian Society wants to get them out of here, send them right into the interior, away from all the tourists and posing for pictures. There's a group of Maca up north who speak Guarani, raise crops, work as cowhands, doing fine. There's no reason these people shouldn't join them."

"And what about you?"

"We shall stay as long as they need us. We've got a nice relationship with them now, and we're making real progress. And we're doing what God wants us to do."

At the door we shook hands. Our two guides went ahead, swinging the lantern, and Pooh and I walked in single file behind. It was eerie going down the track, seeing nothing but the lantern and the dim shapes of our guides, yet aware that the Maca were close at hand. Strange, tropical noises came from all round us, and once, very near, came a fearful strangulated cry, like a child in terror or pain. Pooh, who spoke Spanish, asked the boatman what it was, and he said one small animal killing another.

We came to the landing, got into the boat, and pushed off. I thought, if anything happens to this boat and we find ourselves in the water, the piranha fish will soon gobble us up. I thought, I hope I am unconscious before they reach my parts. Downstream a dull glow warmed the sky, the lights of Asunción. Soon we would be there, cool as Eskimos in our air-conditioned rooms, slumbering sweetly on foam-rubber beds. But Marvin wouldn't be there for another two weeks, and then only for the day. In a way he was a prisoner in a cage of his own making, like the impoverished inheritor of a great country house, free and happy behind his own bars. Yet the gap between his way of thinking and that of the Maca was so huge that in his efforts to impose on them orthodox Christianity, there was something almost farcical. I remembered the line "I am following Jesus," which he had mistranslated as "I am running away from Jesus, and he can't catch me." Did it really matter which of the two versions they sang? And yet, in his efforts to improve their well-being, to lift them an inch from the slough in which they passively wallowed, there was something so splendid and radiant about him that one could only stand and wonder. Somewhere between farce and glory lay the truth. I thought of what Berlioz had said about composing, that he had within him a machine that functioned in a certain way, and that he permitted it to function only because he was powerless to prevent it doing otherwise. In the end, it was a question of semantics. Berlioz took the view that he was inspired from within, Marvin that God was directing him.

It was after midnight when Pooh and I reached the hotel, and I went to the desk for my key and messages. Later Pooh said, "I've just been speaking to that Englishman we met. He said he couldn't wait, but he promised to give me a tinkle. What do you suppose he meant by that?"

"He's going to give you a ring," I said.

"A *ring?*"

"A telephone call. He's going to call you up."

"Well," said Pooh, *"for heaven's sakes!"*

❂

THE WEEKLY Pan Am jet from Asunción to New York screamed skyward; suddenly Asunción became a toy town, the river a shoelace carelessly thrown down; the Chaco came up with the earth's curvature, then blended with the surrounding grassland to make of Paraguay a green blur. There was only a handful of us in the plane, and I had three seats to myself. The hostesses, with time on their hands, gave us special attention, and one, a beautiful young English girl called Tessa, told me she had been with the company two months; she and two other English girls had joined at the same time. When I asked why, she said, "To see the world and have a good time." I said, "Are you?" She smiled and said, "You bet!"

At Caracas a new lot of passengers came aboard, and I gained a neighbor. She was a small, dark, pert and pretty girl in her early twenties, and although she could have sat down only seconds ahead of me, she was already busy scribbling in a large exercise book. Going down the runway most of the passengers looked out the window for reassurance, but she went on scribbling. The plane climbed through the clouds and leveled out, Tessa and her friends offered us coffee or a drink, but my companion never took her pencil from the page.

In the end curiosity got the better of me. Over her elbow, I read: "Education viewed as very important. People will work together and feel pride. Nearest school may be far away—too far for little children to walk—too expensive for parents to pay transport." So here was another stomper for citizenship responsibility; wherever you went, they were never far away.

"You seem busy," I said.

I regretted it almost as soon as I spoke, for she was a girl who gave her undivided attention to whatever she was doing. Up to now it had been the exercise book; from now on it was to be me. She shut the book, smiled a friendly, sexless smile, and said, "Oh, I am. I have *so* much to do."

She told me what it was without prompting. Her mouth was like a bath tap which someone had forgotten to turn off—the words poured out in a continuous flow. "So all these business companies got together and formed this organization called Acción en Venezuela, that means 'Action in Venezuela,' it's a kind of private Peace Corps, really, the object is to do community development work in the *barrios*—those are the slums—and when I got the opportunity to join them I jumped at it. I've been living in a *barrio* these last few months, studying the conditions and needs of the people, and now I'm going home for a month to prepare a report on how things in the *barrios* can be improved—you know, adult education and transportation and proper sewage and so on. Oh, those *barrio* people are sweet. You know, eighteen of them came to the airport to say goodbye. Wasn't that wonderful? And my fiancé is going to meet me at Idlewild, he hasn't seen me for three months, this is the ring he gave me. You know, I'm twenty-two and I've been traveling since I was nineteen. My name's Sally Kroger, what's yours? How do you do? Well, I've been to Africa and Asia and I've stayed with native missionaries and other wonderful people. I started traveling because I wanted to see what other people were like, I knew Americans were different, but I wanted to see just *how* they were different, and after a bit I realized the important thing wasn't just that Americans are different from the rest of the world, but that the rest of the world are different *from each other*. You've got to experience this to realize it, but when you do, it's a big help, I mean it's a big help to know that, say, Venezuelans are different from Filipinos."

It went on like that all the way to New York. After a time I stopped listening; the mind shut off, unable to take any more. But the gale of words blew on, over the canapés and cocktails brought by Tessa and her friends, over the veal from Maxim's, over the coffee and ice cream. It only began to ease up when the lights of Manhattan showed ahead.

In the silence before landing I said, "What are you looking forward to most in New York?" "Making a plan for the *barrio*," she said. Not a word about seeing her fiancé.

Tessa came by with a heap of trays, and I caught her arm and said, "What are *you* looking forward to in New York?" "Oh," she said, stopping, "going out on the town, I suppose. Having a ball." She

smiled across at the other girl, and for a moment their eyes met—
Swinging Britain, you might say, and the Great Society.

✪

ON MY last evening in New York I dined alone at the Gotham Hotel.
There was a time when I used to stay at the Gotham, but as over the
years the charges got larger and the rooms smaller and higher, I
moved round the corner to the Dorset. But I still like dining at the
Gotham. The food and service are admirable, and it is one of the few
American eating places which do not share the popular view that
semidarkness is necessary to gastronomic enjoyment.

I dined, if I remember rightly, on pea soup with croutons, and soft-
shelled crabs, I drank a bottle of Almaden, and I read *The New York
Times*. During dinner I had been aware of three men dining at an
adjoining table, but had paid little attention to them. But when the
coffee arrived and the room began to empty I could not help overhearing their conversation. All three were employed at the United
Nations, all three were Americans. But what was interesting was
this: two of the three were in the process of sacking the third.

The chief sacker, and the eldest of the three, was a clean-shaven,
rather red-faced man of about forty-five, with crew-cut hair and a pair
of steel-rimmed glasses. His name was George. His assistant, a few
years younger, was a smaller, darkish individual with a pointed chin,
a bow tie, and thick eyebrows. He was called Bob. The third member of the group was about thirty, a lean rather weak-faced man with
freckles and hair that was thinning on top. He too wore spectacles,
heavy and horn-rimmed. He had longish fingers, nicotine-stained,
and on the fourth finger of his left hand was a marriage ring. His
name was Pete.

George said, "I'm sorry, Pete, but that's how it is. That's the way
things go."

Pete said, "You mean I'm not up to the job?"

Bob said, "Hell, no, Pete, it isn't like that at all. It's just that the
particular talents you have—and both George and I think you have
one hell of a lot of talents, don't we George?"

"You bet."

"—aren't best suited to this kind of work. Isn't that right, George?"

"Sure."

"You mean," said Pete, "that I'm a kind of a square peg in a round hole?"

"*Exactly,*" said George, grasping this unexpected hostage to fortune, "that's just it. I couldn't have put it better myself. And what we have to do now, Pete, is find you a *square* hole."

Pete said, "When did you decide on this?"

George said, "Don't ask me to put a date on it, Pete. I couldn't if I tried. It's one of those things that's kind of evolved, if you know what I mean."

Pete said nothing, and Bob said, "Listen, Pete. We've all been together a long time now, eh? We know each other pretty well, eh? Now, I don't mind saying that I have the *greatest,* but the *very* greatest admiration for you as a person. I haven't said this before, because I didn't want to embarrass you. But I can tell you this, that everyone back at the office, the stenographers and everybody, Judy and Anne and so on, feel just the same way. I've heard them say it. 'Isn't that Pete just something?' I've heard them say. No kidding. You have real talent, you have qualities which I certainly don't have, and which I daresay George, if he's honest, would admit he doesn't have either." He smiled at George for approval, and George, looking solemnly at his plate, said, "Dead right, Bob." "But the fact is that these talents of yours are wasted in this particular job. Now, we don't want to see your talents wasted any more than you do."

Pete said, "Do you have a new job in mind?"

George was expecting this, and said, rather too quickly, "Well, now, Pete, we don't have anything in mind *right now*. But you know how it is in the organization. There are things coming up all the time, and if you don't find something soon that really suits you—you know, that's really tailor-made for you—I'll eat my hat. And let me say this. If there's anything I can do in the way of a letter or anything, why, you only have to say the word."

Pete puffed at a cigarette and said, "What am I going to tell Mary?"

Bob said, "Hell, Pete, you can manage Mary. She's an understanding kid. Tell her what we're telling you. Say we think you're too good for this job, because that's what it amounts to."

George said, "Sure does," but even he didn't sound convinced.

There was a bit of a pause then, and George said, "Hey, you don't have a drink, Pete! Why don't we all take some brandy?"

Bob said, "Great idea."

I thought, this is not really happening; this sort of conversation happens only in the movies. The brandy came, and cigars. Pete handled his cigar as though it was the first in his life. George and Bob drank Pete's health. After this Pete rallied a little, smiled at his executioners and said, "You know, it's a kind of a shock."

George said, "*Of course* it's a shock, Pete. We understand that. It's bound to be. But you'll look at it all in a different light when you've had time to think it over. And one day, you know, you'll look back and be glad it happened."

Pete looked at his brandy glass and said quietly, "I guess you're right, George." It was the first time he had used George's name since the conversation began.

George said, "Good boy! That's what I like to hear." I bet you do, I thought.

The talk was rather desultory after this, while everyone changed gear, tried to get back to pre-execution relations.

After a bit Pete said, "George, there's something I'd like to ask you, get your opinion on. You too, Bob."

George said, "Sure, Pete. Anything you want. Be glad to help." Bob said, "Go ahead."

"Well, I've been thinking recently about a lot of things—you know, life and the role of the intellect and all that—and there's one thing that's been puzzling me."

George and Bob nodded sympathetically.

"It's this. In the kind of society we live in today, and where true evaluations are increasingly harder to make, we have these two great intellectual pillars, on the one hand Politics and on the other Art. Right?" He made them sound like two boxers, Art in the red corner and Politics in the blue, about to slug it out for the heavyweight title of the world.

"Right," said George.

"Now, then," said Pete. "Which, in your view, and in Bob's too, is the more important, the more significant for our times—Politics? Or Art?"

There was a slight pause, and then George said, rather slowly, "That's a hell of a good question. Politics or Art, eh? That's a real teaser." He looked at Bob for help, and Bob just smiled and said to Pete, "You're quite a pitcher."

But I didn't stay to hear the answer. I thought if I did, I might throw up. It is one thing to see a man being crucified, but another to have to stay and watch him lick the arses of his crucifiers, and them positively enjoying it. I walked back to the Dorset, packed my bags, and went to Africa.

Part Two

AFRICA

NIGERIA
LIBERIA

Five miles above the darkened Atlantic, in the black void between one day and another, the Pan Am stewardess switched off the cabin lights. We wrapped blankets round our knees, tilted back our seats, and attempted sleep. All, except six young Nigerians in the two rows opposite me—you could tell they were Nigerians, because there were also American Negroes in the plane, and these were blacker by far. Ever since takeoff they had been giggling among themselves, commenting on the food and drink, passing remarks on the pretty stewardesses. "Man, those girls certainly work." "Yes, but they go travel lots of nice places." "Yes, but what a life, though!" The one in the front seat nearest the aisle found a switch which turned on a little red light on the back of his seat (I think it was for summoning the stewardesses). When the man behind first saw it, he said to the others in his row, "Man, look at this! What is this?" The one in front leaned back and said, "That's the devil, man, come to remind you of your sins." He turned off the light and the one at the back peered forward suspiciously; but the switch was on the arm rest and he didn't see it. In a little while the light came on again, and the man at the back jumped in his seat. His friends, who by now had been let in on the joke, said, "There's that devil again, man. Man, you must be a *great* sinner." It was a game that afforded them endless amusement. I think

127

the man at the back knew quite well what was going on, but pretended he didn't, to keep the party going. They were still at it when I fell asleep.

In the morning I was woken by a stewardess with orange juice. Of the Nigerians, the man at the back was still asleep, but his companions were all awake, not yet at full giggle, but gently ticking over, waiting for something to happen. The stewardess teetered down the aisle with hot towels. The Nigerians had not seen such things before, and the stewardess had to explain their purpose. They laughed till I thought they would be sick. Then instead of wiping their own hands and faces, they wiped each other's. Their bodies shook with laughter and the tears rolled from their eyes.

The Nigerian at the back woke up and stretched himself. The one next to him said, "Man, you sleep like a dog." Another said, "You don't know what you just missed. You missed a hot towel." The man yawned and looked about him with unseeing eyes. "What you mean?" he said dully. The other said, "Man, I'm telling you God's truth. This beautiful girl came by with hot towels to clean your dirty black face." The man stared and said nothing, utterly uncomprehending. "He doesn't believe us," said the other. "We are telling him the truth about this fine Pan American service, and he doesn't believe us." Another said, "We have all had our hot towels. We are clean and he is dirty." The man said, "Why you wasting my time with that silly talk?" A stewardess went by, and one of them said to her, "Excuse me, miss, but our friend here did not receive one of those hot towels, would you be so kind as to fetch him one?" The girl said, "Certainly, sir," and she went off to get one. The man looked at his companions suspiciously. When the towel arrived, he accepted it disbelievingly, holding it in his hands loosely, staring at it, like a child with a comforter. He didn't alter his expression or position, but just sat there, incredulous. The others laughed fit to bust.

We came down at Dakar in the hot dawn and went to the airport building for free drinks. There was a strong smell of fish about the place. A zany American woman said in excruciating French, "Donnez-moi un spécialité de Dakar!" The waiter said, "All I got is bottled pop. Take your choice." He produced Coca-Cola, Seven-Up, pineapple juice, orange juice, and Fanta. She chose Fanta, thinking it a Dakar brew, unaware that it was a stepchild of Coca-Cola. We climbed aboard with one new passenger, a vast African in green robes and a little red nightcap. The Nigerians giggled all the way from

Dakar to Lagos. A white American in front of me tried to join in their jokes, become one of the party, but his mind worked on a quite different wavelength; they didn't so much ignore him as show themselves totally unaware that he was even there. After a bit he gave up and started reading a book. At ten we landed at Lagos.

❂

WHEN THE British came to Lagos in 1862, they found a malarial swamp, a string of fishing villages whose way of life had not altered in generations; a place where the wheel was unknown, and ritual murder, animal sacrifice and juju were rife. The only previous contact of the people with the Western world had been the tall ships that swam over the horizon, at first to trade for fruits and hides, but later to buy men and women as chattels for the labor-hungry plantations of America and the West Indies. Nobody then could have foreseen the vast consequences of such an action.

The British, inspired by Wilberforce and others, abolished slavery and came to Africa to stay. The tide in human traffic was reversed: instead of black men leaving Africa to be exploited by white men overseas, white men arrived in Africa to exploit black men at home. With their peculiar genius for combining trade, administration and proselytizing, the British spread themselves across the continent. At Lagos they built one of the finest deep-water ports in West Africa, and inland they set up trading posts. They introduced money and medicine and missionaries, and the missionaries introduced schools. In time they penetrated into the interior with roads and railways and a telegraph system, and unified people who had never heard of unity in their lives. In their hundred years in Nigeria the British did much —some people might say too much. They found a handful of savages at the water's edge: they left a country of fifty-five million people.

In Lagos today the legacy of the British is self-evident. First the language. Signs such as "God's Will Engineering Company," "We-We Batteries" and "One Starry Night Inn" greet you on all sides. Perhaps the oddest claim is that of the Irish stout manufacturers whose slogan, "Guinness Gives You Power," is so widely believed that in the heat of the day many Nigerians can be seen swallowing the stuff by the gallon. In the center of the town are bright new department stores, where English products can be bought as easily as at home. Most of the cars are British, and on the outskirts are British-run hotels and macadamized avenues, fringed by frangipani and bougainvillaea. There is even a British-built racecourse. And then there are the British themselves, representatives of trade and culture if no longer of government; the women unmistakable in sandals and trim summer dresses, the men in hilarious mini-shorts, exposing knobbly knees.

But in Nigeria the jungle is never far away. Walk a little into the less fashionable quarter of the town, and the signs take on a madness all their own—"Chief Paramount Water-house, Royal Compound"; "Madame Grace Agogo: Wines and Beers"; "J. Ogofepye: Spiritual Dry Cleaners." Here the crowded mammy-wagons spill out and pick up sweating housewives, in from the country to shop, ebony babies cradled to ebony backs. Here stubby, black-bearded goats, the size of spaniels, roam for garbage. Here are brown boys with navels like oranges, and legless beggars like crabs crawling the dusty street. Pick up the *Daily Times* and read how after a party at the house of Mr. Oforokpe, Mr. Nwankoagu was "found dead in a pool of blood with matchet wounds all over his body." The story repeats itself almost daily: the matchet wounds and the pool of blood are constants, only the names vary. Within the Nigerian body politic the ulcer of tribalism is never far from the surface: it has burst already in Biafra and some say, must soon do so elsewhere. Juju is in the air and, if you know where to look for it, on the ground. And wherever you go and whatever you want, you will not get far without "dash." "Dash" is a tip, a bonus, a gift or a bribe, depending on who is defining it; it is the passport to every worthwhile deal, from a government contract to a table in a restaurant.

In 1960 the British pulled out of Nigeria, and although many educated Nigerians still continued to regard Britain as "the mother country" and to send their sons to English schools and universities, others, heady with a sense of freedom, began to look elsewhere. Inevitably their thoughts shifted across the Atlantic to the country which had not only plundered them of their ancestors and might therefore have felt it had a debt to repay, but was now indisputably the richest country in the world. And America responded. American businessmen arrived with American automobiles and gasoline and films and television programs. American lawyers came to advise on the constitution; American cultural organizations came to spread the word about American scholarships, the truth about the Negro in American society, the desirability of the American way of life. Coca-Cola flexed its muscles and the Chase Manhattan Bank opened casements onto fairylands forlorn. AID came, and the Peace Corps, eight hundred strong, to help with the sudden new demands for education.

It would have been strange if the British community in Lagos had not resented this mini-invasion, had not regarded the Americans as usurpers of their own exclusive preserve. Even so, I was not prepared for the variety and extent of their strictures.

Most, admittedly, were ones I had heard before: familiar garments drawn from a kind of international used-clothing store of current anti-Americana. At dinner at the house of a British government official, a little man with a bald head lit his pipe and said to my host, "Alec, why is it the Americans get such a bad press? Why are they resented so much?" I had not noticed that they had been having a bad press, or indeed, among the community as a whole, that they were being resented. But these vast, airy assumptions went unchallenged. "They've got a lot to learn, I think," said my host, "and they're much too lavish with their money." Well, that wasn't exactly a fresh thought. A woman at the party said, "The Americans will dress up in Nigerian robes at the slightest opportunity, and go to local functions in them. It's really *too* embarrassing and awful. They've no idea how silly they look." And where had I heard that before? Bogotá, wasn't it? But the impression I got from some Nigerians, as I had from some Colombians, was that it was thought rather a nice compliment. One man said, "One of the stupidest things they've done recently was appointing a whole lot of Negroes to diplomatic posts in Africa. They just don't realize how much the Africans resent it."

Other criticisms were more original. One Englishwoman told of an American bishop in the interior who was so alarmed at the diseases he might catch when laying on hands that he wore white gloves. Another, attractive and intelligent, told me a scary tale about AID. "They sent a whole lot of milk up to some pregnant women in the mountains. The women were so undernourished that the milk swelled up the babies inside them, and nine months later they found they had a hundred Caesareans on their hands." But hadn't Karen in Caymito touched on much the same thing, and hadn't she added that she had a special film to show expectant mothers that drinking milk in pregnancy made deliveries easier, not harder?

A few genuinely liked the Americans, but even their praises were cooled with condescension. One woman said, "They're so kind and hospitable and friendly, and they're terribly *aware* of how other people regard them. Here they fall over backwards not to push themselves forwards, if you see what I mean. For instance, the wives of the embassy officials can join any voluntary organization they like, but they're not allowed to take office or become president, or anything like that. We can and do. The Nigerians like us to." And a sweet old retired British district officer said to me, "They're a bit too hail-fellow-well-met for my taste. I was up in Ibadan the other day, and there was an American in the hotel there having breakfast with his driver. Well, I mean to say, one just doesn't *have* breakfast with one's driver, does one?"

But the most bizarre piece of anti-Americanism came from the foreman of a small factory, an Englishman who at home would have been of small standing, but here found himself a person of power. He took me round the factory, and whenever we entered a room where African workers were sitting down he uttered imperiously the monosyllable "Up!" He was a tough, wiry little man who pronounced his *r*'s as *v*'s and *th*'s as *f*'s. After the tour he asked me why I was in Lagos and I told him about my book. He smiled a knowing smile.

"What are you smiling at?" I said.

"I could tell you a thing or two about some Americans," he said.

"What?"

He smiled again knowingly, and I said, "Well, tell me."

"Well, I spent the first three months out on my own before the wife came out, and a lot of us bachelors and grass widowers used to get together, especially on Sunday mornings, and have chicken and potatoes at my place."

"Yes."

"Well, one of these fellows said to me one day, 'Would you like an African woman?' And I said no, that kind of thing didn't interest me. So then he said, 'Well, how about an American girl?' I said, 'How do you mean?' And what do you think he said?"

"I don't know."

"Peace Corps."

"Really?"

"Yes, it seems that some of the girls are running a knocking shop on the side. Making a bit of extra. You'd hardly credit it, would you?"

"What happened?" I said. "Did you have one?"

"No, I told you that kind of thing doesn't interest me. Black or white."

I said, "I think that's very interesting. Who is this chap who told you about it?"

"Ah, well, he's a funny fellow, to tell you the truth. One day he's your best friend and the next he won't recognize you. I don't think he'd like it if I were to give you his name."

"Well, let's try the other end," I said. "Do you know where this knocking shop is, where the girls operate?"

"No, my friend didn't tell me that. So far as I could gather, you couldn't approach the girls direct, you had to go through some African woman."

"Are you seriously telling me," I said, "that some of the Peace Corps girls in Lagos have organized themselves into a brothel run by an African madam?"

"Well, I'm only telling you what my friend told me. I thought it might interest you for your book. But there's no need to go on about it."

"In the end it amounts to this," I said. "You won't give me the name of the man who told you about it, you don't know where the knocking shop is, who the girls are, where the madam lives or anything."

"No, I bloody well *don't,* and if I'd known you were going to go on about it so, I wouldn't have brought it up in the first place. And now for Christ's sake do me a favor and let me get on with my work."

I made such investigations of the knocking shop and the madam as I could; and by the time I had finished, I was as certain as I could be that they existed only in the daydreams of one or perhaps two unhappy minds.

Some Americans are unaware of what others think of them; some are aware and ignore it; a few bitterly resent it. At a party I went to, two little girls from Sarah Lawrence College simpered up and said they heard I was writing a book about Americans abroad. I said I was. One of them said, "Do you like them?" and waited, trembling, for the answer. But such a question is impossible to answer; it is not nationalities one likes or dislikes, but people. Misinterpreting my silence, the girl said fiercely, "Well, don't you *know* what you think about them?" I shrugged my shoulders. She thought I meant, I hate their guts, but I'm too polite to say, so she looked as though she would scratch my eyes out and said, "What the hell's gotten into you, what are you worrying about anyway?" and stomped angrily away.

Happily, other Americans take the broader view. Later in the evening a genial Californian said to me, "When you're the king of the castle, you must expect one hell of a lot of shit to be thrown at you." He beamed from ear to ear, as though being at the receiving end of shit was the most desirable situation in the world.

✪

I HAD not expected, when I came to Nigeria, to find *national* prejudices to the degree shown by some British toward the Americans. I had expected to find *racial* prejudices between blacks and whites. And I was as mistaken about the one as about the other. It is true that Brazil, where I had just been, is also a country of no racial prejudice; but there crossbreeding has produced such variety of skins that racial prejudice is meaningless. In Nigeria there are few such gradations: black is black and white is white; and yet there is almost no racial prejudice at all. (*Tribal* prejudice is, of course, another story.)

It was a Texan who first opened my eyes to it. "When you've been here a time, and find everyone mixing so freely," he said, "you stop thinking of people as Nigerians or Americans or British. A moment comes when you're not *aware* of nationalities any more. You just think of them as *people*." He said another interesting thing: "Every year there's more and more mixed marriages. I see a real hope for world peace there, because once that happens on a big enough scale, we'll all be one people."

My own revelation came at a dinner party in Lagos given by the director of the United States Information Service, Mr. Huntington Damon. This was in honor of a distinguished Nigerian who had just won that year's Eisenhower traveling scholarship in the United States. His name was Dr. Olatunji Adeniyi-Jones, and he was Medical Officer of Health for Lagos City Council. There were twenty-five of us at the dinner, and we sat at little tables of five and six in the Huntington Damons' garden. The party consisted of white Americans, Negro Americans, Nigerians, and Britishers. Most of the Americans were officials from the embassy with their wives, and the Nigerians included past Eisenhower Fellows such as Mr. Boonyamin O. Kazeem, the Acting Federal Solicitor General, Dr. Samuel Cookey of the Federal Ministry of Education, and Chief and Mrs. Omolulu.

There was also a Ghanaian doctor, Dr. Maciver-Sloe from Freetown, now Registrar of the Lagos Teaching Hospital, and the wife of the director of the British Council. Many of the colored women, Nigerian and American, were extremely attractive. I sat next to the wife of the American cultural attaché. She had had her hair Westernized, and was wearing a short, sheath-like white dress; the contrast of white dress, chocolate skin and scarlet nails, combined with a lively and humorous mind, was very stimulating. The Nigerians wore white tribal robes and floral skullcaps, which quite unprepared one for their Western wit and sophistication. Dr. Adeniyi-Jones, in particular, was a most worldly man, and a skilled raconteur of lively stories. He was a tall, youngish, bearded Nigerian, and beneath a polka-dot robe he wore a pair of silk trousers. Soon after the party began he said to some of us, "Have you heard the one about the man who took his dog to a pub and asked the owner if he'd mind letting it play the piano?" We said we hadn't. "Well," said Dr. Adeniyi-Jones, "the owner said he didn't mind, so the dog sat down and played something. When it had finished the owner said, 'What was the name of that piece?' The man who had the dog said, 'Oh, it hasn't got a name. It's just something the dog made up on his own.' So the owner said, 'Is it orchestrated?' and the man said, 'No, it's not orchestrated, it's a bitch.' "

I cannot remember when the talk turned to racial prejudice, but there was no sense of easing into it, of idling the engine of our conversation while we changed into lower gear. By way of warning Dr. Adeniyi-Jones of what he might expect in the States, Mr. Boonyamin O. Kazeem told us what had happened to him. Mr. Kazeem was a happy, tubby little fellow, with big horn-rimmed spectacles and a set of teeth like a fan. He and his wife had been motoring through the South, and they had stopped for the night at a motel at Oxford, Mississippi. At the reception desk they were received correctly if not cordially, but when they reached their room the manager telephoned to say that he regretted they could not be served food in the dining room, and that a meal would be sent to their room. "What did you do?" someone said, and Mr. Kazeem, grinning broadly and opening both hands, said, "What *could* we do? We had our dinner in our room." He beamed cheerfully at us all. As a white man I felt ashamed of this insult to Mr. Kazeem, and I expected his reaction to be one of anger and hurt. But Mr. Kazeem had traveled beyond the reach of such things. He saw this obscene incident for what it was; not as something to be taken seriously at all, but so ludicrous and farcical that one could only sit back and laugh. And I, entering with my imagination into his, saw it in that way, too.

Dr. Maciver-Sloe told us of his experiences in England, where he had spent a year as the first African doctor to be taken on by Unilever. His first secretary asked to be relieved after a day or two; she said she didn't like working with a colored man. "Then they got me another, and she didn't seem to mind. After she'd been with me a few months and we'd got to know each other, she said, 'You know, I didn't think I'd enjoy working with you, but I do. *You're really just like everyone else.*'" Dr. Maciver-Sloe bubbled over with laughter, just as Mr. Kazeem had done. Later, he said, he had had to go to Liverpool for the firm and was told that he would be met at the station by one of their representatives. "His name was Mackenzie, and I expect he thought he was going to meet a fellow Scot." At Liverpool the platform had emptied until there were only the two of them left. "I knew the other fellow must be Mackenzie, but even then it didn't occur to him that I was me." He went up to Mackenzie and said, "Excuse me, but is your name Mackenzie?" Mackenzie said it was. "So I put out my hand and said, 'How do you do? I am Dr. Maciver-Sloe.'" The look on Mackenzie's face, he said, was something wonderful.

Others in the party contributed variations on the same theme. Our host said, "My daughter is studying in New York. She goes out quite a lot with colored boys. Of course her grandmother is horrified." And the wife of the cultural attaché, the lady in the white dress next to me, said, "I was born and raised in the South, but I went to college in the North. I had a white girl friend there who was thinking of visiting the South and I told my father I'd like her to come and visit with us. My father minded terribly my even suggesting such a thing. He thought it a betrayal of everything he believed in."

Then we talked of the misconceptions that Americans and Africans still have about each other's country. The Americans agreed that most of their countrymen thought of Africa as it was two hundred years ago, a place without roads, railways, power, sanitation, where lions roared and people ate each other. One or two admitted that before coming to Nigeria they had had this sort of misconception themselves. The Nigerians said most of their people thought that all white Americans were rich and that most Negro Americans still lived under the lash.

I asked about the affinity, if any, between Africans and American Negroes. Most thought that there was none, that the American Negro considered himself an American first and a Negro second, that he was conditioned to an entirely different and indeed superior way of life. The cultural attaché said he thought that most Africans believed the American Negro would be less likely to exploit them than any white man, and that that was about as far as it went. His wife summed it up: "In our two cultures we're poles apart. There's about as much affinity between the American Negro and the African as there is between the Germans and the English."

○

To PURSUE the question of the American Negro in Africa a little further, I went to see one of the top Negro American administrators in Nigeria, Mr. Jim Jackson, Associate Director of Management for the Peace Corps. Mr. and Mrs. Jackson lived in a trim little house along Awolowo Road, and when I arrived they were having supper on table trays and watching a Western on television. Mr. Jackson was a huge man with flaring nostrils like a dragon, and big red gums, and a lovely smile. He wore a white shirt and black woolen tie, black socks, slacks, and slippers. Mrs. Jackson was on the big side, too, with a solid gentle face and with hair bunched up on top and kept at anchor by a ribbon. She sat me down and gave me a cup of coffee. Mr. Jackson turned down the sound on the television, but the pictures of cowboys and Indians flickered on.

Mr. Jackson said he had been born and raised in Texas. He was now forty-eight, and he had spent most of his career at the Pentagon. "At the Pentagon they looked on me as a kind of invisible man. I did my work and I kept quiet. I didn't cause any difficulties for them or have any chips on my shoulder about hating the white man. But when they said, 'We can't promote this man,' I used to smile and say, 'Why not? Just tell me why not.' Always with a smile. My mother told me you can best catch flies with sugar. So they promoted me. And I kept on at night school, and at the end of ten years I qualified as an accountant. There's not many Negroes who are on the economic level that I am."

I said, "How did you get from the Pentagon into the Peace Corps?"

Mr. Jackson took out a pair of spectacles and started to polish them. On the television screen another redskin bit the dust. "One day I took my wife to watch the Peace Corps playing a baseball game at the back of the White House. At that time my wife was working in the Talent Search Office in the Peace Corps. During the game, the head of the Talent Office came up and talked to my wife, and after she'd introduced us he asked me what I did. So I told him, and a few days later he gave me a call and asked would I be interested in doing a spell in the Peace Corps. My wife and I talked it over, and though I'd never been out of the States before, curiosity got the better of me and I said yes."

"Why do you think they asked you?"

"Well, as I say, I've never hated the white man. I've always been free of prejudice. We've always had all the social freedom we ever wanted. All I've ever fought for is economic freedom."

Mrs. Jackson said, "We've never felt trodden down or abused."

Mr. Jackson said, "I went along to the Peace Corps office, and I was interviewed by about twenty people, and finally by Shriver himself. I liked that. It was a real challenge all the way. Shriver wanted me to go to Latin America, but the African bureau wanted me to come here. In the end Shriver yielded. At that time I didn't know too much about Africa. I'd been brainwashed by all those Tarzan pictures. When they asked me about getting my car shipped over, I didn't appreciate there were any roads for it to run on. I thought it was all bush. My friends thought I ought to get the Distinguished Service Cross for coming to Africa at all. A neighbor wrote the other day and asked would we come home with bones in our noses. They think we see elephants all day and eat elephant meat."

Mrs. Jackson said, "I've never had some of the wild thoughts about Africa that some people have because I've always been internationally minded. I studied international relations as a girl."

Mr. Jackson said, "I think the biggest shock when we came here was the African's ignorance about the American Negro. One day I decided not to give any dash to those little boys who open the car door for you, and they said to me, Negroes in the States don't get dash, they get beaten. So I told them the truth, but they didn't believe me. Another time at a cocktail party I met the premier of Eastern Nigeria. He thought I was a Nigerian and he gave me a handshake like a wet fish. Then he heard my voice and gave me a double handshake. He didn't expect to find an American Negro at a diplomatic cocktail party. He asked what I did, and when he learned that I had authority over white men, he could hardly believe it."

"What about this question of affinity?" I said.

"Many white men ask me do I feel kindred with these people. And the answer is No. I've noticed there are some occasions, like getting someone quickly through the customs, when I can get things done more quickly than a white American. But when I'm with an African, I don't feel this man is my brother. The fact is I'm a Negro with a white man's tongue and a white man's thoughts."

Mr. and Mrs. Jackson finished their supper, and Mrs. Jackson put the trays on the side. On the television screen a stagecoach started out on a journey which, I assumed, would not be without incident.

"Do you have children?" I said.

"We have a daughter here in Nigeria," said Mr. Jackson. "In Lagos we found there was only one school suitable for her, a Nigerian school for ninth grade. But she was the only American girl there, and they discriminated against her, they wouldn't accept her. So I ribbed the schoolteacher. I said, 'You sold my foreparents, so you ought to take my daughter.' " He laughed in the way that Mr. Kazeem and Dr. Maciver-Sloe had done. "So then I sent her to a mission boarding school at Enugu. The pupils there are sons and daughters of diplomats and missionaries and business people. She's the only Negro there, and her best friend is an American girl from the South. She lives in a hostel with other boys and girls, and she's having a ball."

I asked Mr. Jackson if being an American Negro in Africa caused any friction between himself and his white colleagues, and he said he didn't think so. "Some white Americans," he said, "keep their distance. You know, they say they're going on a trip and why don't we go too, and then when I tell them we're ready, they find some excuse. But that's no different from the States." He added, "But you do have to watch out. People here mix so free and easy that you sometimes forget their prejudices. I know a lot of Negro stories, and at one time I used to tell them at parties. But I had to be very careful whom I told them *to*. You know the story about the Negro father who dropped a pot of white paint all over his son. Three relatives tried to scrape it off, but they couldn't. And the son said, 'I've been a white man five minutes and already I hate three niggers.' " He chuckled. "I told that story at a party where there were some white Americans, and they were really shocked."

Mrs. Jackson said, "You should have *seen* their *faces*. They were quite *disgusted*."

"But on the whole," I said, "you like it here?"

"Oh, we like it fine," said Mr. Jackson. "We have a social status here that we would never have in the States. We know people like the ambassador and the head of Lufthansa and members of the cabinet, people we'd never meet back home. We're on a higher plateau."

Mrs. Jackson said, "And I would think that when we get back, the sort of people who would otherwise say 'Hi!' and pass us by would ask us to cocktails and all that."

I looked out the window at barefooted Nigerians slogging along Awolowo Road, and began to understand the Jacksons' lack of affinity with them.

"The only thing we've tried to be here," said Mr. Jackson, "is ourselves. We haven't put on any airs and graces. We haven't tried to hold a cup of tea with two fingers."

"What will you do when you get home?" I said. "Go back to the Pentagon?"

"I don't know," said Mr. Jackson. "It depends on the visibility I have. So many avenues have been opened to us."

Mrs. Jackson said, "Jim's been such a success here that I think he feels that anything is possible."

On the television screen the stagecoach had been ambushed by Indians. But the sheriff's men were coming down fast from the top of a hill. Mr. Jackson leaned forward and turned up the sound, and suddenly the room was filled with war whoops and rifle shots. Mr. Jackson said, "They get some pretty good programs here." Now the sheriff's men had joined battle, and Indians were crashing to the ground like tenpins. I looked at the Jacksons' faces, alight with enthusiasm. There was no doubt whose side *they* were on: two brownskins watching with joy the whiteskins knocking off the redskins, two Americans approving the triumph of law and order over savagery and disorder. It helped to confirm a lot.

A day or two later I met the white wife of the white American ambassador and told her I had talked with Mr. Jackson, and how interesting it had been.

"In what way?" she said.

"As an American Negro," I said, "coming back to the land of his fathers. What he feels about it all."

"Oh, I see. Well, of course, that's *not* the sort of thing *I* would *ever* talk to him about."

I thought, but didn't say, Why not?

✪

A MILE or so from the center of Lagos is Herbert Macaulay Road; in Herbert Macaulay Road is Our Lady of the Apostles School, and teaching in Our Lady of the Apostles School was a young Peace Corps volunteer by the name of Samuel Abbott. I had been given his name by Jim Jackson.

Samuel Abbott was a good-looking boy in his early twenties, with fair, curly hair, a pronounced Ivy League accent, and a quiet, self-assured manner. He taught English literature. He was born in New Jersey, but his home was in Washington, D.C., where his father was an Episcopal priest at St. John's Church, opposite the White House. He thought the idea of the Peace Corps the best thing to come out of America since the early Roosevelt days. "I felt that this was the modern equivalent of people going to the Spanish Civil War, that it was right *in time*."

Like other volunteers he had found the first days in the field difficult. "I was at a loss with my teaching. I found the textbooks inadequate. The heat was sapping my strength, I didn't know many other people, and I hadn't any transport. Gradually the novelty wears off and you realize what a long time two years is." Now, after a year in Lagos, he had adjusted himself to his situation and was enjoying life. "I feel I have made steady progress in my teaching, and I don't end up the day feeling ashamed of myself."

Mr. Abbott and I walked into a classroom where at small scrubbed desks sat twenty little Nigerian girls between the ages of ten and twelve. They looked as fresh and trim as black tulips. They wore neat blue-and-white uniforms, as newly laundered and creased as the American marines'; Mr. Abbott said that other children called them "cops," because their uniforms were like those of the Lagos police. They had a variety of hair styles, most favoring a local coiffure in which the hair is flattened into a series of crisscross squares, like the pattern on a charcoal-grilled steak.

They all got up, and Mr. Abbott said, "Good morning!" The girls chorused back, "Good morning, Mr. Abbott!" Mr. Abbott said, "This is a guest, Mr. Kennedy"; and the girls chorused, "Good morning, Mr. Kennedy!"

When they had all settled down Mr. Abbott said, "Now, in your essays which I've just been correcting many of you have written 'taught' when you've meant 'thought.' You have difficulty in distinguishing between the two, don't you? Let's hear some of you say 'taught' and 'thought' a few times. Philomena?" Philomena, at the back, said "taught" and "thought" correctly, and so did Francisca, Virginia, Elizabeth, Agnes and Rita. "Right," said Mr. Abbott. "Now look at this!" He went to the blackboard and wrote down:

She taught/thought her students

> badly
> foolish
> brilliant
> lazy
> Math
> English
> for ten years
> too noisy

"Now," said Mr. Abbott, "where would you use 'taught,' and where would you use 'thought'?" He went round the class at random, and some gave the correct answers and some did not. Then he went on to verbs and the different meanings of "should." "Should you go out with married men, Francisca?" Giggles all round. *"Ought* I to go out with married men?" said Francisca. "Right," said Mr. Abbott. "Now, *'I shall come.'* " Rita said, "I may come. I hope to come." "No, no!" said Mr. Abbott, "I *intend* to come. I will come." He turned to another girl. "Jennifer, 'I love her'?" Jennifer said, "I am loving her." "Yes," said Mr. Abbott, "I am loving her more and more, and right now I am wishing she were my wife." We moved on to *Animal Farm,* which the girls had been reading. "How did the hens defy Napoleon?" asked Mr. Abbott, and one girl said, "Please, Mr. Abbott, what's 'defy'?" Mr. Abbott said, "If I told you to go out of the room and you refused, that would be 'defy.' " The girl blushed; defiance was not for her.

I had come to see Peace Corps teaching in action, because I knew there were several hundred volunteers in Nigeria working in education, and also because Nigerian education was in a state of flux. A few days earlier I had been to Nsukka University and had seen the Dean of the Faculty of Education, Dr. Fafunwa. Dr. Fafunwa had a grizzled old face like Popeye, and wore lovely yellow robes and puffed away at an old pipe. When the British were here, he said, the whole Nigerian educational system was geared to their system. Stress was laid on the classics, and all points of reference were British ones. "For instance, the flora and fauna we were taught were not our own flora and fauna but yours. We learned about British toads and British frogs and British rabbits. I still remember my secondary-school final exam which had an essay on winter—snow and ice and all that—which we'd never seen. Or take trees. I could tell you now the names of all the English trees, but I don't know the names of any trees here. It was the same with geography and history. We were taught about the geography of Britain and the British Empire, but very little about our own geography. In history we learned about the British colonization of Africa, the drawing up of political boundaries, but nothing about our own history in Nigeria before colonization took place. Of course, the people who set the syllabus and the exams lived in London and had never been here."

Dr. Fafunwa told me it was the narrowness of the British education that had made the educational authorities in Nigeria turn, after independence, toward America, to accept the increasing number of American scholarships offered them, and then to apply for Peace Corps volunteers to help put American educational methods into practice. "We felt that while British education gave a certain depth, it didn't have the flexibility of American education, it laid too much stress on the classics and so on. Also we felt that America was less culture-bound, was a newer country, like our own, and so had something special to offer."

Dr. Fafunwa said that before independence he himself had won a scholarship to America, and that when he applied for a passport, the British officer in charge had said to him, "Why do you want to go to America? Half the people there are illiterate." "So I just said, 'Well, they may be, but they helped pull Britain through the war, and through the peace afterwards, so I'd just like to go and see the place for myself.'" Before he went to America, he had never seen an American Negro in his life and thought they all lived in the South. "So when I arrived at the airport in New York, and saw this colored fellow helping with the bags, I thought he must be an African. I went up to him and said, 'Hullo, brother, how are you?' He looked at me very coldly and said, 'What do you want, buddy?' That just shows how ignorant I was about America."

Dr. Fafunwa said that since independence the educational syllabus had changed drastically. Points of reference now were Nigerian points of reference. English was no longer taught as the mother tongue but as a secondary language, and a failure in English did not necessarily mean a failure in the whole examination. In English literature, set books included works by American as well as English authors, and a modern Nigerian novel. "We are trying to draw the best from both worlds, and yet create something entirely our own."

What I had been told at Nsukka was in my mind when Mr. Abbott took me back to his flat on the other side of Macaulay Road. He lived on the upstairs floor of a Victorian colonial-style house; the sitting room was full of ferns and plants in tubs, and outside the window was a huge bougainvillaea. Waiting for us were two friends, Marianne Burgbacher from Chicago, and Mrs. Casey. Miss Burgbacher held a B.A. from the University of Illinois and had majored in linguistics. Like Mr. Abbott she taught English literature. Mrs. Casey was forty-five and was teaching at a teachers' training college.

I told them what Dr. Fafunwa had said, and while they all agreed that British education in the past had not been suitable for Nigeria's needs, they thought this less a failing of British education than of the colonial system generally. Admittedly the British thought their culture and values superior to those of the Nigerians, but they also knew that any undue emphasis on Nigerian history, geography, achievements, culture, et cetera, would have generated a pride of country which it was not the business of a colonial regime to foster.

Miss Burgbacher said, "I think one of the most basic mistakes the British made was not teaching English properly. So much of our work here is *remedial*, getting people to unlearn all the things they've learned wrong. Now, you don't find that in French-speaking African countries, because the French have always insisted on correct pronunciation and grammar from the very first day."

"What kind of wrong things?" I said.

"Well, for a start, in not differentiating clearly enough between words that sound alike—"

"Like 'taught' and 'thought,' " said Mr. Abbott.

"Yes, and 'pull' and 'pool,' " said Miss Burgbacher, "and 'bit' and 'beat,' and so on. I have to work out all sorts of exercises with my students to help them overcome this."

Mr. Abbott said, "A lot of them say things like 'have went' instead of 'have gone,' and you have to take a lot of time putting things like that right. Then, they don't understand the negative. If you say to them, 'You didn't go downtown, did you?' they'll maybe answer, 'Yes, I did,' meaning 'No, I didn't.' What they *think* they're saying is, 'Yes, I did not go downtown.' "

"They have one pronoun for 'he' and 'she,' " said Miss Burgbacher, "and two words for 'you,' and they can't make this distinction in English. They get confused."

I told them Marvin Cole's story about mistranslating the hymn, and Mr. Abbott said, "We have just the same problem here. The word for 'husband' is the same as for 'bastard.' The pronunciation is different. But you can imagine the kind of trouble that that can lead you into."

Mrs. Casey said, "Their real trouble with English is that they can't control the language."

"One reason they can't," said Mr. Abbott, "is because in the past they've had this excess of the classics—Shakespeare and the Bible and all that. That's what the missionaries, who were the first teachers here, used to give them. They learned it, but they couldn't absorb it; they had no means of distinguishing between the archaic and the modern colloquial. That's why you still find them using quaint expressions like 'firmament' for 'sky,' and 'Except you go, I will not go,' which is straight out of the Bible."

"Where does American teaching of literature differ from British teaching?" I said.

Mr. Abbott said, "First, the emphasis now is on modern literature rather than on the classics. You heard my class discussing Orwell's *Animal Farm* this morning, and with another class I'm doing Hemingway's *Old Man and the Sea*. In the old days here they used to do *Mill on the Floss*. Well, that kind of change is accepted now, and the British and everyone go along with it.

"Then there's this question of retelling a story, which I regard as one of the most pernicious aspects of British education. You know, you give a child a story to read, and the next day you get him to tell it back. Well, that's just a test of memory and concentration. There's no enjoyment to it and it doesn't lead anywhere. It's almost as arid an exercise as learning by rote, which is another thing British teachers go for. What we try to do is ask the child questions about the story, what ideas it triggers off in his mind, how he can relate it to his own experience."

I asked about other differences between British and American teaching, and he said, "The British taught that the teacher should be in a position of absolute authority, which is all right if you happen to have the authority, but most Nigerians don't. Then in some schools they still have caning and prefects, which are not things we go in for. And there's still a lot of snobbery as regards the difference between U.K. and U.S. higher education. There've been several cases of Nigerians getting Ph.D.'s in the States, and then not being able to get a job when they come back here."

Before I left Lagos I spent some time with members of the V.S.O., the British equivalent of the Peace Corps. They confirmed almost everything that Dr. Fafunwa and Mr. Abbott and Miss Burgbacher had said. Mr. David Waterhouse, of the British Council, said, "I find the Peace Corps here to be both aggressive and intelligent, and that is a very attractive mixture. I think the whole U.S. educational system is far better suited to Nigeria's needs than ours. At Nsukka they have started a course in secretaryship and another in business, which are just the sort of practical things this country wants." They agreed, too, with what Mrs. Casey had said about Nigerian inability to control the English language. I spoke about this to two young English teachers of French at Nsukka University. Judith told me that her class were supposed to converse in French, and one day a student said something to her that she didn't understand. "Say it in English, George," she had said to him; and he replied, "But I am." And the other girl, Virginia, told me how sometimes the students invited them out to supper, and that this was often followed up by a letter. She had kept some of these letters, and she showed me one.

I am seizing this chance to signify my willingness to be on cordial terms with you. I admire your cheerful appearance. This bold attempt perhaps will be the beginning of a friendly and symbiotic association between us. Kindly elicit a reply so that I know what your opinion is.

"And that," said Virginia, "is what all of us—British and Americans alike—are basically up against."

✪

THE READER will remember that on my first visit to New York the Coca-Cola people had promised to give me a letter of introduction to their area representative in Lagos, Mr. Parissis.

Mr. Parissis' office was on the top floor of the Philips Building. It was an impressive office. I think it would have impressed the people back in New York, who the reader may recall, had rather dingy offices. This one had a red carpet, green plants in tubs, African carvings on the desk, and African paintings on the wall. Mr. Parissis was in keeping with the office. He was a vibrant, graying Greek who wore a big gold ring on his little finger, a smaller gold ring on the fourth finger, a gold watch and gold cufflinks; and he smoked cigars in a holder. I remembered what they had told me in New York, that it was the policy of the firm to let everyone share in the profits. Mr. Parissis seemed a living proof of this policy.

"How is Coca-Cola doing in Africa?" I said to him.

"You wouldn't believe it," said Mr. Parissis, "but one of our greatest competitors now is water. People get our old bottles, put water in them, ice them, and sell them at a penny a time."

Mr. Parissis said that he was area manager for twenty-eight African countries, but even this did not entitle him to visit any factory which made the concentrate. The concentrate, he said, was all that Coca-Cola actually *owned,* though they were responsible for training, advertising, sales and distribution; the bottles, water, crates and everything else were owned by the people who had the franchise. I asked Mr. Parissis how many Americans were employed in his twenty-eight countries, and he said two. "Our policy is to Africanize as much as possible—to have as many Africans working for Coca-Cola as we can. At present we are a long way from this, because we need people who can travel about and speak languages. So we employ Dutch and English and Egyptians and Irish and Greeks. But the idea is eventually to have all Africans. When you have all Africans, then people will start thinking of Coca-Cola as an *African* drink—"

"Oh, surely not?" I said.

"Yes," said Mr. Parissis, pointing a well-groomed finger at me. "Wherever we go we try to identify Coca-Cola with the country that we are in. All the time we play down its American origin."

"Well," I said, "it'll surely be a long time before people here start thinking of Coca-Cola as African rather than American?"

"Africans," said Mr. Parissis, "are very superstitious about drinks. They want to *identify* a drink with something. You've heard about Guinness here and how they believe it gives them power. They also believe that quinine tonic water cures malaria. And before the war, in Egypt, the idea got around that Coca-Cola contained pig's blood, and they had to photograph the Aga Khan drinking a bottle to show it didn't.

"Now we have two drinks here, Coca-Cola and Fanta. Fanta, as you know, is the orange drink, and we sell twice as much of it as Coca-Cola. The native has a natural inclination toward orange as a source of refreshment, which we recognize. The further into the bush we get, the more Fanta we sell. The average native thinks that Fanta is his own local brew; he doesn't associate it with America at all. Because Coca-Cola and Fanta are sold together—whoever has the franchise or agency for the one has it for the other—the idea that Coca-Cola is something essentially American is going.

"And," said Mr. Parissis, pointing a finger again, "it is right that it should go. All that's American about Coca-Cola today is the concentrate. Everything else—the bottling, advertising, marketing, et cetera —happens locally. The only money that goes back to Coca-Cola in America from all its huge sales abroad is the money paid for the concentrate. So you see, Coca-Cola is *becoming* a local drink, in practice as well as in theory."

Later I went out on a Coca-Cola delivery round in a small truck owned by an African called Raymondo Adebo Awale. He said he called himself R. Ade for short, but I called him Raymond. South of Lagos, on the outer limits of the town, is a beach where people go for bathing. The road ends at the beach, and Raymond had a small shop near there, where he sold Coca-Cola and Fanta and chocolates and nuts. When I arrived at the shop, Raymond and an assistant were loading up the truck with Coca-Cola and Fanta. Raymond had the agency for an area south of Lagos, and when the truck was loaded up and we were all aboard, he drove straight onto the beach, turned left just short of the sea, and headed south.

It was marvelous careering down that golden beach, with the sea all green and shining on the right, a cool offshore breeze coming in through the truck windows, and Coca-Cola and Fanta clanking about in the back. In a mile or two we came to a fishing community, a

collection of shacks made of bamboo and wooden planking set down
on the shoulder of the beach. The shacks had been laid out symmetri-
cally, like New York, with sandy lanes between the blocks. The people here were jet-black, with skins like oiled tar; Raymond said they
were Ghanaians or, as he called them, Ghaninas. Many of the women
had naked breasts, and when they saw me they ran inside to cover.
Others were sitting at street corners, cooking a dish called *mussa,* a
mixture of flour and bananas, fried in oil.

Raymond's assistant showed me the inside of one of the huts. It was
spotlessly clean. There was a rush mat made of palm leaves on the
sandy floor, and little else; and the palm leaf and bamboo walls
were covered with magazine pictures from all over the world. There
was one picture of the Beatles singing, and another of President
Johnson getting his hair cut.

Raymond left twenty cases of Coke and Fanta in this village, also a
quantity of ice. The ice was put into boxes and covered with palm-
leaves. Raymond said he always delivered ice on a Saturday, so that
friends of the villagers who came out from Lagos on Sunday could
have a cool drink. On the way out of the village we saw the fishermen's boats, long, lean vessels carved from a single piece of mahogany, drawn up on the sand. Some of the fishermen were lying on the
sand beneath them, sleeping in the shade. Others were up to their
necks in the sea, pulling a long crescent-shaped net toward the shore.
They were magnificent-looking men, long and supple and ebony, and
I thought that if I were a girl I might like the idea of one seducing
me. Raymond said that they fished in communes of twenty, and that
they would sometimes share out as much as £200 for a single catch.

We drove on down the beach, and soon there was nothing but the
green sea on the right, the green bush on the left, and the golden sand
ahead. On the horizon were a string of ships, hull down, waiting to
enter Lagos harbor. We came to a grove of palm trees running down
to the water's edge, and stopped. Raymond's assistant fetched three
Cokes from the back, and we all had a drink. Then I took off my
clothes and plunged into the surf. There are few places now where
one can swim naked in the sea, and it is a liberating experience, making you feel at one with God and his fishes and giving an insight into
what nudism is about. But I was glad there were no piranha fish
about.

We went on down the beach for another mile or so, then swung left
into the bush, along a hardly visible track that lay between two salt-

water lagoons. Presently, we came to a village full of goats and chickens. The children ran out of the houses and crowded round us. Some of the smaller ones started crying, and Raymond said, "It is you. You frighten them. They have not seen a white man before." Some of the older children pushed the crying ones toward me, and others broke into a sort of rhythmic chant, jumping up and down and laughing. Raymond said they were chanting *"Oyinbo,"* which meant "White man." I asked Raymond what "black man" was, and he said *enyadoo-doo.* So I began chanting *"Enyadoodoo"* back at them. The crying and the chanting stopped; a dozen little faces stared at me; then they got the joke and we were friends.

We unloaded four cases of Fanta and three of Coke at this village, then worked our way northward, round to the outskirts of Lagos, where Raymond did most of his trade. The bush ended here, giving way to a sprawling shantytown, all wooden planking and corrugated tin roofs. We drove into the center of the place and found a dozen tumble-down wooden shops, all jostled together. There were scores of signs, Coke and Fanta, Seven-Up and Sprite, Pepsi and Guinness, Tango and Star Beer. Outside one ramshackle building a notice said: "Sani Oseni. Native Doctor for Women with Pregnancy. Children's Sickness or any other kind of Sickness. A Trial will convince you." Another said, "Goodwill Commemmorial Service"; and a third, "Bright Day Photography and Barber Service. Napoleon Buonaparte." A small tin hut advertised itself as "Oluwa Loose Lodge. God First," and next to it was "Sunday Afun. Wine and Beer Licence."

Here we had several shops to supply, so I got out and wandered around. Most of the shopkeepers sat in the shade outside their shops, chatting with friends or swatting flies. I went into one shop called "E. G. Ogundare," which seemed full of tins of Ovaltine, notebooks and rubbers, and bottles of ground-nut oil. At the counter was a very drunken African woman wearing a yellow brassiere, swilling Guinness from a bottle. She asked me if I would buy her another Guinness, and I did.

Raymond and his assistant came in with cases of Coke and Fanta. The owner of the shop said something to Raymond, and they started up an argument. Raymond said, "She wants a sign. Everybody wants signs. But they do not give us enough signs." I said, "What sort of signs?" and Raymond said, "Coca-Cola signs. To put up outside the shop. Big ones." The argument started again, so Raymond sent his assistant to the truck to get a sign. When he brought it, the woman was not pleased. "She wanted a big one," said Raymond, "Seven-Up gave her a big one. But we do not have any." Raymond left two cases of Fanta in the shop, and one of Coke. I asked him what profit the shopkeepers made on each delivery, and he said, "I sell each bottle to them at five and a half pence, and they sell to their customers at seven pence. Out of their profit they have to pay for kerosene fuel for the fridge, so they do not make much." This shop also stocked two drinks called Trikola and Krola. Raymond said these were locally made drinks which the Nigerians used to buy before Coke and Fanta arrived. "Now," said Raymond gleefully, "we are driving them off the market."

Back at the truck, a crowd had gathered, including several boys. These boys had caps from Coca-Cola bottles, and Raymond said that anybody who could produce twelve caps got a free plastic cup. Raymond's assistant counted the caps as carefully as if they were golden sovereigns, and then handed out the cups. One boy had only nine caps, and when he was refused a plastic cup he went away crying. By now the village had got the idea that I wouldn't be riding in the truck unless I were a big shot in Coca-Cola. One man came up and said, "Sir, I wish you would tell your company that we are most bitterly disappointed at not getting any Christmas dash from them. Look at this fine calendar I have here from the Nigerian Tobacco Company. Why can't Coca-Cola give us dash like that? And tell me, please, why cannot we have the symbols? Seven-Up bring us fine symbols. We have a need for symbols. And, please, what about straws and cups? We badly want straws and cups. Why doesn't Coca-Cola give us good dash, same as other people do?"

On the way out we passed E. G. Ogundare's, and I saw that the Coca-Cola sign had already been nailed up, but upside down. Raymond said, "They don't want the signs for advertising. They just like collecting them. Everyone wants to have better signs than his neighbor."

✪

DASH HAUNTS you in Nigeria, from the moment you arrive until you go. When I went to the airport to fly to Liberia, the passport control officer, a young Nigerian in khaki shorts, took my passport and said, "Wait a moment, please. Your passport is not quite in order."

I waited, fretting, wondering what was wrong. The other passengers all filed through, and the officer and I were left alone. The officer picked up my passport and said, "You had an entry permit for seven days, but you have stayed two weeks."

"I put in for a stay of a month," I said.

"Yes," said the officer, "but when you showed your passport on arrival, I gave you a permit for a week. See, it is stamped here in your passport."

He showed me a blurred stamp and, in handwriting so illegible you could hardly see it, the figure 7.

"You never told me you were doing this," I said. I nearly added that it was not he but another man who had stamped my passport on arrival, but I couldn't be sure.

"You should have looked at your passport," he said.

"Well," I said, "does it really matter?"

"I must respect the regulations," said the officer. "There will be formalities to see to. But they will take time. You will have to cancel your booking on the plane."

I exploded. There wasn't another plane for three days. I was due to meet someone in Monrovia that night.

The officer looked at me impassively, and said, "I see you are a very busy and important person, so I might be able to make some special arrangements for you. Of course, it is against the regulations."

I got the message.

"You want dash," I said, "don't you?" I said it as loudly as I could, but there was no one around to hear. The officer had seen to that.

He winced and said quietly, "Thank you."

I pulled out my wallet and counted some dollars. He glanced around shiftily to see if anyone was watching, and took the money.

"Can you give me pounds?" he said.

"No," I said. It was true. I didn't have any.

He shrugged his shoulders, stamped the passport, and let me through. Later, in the plane, when a Pan Am cocktail had restored my equilibrium, I thought, What a bloody marvelous racket.

✪

THE AIRPORT of Monrovia is fifty miles from the capital, at a place called Robertsfield, near the headquarters of the vast Firestone rubber plantations. When we arrived, a group of young planters were waiting at the end of the customs shed, their faces pressed against the wire grille, like prisoners waiting for release. A man on the plane told me this was a regular occurence: the planters had little feminine company and now, like panting bulls, were waiting for the Pan Am girls to come and assuage their thirst. This man and I shared a taxi to Monrovia, driving for the most part through huge Firestone forests, passing regiments of rubber trees, each wounded in the side and supporting a little cup to catch the dripping rubber.

If Paraguay is as unreal as Ruritania, Monrovia has the unreality of some surrealistic film set. Despite the sun that shines all day, and the soft sea that washes its western side, and the milk-blue sky above, it is one of the eeriest places I have ever visited. The town, with a population of ninety thousand, is dominated by two hills. On top of one stands the plush new American Intercontinental Ducor Hotel, replete with air conditioning and marble and iced water. On the other is the equally new and startling twenty-million-dollar Executive Mansion, a massive, gaunt, square, black palace, which has been set down on a patch of wasteland overlooking the sea, and bears as much affinity to its surroundings as a robot in a roomful of humans. Here sits and works the timeless President Tubman, a jolly black spider at the center of his country's web.

Between the Executive Mansion and the Ducor lies downtown Monrovia, with the main shopping center, Ashmun Street, as its spine, a pleasant boulevard of one- and two-story buildings with a row of trees down the center, and inhabited mostly by Lebanese shopkeepers, a stunted, unattractive lot. But behind Ashmun Street, as behind the Stalinallee in East Berlin, is drabness and decay; old wooden plantation-style houses, crumbling, unpainted, unrepaired; gaping patches of wasteland; dumps for cans and garbage. The streets are patrolled by American-dressed cops who look as unreal as film extras. Everywhere mangy dogs roam, singly and in packs; at night they squat in the road, scratching themselves to a standstill. Down aptly named Gurley Street are sleazy nightclubs and bars, where pretty Bassa girls will give you whatever you desire. One night, in one of these bars, I met two Peace Corps volunteers, who took me back to their flat for a nightcap. While one played the Brandenburg Concertos in the bedroom, the other told me about Liberian women. "I've had a lot of them," he said, "and mostly they're like logs. See, it's an old tribal custom here for little girls to have their clitorises removed, so that when they grow up and get married, their husbands can go off hunting without having to worry if they're having a ball with anyone else. And they don't understand about breasts. You can fondle their breasts as much as you like and it doesn't mean a damn thing to them. One or two have these marvelous tight skins, though, which I find very exciting, though you have to go in real deep to get any fun."

Despite this, sex in Monrovia seems to be much enjoyed. Morals are not so much lax as undefined. "Outside marriages" are commonplace, and it is quite customary for the mother of a family to bring up her husband's bastard children alongside her own. This is perhaps a rather more civilized way of coping with the problem than the orphanages and foster homes of the West. Members of the cabinet are said to have enjoyed several outside marriages, and among Westerners in Monrovia there is a saying that they are the only cabinet in the world of whom it can be said that they are, literally, the fathers of their people.

There are many reasons for the sense of unreality and eeriness that pervades Monrovia. One is that while there is a television station, there was not yet, while I was there, any telephone system. There was a telephone in my bathroom at the Ducor, but it was only for internal use. Every message has to be relayed, and every conversation conducted, in person. But on a deeper level what Monrovian society suffers from is a lack of structure, almost a lack of identity. In 1822 the place was chosen by the American Colonization Society as a settlement for returned American slaves. These people, having acquired some experience of Western know-how, saw themselves as superior beings to the primitive tribes in the hinterland (who still compose 99 percent of the population) and so became the first black colonists. But unlike the white colonists, with their careful gradations of class and status, ranging from governor general down to telegraph clerk, the Americo-Liberians had no historical or social base to work from. So they created it, with a proliferation of religious and semireligious, secret and semisecret, organizations. Today in Monrovia, churches for

Catholics, Baptists, Methodists, Presbyterians, and Seventh-Day Adventists all flourish. And then there are the Freemasons. There can be few Westerners who have not seen pictures of Monrovian dignitaries dolled up in top hats and tails and clutching silver trowels, wending their way to some Masonic jollity. The social position of a Monrovian today is determined largely by the office he holds within his church or lodge. President Tubman, not surprisingly, is Grand Master of Monrovia's Freemasons.

Nothing in Monrovia surprises one. One day I attended a murder trial in the city's Hall of Justice. During an address by counsel it was found that one of the jurors was missing. He had found the proceedings increasingly tedious and had gone off to the liquor store to have a drink. Next day I read in the *Liberian Star* that the judge had fined him ten dollars. "The judge in imposing the fine, said that he had previously warned the juryman against his perambulating activities, but he apparently did not heed the warning." And the day after I arrived there was a curious incident regarding a Mr. Heinz, proprietor of what was said to be the best restaurant in town. It seemed that President Tubman was giving a party at the Executive Mansion, and they had run out of champagne. An aide was sent down to Mr. Heinz for more. Mr. Heinz refused to give him more than three bottles on the very sound grounds that (a) the aide refused to identify himself or sign for the champagne, and (b) Mr. Heinz had not yet received payment for a similar consignment ordered by the Postmaster General. The aide asked Mr. Heinz if, were he living in West Germany, he would refuse to send champagne to the West German President; to which Mr. Heinz replied that the President of West Germany was not in the habit of sending out for champagne. The upshot was that although the Heinzes had been in Monrovia thirteen years, they were deemed to have been guilty of "gross insult" to the President, and were ordered to leave the country within thirty days. In a way the name of the British ambassador's yacht summed up Monrovia. It was called *WAWA*. When I asked him what it meant, he said, "West Africa Wins Again."

❂

LIBERIA IS the African headquarters of the Voice of America, and its director was a man called Hank Miller, about six and a half feet tall. He sent me in a car down to Careysburg, twenty miles from Monrovia, to the transmitting station which picks up V.O.A.'s signals from Washington and beams them all over Africa. It was a big, dull, building tucked away in the hills and surrounded by groves of antennas, two hundred feet high, like something out of science fiction.

An Englishman called Mullins and an American called Ferguson took me round. At one point we found a sort of tub resting at the foot of one of the antennas, and Ferguson invited me to get in and go up to look at the view. He pressed a lever, and the tub and I went up a hundred feet: he pressed another, and we went sideways thirty feet. I peered over and saw Ferguson, the size of a doll. "How's the view?" he shouted. "Fine," I shouted, looking at my feet. He let me look at the view for an age, and then hauled me down. "Isn't that view something?" he said, "I knew you'd enjoy it." Ferguson said one reason he liked the job was the view, and another the isolation. Mullins said, "Give my love to Blighty."

On the way back to Monrovia in the car a voice said from nowhere, "Where is Mr. Kennedy?" I thought I must be hearing things. The driver picked up a hand telephone from the dashboard and said, "Just passing Bernard's Beach. We'll be back at the office in ten minutes." He put back the telephone and said to me, "They like to keep their tabs on you."

Back at the office, Hank Miller showed me a copy of that week's African program schedule, with items like "African Panorama," "News in Special English," "Report to Africa," and "Music U.S.A." I said, "All the stuff you broadcast here originates from Washington, or from V.O.A. reporters in Africa who transmit to Washington. Isn't there anything you do locally, something that is specifically African?"

Mr. Miller said there was. In Monrovia there was a V.O.A. man called Sarkisian who was compiling a library of tribal music from all over Africa. He was leaving shortly to record what he called a "town meeting" between the AID man and some tribal chiefs in a place called Foya, about a hundred and fifty miles into the interior, near the Sierra Leone border. If that interested me, why didn't I meet Sarkisian and fix up to go with him?

I met Mr. Sarkisian the next day. He was an Americanized Armenian, and looked the image of Britain's Mr. Punch, a short, stubby man, with bald head, hook nose, and thin mustache. He was surrounded by tape recorders, microphones, and yards of cable and tape.

When the tangle had diminished, I asked him how he had got interested in this work. He said he had learned music originally from his father, who had emigrated to Massachusetts from Armenia in 1900, after the Turkish massacres, in which his father's parents were killed. "Ever since a child I have played Turkish and Arabian instruments. I can play the Egyptian harp and the Arabic lute and the Persian dulcimer, and pretty well all types of flute and clarinet and drums. When I go to record in a new village, I start off by sitting down in the middle and playing the drums myself. They all crowd round and listen and say, well, that's fine, now we'll show you how it's *really* done. Which, of course, is just what I want."

I said, "Hank Miller tells me you're compiling a library of African music?"

"That's right. We've amassed a tremendous amount of material already. The last few years the U.S.I.S. officers all over Africa have been sending in tapes of local music which mostly has been recorded by local radio stations. Frankly, the quality of these recordings isn't too good, but we don't say too much about that because a lot of these people are very sensitive. I visit the area later, and then arrange to make my own recording."

I said, "How much of what you collect is actually broadcast on V.O.A.?"

Mr. Sarkisian said, "Every day, seven days a week, we put out African music. Some of it I've recorded, and some of it others have recorded. Then, about twice a week, I take part in a program myself, play the drums and so on, and talk about rhythms and histories of the various instruments."

I said, "I haven't heard much African music, but I find it incomprehensible."

"So do most Westerners," said Mr. Sarkisian, "and most of it is. But a lot isn't. A lot of it has just the same scales as Western music. But it takes time to get to know."

Two days later Mr. Sarkisian and his wife left for Foya by car, and I arranged to fly there later by charter plane and meet them. The charter firm had a small office at the airport, but when I arrived at 7:30 A.M., it was still closed. So I went to the airport café, and presently this young Greek god came in, with blue eyes and fair hair, a slim figure in khaki shirt and trousers. Greek god, hell! He was the all-American boy.

"You Mr. Kennedy?"

"Yes."

"I'm McTeague. How are you, sir? I'm going to take you to Foya. You ready to go?"

We walked to the plane. It looked like a clapped-out dragonfly. There were patches of tape on the windows, and McTeague said a big battery he had been ferrying a few days before had got loose and partly gone through the window. I seized a strap to pull myself into the plane, and it came away in my hand. McTeague hauled me up and started the single motor. It wheezed and spluttered into life. We trundled onto the runway and turned down it, and took off.

We circled once, over the sea, climbed to a thousand feet, and headed east. Monrovia dropped away, and soon there were no roads beneath us or anything, just little clearings in the trees and groups of conical native huts clustered like autumn mushrooms.

A group of mountains appeared ahead, and McTeague said that Foya lay beyond them. Now there was nothing beneath us but thick forest, not a trail or a clearing or a hut in sight, nothing but this huge carpet of trees. I wondered what McTeague would do if the engine packed up.

"McTeague," I shouted.

"Yes?"

"What do you do if the engine packs up?"

"Try to land."

"Where?"

"On the treetops."

"You're joking!"

"No I'm not. I'd rather try to land on the treetops than on water or in a swamp. When you land in a swamp with a fixed-wheel aircraft, the first thing that happens is the aircraft turns on its back. But the treetops should give a nice cushion."

"How do you get from the treetops to the ground?"

McTeague pointed a thumb behind him. I turned and saw, at the back, a huge coil of yellow rope like a sleeping snake.

"Have you ever had to do it?"

"No, but I heard of a guy who did, and he got away with it."

We cleared the mountains and McTeague lost height. In about five minutes a road appeared, and we flew along it until we came to a village. We circled the village and saw a landing strip, like a swathe of bandage, in a field of sugar cane. "I think that's Foya," said McTeague, "but we'll go down and find out."

We made a nice landing on the strip and taxied to a stop. A crowd of boys gathered round us. McTeague got out and said, in a kind of broken Italian, "Vot is zis town, please? It is Foya, yes?" The boys stared and said nothing. "I guess we'd better go into the village," said McTeague. He locked the plane, and we set off toward the village, followed by the boys.

In the center of the village was a store that sold Coca-Cola and Guinness and tinned sardines and brassières and toys and Scotch and baby powder. The woman in the store confirmed that this was Foya. But she hadn't seen Sarkisian. "I'll tell you what we'll do," said McTeague. "We'll stick around here for maybe a half hour in case they're late, and if they haven't shown up by then, we'll fly along the road to Voinjima and see if we can pick them up there."

So McTeague and I ordered bananas and Coca-Cola and he told me about his life. His home was in New Jersey, and he had dreamed about flying ever since he was a boy. On leaving college, he had taken a job with an air charter firm in Guatemala, mostly spraying crops. He stayed there seven years. "That was a great job. I earned between fifteen and twenty thousand bucks a year. I lived well, with a house and servants on five thousand, and I saved the rest."

"Why did you leave?"

"The accident rate was getting uncomfortably high. One year we had a hundred planes and lost forty-eight of them. Otherwise it was great. I married a Guatemalan girl just before I left. She's with me now in Monrovia. Before that I had some fabulous girl friends. Oh, boy!"

"Really?"

He turned to the counter. "Hey, Mama! You want to give us two more Cokes?" He turned back to me. "I was in charge of maintenance in this company, and there was another guy who took care of administration. This guy had a Guatemalan secretary who was a real peach. She was only nineteen, and she was married to a Guatemalan boy of twenty. I got pretty friendly with her, and after a while I said, 'Why don't you come with me to Miami for a week?' And she said, 'Fine.' She told her family that her boss was going with his family, so everything would be all right. Well, we were going in my plane, but the week before a friend of mine borrowed it, and he was chasing his girl friend down the road, trying to touch his wheels on the top of her car, when he hit a telegraph pole and got killed. So that meant we had to go in the commercial plane. And what do you think? This girl's whole goddam family—husband, mother, father, brother, sisters—all turned up at the airport to say goodbye, and I had to go right down the line shaking hands with them. The girl's boss was mad as hell when he found out what I was planning to do—I think he fancied her himself—but it was okay, and he saw me through."

"How was Miami?"

"We had a great nine days. I guess I must have bought her four to five thousand dollars' worth of dresses. We ran around in a Ford convertible and really lived it up. Boy, *did we live it up!* And then the nine days came to an end and that was the end of that."

"She went back to her husband?"

"That's right. He wasn't a bad little guy at all."

"How do you like it here?"

"It's not bad, though I don't go much for these Liberians, they're kind of spooky. I bought a couple of guns when I came here, one for the plane in case I have to land in the jungle, and another for my wife, because she's often on her own. Well, this Liberian F.B.I. man came to see me and tried to make out I'd promised him one of the guns. He was real mad at me, so I said, 'Well, doesn't the government give you a gun?' And he said it did, but he wanted one for himself. These guys are quite illogical. I don't understand the way their minds work. I guess it's got something to do with the color of their skins. You take this restaurant of Heinz's which they say they're going to close. *Why?* It's the best restaurant in town. The guy built it up from nothing. That just shows how crazy they are."

I said, "You like the job?"

"Sure. It has lots of variety. You never get bored. We pilots are a funny kind of breed, really, we like to feel we're more or less our own masters. But I don't believe I'll stay here too long. The pay's about fifteen percent less than in Guatemala, and with the cost of living what it is, I use every penny of it."

"Where will you go?"

"I've had a few offers. There's quite an interesting outfit working from Bombay. I might go there. And then I've been working on an idea to ship meat over to West Africa from Brazil. Meat in Brazil is cheap. In West Africa it's expensive. That's the basic idea."

"What do you do in your spare time?"

"I don't have too much spare time. I use a camera, two in fact, but I'm a strictly Sunday photographer. I read a little, mostly flying stories of the war. Right now I'm reading a book called *Nine Lives*—about a pilot called Deere. It's really great. And I keep my eyes open and listen. A day in which I haven't learned something I regard as an unprofitable day. But there's two things I won't discuss with anyone."

"What are they?"

"Politics and religion."

"You don't have any views on them?"

"I have plenty. I'm a Protestant and a Republican. But I don't like talking about them."

"Do you see many other Americans in Monrovia?"

"Not too many. I make friends as they come, and I don't give a damn where they come from. Frankly, I'm not greatly impressed by American representation abroad. I've seen ambassadors come and ambassadors go, and this whole diplomatic deal seems to me a load of nothing. As for the Peace Corps, they make me ashamed I'm American. All those beards and scruffy beatnik clothes. They represent America, don't they? Why can't they be decently turned out?"

We returned to the plane and took off for Voinjima. About ten minutes out of Foya, McTeague suddenly banked the plane and dived toward a bend in the road. He pointed out the window, and in a clear patch of road I saw two stationary cars and beside one of them Mr. Sarkisian's unmistakable bald head. McTeague made a run over the cars, waggling his wings in the direction of Foya. Then we flew back and landed, and presently the cars arrived.

✪

THE "TOWN MEETING" was scheduled to take place in a small village called Karwohun, some ten miles out of Foya; and the object, as far as I could make out, was for the local AID man to have a kind of dialogue with the local chiefs about the benefits AID was bringing, and for Mr. Sarkisian to record it. The AID man, who was traveling in the second car, was a Southerner called Hutton. He had a face like an old dead moon, spectacles, and fur on his arms and chest like a bed of watercress; you could have put a pin into it and not found it for days.

We assembled in the village hall, which was made of wood with a tin corrugated roof. There were a lot of people there: Hutton and his wife, Mr. Sarkisian, now wearing a little black-and-white-striped, tasseled hat that looked like a pillbox, Mrs. Sarkisian, who had red hair scraped back in a bun, a Mr. Moore, who was Mr. Sarkisian's Liberian assistant, and a whole lot of chiefs and villagers. The chief chief was a fine-looking old man called Thomas Kollie, who wore an old pair of khaki trousers and a loose khaki shift buttoned up to the neck. Mr. Sarkisian said he reminded him of Jeff Chandler, the movie actor. He had seventy wives, and most of the villagers were his relatives.

On arrival in the hall we were given a little white napkin and a glass of beer or Fanta. Mr. Moore said that the customary gifts of chiefs when entertaining strangers in these parts were "white heart" and "cold water." "White heart" was anything white, like the napkins, and signified peace; and the beer and Fanta represented "cold water." Then we had lunch, a huge bowl of what looked like Irish stew. It tasted of nothing in particular, but as I hadn't had anything to eat all day except two bananas and a doughnut, I ate mine with relish.

After lunch, Mr. Sarkisian set himself up behind a battery of tape recorders, microphones, and boxes marked "Virgin Tape," and we were ready to get on with the meeting. Mr. Hutton walked over to one of the microphones and opened the proceedings. I had a feeling that he was going to make a real meal of the occasion, and I was right. "Chief Kollie," said Mr. Hutton ponderously, "it is *so gracious* of you to welcome us here today and give us your hospitality and make this town meeting possible. And I want to say right away how grateful and pleased we all are." He beamed. One of the Chief's relatives translated this, and everybody nodded and then clapped. "And now," said Mr. Hutton, "I would like to introduce ourselves to you." At great length he then introduced Mr. Sarkisian, Mr. Moore, me ("Mr. Kennedy is an English writer, and we are so honored to have him with us today"), and his wife. All this had to be translated and told a second time. "And now—" said Mr. Hutton, and then he stopped. "Oh, my goodness," he said, "I made a terrible mistake. I forgot to introduce *Mrs.* Sarkisian." Sarkisian, from behind his tape recorders, said, "She's the one who carries the boxes." Mr. Hutton said, "She's his head wife, and his *only* wife."

We all laughed to please Mr. Hutton, who then said, "And now, Chief Kollie, we would be happy if you would introduce your people to us. We know you are the paramount chief, and therefore the greatest of the chiefs, but we would like to meet your town chiefs." There were a dozen town chiefs, and Chief Kollie started wading through them. At one point the translator got so muddled that Chief Kollie pushed him away and took over the translating himself. Mr. Hutton said, "This is one of the problems we have brought you, I fear. We wish we could talk with you in your language, and we are so sorry we can't." After what seemed a lifetime, the introduction of the town chiefs came to an end. Mr. Hutton said, "Chief Kollie, it is most gracious of you to let us meet all these people, because we want to get to know them by name. And now let's talk a little about the school."

It seemed that AID had a plan, or Mr. Hutton wanted AID to have a plan, to build a school. But at the moment it appeared to be no more than a germ in Mr. Hutton's mind. "I can't say when the school will be built," he said, "but I can say it will be built, and I know that's the thing in most of your minds today. Now let's see how many boys and girls would be likely to go to school to read book."

Everyone was asked how many children he had, and one or two chiefs said they had lost count. One old chief, who was Chief Kollie's uncle, said he would like to read book himself.

"Ask him," said Mr. Hutton to Chief Kollie, "why he would like to read book."

The old man muttered something, and Chief Kollie said, "He would like to read book to tell more English."

"Chief Kollie," said Mr. Hutton, "do the chiefs think that reading book is going to cause all the boys and girls to leave family and go to Monrovia?"

"No," said Chief Kollie, "that is not in their minds at all."

"Well," said Mr. Hutton, "we've talked about the school, what's the next most important thing?"

"The next thing is roads," said Chief Kollie.

Mr. Hutton looked round the chiefs as though they were a class of five-year-olds, and he said, "Now, why did you need roads?"

"We need roads," said Chief Kollie, "to send our goods to market and the children to school."

Mr. Hutton nodded, as though to say, Good boy, go to the top of the class.

"I can't say when you will have roads," said Mr. Hutton, "but I know you will have them. I know that roads are very much in the front of your President's mind." A chief in a peacock-blue robe said, "We know what the President has done for us, and we pray God to grant him a long and healthy life. Before, we had no money. Now we have thirty dollars."

Mr. Hutton said, "That certainly is a great tribute to your great leader, and I'm sure he'll hear of that one way or the other, and it is certainly a fine tribute for all the great things the President has done for you."

Chief Kollie said, "Our love for President Tubman is in every Liberian heart. He is showing the way we must follow."

"Well, now," said Mr. Hutton, "we're going to have to close this meeting soon, because I know that some of us have to go in not too many minutes. Let me say this to you. I am not a big man. I am just an adviser. I will pass on your message to my people and to your government. I understand that your first need is for the school, and the second is for roads."

Chief Kollie said, "And we also need a clinic."

Mr. Hutton paused and looked at Chief Kollie with his moon face as though to say, *That* isn't on the program *at all*.

"Now, why do you need a clinic?" he said.

Oh, Christ, Hutton, I thought, do take a pull on yourself.

"Many children sick," said Chief Kollie.

Mr. Hutton nodded again. "Well, thank you for interrupting me, Chief Kollie," he said. "I'm very glad to know that. All I can say is that with your drive and your determination (half of them, by this time, were asleep), you will get the things you want." "I can't say when you will get them, but I know you will get them for certain. To talk with men like you makes one very encouraged. So let me thank you, Chief Kollie, and all these other fine, gracious people, for this very wonderful town meeting."

Chief Kollie said, "Thank you. Now we are happy. We are thankful to the President and the American people for all the interest they have shown in us."

Mr. Sarkisian sat behind his recorders with earphones on his head, adjusting levels. I felt as I had felt at Father Vermilion's meeting in

New York. What had been said was wind and warm air. Who was going to *listen* to it all, and what would they gain if they did?

Three villagers now came forward to sing to us. One wore a brown astrakhan hat, a pair of khaki shorts with half the fly undone, and a striped shirt; the second wore khaki shorts and a red fez with a gold star in the front, and was carrying a huge fly whisk; and the third had on a yellow satin cap, of the kind used by goalkeepers in England, a black-and-white-striped robe, and bathing trunks. Each was holding a hollowed-out piece of tin and a stick, which they used for accompaniment. The noise was awful. The man doing most of the solo singing, the one with the fly whisk, was on the left, and Mr. Sarkisian had to stop everything and shift him to the center, to be nearer the microphone. ("I guess the lead singer turned out not to be the lead singer," said Mr. Hutton.) They started up again, and Mr. Sarkisian bounced up and down, shouting, "That's great!" It went on for ten minutes that seemed like about a hundred. Then Mr. Sarkisian rewound the tape and played it back. They loved that; it was real white man's magic. They crowded round and laughed and listened, and listened and laughed. "The playback is always a cinch," said Mr. Sarkisian. Afterward Mr. Hutton said to the room at large, "I'm going to make a copy of the tape of this whole meeting and send it to our director in Washington." Did he mean the director of AID, I wondered, and did he seriously think that that busy man was going to give up an afternoon listening to it?

Later I asked Mr. Hutton this, and he said, "Well, that was a public-relations gimmick. The real reason I'm recording this meeting is for my doctoral dissertation."

"Your what?" I said.

"My Ph.D. I'm working for a doctorate in education, and I shall send this in as part of my field work." He beamed and looked round the room, and said loudly, "Now it is time for us to go, but we shall be back, I can promise you. I don't know when we shall be back, but I know that we will." He took a five-dollar bill from his wallet. "We all know how generous Chief Kollie is with his white heart, and we'd like to conclude by giving him some of our white heart, too."

He handed Chief Kollie the bill, and the chief looked rather embarrassed. He tried to refuse it, but Mr. Hutton pressed it on him. To me he said, "That's the common practice here."

"I thought he seemed rather offended," I said.

"Oh, no," said Mr. Hutton. "They all do it. When President Tubman was here the other day, he gave him one thousand dollars. It's not payment, but a recognition of what's been done."

"Wouldn't it have been better," I said, "to have given him a bottle of whisky?"

Mr. Hutton thought. "I guess it might," he said, "but I didn't have a bottle of whisky with me."

We drove to the Huttons' house at Voinjima for supper. Mr. Hutton said grace, and then we had country chop and cold tea and noodles and rice, prepared by Mrs. Hutton. Mrs. Hutton was slim and shy and had a pretty, little-girl's face. The Huttons had been married fourteen years; they didn't have any children of their own and had adopted a boy of three. Mr. Hutton said, "We like living here. My wife doesn't want a social life like most American women. She goes down to Monrovia about once every three months. I guess I miss the social life a bit, but not all that much."

After supper, Mr. Sarkisian collected some of his recordings, and we went off to a block of flats to pay a call on Superintendent Kennedy, the governor of the county. Superintendent Kennedy was a Liberian of about fifty, and wore a smart lounge suit. He gave us whisky and beer. Mr. Sarkisian produced a book about President Kennedy and handed it to Superintendent Kennedy. It was a present, he said, for the cooperation he had had from everyone in the county. Superintendent Kennedy was very moved. He stood up and said, "I feel this is an occasion when we must all stand up." We all stood up. Superintendent Kennedy looked at the book lovingly and fondled it, and tears came into his eyes. I began to feel a bit tearful myself. Superintendent Kennedy said that he would treasure the book always. He was sad that President Kennedy's office had been so brief. He was a very good man. The book would help to keep his memory fresh.

Mr. Sarkisian unpacked his recorder, and we listened to some of his tapes. One tape was of another town meeting, and suddenly we heard Hutton's voice saying, "Chief Zugbe, you are so gracious to cooperate with us in this town meeting, and we want you to know how grateful we are. We have a saying in our country that he who would be greatest must be the servant of all, and that's why Chief Zugbe is the greatest among you, because I know he truly is the servant of you all." And later, "I don't know what the answers to your rice problems are, but I'm going to have a word with our agricultural people and see what they can do." There was something eerie in hearing Hutton's unctuous voice saying almost word for word what he had been saying that very afternoon. He sat quietly in a chair, listening to himself, his moon face impassive, tufts of hair sprouting from the crannies in his shirt. Perhaps he was thinking of his doctoral dissertation. Superintendent Kennedy looked at his feet and nodded appreciatively.

Then we had tapes of Liberian music which Mr. Sarkisian had recorded up and down the country. To my untrained ear it all sounded the same, but the others caught the nuances. Mr. Sarkisian said, "That's great" several times, and once Mr. Hutton exclaimed, "Listen to that. That's real artistry there. It's just like the Andrews sisters." To me it was about as far removed from the Andrews sisters as one could imagine.

After the music Mr. Hutton beamed at the Superintendent and said, "I do feel, Mr. Kennedy, that the kind of town meeting we have today is the real *key* to the kind of thing we're trying to do. We're trying to get changes here, but your people have a different way of communication from ours, and we have to try and understand this, we have to pay attention to it. I'm sure you understand this, Mr. Kennedy, as one who has had a great success in the field of education yourself." At large he said, "Mr. Kennedy has a great reputation in that field. I don't know if he knows it, but he has, and it's a very fine thing."

The Superintendent made a conciliatory, embarrassed smile. I thought, Oh, come off it, Hutton, you old creep.

But Hutton was in full flood, and there was no stopping him. "Let me say," he said to the Superintendent, "let me say that when the Chief Justice came up here to swear in the new superintendents, he was so gracious as to take me along with him, and I was able to see for myself the fine relationships these people had with their new leaders, and I want to tell you that this impressed me very much. It made a real impact on me, because I've seen with my own eyes, Mr. Kennedy, the sort of respect and admiration you command."

It was time to go. Mr. Hutton thanked the Superintendent profusely and then said, "Oh, Mr. Kennedy, I don't believe I properly introduced the *other* Mr. Kennedy to you. I don't know if I mentioned that the *other* Mr. Kennedy is a British writer. He's writing a book about Liberia, as I understand, and we think it's very gracious of him to come along with us. In his own country Mr. Kennedy is a ♦ . . ."

But I had sensed what was coming and was already heading for the door. Mr. Hutton's voice trailed away. I never did hear what I was in my own country. A prophet without honor, maybe.

❂

ALSO STAYING at the Ducor was a lady who breakfasted by herself each morning, using her own tin of Nescafé instead of the hotel coffee. She could have been any age between fifty-five and seventy. She had neat auburn hair kept in place by a kind of diaphanous veil spattered with little colored dots like hundreds and thousands, and she wore pearls and amber spectacles.

I might have left Liberia without exchanging a word with her; but one day the local radio station arranged to interview us in the hotel lobby. Her name was Edna McKinnon, and she was going round the world preaching family planning. I made a date with her for breakfast the next day.

She was there when I came down, the pot of Nescafé on the table. The waiter came to take my order, and Mrs. McKinnon said, "Have you finished reading that book I gave you?" The waiter said no, he hadn't, and took my order for boiled eggs. When he had gone Mrs. McKinnon said, "I lent him *No Room in the Ark,* which is perfectly marvelous. He's a darling boy and so bright."

Mrs. McKinnon said she was seventy-one, but I wouldn't think it, would I? I said I wouldn't. She had been in family planning for most of her life, but now she was semiretired and was visiting a few countries on behalf of her old friend Dr. Clarence Gamble. Dr. Gamble was one of the Procter-and-Gamble Gambles, and had used his private wealth in the cause of family planning. "Dr. Gamble has a real obsession about birth control," she said. "He's an absolutely fabulous character. Back in the twenties he had this vision that no one else had, of what birth control could do, and he's given his time and his money to it ever since. He did family planning in the States to start with, and then we all went to a big international conference in Bombay in 1952, and that started his international interest. He now has doctors all over the place which his foundation finances entirely, and about seventeen different organizations which he keeps supplied with contraceptives. If I go to some country where they need contraceptives in a hurry, I send him a cable, and they're sent immediately. Not even

World Health or International Planned Parenthood can act as quickly as that."

Mrs. McKinnon took a spoonful of Nescafé, and I asked her if Dr. Gamble advocated any particular kind of contraceptive. No, she said, all Dr. Gamble was concerned with was preventing the sperm and the egg from meeting, and different countries favored different ways of achieving this. "In Japan now there is a great demand for condoms. No one there thought there would be, because no one thought the men would stand for it. But it turned out that men preferred condoms to anything else, because they retained control. They send their wives to the clinics to get the condoms, but they take care of the condoms themselves.

"Well, I told them this in Malaysia, I said to the Malaysians that seventy-five percent of contraceptives in Japan were now condoms, and they said, well, that may be all right for the Japanese, but the Chinese and Malayans are different. So I said, 'Well, why not give the women free samples when they come to the clinic, and see what happens?' And do you know what happened? They switched right over from diaphragms to condoms. They went from eighty-five percent diaphragms to sixty-three percent condoms. Of course, that was a few years back, and the position may have altered with the coming of the pill."

"What other contraceptives does Dr. Gamble recommend?"

"We don't really *recommend* any particular one. I tell people what is available, what the advantages and disadvantages are, and then it's up to them to choose. For example, I tell them that the natural rhythm method is the simplest of all, but that it's no good at all for people who can't read a calendar. Then I tell them about vaginal foaming tablets and cream, and that these have to be used just before intercourse, and a lot of people don't want to be bothered. And I also tell them about the aerosol cream, which is like shaving cream— when it comes out it spreads all over. Now, that is *highly* effective, and very easy to use. The manufacturers give vast quantities to the Church World Service."

The waiter brought my eggs, and I said to Mrs. McKinnon, "What about the diaphragm?"

"I don't mention the diaphragm now unless I'm asked about it. I think you'll find that the diaphragm is on the way out, and most women in the States who used to use it have gone over to the pill.

The trouble with the diaphragm is that there's a wide range of sizes, it has to be kept clean or you get infection, and the average physician doesn't know how to fit it. Frankly, we don't think it's safe enough."

"And the pill?"

"The pill is the most effective contraceptive yet invented. It's almost a hundred percent foolproof, and it regulates the period. I know some women are afraid it will make them fat, but there's no scientific evidence that it adds to the avoirdupois at all. My theory is that it relaxes you so you're no longer nervous, and you put on weight that way. My daughter's just gone onto it, and my son-in-law tells me she's a completely different woman. But it also depends on being able to read a calendar, so for primitive people it isn't much good."

"What do they get? Condoms and foaming tablets?"

"Yes, and the coil. I'm *very* keen about the coil. You know about it?"

"I've heard of it," I said. "I'm not too sure how it works."

Mrs. McKinnon said, "I have one right here, and I'll show you." She opened her bag and pulled out a crumpled airmail envelope and laid it on the table. From it she took what looked like a white plastic worm curled up for sleep, a small, very thin pipe, and a thing like a knitting needle. She put them on the table between the tin of Nescafé and the marmalade.

"The basic idea," said Mrs. McKinnon, "is to get the coil into the uterus. It's shaped like that because it's been discovered that's the best way for staying there. Once in, it's impossible for the woman to conceive. We don't know why this is so, whether the sperm breaks up when it hits it, or takes fright, or what. But the beauty of the system is that once the coil is in, there's nothing to worry about. It can stay there for years, and any time the woman wants a baby she just gets her doctor to take it out."

"How," I asked, "does he get it in?"

Mrs. McKinnon picked up the thin pipe and said, "This is a little old beat-up introducer, and this"—picking up the thing that looked like a knitting needle—"is the plunger. The doctor pushes the coil into the introducer, then inserts the introducer into the vagina until it reaches the uterus." She picked up the coil and threaded it into the pipe. "Then he puts the plunger into the introducer to carry it all the way."

I said, "But I thought the whole point of the coil was its unusual shape. Now it's inside the introducer, it's gone straight."

"Look!" said Mrs. McKinnon. She pushed the plunger right up the introducer. The coil came out the other end, and sprang into its former shape. "Hey presto!" said Mrs. McKinnon. "That's how it settles down in the uterus!"

I reached for another bit of toast. "Well," I said, "I see how you get it in, but how do you get it out?"

Mrs. McKinnon pointed to one end of the coil, on which were three little beads. "This end," she said, "hangs down from the uterus. All the doctor has to do is pull it out with his finger. As a matter of fact," she said, chuckling, "this is a *modified* coil. We had to shorten this end a little bit because it was hanging down so far that some of the husbands were finding it uncomfortable and getting to complain.

"Basically," said Mrs. McKinnon, "there are two kinds of coil, the Margulies Coil and the Lippes Loop. Dr. Lippes is a darling boy. He thinks it's the most important thing in the world, and he doesn't want to get a dime for it. There's another device called Birmberg's Bow, but that's a little more complex, as you have to use a crochet hook to get it out. The great advantage the coil has over the pill is that once it's in, you can forget about it. Taking pills is the biggest bore in the world."

I asked Mrs. McKinnon when she had first got interested in birth control, and she said a very long time ago. She had got married at the end of the First World War and had had three pregnancies, the last of which was a miscarriage. Her husband, who was a lawyer, had died in the early thirties. "It was the Depression at the time, and I was in need of a job; so my sister, who was very influential in Washington, got me a job in government. Well, one day a fellow in the office said to me, 'Are you going to this luncheon?' and I said yes, not really knowing what it was about, but feeling I ought to be going. And we had this lecture by Mordecai Ezekiel—isn't that a marvelous name?—and it was a real eye-opener to me. The whole idea of family planning was brand new to me, and I asked a lot of questions. I felt that if I'd known before what I was told then, I'd probably not have lost my third child. Well, Mr. Ezekiel was lecturing on behalf of Margaret Sanger, who was really the founder of the birth-control movement in America, and soon after that her secretary called me up and said, would I be interested in working for her and helping to get the law changed? You see, at that time the law equated contraception with obscenity, and it was an offense to send a contraceptive through the mails. So I went to New York and spent a fabulous day with Margaret

Sanger, and I said I'd help all I could, and after that I just boned up on everything I could lay my hands on.

"Later on I met Dr. Gamble, who was then director of field services for Margaret Sanger, and he invited me to help set up clinics in the South. I accepted, and for the next ten years I was one of their field consultants. I traveled all over the United States, advising people on family planning. I never had any medical training and I think this helped, because people knew I could be objective."

"How about the Catholics?" I said. "Did you meet much opposition from them?"

"I'll tell you a funny thing about the Catholics. For years we used to ask people their religion when they came to the clinics, because we thought that the Catholics were only permitted to use the rhythm method. But we began to find that they wanted to know all the methods available, the same as everyone else. So then we stopped asking people's religion, so as not to give the Catholics a sense of guilt. We even had *priests* sending people to the clinics. It's the Pope and the Church who are still against anything except the rhythm method, not the ordinary communicant."

Mrs. McKinnon worked for ten years as a field consultant, then spent eleven years in Chicago as director of the Planned Parenthood Association. "In the late 1950's I decided to retire, and become a lady of leisure, and take a little trip round the world. When Clarence Gamble heard about this, he said you can't just wander round the world on your own, you must work for the Pathfinder Fund, which is the family-planning foundation he and his family have set up. So I said I wouldn't do anything full-time, but I'd look in at places here and there and do what I could for them. And I just love working for them, because they look after me and see I have enough leisure and all that. On this trip I've been to Sierra Leone and Nigeria, and I'm going on to Lebanon, Egypt, Jordan, Saudi Arabia and Afghanistan. Dr. Gamble is not too keen on my going to Afghanistan. He says it's dead from the neck up, but I tell him we have to make a start every place."

"All these countries you go to," I said, "are they glad to see you?"

"Not always, and usually not at first. In many countries there's a resistance to Europeans preaching about birth control. They think we want to keep their population down, to *stop* them from having babies, and I have to explain over and over that we want them to have babies, but healthy ones, not dead ones. Some places *have* a pop-

ulation problem—like India and Egypt and Japan and Hong Kong—
but most places don't have a population problem, but a *health* problem, and that's what I keep telling them. Now, here in Liberia the
government has launched 'Operation Production' for more babies,
because the country needs to increase its population. But what's the
use of more babies when seven out of ten die?

"Often, when I go to a new country, they say, 'The Minister is
unalterably opposed to family planning, and he doesn't much like
white faces either.' So I say, 'He's the man I want to see.' I always find
that if you go to the top you can get things done you never can on a
lower level. At the lower level they think family planning is a population problem and therefore requires a political decision. I tell them
it's a public-health problem, and no more requires a political decision
than having your appendix out.

"In Ethiopia, now, I was told that the Minister of Health was dead
against it, and so was his deputy, and neither of them wanted to see
me. So I went and talked to our ambassador's wife, who was a perfectly darling young Roman Catholic, and she told me the people
who would help me, and finally I got an appointment with the Minister. They all told me he was a five-minute man, but I was there forty-
five minutes, and he wanted to hear everything. And that's how we
started our program in Ethiopia."

"Do you get this sort of resistance in most countries?"

"It depends entirely on whom I meet. *Most* people in *any* country
are embarrassed by the subject. They shy away from it. They haven't
got any curiosity or imagination or courage. And I'm sorry to say the
Americans I meet are among the worst. They're just the *scarediest*
people. They're afraid of losing their jobs and daren't say anything.
But in the end I usually meet someone who's willing to think inde-
pendently and has the courage of his convictions, and when that happens I can start getting things done."

"I suppose," I said, "you must sometimes find yourself in some
quite funny situations?"

"Oh, I do. I remember in Katmandu once we had a family-planning board meeting on Christmas Day, and the room was full of posters which combined information about family planning and *flies*. Another time I arrived in Indonesia with two large cartons. The customs
man said, 'What's in there?' and I said, 'Ten thousand condoms.' So
he went away and fetched a friend, and the friend said to me, 'Who
are they for?' And I said, 'They're all for my own personal use during

the two weeks I'm here.' Well, of course that made them both *hysterical,* and they let me in right away."

"It must be very satisfying work," I said.

"It is. You've no idea how ignorant many doctors are in this field. Half the doctors I meet haven't even heard of the coil. There are many doctors, too, who don't realize what a dreadful thing it is for a woman to lose a baby. The average *man* is more understanding than the average doctor. Doctors get immune to it. I often think that every doctor should have a baby himself! Wouldn't that be marvelous?"

✪

AT A party the night before I left Monrovia, I met an American from Firestone called Rimmer. He asked me what I was doing in Liberia, and when I told him he said, "You know what some of the Peace Corps girls here are doing?" I nearly dropped my drink. "You mean about the brothel?" I said. He looked faintly surprised. "I see you've heard about it," he said. "Oh, yes," I said; "as a matter of fact, they have them in most countries." He looked at me uncertainly, not knowing whether I was joking. "Where is the one here?" I said. "I'd like to see it." He seemed uneasy, just like the man in Lagos. "Well, I haven't been there myself," he said, "but there's a Lebanese in my office who knows about it." I said, "What's his name?" and Mr. Rimmer said he thought it was Gain or Gaim, or something like that. I said, "I'd love to meet him and have a chat, but I'm off in twenty-four hours. I bet he's had some rare old fucking." Mr. Rimmer winced a little, as I hoped he might. We looked at each other hard for a moment, and then Mr. Rimmer looked at his drink. I waited for him to say something, but he had nothing more to say.

✪

THERE WERE six of us in the plane from Robertsfield to Lisbon, and six Pan Am stewardesses, so it looked like a nice flight. I had three seats to myself, and another man took the three seats on the opposite side of the aisle. He was a small middle-aged man with a balding head and spectacles and a sharp, foxy little face. He looked as if he might have a bit of a temper.

They gave us lunch after takeoff, and then I read for an hour. Yet all the time I was aware of Foxy's presence. He had hardly touched his lunch, and I lost count of the number of cans of beer and of menthol cigarettes he had had since the bar opened. Although he had been given a glass for his beer, he seemed to prefer drinking it from the can. He just sat by the window, swilling down the beer and puffing at the cigarettes. He looked as though he had something on his mind.

I put down my book and glanced in his direction at the very moment he was doing the same to me.

"Care to have a drink with me?" he said.

I moved to the seat beside him, and the stewardess brought another can of beer and a glass of brandy. Foxy took the cigarette packet from his tray and flicked a cigarette toward me. I said I didn't smoke. He took one himself and said, "Been in Liberia long?"

"Two weeks," I said. "And you?"

"Five months. Boy, am I glad to be getting out!"

"What were you doing?"

"United States Seabees. You heard of them?"

"They're the naval construction corps, aren't they?"

"Right. I'm a petty-officer instructor. There was a group of us sent there to teach Liberians about mechanics. Or I should say to *try* to teach Liberians about mechanics. They're unteachable."

"Really?"

"Sure. We were stationed way out in the boondocks, about a hundred miles from Monrovia, near a place called Foya."

"I know it."

"Yeah? Well, there were thirteen of us, and we lived in these Quonset huts, and gave these guys lessons. I'd say to them: 'In an internal-combusion engine there are four strokes to make up the cycle. The first is the intake stroke, the second is the compression stroke, the third is the power stroke, and the fourth is the exhaust stroke.' Well, I'd go through it all with these guys and then I'd say to the first man, 'What is the first stroke?' And you know what he'd say? 'The *crank shaft*'! Christ, I must have gone over that routine at least twenty-eight times." He took a pull on his cigarette and said, "I don't know how I'd *describe* Liberians if anyone asked me. It would take a week. They gave us some books to read about the place before we went there. One of them was by this fellow John Gunther. I don't recall the name of it, but I thought he was exaggerating. Turned out he was *under*-exaggerating. That's a fact."

"In what way?"

"Liberians are about one remove from the monkeys. I'm telling you. I've seen things no white person has ever seen. One night I saw a boy of nine initiated into manhood. He came into this hut, all wet and with nothing on, and this old man who was sitting there picked him up and put him over his knee and cut his shoulders and chest with this sharp steel knife. You should have seen the blood that came out. Christ, the *blood!* And when he was through with that, he turned him over and circumcised him. The boy didn't make a sound. I don't think he had anything to deaden it, but he didn't make a sound.

"Then they used to get drunk regular on this cane juice. God, does that stuff drive them out of their minds! Cane juice is a kind of ruin. I'd say it was around a hundred eighty proof. You can put a match to cane juice. You won't see it burn, but you can't put your hand over the top of it. The area gets smaller and smaller and then it's all burnt up and there's nothing there."

"Did you ever try it?"

"God, no! I don't drink nothing that don't come out of a can or bottle or hasn't got a label on it that I can read. I don't believe in that homemade stuff."

"Did you ever get down to Monrovia?"

"Not too often. About once a month we'd make a trip there and walk around and do the nightclubs. The women there are dead, though. They're like logs."

"So I've heard."

"I used to spend my leisure time on the ham radio. I'm a great ham enthusiast. There was a guy in some AID educational outfit at Foya, and he didn't live too far from the camp. He was a great ham enthusiast, too. I'd go over there weekends, and we'd have a great time. We used to call up people all over the world—Japan, Korea, Australia. That was great."

He looked out the window and said, "Christ, we're a long ways up." Then he stubbed out his cigarette and said, "You on a business trip?"

"No, I'm a writer," I said.

He looked at me with sudden interest, as if I were a new arrival at the zoo. He pulled out another cigarette and said, "Anyone tell you about Careysburg?"

"You mean the V.O.A. place?" I said.

"No, I don't mean the V.O.A. place. I mean the area around."

"No," I said. "I don't think anyone mentioned that."

"It would interest you, being a writer. Boy, that's quite a place! You don't want to break down there at night."

"Why?"

"People just disappear."

"White people?"

"No, blacks."

"What happens to them?"

"Nobody knows. But ask any Liberian about Careysburg, and he'll tell you the same thing."

"What do *you* think happens to them?"

He took a puff at his cigarette, looked me hard in the face and said, "I think they get eaten."

I ordered another round of drinks, and when they had come, Foxy said, "I haven't told you why I'm going back to the States."

"No."

"As a writer, it might interest you. I'm in disgrace. I'm being *sent* back."

"What for?"

He took a long pull and said, "You don't know my name and I don't know yours, and we're not ever likely to meet again, so I'll tell you.

"I got up this training program for the Liberians I was telling you about, and the shop steward liked it and I liked it and everybody liked it. It was a good program. But after a few months, living up there in the jungle got to be quite a strain. There was the heat and the insects and the general lack of utilities. And then to add to that, there was this ball-up about our papers, so for two months we didn't get paid. And that wasn't any good, because we had to pay for our food and there were other expenses.

"It was all the fault of this new officer. He was twenty-three years old and about the most prejudiced and obstinate man I've ever met. He insulted at least ten Liberians within a week of getting there. He just didn't know how to talk to people. One of the Liberians said to me, 'I went to the States for my education. I got kicked around there because I was a black man. But I don't expect to get kicked around here. This is a black country.'

"So at the end of the week, when we hadn't been paid for two months, I went to this officer and I said, 'Will you fix up these papers over the weekend and send them off to base?' And he said he would, and I went over to Foya and spent the weekend on the ham radio with this guy I was telling you about. I came back on Monday and went into the office and the first thing I saw was the papers, which were still on the desk and hadn't been touched. So I went into this little cubicle the officer had, and I said to him, 'You haven't done the papers?' And he just sat there on his ass and said, 'No, I haven't gotten around to it yet.'

"So then I blew my top. That's all there was to it. I called him about every name in the book. I know I shouldn't have done it, but I guess I couldn't help myself. A man can only take so much. So he waited until I'd finished and then he said, 'Okay, pack your bags, you're going home.' Well, that really loused me up, because I'd worked out a good training program, and the only reason I'd volunteered for Liberia was to do a good job and help people."

"What happens now?" I said.

"Right now I have to go to Providence, Rhode Island, which is where my base is. The plane I'm booked in goes to Boston, which is only thirty-eight miles away, but this officer has routed my luggage through New York, so I guess I'll have to go there first, and then back to Providence. He fouled that up like he fouled everything else."

"What happens when you get to Providence?"

"I'm going to ask for a court-martial, because I want the whole situation looked into. I want them to hear my side of the story, not being paid and everything, and what sort of a guy this officer is. I've been seventeen years in the Navy, and I've only got another three to go, so I don't want this to mess me up. I'm afraid it may mess me up a little. I know I shouldn't have said what I did. But I guess I was mad at the time. If I'd been a dog I'd have bitten that officer."

"Do you think you will get a court-martial?"

"Yeah, I guess so," said Foxy. He pulled out another cigarette, and said, "See, one of the commanders at the base is a very good friend of mine. He's a fellow that knows me well, and that I wouldn't do anything stupid unless I had good reason to. I've already told him what happened."

"You've written to him?"

"No, I haven't written to him. I called him up on the ham radio."

"Is he a ham radio enthusiast, too?"

"No, but there's a friend of mine in Providence who is, and I called him up and said I'd like to speak to this commander, and so he got hold of him and I spoke to him the following night."

I mulled it over for a few moments, and the more I did so, the more curious it seemed. "In the British Navy," I said, "it would be very unusual for a petty officer to call up a commander in this sort of way."

Foxy said, "Yeah, I guess it is kind of unusual." He paused for a moment and then said, "See, this commander and I are very close. We have a special kind of relationship." He glanced at me in an odd way, and the thought flashed through my mind that they might be a couple of queers. Foxy said, "I don't know why I'm telling you this, but this commander is a very good friend of my wife's. He sees a lot of her while I'm away, takes her out in my automobile and things like that, which is very nice for her and okay by me." He gave me another quick glance and said, "They're real close, if you understand what I mean."

I nodded. "He's a good friend," said Foxy, "and he'll want to help me all he can."

"Yes," I said. "I can see that."

Foxy turned toward the window and looked down. "Christ" he said. "That must be the *Sahaira* down there."

Part Three

 EUROPE

SCOTLAND
LONDON
PARIS
GERMANY

IN SCOTLAND the river was tar-black, treacle-thick; gobbets of giant spittle floated on its oiled belly. Dark green and dank were the banked trees, tall as masts, still as stage scenery. It was quiet, like Switzerland or an empty church. We waited for the thunder, but it never came. Away up the hill stood the purple castle, solid as Everest, cold as death.

Mrs. B. Y. Hackenberger, of Clarence, Connecticut, had taken the castle again for August (and the fishings and shootings) for an estimated thirty-five hundred pounds, or, at the then rate of exchange, around ten thousand dollars. She had been doing this for years, an arrangement which suited her admirably and the laird even better. A mutual friend had fixed up for me to stay with Mrs. Hackenberger for the weekend; but she was away on a visit to Edinburgh and had left word that I was to fish for salmon till she returned.

My companion in the boat was Hamish Howie, gillie, who had a face like crumpled parchment. At the end of my line was his favorite fly. I had fished with it for an hour and a half; two salmon had brushed their lips against it and departed. "Why?" I said to Hamish Howie. "Why?" Hamish said. "When I was sixteen, I could have told you why. I knew everything when I was sixteen. Now I am an old man I know nothing."

183

I said it was ridiculous to call himself an old man, and he said he wasn't as old as his father, who was ninety-five when he died. "He was a grand old fellow. When he was ninety-three the cinema came to Inverness, and we took him along to see it. This would be about forty years ago. Well, we settled down in our seats and presently I heard him say, 'These are damned uncomfortable seats, Hamish, forby.' So I peered through the dark and I saw that he hadn't tipped the seat down but was sitting on the upright bottom edge of it. We set him to rights, but he didn't stay long. I don't recall much about the picture, but after a wee while he turned to me and said, 'Hamish, this is the work of the devil! Let's away.' That was his experience of the cinema."

Hamish said he read a lot and at the moment was reading a book about fishing called *You Should Have Been Here Last Thursday*. I asked him the size of the biggest fish ever caught in the river. He said *one* of the biggest had been hooked a long time ago by the castle's French chef. "There were American tenants here then too, and they had engaged this chef for the time of the lease, you understand. Well, he made friends with one of the gillies, and this gillie had been asked to go and catch a salmon for a dinner party they were having, and as the chef had an hour or two off, he said, could he go too? So the gillie said, aye, surely, and they came down to this very pool we're fishing now, and got into the boat. Well, the gillie had to go ashore for something he'd forgotten, and while he was away the chef dangled the rod over the side, just for amusement, you might say. The next thing he knew was the reel screaming out like a banshee, himself nearly in the water, and the gillie haring back to the boat. Three hours later and a mile downstream, they got the fish ashore."

"How much did it weigh?"

"Sixty-three pounds."

"Good heavens!"

"The gillie wanted to have it mounted, but the Americans said no, they were going to eat it for their dinner. So I suppose the chef cooked it for them. I'm thinking it would no have been very tasty."

Around five o'clock word came down that Mrs. Hackenberger had returned to the castle. Hamish Howie rowed me ashore and a car took me up. I was about to ring the bell when the door opened and a thin, elderly, rather distinguished-looking butler came out.

"Good afternoon," I said.

"How are you, sir?" said the butler, putting out a hand. "We've met before, actually."

I shook his hand and looked at him uncomprehendingly.

"I used to live next door to Pamela Rumble of the BBC," he said, as though that explained everything.

"Pamela Rumble?" I said. I had hopes that saying the name out loud might tell me something. It didn't.

"Yes," said the butler. "She used to talk about you a lot."

I left it there and followed the butler into the house. He put my luggage in a corner of the stone-flagged hall and led me down a long tartan-covered passageway. Pamela Rumble, I thought; who the hell is she?

We came to a door and the butler said, "Mrs. Hackenberger is in the library." He opened the door, announced me, and left.

I looked around, unseeing, dazzled a little by the light. I was aware of many bookshelves and a lot of flowers, and then there was a sort of rustling noise over on the right, and a very small, very stout old lady rose from the depths of a sofa. She had square features, humorous eyes and surprisingly brown hair; the general impression was that of an amiable bun. When she got up I saw that she was wearing silver slippers and a long black dress that reached to the ground. "Mr. Kennedy?" she said. "How nice to see you!" And she shook me warmly by the hand.

We sat down, and Mrs. Hackenberger dispensed tea and honey and scones, like any English dowager; I wondered whether she had them every day or had ordered them specially for me. Then I asked her about her early life and how she had come to the castle.

She was born on the East Coast, she said, and had been educated at Miss Spence's in New York. She had taken a Mr. Bull as her first husband and later (she didn't say what had happened to Mr. Bull) Mr. B. Y. Hackenberger. "Mr. Hackenberger inherited this lumber business from his father, and by the time he died he owned practically all the redwoods in California. In the early days of our marriage we used to go and live in the lumber mills. I went there thinking I'd be the Lady Bountiful, and it took me three years to make a friend. My husband wanted to wear clothes like the men did, but they wouldn't have liked it, so he had to wear a suit like in New York. When he died we sold the whole business and got a huge price for it."

"When was that?"

"That was twenty years ago. When all his affairs had been settled up, I sold this big mansion we used to live in outside San Francisco and decided to travel. I've always liked travel. I traveled all over England and then I came to Scotland, and I liked it so much I decided to rent a house. One day I was brought to lunch here by some friends, and I told them what I was thinking, and they said, well, why don't you come here? So I rented it there and then and I've been coming each year ever since."

"Some years, I believe, you don't come?"

"I'd like to, but my advisers tell me it could make things difficult from a tax point of view. So every five years or so I go to some other country. I've taken castles in Ireland, and one year I tried to take a castle in Holland, but it seems all the castles there belong to the royal family." She laughed, as though aware of the absurdity of the thing.

"Isn't this rather a large place for just one person?" I said.

"Well, one reason I took it originally was for my grandchildren to spend their summer vacations. I have one son, he's now fifty-five, and he has four children of his own and two grandchildren. So that makes me a great-grandmother. My son's eldest boy is twenty-five now, but he first came here when he was a little boy of five, and he learned to fish and shoot and everything. The children just loved it. Now they don't come so much, but I have plenty of friends who like to come and stay!"

"Americans or English?"

"Both. I have one or two California friends who come, and they're not happy unless they're doing something every minute of the day. Of course, quite a few of my American friends don't know the correct etiquette, and I have to tell them. They put on red coats and red caps for hunting and then wonder why they don't get a stag. Last year an American Air Force general came to shoot. He was a friend of a friend. He was on his way somewhere, and he landed in one of the fields in his helicopter. Mr. Kennedy, that man was wearing a green waistcoat with fishhooks in it and a green cap with his medal ribbons on it and a feather sticking out. It was *pitiful,* just *pitiful.*"

"Are there many people staying here just now?"

"No, at present there's only one houseguest besides yourself, and that's a very dear neighbor of mine from Clarence, Connecticut, called Eric Duvivier. He's a young California boy and quite brilliant at landscape gardening. He did my garden over last year and made a wonderful job of it. So there'll be just the three of us and I hope you won't be bored."

I murmured something complimentary and Mrs. Hackenberger said, "And now I'm sure you'd like a drink?" She indicated a tray of bottles in the corner. I thanked her and began to move toward them. "Oh, *no*," said Mrs. Hackenberger, rising, "you mustn't help yourself. May will do it for you."

I stopped in mid-passage and Mrs. Hackenberger glided over to where a very ancient telephone was nailed to the wall. In her long dress she moved as though on wheels. The telephone had a handle, which she cranked several times. Then she said into it "May, will you come and serve drinks, please?"

"Where does that telephone go to?" I asked.

"It goes to the pantry. That's where May works."

"It seems a long way to come," I said, "just to fix a drink."

"Oh, May *loves* fixing drinks. He wouldn't want anyone else to do it."

"He seems to think he knows me," I said.

"Oh, May knows everybody," said Mrs. Hackenberger.

May arrived and poured me a whisky and water. Mrs. Hackenberger said, "May, have you telephoned to Belvoir yet?" May said, "Not yet, madam. I thought of doing it this evening." To me Mrs. Hackenberger said, "It's the Northern meeting ball at Inverness next week. I don't take a party any more myself, but I've said I would put up one or two guests of local house parties. Lady Charlotte Manners is coming to stay, and so is Lady Mary Kerr. I'm told they're both very charming girls."

May handed me a drink and said to Mrs. Hackenberger, "Have you finished with the tea things, madam?" Mrs. Hackenberger nodded and said, "I don't suppose you know anyone at Belvoir now?"

"No, madam," said May. "I haven't been at Belvoir for forty years."

I wondered if Mrs. Hackenberger would tell me that Belvoir was the home of the Duke of Rutland and that Lady Charlotte Manners was his daughter. But she didn't; and that, I thought, was a good measure of how superbly British upper-class she had become.

"I just love having young people to stay," said Mrs. Hackenberger, "because they know how to entertain themselves. People of one's own generation always want to be entertained, and that can be perfectly exhausting."

May said, "Is that all, madam?"

Mrs. Hackenberger said, "Yes, thank you, May. Where are Mr. Kennedy's bags?"

"Arthur has taken them to his room, madam."

When May had gone, I said, "Who's Arthur?"

"He's the footman and he's May's stepson," said Mrs. Hackenberger. "They work as a team and they're perfectly splendid. They're both coming back with me to the States in the fall, and I can tell you they're going to solve all my domestic problems. By the way, you're sleeping in Princess Margaret's room, and I hope you'll be comfortable."

The door opened and a pale, thin young man came into the room. He had a ginger crew cut and glasses with heavy lenses and a polo-neck sweater and very narrow trousers; he looked the spit and image of Woody Allen.

"Hullo, Eric," said Mrs. Hackenberger. "Come and say how-do-you-do to Mr. Kennedy."

There was something in the tone of Mrs. Hackenberger's command —like a parent admonishing a child—that explained their relationship right away. Eric teetered across the room and gave me a damp hand. "Well, hello!" he said. "Glad to *know* you."

Eric fixed himself a drink (no summoning of May for him!) and sat down and started talking about a book he had been reading. After a while Mrs. Hackenberger got up and said, "I'm going along to have a little rest before dinner. Eric, you see that Mr. Kennedy has everything he wants and then show him his room, will you?"

When she'd gone, Eric said, "Well, I'm not sur*prised* she needs a little rest. The pace she's been going the last three days has been fan*tas*tic. We've been visiting in Edinburgh, did she tell you? We made motor trips to three houses, Marchmont, Mellerstain and Traquair. We went to the opera and the picture gallery, and we had drink parties and lunch parties *as well.* You know, she's nearer eighty than seventy and frankly I don't know how she *does* it. She packs more energy into a week here than I do in *six* weeks back *home.*"

"I believe you live near her?"

"That's *right.* She has this *beau*tiful property in Clarence which I've been advising her on, and this perfectly *fab*ulous *gar*den."

"Does she take things easier back there?"

"My *God,* I wish she did. Sometimes she does what we call a *back-*

breaker. We leave her home in Clarence at six in the morning and arrive in New York at eight. She shops in New York all day, goes to the Drake at four for a rest and to change, at six-thirty has drinks and something to eat, goes to the theater, has supper after, and then I have to drive her back to Clarence, where we arrive around *one*. I tell you, it's *killing*."

If it was as killing as all that, I wondered, why did he do it? But to ask this would be exploring deeper into his relationship with Mrs. Hackenberger than I, and probably he, wished to go.

"But isn't she a *lovely* person? She has this fan*ta*stic knowledge of *his*tory. I tell you she knows more about Scottish history than the Scots who *live* here. You know, when she's talking about history, she'll suddenly slip in a fast one, like saying that Charles the Second had a French *mis*tress or something, just to see if the person she's talking to is *lis*tening."

Eric and I finished our drinks, and then he took me up to my room which looked out over the garden. May was in there fiddling with my clothes.

When Eric had gone, I said to May, "I've been trying to remember Pamela Rumble, and I can't."

May said, not looking at me, "Oh, she's a very charming person, sir." I knew then I had never set eyes on him or Pamela Rumble before.

"I'm told this is Princess Margaret's room."

"Yes, sir," said May. "It's where she slept when she came and stayed here with the King and Queen just after the war. But that was before my time."

"Have you been here long?"

"I've been coming up each summer to help Mrs. Hackenberger for several years."

"And what do you do the rest of the time?"

"Temporary jobs, sir. I don't like staying in one place too long."

"But I gather from what you said downstairs that you've been in service all your life."

"Only on a temporary basis, sir. Holidays and weekends."

"Really?"

"As a boy it was always my dearest ambition to enter service. In fact, I ran away from home twice to do it. But each time my father found out where I was and had me brought home. In the end he put me into the probate section of the income-tax office, and I stayed there all my working life. Of course, I'm retired now. I'm nearly sixty-three."

"Do you wish you had been in service always?"

"I don't say that, sir, but that is what I would do if I had my time all over again. I'm inclined to be artistic by nature and I find that service satisfies me in some way. I like arranging flowers, for instance. All the flowers you see here have been arranged by me. But I can't really complain. I've had some wonderful times. I've been to all the best houses and attended all the best people. Belvoir, Woburn, Chatsworth, Longleat, Hatfield—I've seen them all."

"And now?"

"Well, now that I've retired, I can afford to pick and choose. Now I just go to those places that interest me. I've got my civil-service pension, and I have quite a little put by. A few years ago I bought a number of derelict cottages for twenty-five hundred pounds, and recently they've been valued at twenty-four thousand. There's no doubt one can do some very nice things with property."

"Mrs. Hackenberger says your stepson is here with you."

"Yes. He's a very nice boy, and he has a real aptitude for service. Of course, I've taught him everything he knows. Sometimes we do jobs together at weekends, and then every summer he takes two months off to join me here."

"Two months off from what?"

"He's a free-lance chartered accountant, sir."

It was on the tip of my tongue to ask how Arthur's chartered accountancy would fare when they went to Clarence, Connecticut. But May was at the door.

"I've turned your bath on, sir. Dinner will be at eight."

★

WE HAD an excellent dinner, artichokes and lamb and creme caramel, which I would have enjoyed rather more had not May and Arthur, immaculate in white tie and tails, spent most of the meal standing watching us. I found the idea of being waited on by two men who were, in their own ways, wizards of finance quite unnerving. The further grisly thought that there might have been a time when Arthur

had had a hand in preparing my tax returns and May in assessing
them upset me so much I could hardly finish my food.

After dinner we went to the library for coffee, and I asked Mrs.
Hackenberger what was the main difference between life in Clarence
and life at the castle. "Except for the shooting and the fishing," she
said, "not much. A lot of people back home are always craving for
activities like drinking and playing bridge, which I don't like. I think
the people round here have a much better knowledge of the world.
They're better educated, I would say. But it's the fishing and shooting
that counts."

"Do you shoot, yourself?"

"Yes, I do. One day I went up on the hill to shoot a grouse. The
dog put up a covey all right, but the keeper who was holding my gun
forgot to release the safety catch. So I didn't get a shot after all."

"What else do you do?"

"Well, I read a lot. May calls me at six and I start my reading then.
And then maybe I'll go out for a drive or to have lunch somewhere,
and then, later, friends may drop by for drinks. The Duke and Duch-
ess of Gloucester used to come over and see me when they took Farr.
Isn't he a charming and delightful man?"

"What is it about Scotland," I said, "that you find so particularly
appealing?"

"I would say that people here are still able to practice the art of
gracious living. They've been doing it for so many hundreds of years
that it's second nature to them. Now, in America we've lost that art, if
indeed we ever had it. For instance, no woman here would dream of
wearing diamonds in the daytime. In Texas they do it all the time.
Here, all a gentleman needs to know is how to fish and shoot and
dance. And the style with which they do it is something that I find
very pleasing."

"Did you do the Highland dances yourself?"

"Oh, I just adored them. All those wonderful Northern meetings
we used to go to. Of course, when I first came here, I didn't know the
correct way of doing the Scottish dances. But I was taken in hand by a
very dear lady and told that the first rule for a woman was to keep
one's eyes on the floor and not look at one's partner, and generally
comport oneself in a modest and becoming way. It was only the men
in their kilts, I was given to understand, who were allowed to be great
peacocks. And later on I was able to put other poor ignorant Ameri-

cans to rights. I remember one time I had to go up to a woman who was clicking her fingers and jigging about and making a perfect fool of herself and tell her to stop it. Well, it was very embarrassing at the time, but afterward she thanked me for it."

Around ten-thirty Mrs. Hackenberger went off to bed, but Eric and I sat up talking and drinking for another hour. He was quite an entertaining companion. Just as I was finishing my last whisky before going up, he said, "Do you come *often* to the United States?"

"I used to," I said, "when I was doing television. Now I come about once a year."

"Where do you *stay* when you're there?"

"I used to stay at the Gotham, but recently I've been at the Dorset. Why?"

"Well, I was thinking, you know, how ex*pen*sive New York hotels can be, and I was thinking, *next* time you come, why don't you stay with *me?*"

"That's very kind of you."

"I have this little apartment, it isn't very *jazzy* or anything, but I think you'd *like* it. You could really *relax* there."

"Well, thank you."

"The *only* thing I would ask is give me a few days *no*tice, as there's only one *key*."

"Of course."

He pulled out his wallet and handed me a card. "That's the *ad*-dress." I took it, and while I was reading it he said, "By the way, that is *strictly* entre nous."

"How do you mean?" I said.

"You know," he said, "between *us?*"

"Why?"

He giggled.

"Good Gracious me!" I said.

✪

WHEN I came down in the morning, Eric was already in the dining room, natty in polo-neck and cavalry twill, swilling down cornflakes. "Breakfast here is a kind of walking deal," he said, indicating a row of silver chafing dishes on the sideboard. There were porridge and trout and eggs and kidneys and tomatoes and bacon. I took a couple of eggs and sat down. Out of the window was a stunning view to the river and the hills beyond. In the center of the table was a big bowl of flowers, newly arranged by May, mostly fragrant sweet peas. Eric, looking at it, said, "Isn't that a *beautiful pott-paree?*"

After breakfast Mrs. Hackenberger appeared, wearing the same tartan cloth that covered the passageway. This was the laird's tartan and he had given her special permission to wear it. "I'm very proud of that, I can tell you, Mr. Kennedy. This is a privilege he has granted to nobody else."

Mrs. Hackenberger was in a state of high excitement, as a great friend of hers from Clarence, Connecticut, had just called up to say that she and another friend were on a coach tour of the Hebrides and would be passing by the castle later. "So I've asked them both to lunch," said Mrs. Hackenberger, "and then Emil can take them to wherever the coach has got to afterward. The name of my friend is Mrs. Truffaud, and she is very well off and has a beautiful estate. Her friend is called Mrs. Fingleton. She's not well off at all, but I believe she comes of a very good family, though I don't know where."

Mrs. Hackenberger took me on a conducted tour of the castle. There wasn't much to see, because the castle had been built in Victorian times, previous ones having been burned down. I thought it a pretty characterless place, but Mrs. Hackenberger made the most of it. One of the laird's forebears had helped Bonnie Prince Charlie during the 'Forty-five, and there were various relics, such as his wig and waistcoat, in a glass case. Mrs. Hackenberger said she had been to Culloden House and seen the room that Prince Charles had slept in the night before the battle and the Duke of Cumberland had slept in the night after it. "Just think of it, Mr. Kennedy, those two boys were both under twenty-five and yet they were commanders of two armies."

We visited the chapel and the hall, and then we had a look at Mrs. Hackenberger's bedroom. There was a huge double bed there, as broad as it was long. Mrs. Hackenberger said that King George VI and Queen Elizabeth had used this room when they visited the castle after the war. "But the King didn't sleep here. He said he wanted to sleep in this little dressing room next door." We had a look at the dressing room. It was a tiny, ugly room with a tiny, shabby bed. "At that time," said Mrs. Hackenberger, "the carpet had holes in it, and the curtains hadn't been changed since 1860 and were all frayed. Yet the King of England slept there. Just think of that."

We finished our tour and Mrs. Hackenberger said, "I *must* go and tell Eric to put a coat and tie on for lunch. It's Sunday today, and Sunday in Scotland is something." I said I would go and pack, as I was leaving after lunch. Mrs. Hackenberger said, "Now, don't you pack a thing, Mr. Kennedy. May will do all that for you, and he'll do it just beautifully."

So I had a wash instead, and when I came down to the library the sound of female American voices told me that Mrs. Truffaud and Mrs. Fingleton had arrived. No need to inquire which was which. The large chic one engaged in animated conversation with Mrs. Hackenberger was Mrs. Truffaud; the small mousy one engaged in small talk with Eric was Mrs. Fingleton. It occurred to me then that Mrs. Fingleton had much the same relationship with Mrs. Truffaud as Eric had with Mrs. Hackenberger. They were both, as it were, other people's poodles, going along for the ride.

We went in to lunch. There were two places laid facing the river, one facing the wall, and one at either end. I assumed that our visitors would be given the two places facing the river. But, no; Mrs. Hackenberger and Eric were at either end, Mrs. Truffaud and I had the view, and poor Mrs. Fingleton faced the wall. At lunch she got the bum's rush again. Although Mrs. Fingleton was next to Mrs. Hackenberger and Mrs. Truffaud wasn't, it was to the latter that Mrs. Hackenberger addressed herself. I did what I could across the table with Mrs. Fingleton, though against the gale created by the other two it wasn't easy. Eric, sulky in a silky suit, said nothing.

The conversation, as I recall it, was centered almost entirely on the affairs of Clarence, Connecticut. There were two matters uppermost. The first was the water shortage. This was discussed for the first two courses, and I think it might have lasted the meal if Mrs. Fingleton hadn't piped up that she was going to be robbed of her water altogether. This made Mrs. Hackenberger say rather grandly to her, "Mrs. Fingleton, as I've said before, I'll guarantee you *all* the water you want." I wondered how she was going to do this, and I assumed that in America, if only one had enough money, one could buy up even water.

The other matter was the building of a school for mentally disturbed children. Mrs. Hackenberger and Mrs. Truffaud were against this. "A small place like Clarence is so unsuitable for it," said Mrs. Truffaud. "There must be plenty of other places they can find. It's not as though the state weren't big enough." Mrs. Hackenberger said, "I *so* agree. I don't know if you know about the petition that's being got up against it. My son has advised me not to sign it, but I guess I will. I hear the most terrible stories of other places where they have these schools, and the children break out all the time and set fire to things." Mrs. Fingleton said, with a little nervous laugh, "Well, the children do have to go *somewhere*" and Mrs. Truffaud said, "Well, of course, dear, but it doesn't have to be Clarence."

After this we got on to politics and President Kennedy. None of them liked President Kennedy, Mrs. Hackenberger least of all. "What did he do?" she said. "Nothing at all!" I said, rather hesitantly, that the world had wept for him when he died. "He was just shanty Irish," said Mrs. Hackenberger, "and his origins were shanty Irish, and in politics, as in everything else, a person's origins are important."

After lunch we had coffee, and several times Mrs. Hackenberger gripped Mrs. Truffaud's arm and urged her to stay the night. But Mrs. Fingleton said they had to get back to the coach. Eric went off to get the car, and the rest of us trooped down the tartan passage to the hall to say goodbye. Mrs. Truffaud, inevitably, got into the front of the car beside Eric, and Mrs. Fingleton climbed into the back, where she soon disappeared from view. Mrs. Hackenberger, standing on the steps beside me, said, "What a funny little person that Mrs. Fingleton is!" The car moved off and we waved goodbye. "Fancy going on a coach tour," said Mrs. Hackenberger, as we went back into the house. "Can you think of anything more dreadful? I'm sure I shouldn't like it at all."

It was time for me to go, too. I went up to my room and found May packing the last of my things. "Well, May," I said, "it's been a nice weekend, and thank you for looking after me." May folded a shirt and said, "It's been a pleasure, sir." I said, "I hear you and Arthur are going back to the States with Mrs. Hackenberger?" May stopped packing and looked up. Then he walked over to the door and quietly closed it. On the way back he said, "I'm sure you're a shrewd man, sir." He went on packing. I waited, expecting him to go on, which after a bit he did. "I like her very much, sir," he said, "but these old people are so exhausting. They suck the energy right out of you. My mother was the same." He closed the case and locked up. "I was over there for ten weeks last year, sir, and I can tell you it damn near killed me."

"But oughtn't you to tell her you're not going?"

"Oh, I shall, sir. But all in good time."

One way or another, I wasn't sorry to leave.

○

IN LONDON there are always many Americans. Some are on holiday, some on their way elsewhere, and an increasing number have come to work and live. They call it a "civilized" city, a term they no longer feel able to apply to New York and Chicago and Los Angeles. They appreciate the absence of language difficulties, they find the quality and tempo of life soothing, and they are much relieved to find that the blacks, while clearly a social problem, are not yet, as they are at home, a menace to Anglo-Saxon life and property.

Among those who visit Britain briefly but regularly are the representatives of American business and industrial firms that are short of skilled technicians and have come to seek fresh blood. These operations, which have been successfully conducted for some time now, have been dubbed by the British press as the "brain drain." When news of the brain drain first broke, it caused unease among the British people. The press having now lost interest in the subject, as it does eventually in everything, it is no longer discussed. The brain drain, however, continues.

Prominent among companies at the receiving end of the brain drain are American aircraft combines such as Sikorsky Aircraft, of Stratford, Connecticut, a division of United Aircraft Corporation; and at the time of which I write, six of their number had taken a suite and several adjacent bedrooms at the Royal Garden Hotel, overlooking Kensington Gardens. The names of the representatives were Mr. Shalvoy, leader of the expedition and Sikorsky's chief technical recruitment officer, Mr. McCullough of the personnel department, and Messrs. Oakes, Sonneman, Paul and Albert of, respectively, electronics, surface systems, analysts and design. The walls of the sitting room of their suite had been hung with pictures of the helicopters the company makes, also a large map of the state of Connecticut. Outside in the gardens on this summer afternoon were children playing, a colored lady sitting on a white seat, and, directly beneath the window, a very beautiful blonde in a bikini, offering her oiled torso to the sun. Up the hill was the Round Pond of which Mr. A. A. Milne has lovingly written, and also Kensington Palace, where Princess Margaret and Lord Snowden at present live and love.

I arrived in the sitting room at about the same time as an applicant called Dickson, who had just spent an hour being interviewed on technical matters by Dr. Sonneman. Having satisfied Dr. Sonneman that he was competent in the field for which he had applied, he was first shown into Mr. Shalvoy's bedroom to be told of the financial prospects, and then returned to the sitting room to be given a run-down by Mr. McCullough on Stratford and its environs and the community in which he would live. "Where a man is going to live," said Mr. Shalvoy to me later, "is the most important single thing to him."

Mr. McCullough wore a black suit and a tartan tie and was clearly a very nice man. "I don't know how much Al has told you about our location," he said kindly, "so why don't you step over here and take a look." Dickson moved over to where Mr. McCullough was standing beside the map. He was about thirty and looked like a suet pudding. "This is a bedroom community, to use our jargon," said Mr. McCullough. "Stratford has a population of about forty thousand, is six miles long and three miles wide. The plant is in the north of the town. We're sixty-seven miles northeast of New York City, which is near enough to the bright lights if you enjoy them, and yet far enough away if you don't like density living. Here is the Merritt Parkway, which goes diagonally across the state, and here is the Connecticut Thruway, which is like your M4."

Dickson had a good look at the map, and Mr. McCullough said, "Why don't you sit down and relax?" and went over to the window and drew the curtains. Dickson sat down like a lead weight. "Our summers are warmer than yours," said Mr. McCullough, "and our winters are colder. You need heavy clothing in winter and a light suit in summer. We have snow, but never more than six inches. We nearly always have a white Christmas. May and June are lovely. July, August and September are inclined to be warm and sticky. November is kind of grim, and December, January and February are snowy and wintry."

Mr. McCullough put in the first slide and said, "Here, now, is our plant, one and a half million square feet on a two-hundred-fifty-acre site. It was built in 1956 and enlarged in 1958, and all our engineering is housed here. . . . By the way, the workday commences at seven forty-five and ends at four-thirty. . . . Here is the Town Hall of Stratford, which many of your countrymen think looks quite familiar as regards architecture. The community here started in 1639, which we think is quite old, but I sat in your Westminster Abbey on Sunday night, and gee whiz, that place was standing before we were even thought of. . . . Here's the Connecticut Thruway I was telling you about. You throw in a quarter for an automatic toll. . . . Here's a picture of boating, which is a very popular summer pastime with us. . . . And here is our Shakespeare Theater at Stratford, which we're all tremendously proud of. It's a big thing with us. It opens in April and the children are brought in buses from miles around."

There followed pictures of shopping centers and streets and the village green at Milford ("where many of your countrymen have made their homes"), and schools and churches ("we thought we ought to bring in the religious aspect"), and American football ("this is a distant relative of your Rugby; it's a big thing on Saturdays and Sundays and always heavily attended"). Then came housing, and after showing slides of houses and apartment blocks in different price ranges, Mr. McCullough showed a picture of his own house. "I bought the lot with an initial investment of ten thousand dollars, and then I subcontracted to the mason, joiner, etc. It's now worth around twenty-three thousand dollars. I pay just over three hundred dollars in property taxes, which are the equivalent of your 'rates,' about three hundred thirty dollars a year on heating, and light works out at around nine dollars a month and gas at about three. . . ." I thought, how admirable and open of Mr. McCullough to give such personal details of his life; in Britain that kind of frankness is almost unknown.

Finally, we saw slides of an attractive-looking motel. "If you decide to join us," said Mr. McCullough, "we arrange for one of your countrymen who is now with us to meet you at the airport or boat and take you to this motel for a week. It's located about five miles out of town." He switched to a slide of the interior of the motel, a snazzy-looking bedroom. "We find you need this time to orient yourselves. We meet your expenses there, and during that week you don't do any work."

On this happy and attractive note Mr. McCullough finished his rundown and drew back the curtains. The colored lady had gone from the seat, and the blonde in the bikini had turned over to toast her bum. "Have I prompted any questions?" said Mr. McCullough. "It's an awful lot to listen to." Dickson sat silent for a moment and then said, "Can you get a driving license easily over there?" Mr. Mc-Cullough said, "Your own will do for thirty days, and then you have to take a test." Mr. McCullough asked if there were any more questions, but the thing about the driving license was all Dickson could dredge up. "There's so much to think about," he said. "Of course there is," said Mr. McCullough nicely, "and the last thing we want is for you to rush yourself." He reached for a large camera and said, "Now I'm going to take a picture of you. This is so that if you do decide to join us, our representative will be able to recognize you easily when you arrive by plane or boat."

After the photograph Dickson went back to Mr. Shalvoy's bedroom for a final session, and then left by another door. There was a little time to wait before the next candidate appeared, so Mr. Shalvoy came in and one or two others.

"How long have you been doing this?" I said.

"This is our seventh trip," said Mr. Shalvoy. Mr. Shalvoy was smaller than Mr. McCullough and wore a black suit and striped tie. "We started these trips three years ago when applicants were coming to us from Canada, and we learned they'd been trained in England."

"How many people have you engaged?"

"Sixty-three all together, not including this trip. Four have left and two have returned to England. On this trip so far we have done forty interviews and made twenty-five offers. At present we're waiting for about ten applicants to decide."

Mr. McCullough said, "The whole effort has been very worthwhile. The people we've had so far have worked just beautifully. They've liked us and we've liked them."

"We send teams to Dallas and Los Angeles and other places as well," said Mr. Shalvoy. "Here we only hire people we can't get in the States."

"Do you go to other countries too?"

"No. The language problem is too great."

I asked Mr. Shalvoy how they contacted applicants, and he said they used the services of an American organization called Careers Inc., which acted as a clearinghouse for several American firms. They put an ad in the papers, the applicant wrote in and was sent a form, and on the basis of his record, they decided whether to interview him or not. As well as the interview, there were a medical examination and a security check, because of Sikorsky's government contracts.

"Why do you think so many apply?" I said.

"Because they feel the opportunities here no longer exist. They think the aircraft industry here has no future."

"What salaries are you offering?"

"We're offering jobs in the ten-thousand-to-fifteen-thousand-dollar-a-year area. Here they'd be getting between fourteen hundred and two thousand pounds."

"That's almost triple."

"Yes, but you have to remember the difference in the cost of living, though we do find some things here which are almost as expensive as in the States—TV sets, washing machines, things like that. We've been quite amazed."

"What are they most concerned about?" I said.

Mr. Albert, who was short and bald and hadn't said anything up till now, said, "The fear of leaving the U.K. and not knowing what's at the other end. The women fear tornadoes and riots. The younger men fear the draft and Vietnam, because anyone under twenty-five who has lived in the States six months is eligible for the draft. You get all types. You get the suave ones and those scared out of their wits. Some are meeting Americans for the first time. I had one this week who was so scared he could hardly speak."

A new applicant came in. His name was Pratt and he looked burly and surly and carried a little green hat. After he'd seen Mr. Shalvoy about the salary, Mr. McCullough took him through the slide routine. When they came to the slides of the churches Mr. Pratt said, "I never realized till I went to the States what beautiful churches you have." I think he said this just to let Mr. McCullough know that he'd been around. "Yes," said Mr. McCullough, "we certainly do have some nice churches." After this Mr. Pratt kept quiet until we were looking at the town center of Stratford, when he said, "When I was in Hartford, I passed an Indian at three in the morning. He was in full war paint, feathers and everything. I nearly fell off the parapet." I thought this an odd thing to say, and so did Mr. McCullough. He didn't answer at once, and I imagined he was thinking what I was thinking, either that Pratt had been stoned and was seeing things or that he'd met a man walking home from a fancy-dress party, or a mixture of both. But he wasn't taking any chances. "We haven't seen an Indian in years," he said, "so you're not to feel concerned about that."

When everyone had finished with Mr. Pratt, I asked Mr. Shalvoy if he'd mind if I went with him down to the lobby and asked a few questions, and he said no. On the way down I said to Mr. Pratt, "Why do you want to go and work in the States?" and he gave a surprising answer. "Because I've always worked there," he said. "I've never had a job here. I'm going to go back there anyway." It was then I noticed he had quite an American accent.

"Why?"

"Because the aristocracy has governed this country too long. For two hundred years the power men in this country have mistreated the working men. If they hadn't, you wouldn't get the union situation you have today. Now, in the United States the power men have a healthy respect for the workingmen. I'm only here seventy years, so I haven't got time to wait around. I'm against this country pouring all that money into the military, and I'm against it in other ways too. I'm a happier guy in the States than I ever was here. So that's why I'm going to stay over there."

Mr. Pratt told me a few personal facts, such as that he'd been brought up in Southampton and that his father was a chemist, et cetera, but by this time I'd decided he was a bit of a nut, and I said goodbye in the lobby. When I got back to the suite the team were discussing an applicant called Boag, an expert on vibration.

"Boag isn't too sure," said Mr. Shalvoy. "He has a good job here, two cars and personal access to the director of engineering, who has a seat on the board. He wouldn't get that with us. He's afraid of losing status and not gaining too much money in return."

Mr. McCullough said, "I think his indecision came through."

"Right," said Mr. Shalvoy.

"He told me," said Mr. Albert, "that he doesn't like the government, and they've passed a whole lot of legislation he doesn't agree with."

"It all added up," said Mr. Shalvoy. "So I didn't encourage him. He's going to talk to his wife about it and call me up tomorrow. But I don't think he'll be joining us."

There was one more applicant to come, at present having a technical interview with Dr. Sonneman. This was the last applicant of the tour. The day after tomorrow the team were flying back to the States.

I went over to the window. The shadows were already falling over the park, and most people had gone. One park attendant was going round picking up bits of paper with a prong and another was folding chairs.

"What are your work hours here?" I said.

"We start at twelve noon," said Mr. Shalvoy, "which gives the applicants time to get up to London if they live in the country, and gives us time to get acquainted with their particulars. We see each applicant for two hours, and we take the last one at eight."

"That's a long day," I said.

"We don't complain," said Mr. Shalvoy. "We give ourselves a day off at the end to do some shopping and relax."

The last applicant came in and went through to Mr. Shalvoy. His name was Hennigan. He looked very young and fresh and innocent, though Mr. McCullough said he was in his thirties and had served with the R.A.F. for fifteen years. "He joined when he was fifteen years old," said Mr. McCullough. "Fifteen! Now, isn't that something?" Mr. Albert shook his head in disbelief. "Child labor," he said.

Hennigan came through from Mr. Shalvoy's room, and Mr. McCullough invited him to step over to the map. Hearing him going through his routine for a third time was an odd experience, like listening to an old gramophone record and knowing what to expect. He made it fresh and interesting, but the propaganda bits were more obtrusive—the slides of boating and skiing, and the punch line about staying the first week at the holiday motel at Sikorsky's expense. The general impression was that Sikorsky was out to give you a good time. I couldn't recollect seeing pictures of men *working* at the plant at all.

When they'd finished with Hennigan, I asked again if they'd mind my putting some questions of my own. Mr. Shalvoy said they didn't, so, as Hennigan was the last applicant, I shook hands with the team, thanked them for letting me sit in with them, and took Hennigan downstairs. We went to the bar, and I asked Hennigan why he wanted to go to the States.

"Because the opportunities for someone of my qualifications simply don't exist here any more." He said that after leaving the R.A.F. as a sergeant fitter, he went to the College of Aeronautics at Cranfield for a postgraduate degree in aircraft engineering, including jets. He wanted to go from there into the aircraft industry, but there were only two firms needing people with his qualifications—Hawker Siddeley and Bristol—and neither was offering enough.

"Were there no other firms you could have tried?"

"The only other firm in the running at all was Rolls-Royce, and they did drop a hint that they *might* have given me a job at eighteen hundred pounds a year, which was more than the other two were offering. But by this time I'd already started thinking in terms of overseas, and once you've done that you don't look back."

"Will you accept the Sikorsky offer?"

"No."

"Why not?"

"I've had others that are better."

It had never entered my head there might be others. Hennigan wasn't as dumb as he looked.

"What others?" I said.

"All the other American aircraft companies that have advertised in this country. There were several Americans studying at Cranfield when I was there, and they advised us to try the lot."

"Whom else have you seen?"

"Oh, a whole lot of them. And I've had offers from Boeing and Macdonald Douglas and General Electric, and half a dozen firms dealing in agricultural or heavy industrial equipment."

"What was the best offer?"

"General Electric. They're prepared to start me at thirteen thousand five hundred dollars."

"Will you take it?"

"Yes, I've more or less decided."

I looked at Hennigan's boyish, open face and was amazed. When he finished his drink he looked at his watch and said, "Will you excuse me? I have to catch a train back to Manchester."

As I watched Hennigan disappear through the door, I was glad I didn't have to go up and look Mr. Shalvoy in the face. I knew something about Hennigan that he didn't know; and, knowing it and not being able to tell it, I'd have felt a terrible heel. Perfidious Albion, the French called us, and perfidious Hennigan was a splendid example. And yet one couldn't help admiring him. His cunning and duplicity were an indication that Britain wasn't beaten yet; that if only he and his kind could be persuaded to stay at home, we might yet survive and prosper.

✪

PARIS WAS much as usual, sensual and clockless, and wonderfully spruce after Mr. Malraux's spring cleaning. I called up the American embassy, and a Miss Mim Johnson said why didn't I come on over? I found her office already occupied by what I took to be a visiting Frenchwoman, chic and small and elegant, who was saturating the telephone with a cascade of lovely Gallic words, like the waters of the Loire over gravel; with her left hand she made tiny, exquisite gestures to help the conversation along, in that peculiarly sexy way which comes to Frenchwomen so naturally. This was Mim Johnson. We went to lunch at a restaurant called Le Petit Coq, in the Rue Budapest. It was a small restaurant on a hill, and when we got there Miss Johnson said, "I come here evenings and take cooking lessons. But they won't accept a penny for it. So I bring along all the latest cooking gadgets and give them to the chef. They don't have any. To-morrow I'm going to take along a grapefruit knife. Can you believe it, they don't even have that?"

We sat by the window, and Mim Johnson said, "This is a great street for prostitutes. They have three shifts. The grannies do the early-morning shift. They have a very strict code of honor among themselves. One night one was caught stealing a wallet from another, so they ripped the clothes off her and left her naked in the street. She had to take a taxi home."

In the course of our lunch Miss Johnson suggested various contacts I might make in Paris, including a body called the Association of American Wives.

"Do you have any French blood in you?" I said.

"No," said Miss Johnson. "Why do you ask?"

"Well," I said, "you speak like a Frenchwoman, dress like a Frenchwoman, eat like a Frenchwoman. Anyone who didn't know you would think you *were* a Frenchwoman."

"I'm American through and through."

"But you like it here?"

"I love everything except one thing."

"What's that?"

"The people."

"Why don't you like the people?"

"They're not kind people. They don't give a damn about you. Now, in America we are kind people. We look after each other."

I said nothing, uncertain whether to agree or not.

"Let me give you an example of what I mean. Soon after I got here, I had to represent the embassy at some reception. I didn't know a soul, and nobody talked to me, and after about twenty minutes I felt so miserable I decided to go home. But when I got to the vestibule I thought, Dammit, I won't be beaten, and I went right back to the party and said to the first man I saw, 'I'm Miss Johnson from the American embassy. May I talk with you?' And after that I had a ball. Well, a little while later, when our ambassador was having one of his parties, a French woman journalist whom I'd got to know called me up and said she'd been invited and would I be going? When I said no, she said she didn't think she'd go, as she didn't know anyone. So I said, 'Don't be silly, you'll have a marvelous time, because I can guarantee there'll be loads of people who'll look after you.' And next day she called up to say she'd had a wonderful time. That's the difference between us."

"Anything else?"

"Yes, the status of married women. They're subjugated to their husbands, and when their husbands set up another establishment for their mistresses there's nothing they can do about it. I prefer the American way."

"What's that?"

"When a husband goes on a trip, he finds a girl to spend his evenings with. But he doesn't talk about it. And his wife thinks every other husband in America who goes on a business trip has a girl to spend his evenings with, except him. That's a much better way."

Back at the embassy, Miss Johnson went off to arrange an appointment for me with the president of the Association of American Wives, and I made a call on Mr. Coleman, of the Passport Section. Mr. Coleman was a nice, friendly man, who wore a tartan waistcoat which just failed to reach the top of his trousers. He said, "Come on in and shoot the breeze."

"What about passports?" I said.

"Oh, we have a *lot* of trouble with passports," said Mr. Coleman, "because we have to handle so many. There are about twenty-five thousand Americans living in the Paris district alone, and about half a million tourists come through here every year from the States. In the summer months about a hundred passports a month are reported to us as stolen or lost. Most are lost by people between twenty-two and twenty-four years of age. But eighty percent of them are found. Some of those that get stolen are altered. We don't get these canceled, because it would take too long to pass the word around, and most immigration people don't look too closely at passports anyway."

"Who alters them?"

"Oh, rogues and swindlers of every kind. We have a lot of rogues and swindlers. There's a guy by the name of Jo Garten who's the biggest rogue I ever met, but a doggone pleasant one. He knows we know all about him, but that doesn't make any difference. He's not a smooth talker like some, he jokes and laughs and all that, though he has just a touch of vulgarity in his voice, if you know what I mean. He was in here the other day to get his passport restored, and he sat right where you're sitting now. I said to him, 'I'm writing to the State Department and I'm saying this: Jo Garten is a rogue and a swindler and an embezzler.' And he laughed, he saw the joke, and he said, 'Fine! What else are you saying?' If I could write, this is the man I'd write about. He's an unforgettable character. He swindled a guy in the embassy here so bad the poor guy had to postpone his retirement until he was seventy. He dropped by at a lawyer's one time and said he wasn't sure if he could cash a Swiss check in Paris, could the lawyer let him have a French check for the equivalent amount? The lawyer did and never saw him again. He told a girl I know that he wanted to marry her. I said to the girl he'd never marry her in a hundred years. She said, 'Oh, but he's already wired my mother about it. I paid for the telegram.' He married her, robbed her and left her."

"You certainly have some problems," I said.

"We do. Another problem we have is American girls who come here to have illegitimate children. That raises problems about citizenship. Oh, we have many problems, yes."

I left Mr. Coleman to his problems and went to see Mr. Kautsky in the Consular Section. Mr. Kautsky was a quiet man who wore a sober gray suit and a red-and-blue-striped tie. He said his job covered mental cases, repatriation cases, families looking for lost children, Americans arrested and put into jail, accidents and hospital cases.

"We had an interesting accident case just a couple of weeks back," said Mr. Kautsky. "There were these two women traveling around the country and buying antiques. One was middle-aged and the other elderly. They got killed in an automobile accident, and the police doctor who undressed them found two thousand dollars inside the corset one of them was wearing. There's an interesting question of probate here, because one had left everything to the other. Who's going to say who died first?"

"What about the mental cases?"

"We have quite a few. Some are really sad. We had one boy who'd just taken his discharge from the army. He went skiing in Austria and Switzerland and then he came here and broke down. He thought he had a radio in his head. He kept hearing voices, some from outer space and some through the springs of his bed. Then we have a woman who comes every week to tell us her life is in danger and powders are being put under her hotel door. Everyone she meets is in the conspiracy against her, including us."

"What do you do with these people?"

"We try to find out who their relatives are and whether they're prepared to take care of them. Often we can't locate relatives, or if we do, they don't want to know about it. Then relatives sometimes ask us to trace someone who is missing. We can get into a hornets' nest of trouble there, because often we find that such people have gone missing on purpose, and by law we can't divulge where they are unless they're under twenty-one. Attempts at suicide are another problem. They become deaths if they succeed, and repatriation cases if they don't. I had one attempted suicide call me the other night. Said he'd taken an overdose of sleeping pills and gashed his wrists with a penknife. I went and fetched him in a taxi. All he wanted was to be taken notice of. He'd been reading a lot of psychiatry and was too glib about it. He was fascinating to himself and a bore to everyone else."

"What is the commonest problem you have?"

"The repatriation cases, I should say. There seems to be an entirely new group of tourists among the young people, who buy a one-way ticket and are ready for repatriation almost as soon as they step off the plane. Some of them have the weirdest ideas—like the sun in France is always shining, and everybody speaks English and there are plenty of jobs. They spend a week or two in Paris and then come to us and say they're broke, they want to be repatriated. We have to exhaust every possibility of getting money from their relatives, so we tell them it'll take three to four weeks to arrange repatriation and until then they'll have to stay in the Salvation Army hostel. When they hear that, a lot of them manage to find *other* ways of getting the money. I'm sorry to say there's an awful lack of veracity among some of our customers."

"What happens if they can't find the money?"

"They stay in the Salvation Army hostel, and then we send them to Bremerhaven and ship them home by military boat. They don't like that very much. Then when they get back to the States, their passports are taken away until they've paid back the repatriation fee. They don't ever do it twice."

✪

THE PRESIDENT of the Association of American Wives was a Madame Michaux, and she received me in a gloomy office in the American Chamber of Commerce, where she had a job. She was a woman of about fifty, with graying, untidy hair, and wearing a white blouse and black skirt. Her husband was a French businessman by whom she had a son and a daughter. She had two gold rings on her wedding finger, and a nice dead-pan sense of humor.

"*Alors,*" said Madame Michaux, "the whole darn thing started with an ad in the New York *Herald Tribune.* There was a small group of us wanted to find out how many other American women were married to Frenchmen, whether they had the same sort of problems and what we could do to solve them. The ad went in during April. By May we had thirteen members, by June thirty-five, by October sixty. Now there are a hundred and twenty of us out of a potential four hundred. And among us we have a hundred and seventy children. *Bien!*"

"What are the problems?"

"*Alors,* the *basic* problem is the American Nationality Act. If you want your children to have dual nationality, and we all do, the Nationality Act says they must spend five consecutive years in the United States between the ages of fourteen and twenty-eight. *Alors,* that raises a financial problem. Where's the money to come from? One of our members is married to a plumber and another to a tailor. We're none of us exactly in the Grace Kelly class."

"What did you do?"

"We wrote to three hundred universities and colleges all over the States, to ask about scholarships, and we got a wonderful response. In fact, we overreached ourselves. This year we got two more scholarships than we could use. But it has all been valuable pioneering work. Every year there are more and more mixed marriages everywhere, and we think the problems apply equally to a Belgian who marries a Brazilian and to an Eskimo who marries a Chinese. By the mid-seventies America will have a whole new generation of mixed-marriage children to care for."

"What other problems do you have?"

"French conformism," said Madame Michaux, "than which there is nothing more boring. *Alors,* many of our wives come over as third-year college students and marry into French families. The French families are delighted. It is *à la mode.* This is America's century. But when the honeymoon is over, they expect the wives to keep absolutely to the French way of doing things. At first the wives accept this. They identify completely with their husbands and their homes, and that keeps them from being too homesick. And then after two or three years they go completely anti-French and start asserting their Americanism in a big way."

"Why?"

"*Alors,* because some French people are very stupid and *make* them. They have an *idée fixe* about how Americans live and behave, and nothing in the world will change it. For instance, they have this ridiculous thing that all American women are dominating. My God, you ought to see how some *Frenchwomen* carry on! One evening soon after I was married, we had company to dinner, and afterward my husband was helping me clear away the things. So his friends said to him, 'There you are, she has already domesticated you.' Such a *stupid* thing to say.

"And you wouldn't believe this, but after nearly twenty years in this country I can still go out to dinner and find myself next to people who say, 'Do you like French cooking?' When I hear that, I move away fast. Of course, the way they look at the American racial thing is enough to kill you."

"How do they look at it?"

"They love to needle us about it. They're still mad over our having championed the cause of the independent countries and taken away their colonies. Well, I've found a good method of dealing with this. *Bien!*" She opened her bag and produced two faded photographs of a Negro maid in a back garden. "*Alors,* whenever they start asking why we have segregation, I show them these, and I say, 'That's my cousin; she used to be a maid, but she isn't any longer; she went to high school and *improved* herself and became a secretary and got married. She's coming to Paris next month and is just dying to meet French

people, so will you be very kind, please, and do something for her?'
That's the last I ever hear about segregation."

Madame Michaux had another photograph in her bag, of what
looked like a boy standing on a crocodile. "I keep that one," she said,
"for those who tell me that all Americans are rich. I say it's another
cousin, but he's fallen on hard times and has to earn a living fighting
alligators. You should see their faces. Actually, it's a photograph of a
friend who works on an alligator farm in Florida."

"What about the children?" I said. "Do they find themselves getting pulled in two different directions?"

"*Alors*, no. In fact, another reason for our forming the club was
that their orientation is so exclusively French. Our children are born
in France, they learn to speak French as babies, they're brought up in
a completely French atmosphere. When they come home with pronunciation tests, it's their fathers they turn to, not us. My children
were proficient in English when they were six, but they didn't like
speaking it with me in front of other children, because that made
them different, and they didn't like speaking French with me in front
of others because I speak it with an English accent.

"So we started these English classes, where the children soon found
that there were other mothers who spoke French with an American
accent, and where they could develop an equal respect for both
languages. And we've taught them other things, like George Washington and the Civil War and nursery rhymes and Halloween and
Thanksgiving Day dinner. Our husbands accept all that—though
they usually turn up their noses at cranberry sauce. I wish it could be
like that the other way round. I'd love to hear a German war bride
talking German to her children in the Safeway market in Levittown.
But today she'll be talking English. There's *American* conformism
for you."

"You don't think the children feel any conflict?"

"Well, we certainly hope they don't. There's going to be a party for
the teen-agers on a houseboat down the river next week. Why don't
you come and look at them for yourself? I tell my children not to
think of themselves as half French and half American, but both
French *and* American. It's more positive, *bien?* We want our children
to make use of *both* their cultures, to feel loyalty to *both* their countries, and that way to become truly international people."

The houseboat was moored to a bosky bank near the Porte Moli-
tor, and you reached it by a long flight of steps. Inside, was like a

rather avant-garde nightclub. There were shaded Chinese lanterns and an old stove and modern pictures and bits of pottery. In the center room some twenty Franco-American teen-agers were twisting to a gramophone, watched by perhaps a dozen mothers. In clothes, hair style, movement, et cetera, they *looked* more French than American, though in the bone structures of one or two there were undertones of GI Joe. I thought they seemed strangely shy and ill at ease, and Madame Michaux agreed. "They are not nearly so forward as American children of the same age. American children of the same age would be dating and going steady. Yet they talk about things in a sophisticated, mature sort of way that American children could never do. They are *au courant.*"

The gramophone stopped, and there was a move toward the room at the stern, where salami and pâté and deviled eggs had been laid out, and about fifty bottles of Coke.

While the children ate, I talked with them. They had none of the brashness of the average American teen-ager: they were painfully, charmingly shy. I asked if they felt more drawn toward one country than the other, and they all said oh, yes, France, living there made that inevitable. "But if the talk turns to America and Americans," said one girl, "then I become an American immediately." The others agreed. Without exception, though in varying degrees, they spoke American with a French accent. Some had been to America for vacations, and they said it always required a few days' adjustment to the different way of living. They agreed that they thought in the language which they spoke. One girl said, "When I'm in America, I dream in English." I had expected to find a schizophrenic attitude, a not-knowing where they belonged, but there was no doubting their mongrel pride. Dual nationality made them unique, gave them life membership in an unusual and exclusive club.

After supper Madame Michaux said she had to go, and handed me over to her friend Dorothy. Dorothy was a pretty, willowy creature in her late thirties, quiet and gentle in an un-American way. She told me she had been a beatnik in Greenwich Village when she was seventeen, then a model. She had a sixteen-year-old daughter at the party, by her first husband.

Presently Dorothy's second husband appeared. He was an advertising man named Belon. Dorothy told him her daughter was going on somewhere with friends, so he said *bien,* why didn't we go on somewhere, too? We drove back to their flat and Monsieur Belon and I had a drink while Dorothy changed. "By the way," he said, "Dorothy isn't really American at all. She comes from the South. My God, by the way, I wouldn't even have considered marrying one of those snobbish northern American women. They have nothing to offer a Frenchman, by the way."

We went up to Montmartre ("Montmartre," said Monsieur Belon, "is now very bourgeois and commercial; by the way, the St.-Séverin area is how Montmartre used to be") and went into a place called Buttercup's where I had been a few nights before. Buttercup was a big American Negro woman who sang, or used to sing, and was married to a jazz musician called Bud Powell. She ran the place as a rendezvous for itinerant jazz groups, and because it was cheap, students and GI's and even tourists used to go there, too. There was a big photograph of Thelonius Monk behind the bar, and two or three Vat-69 bottles with red lampshades on the bar counter, and a big sign which read: "SOUL FOOD. Chicken and Chips 10 NF. Hamburger and Chips 5 NF."

Buttercup remembered me from last time, and I introduced her to the Belons.

"You seem pretty busy tonight," I said.

"Oh, we have some real characters tonight," said Buttercup. "There's a group of college girls over there, and they're very particular who *touches* them. One of them just said to me, 'I was touched.' I said how, and she said, 'Well, this fellow asked me to dance and when he asked me, he *touched* me.' I told her, 'Honey, he was French and he didn't understand.' "

Buttercup showed us to a table and said, "In a few moments a lousy French combo is going to play. I don't mean they're lousy because they're French, they'd be lousy whoever they were."

We ordered drinks, and when the lousy French combo started up Mr. Belon and I danced with Dorothy in turns. Once Mr. Belon said, "My God, this band is awful, by the way." Later he said he had an early train to catch in the morning, and would I excuse them, and they left. The lousy French combo packed it in, and a pianist took their place. Buttercup came by, seeing that everybody was all right, and I said, "Why don't you sit down and rest your feet?"

"Okay," said Buttercup, "but not for too long. I have things to do."

"How did you start this place?" I said.

"I don't know if you know about my husband, Bud Powell," she said. "He's a great jazz musician, but unfortunately an alcoholic and a schizophrenic too. We first knew each other in the Village. In 1958 he was in the hospital and when he came out he got this offer of touring Europe. I thought the change would do him good, and for a time it did. He didn't drink so much and he wasn't so nervous. We got my son over from New York—he was three and a half then—and we toured Europe and your country with this trio my husband had.

"But around 1963 we had a breaking-up period, a disagreement. I wanted him to go into the hospital to have his teeth fixed—he was always onto me about his teeth—but a friend of his said he didn't want that, he just wanted to play his piano. Well, soon after that he developed tuberculosis and then he *had* to go into the hospital.

"While he was in the hospital I started looking for a place that would support him when he came out and would let him play when he wanted. I found this place. It was a segregated GI joint then and had a very bad reputation. They used to throw out French Negroes and kick holes in the wall. I got into a partnership to buy it, and I have a third interest. Now I'm very involved in it and want to make it work. I want to make it a meeting place for young musicians, a place where a guy can bring his instrument and sit down and learn to play with the great. That's how my husband learned to play, sitting in with Duke Ellington and others."

"Where is your husband now?"

"Back in the States. He went right back there after he got out of the hospital."

"Why?"

"A lot of guys persuaded him it was best for him. They said I wasn't doing him any good. But I understood him. I had to be a little rough with him sometimes, but that was for his own good. Right now he's running around the streets like a bum. If I could find him I'd bring him right back here and put him into the hospital and look after him. Only I don't think he wants to come, and if a fellow don't want to come, you can't force him. Do you know what he said to me once? 'Buttercup,' he said, 'why do you try to save me? I'm not worth it. I want to die.' That's his trouble. He's always looking for some alley to escape down." *

"And your son?"

"He's with me now."

"Here?"

* Bud Powell has since died.

"In the hotel, sleeping. We live in a hotel rather than an apartment, so he doesn't have to be alone when I'm working. I'll see him when I get home. I get home around six, mostly, and have a shower and coffee, and then I get my son ready for school. He talks French fluently. He can talk English too, but he can't read it."

"What's his name?"

"His full name is Earl Douglas John Powell—Earl after his father; Douglas, which is my name; and his own name of John, which is strength, the strength of our love. We do many things together. Between six and eight-thirty is the time when I don't see people. I save it for my son. We spend that time communicating. Sometimes we talk or I read to him or he reads to me. Then at eight-thirty he goes to bed. He's had a long day and he's tired."

"When do you sleep yourself?"

"When my son's gone to school. I sleep till around one or two, and then I have telephone calls to make and letters to write and socks to wash. I tell my son he ought to wash his own socks, but he always gets around it by doing something else. Then about four I go down to the Café Seine, which is off the Boulevard St.-Germain and right near my hotel, and I stick around there till my son comes home at six-fifteen. Excuse me."

A rumpus had started at the bar, and Buttercup went to sort it out. One huge GI who looked about twenty years old and seven feet high, was shouting at someone, "But she *slapped* me, I tell you. She *slapped* me. I'm not going to stand for that." Someone said, "Oh, shut up!" and the GI said, "Well, *you* shut up. You're not even a goddam American, and you don't know what you're talking about."

Buttercup quieted them and came back. "Did I tell you my father was white?" she said.

"No."

"He was painting the church in Richmond, Virginia, where my mother was the organist and my grandfather the pastor. They got married and went to Washington, D.C. After my sister and I were born they moved to New York and lived at One Hundred Thirty-third Street and Lenox. My father was a wild character. He liked drinking and gambling, and one night a Negro came in and there was a fight and my father fell out of the window. But he loved my mother and she loved him. He set up trust funds for all of us. Later my mother married again. She's fifty-nine now. She has a nice body and a nice personality and a nice home in Long Island. My sister has a nice home in Long Island, too. She's married to a man from the Baha-mas."

"Has being of mixed parentage made any difficulties for you?"

"No. After my father's death I grew up in a strictly Negro society. And here in France, and in the kind of circles I move around in, nobody cares where you come from."

"Don't you ever find it gets monotonous coming here night after night?"

"No, because one night's never the same as the next. There's al-ways new people to meet—like yourself, for example—and I like that. And then there's problems to overcome, like staff and drunks and customers who don't like being touched. Do you know, I get some crazy letters. I had one from a man the other day asking me to find him a wife and send him some books on the art of making love. He sent a blank check and told me to take whatever percentage I wanted. And a singer who wanted to come here from the States sent me a twelve-page history of herself and a lot of pictures, and said would I find her a job. So I wrote back and told her, 'Honey, if you want to make it in Europe, you've got to come on over and make it on your own.' "

"Do you miss anything?" I said.

She thought. "I do miss people of my own age. I'm forty-two and most of those who come to me here are in their twenties and thirties." And then she added, "I miss being married, too. I miss having a hus-band to take me out to dinner sometimes in the evenings."

⭐

IN PARIS always there are all kinds of students. At the top, so to speak, are the girls of the Académie, a finishing school run by Ma-dame Vaudables, wife of the owner of Maxim's. The Académie is not a bricks-and-mortar establishment, but the name given to a group of girls, mostly American, who live with French families and meet daily for a program of cultural and social activities arranged by Madame Vaudables.

Madame Vaudables received me in a room above Maxim's, in which were a very large Empire divan with very steep sides and, above it, a framed oil painting of what appeared to be an inkblot. Madame Vaudables had been described to me by Mim Johnson as "a tough little cookie," and the description was apt. She was short and stocky and had very red hair, a shrewd, leathery face and lips that were thick, red and wet. "It is nice to meet a serious writer," she said. "They did a story on me in *Time* magazine the other day. It was very silly and did me no good with the professors. We have some very able and charming professors here, you know."

"Tell me about the Academy," I said.

"I used to call it the Académie Maxim's," said Madame Vaudables, "but people got the wrong idea and thought it was only to do with cooking. The girls are very high-class girls from very high-class schools. We have the best of Bryn Mawr and Wellesley. This year we have sixteen girls. They are between eighteen and twenty-one. If they do not have good enough French on arrival, they are put through an accelerated course. This year's course costs twenty-four hundred dollars, and they get ten dollars a week pocket money."

"What do they learn?"

"They are taking a special course at the Sorbonne on *la civilisation française*. Every day they have lectures on art and music, painting, literature, and so on. The music lectures are given by the best music critic in France. Did you know that the professors *repeat* their lectures? That is good for a girl who wants to hear it again, or has missed it the first time. In addition they do political science, but I try to make the course more lively than the usual academic program. Once a week they go to the gas company's kitchens to learn French cooking. They are supervised then by the Comtesse de Toulouse-Lautrec—"

"Any relation to the painter?"

"Her husband is his great-nephew. They have the best cream, the best lobsters, the best brandy. There is a charwoman to prepare the vegetables, and at noon they eat what they have cooked, served by the charwoman. Also I arrange for them to visit museums and private collections on days when they are closed to the public. At the end of the year, they take a special examination, not in a hall with two thousand other students, but together in a little room. There are no privileges they do not have."

I went to the gas company's kitchens, housed in a long, low, austere building with "CUISINES DU GAZ DE FRANCE" on the face of it. The kitchens were as light and airy as the girls themselves, six of whom were there when I arrived, wearing pink-striped aprons and making the base of a pudding. Two assistants were helping them

(Madame Vaudables's "charwomen"); *they* were wearing *green*-striped aprons, a very delicate distinction.

The girls were polite and reticent and self-possessed in a conventionally upper-class way; they reminded me of Mary McCarthy's *The Group*. Most came from Chicago. The father of one was a grain broker, of another a textile banker, whatever that might be. I asked where they had been to school and two said Briarcliff, two Finch College, one Chapin School in New York City, and one Bradford Junior College. So much for the best of Bryn Mawr and Wellesley.

Presently a large woman arrived, wearing a smart green linen dress and an enormous green hat. This was the Comtesse de Toulouse-Lautrec. ("She always wears the hat," said the girls.) "Come along, girls," said the Comtesse, "the meat has now arrived." So the girls left the pudding and turned their attention to the meat.

The Comtesse showed me the menu for lunch which was *dartois de sardines, sauté d'agneau au citron,* and *poires Bourdaloue.* "Some of the girls," said the Comtesse, "have more talent than others, and I could tell which were which on the first day they came." Most of the cooking was being done by the two assistants, and the girls took frequent breaks to gossip or puff at cigarettes. One girl was gingerly wrapping some sardines in pastry. "When the girls first came," said the Comtesse, "they weren't used to touching fish with their hands. They didn't like it much, but now they don't mind." I said to the Comtesse, "Do you teach cooking to other students here?" She appeared quite shocked. "Oh, no," she said, "I am not a teacher of cooking at all. I just do this as a favor for Madame Vaudables."

When the food was ready, we sat down and ate it, and it was very good indeed. I asked the girls about the Académie. One said, "We're getting an experience that is absolutely unique"; but another added, "Maybe we're missing something, too." When I asked what, she said, "I guess all this is a bit rarefied." They described the families they were staying with as "darling." They could come and go as they pleased. A pretty blonde called Diane said, "We all have our own keys"; and she laughed. "What are you laughing at?" I said, and Diane said, "Nothing *méchant.*"

All found the formality of French life a great bore after America's easygoing ways. Louise, a dark girl with spectacles and the hint of a sexy mustache, said, "Last year six of us went to Courchevelle for the skiing, and the woman we stayed with was horrified that we didn't have a married woman to chaperon us. And she kept saying things like 'In France one does not go into the house with snow on one's boots.' "

A girl called Jean said, "The day I arrived, the father of the family said, 'Have you ever been out with a Negro?' So I said no, I'd never had the opportunity. So then he said, 'Would you ever marry one?' That really threw me, because I'd never thought about it."

The girls had a long day. They got up soon after seven to be at the Sorbonne for the first lecture at nine but all made a point of going back to their French families for lunch. Most of them now spoke French well enough to go out with French boys, whom they found a little overserious and hard to know, but preferable to the American Army officers stationed in Paris. "These officers don't have much education. They take us to dinner at the officers' club, because it's cheaper. They get steak and champagne there for five dollars. But they're bitter. They don't speak the language and they don't want to speak it, so they can't understand or be understood. As a result, they don't like the French and the French don't like them."

I asked the girls if they thought in French when they spoke it. Most did. One said, "I dream in French sometimes." But another said, "For me that's a bad dream. I dream I'm talking French and no one can understand me, or that everyone else is talking French and I can't understand them."

After lunch Daphne and Louise and I went to a lecture on art. Two other girls were coming, too, but one said she felt cold and the other disappeared. The lecture took place in a building near the Eiffel Tower which, Daphne said, was used for railway conferences. There were four other people at the lecture. The lecturer was a small, dark Frenchman with big black-rimmed spectacles and a fine array of teeth. He spoke nonstop for an hour and a half in a voice that never varied in pace or pitch. He, and the lunch beforehand, commanded sleep, and I woke a few minutes from the end, refreshed.

Later I went back to see Madame Vaudables. "Only six girls at the cooking and only two at the lecture on modern art?" she said. "I'm afraid that some of them are a little *amateur,* they lack the right *esprit*. But next year it will be different. Next year they will get credits for attending, and then they will come."

"The Comtesse de Toulouse-Lautrec," I said, "says she is not a teacher of cooking but a writer."

Madame Vaudables laughed. "She is a writer," she said, *"on the cooking things."*

✪

And then there are all the middle-ground students, those who come to France in their thousands every year and take a course of studies at some French university or college.

In the basement of a house in the Rue du Puits de l'Hermitage in the Fifth Arrondissement, I met three American eggheads, Don and John and Peter. Each had a bed-sitting-room of his own, and they shared a windowless kitchen. There was an odd smell in there, and a lot of bamboo screens and a gas water heater and a massive old dresser covered with bottles. Some of the bottles were full, and the cork in one of them suddenly popped while we were speaking. The room was lighted by a single naked bulb hanging from the ceiling, and beneath it was a round table with a vase of yellow flowers.

Don was twenty-three and came from Massachusetts. He had a wispy beard and two spots on his forehead and had got a Master's in science at M.I.T. Here he was on a Fulbright, studying mathematical logic at the Institut Henri Poincaré. "The teaching of math is somewhat different here from what it is in the States. I am making a study of this difference in pedagogical approach, and I find it very interesting."

John was twenty-four and came from New York. He smoked a pipe and had curly hair and a boyish face, which belied his maturity. He wore an open-necked shirt, a navy-blue sweater and gray flannels. He had got a Bachelor's at Fordham in Latin and Greek, and a Master's in the Romance languages at Yale. Here he was doing a dissertation for his doctorate on French literature of the nineteenth century with particular reference to the effect on literature of the *coup d'état* of 1851. He read and spoke French fluently and was devoted to the ancient classics. "A lot of people would like to see the Greek situation improve," he said. "I think the fault originally was teaching Latin to the masses."

Peter was thirty, the eldest of the trio, and he also came from New York. He had wavy hair and a tartan shirt; and a slight Brooklyn accent made him the most obviously American of the three. He had got his B.A. and his Master's in music in the States, and was now doing a dissertation for his doctorate on an obscure Czech composer called Anton Reicha. "He taught at the Conservatoire here. He was a friend of Beethoven and Haydn, and he taught Berlioz, Franck, Gounod and Liszt. Most of his manuscripts are here. He interests me primarily because he wrote a number of experimental works and a number of treatises which verbalize his musical ideas. Apart from the Czechs, about the only people who have heard of him are individual players. He wrote about twenty-four woodwind quartets."

I asked Peter if he spoke French, and he said, "I didn't speak it at all when I first came, and I'm still picking it up. It's no problem with my work, because I can read it fairly fluently. I think I would be speaking it better now if I'd gone to live with a French family instead of here with the other two. But living here does have certain advantages—for example the economy in sharing the apartment. I know a lot of American girls who share apartments and make a pact not to speak English, and they fine themselves a penny if they fail."

Don said, "Girls can keep up that sort of pact. Men don't seem able to."

Peter said, "When I take a French girl out, although I know she speaks better English than I do French, I insist on speaking French—until suddenly something crops up that I badly want to say, and then I break into English."

John said, "I think, to learn French, you do need someone who *is* French to bounce the language back on."

Don said, "Yes. If we speak French among ourselves, we're saying American things in French and not really using the French language. We're just using the language to communicate with and not for all the other things."

John said, "The French do a lot of linguistic banter when they first meet you. American humor is based on invented situations, but the French has more to do with linguistic things. If you go along with this for a while it can be very rewarding."

"That shows the real importance of language in any relationship between people," Don said. "I found it wasn't until I could speak French reasonably fluently that the French started asking me along to their homes. One has to share that much with them, so to speak, before they fully accept you. Now I have a lot of French friends—there's an older group of young businessmen whom I play bridge with and stay with on weekends, and a younger group of fellow students whom I meet at university."

John said, "My friends tend to be people just starting business careers, and teachers, and young officers in the Army."

Don said, "I think the friendships one has here are more durable. I have a lot of friends in the States, but it's a kind of a movable thing."

Peter said, "I wouldn't agree with that as a generalization. I have many *very* good friends in the States."

Don said, "Of course, you have to watch out. There's a whole class of Frenchmen here who are on the lookout for you. They're Americophiles. They're determined to meet you."

"That's right," said John. "They're constantly dissatisfied with France, always complaining about it and saying America is much better. Well, we know there are many things not right with the U.S., but we accept them, we don't go endlessly talking about them."

Don said, "I find them a bit jarring after the ordinary French people. They will insist on saying things like 'Bye-bye' instead of *'Au revoir.'* "

"What about girls?" I said. "Which are best, French or American?"

Don sighed and said, "American girls who share my interests are very rare. There must be some. No, I much prefer going out with French girls."

John said, "When you see American girls alongside French ones here, they do seem to lack poise, even if they are bright."

Peter said, "I think there are some who have poise. It depends on the girl. I don't think any nation has a monopoly of femininity."

Don said, "They're not *serious*. They're here for kicks."

John said, "A French friend of mine said that *moralement* they're quite ungrown-up. If, for example, you say you're interested in chess, an American girl will say, 'Oh, really? Oh, chess?' and not have any idea what you're talking about."

Don said, "Mind you, there's a whole class of French girls of twenty-eight who are just as immature as American girls."

John said, "Yes, but what I really like about them is that there's a real respect between the sexes. There's real equality and there's a lot of humor. We talk about equality between the sexes, but it isn't there. My summing-up of France is that it's a really healthy country. It's *sain*—sane and healthy."

Don said, "Yes, the fact that you can serve beer at a teen-age party. Try getting away with that sort of thing in the United States."

John said, "Sex is something you don't talk about here, because you don't need to talk about it. It's normal. That's how it ought to be. One shouldn't ever have to talk about sex."

✪

AS POSTGRADUATES with organized lives, Don and John and Peter could afford to dwell on the subtler implications of *la vie américaine* in Paris. But down at the Cité Universitaire, where life was real and earnest, I found another group of American students preoccupied with the sheer business of living. Sue and Terry and David, all in their early twenties, all complained of bureaucracy and red tape. "You have to have about eighteen cards before you can start," said David. "A subway card, a restaurant card, a registration card, and a card for every library you want to visit. You end up by spending all your time in photomotion."

Terry said, "One day I lost all my cards. I didn't exist."

Sue said, "The classes never start when they're scheduled to. So you have to go and ask every day. Some students get weary of asking and drop out. My classes didn't start till December, then it was almost impossible to get a seat. The Sorbonne was built for three thousand, and there are sixty thousand there now. To be sure of a seat for a class that starts at four, you have to go and sit through the one at two and the one at three. Not many students are prepared to do that."

Inevitably the conversation came round to the language question, and the difficulties in tackling it. "One phenomenon among Americans when they first come here," said David, "is to start practicing their French wherever they can, because they want to get into the ball game as soon as possible. Then after about a month they just give up. And you see boys sitting around in the lobby reading *The New York Times* or booking plane tickets to Sweden."

"Why do they give up?"

"They can't be bothered. They think, aw, what the hell, what's the use?"

"One thing that makes it difficult for them," said Terry, "is that English is now the international language, and the French students want to practice it on us all the time."

"If you have a French friend," said Sue, "that's a very good motivation for speaking French."

"Yes," said Terry, "but how do you get the friend? You don't know the language because you don't have friends, and you don't have friends because you don't know the language. How do you get over the hump?"

"When I first came to Paris," said David, "I stayed here two months, and I didn't know anybody and I was miserable. So I got out of Paris and started hitchhiking round France for about ten weeks. I had a fantastic time. People were always inviting me into their homes, which they never did in Paris. At one farm where I asked for a bed in the barn, the farmer asked if I would stay on for a bit and teach his son English. I learned French fast that way."

Terry said, "You never see a Frenchman hitchhiking. They think it's too risky."

"And too uncertain," said David. "When they travel they have the whole thing scheduled in advance."

"We went through France in a rented car," said Sue. "Four girls. Everyone was shocked."

"There are a lot of things I like about the French," said David, "but I do get a little tired of this endless holier-than-thou attitude. You know, Americans have washing machines and television, but they don't know how to enjoy life, they don't have the *joie de vivre* or the *savoir faire* and all that. It's a load of crap."

"Some French people," said Terry, "live on a kind of myth that all Americans are morons—and you have to keep exploding that all the time. Not by *denying* that we have morons, but by pointing out that they have them, too. For example, few Frenchmen seem to know that the French read millions of comics every year."

"There's one thing about the French," said David, "that I really like. You go out with an American girl and she expects you to light her cigarette for her. But you go out with a French girl and without your saying anything, she lights yours. Now, that's good."

✪

FINALLY, THERE were what you might call the students of life, who, every evening at around seven, make their way to a narrow street across the river from Notre Dame, where friends of the Église de St.-Séverin dish out free soup. Most are young, many are bearded, and all look unclean. They are of various nationalities and include one or two girls. They stand patiently in line in their filthy clothes, and when each has been given his bowlful he takes it away to a corner, proud as a mongrel with a bone.

One evening I invited some to a nearby café (the only café in the neighborhood which would allow them in) for a drink. They all had long hair and matted beards and dirty sweaters. A small one in an old overcoat with anchor buttons and a nuclear-disarmament badge was an American-born Scotsman called Jock; another, blonder and a shade less foul-looking than the rest, was an American called Richard; a third, with a black beret on his head, was an Englishman called Jim; and there was a massive German called Klaus.

Jock said he was thirty-four and had been on the road since he was seventeen. The year before, he had been working in a shipyard in San Francisco. He had bought a scooter, driven it across the States, sold it in New York, and made his way to Britain. In London he had got work as a potman in a public house in Hampstead. "I used to get a lot of tips there, five quid on Saturday and five on Sunday. I had a Swedish girl friend, and when she went back to Sweden I went with her. I stayed with her family in a house near Stockholm. I used to share her room. The family didn't mind. Sometimes I'd actually be on the job, you know, doing her, and the mother would walk in and say, 'Oh, excuse me!' and go out again."

Klaus said, "It is impossible to do that in Denmark. Denmark is very conservative."

Jim said, "I had an experience like that myself once. In Torquay, it was. When the daughter went away to visit a friend, I moved in with the mother. The daughter was ten years younger than me and the mother ten years older. I could never make up my mind which I liked best."

"Anyway," said Jock, "I stayed there five weeks and then I went to Istanbul."

"Why?"

"Because I speak Turkish. I'd been there before in the Navy. I stayed a month, writing and fishing, and then I moved to Israel. I worked on a *kibbutz*. I'm half Jewish, you see. I'd forgotten about the Swedish girl by this time. I found others—you do as you go along the road."

Just then some people sitting at the next table got up to leave. Jock saw a sausage on one of their plates, and he leaned over and grabbed it. "Excuse me," he said, "but I do hate seeing food go to waste."

"What happened after Israel?"

"I went back to Istanbul," said Jock, "and I started painting on the sidewalks. The first day I wrote 'Ban the Bomb' in Turkish I made thirteen dollars. Then I got better at drawing, and on New Year's Eve I made twenty-eight dollars, so I had a very good New Year. I went on to Munich, where I made two hundred marks in two days, hustling. I sold some cigarettes and things I'd brought in a suitcase from Turkey, and I sold the suitcase too. Then I tried to get to England, but I didn't have enough money and they wouldn't let me land. I got as far as Dover and then went back in the ship I came over in."

"Next time," said Jim, "you want to go to Jersey first. You can get over to England from there without any trouble."

"That was three weeks ago," said Jock, "and since then I've been here, working the snake."

"What's that?"

"The Métro. The other day I drew a picture of the old mushroom cloud on the platform, and I wrote beneath it: 'Beware of the H-bomb, whom it may kill/If the blast don't get you, the fallout will.' I made forty-five francs in three hours with that. That's good money. Some days you make it and some you don't. As a writer, what do you think of the verse?"

"It's a bit gloomy."

"I write quite a lot of poetry." He fumbled inside his filthy coat and brought out a ragged piece of paper. "Here, read this."

I took it and read:

LIFE'S COWARD

Oh, grim-faced fool,
Doomed drudgery's slave,
What things you'll do for pay.
You'll sweat, you'll toil,
Just have your boss command
The fear of pain or deaths unknown,
Should you lose that job,
The work you loathe,
The boss you hate,
But quit you never can.

"Did you get the point?" said Jock. "It's about a chap trapped in a job, see?"

"What about your future plans?" I said.

"This summer I'm going back to Turkey. There's a girl there I like very much. I think I might get married and settle down."

"Where?"

"Well, it doesn't really matter. India, perhaps. Or we might open a coffee bar somewhere, or go to Israel and live on a *kibbutz*. It's up to her, really. I can make myself more or less understood in about fifteen languages."

I ordered another round of drinks and some sandwiches and said to Richard, the American, "What about you?"

"I don't have a case history like him. I'm twenty-one and I've been traveling about a year. I was at school in Vermont and I decided to take a year off. I didn't have much money, but I came over and stopped off in Sweden and just traveled around. If the weather was nice I slept out; if it wasn't, in youth hostels or other people's houses. I had my guitar, and I made a little money playing that.

"Then I went over to Norway and ran out of money completely and got a job as a deckhand on a ship going to Archangel. We were away a month, and then I started hitchhiking across Europe. I got to Paris, worked in a bookstore, went down to Madrid for a month and improved my Spanish. Then I crossed over to Morocco and ran out of money again and just lived off the land. I got pretty hungry there. I sold my clothes and even my guitar, just to eat. I could have asked my parents for money any time, but at twenty-one I guess I should look after myself. It's a matter of pride. So in Casablanca I signed on another ship and went to England, and Odessa on the Black Sea, and Dieppe, France. I hitchhiked down to Spain again three weeks ago to get another guitar—you get the best guitars in the world there—and now I've teamed up with an American girl who sings. Day before yesterday we played to a whole lot of tourists on the roof of Notre Dame, but otherwise we just play along the Seine—"

"I've seen you," said Jock, "and I want to tell you something, mate. You've got to get some volume in your voice. Two feet away you can't hear a thing."

"I know, I know," said Richard quickly. "Anyway, I aim to take this girl down to Switzerland and Greece, and then in the fall she'll have to come back to her studies at the Sorbonne. I guess I'll go on to the Middle East and India and get a ship back to the U.S. from there."

The sandwiches came. Everyone waited politely for me to hand them round, like spinsters at a tea party.

"What are the worst things about this kind of life?" I asked.

"Finding a place to sleep," said Jock.

"Where do you sleep?"

"Under bridges, in derelict buildings, in friends' houses—anywhere."

"Incidentally," said Jim, "where's anyone sleeping tonight?"

Klaus said, "I have found two rooms in a condemned building. There's a toilet and a tap. Any of you who want to can come there."

"Sometimes when I've saved up a little money," said Jock, "I go to a hotel for two or three days to build up my strength. I went to a hotel last week with a girl I met in the soup line. We stayed in bed three days. It was great."

"If you're really pushed for money," I said, "what do you do?"

"Sell blood," said Jock. "You can sell blood almost anywhere."

At one time or another they'd all sold their blood, and they knew the European market rates. Klaus said, "In Spain they take it out of you till you faint" and Jim said, "I once sold mine in Morocco three days after I'd been cured of dysentery. They can't be too fussy." Jock pulled at his tangled hair and said, "When this grows to eleven inches, you can sell it too." I wondered what anyone would want it for. Klaus said that the cheapest place to live was the Canary Islands. "I was there this February," said Jim. "There were three of us, and we lived very well on three pesetas—that's about fourpence halfpenny, or five cents—a day. We made cufflinks and things like that for the tourists."

They finished the sandwiches, and Richard said he had to meet his girl, and they began to move.

I said, "What's the real attraction about the life?" and almost together Jock and Richard said, "The freedom." Jock said, "The more you've had it, the more difficult it is to adapt to any other way of life. It becomes a way of life in itself. The only time I thought of giving it up was in that *kibbutz*. There was real freedom there and a complete absence of greed. I think if I get married this summer I could settle down in a *kibbutz* quite happily."

Richard said, "It's great being on your own after all the social pressures in the States—not having any responsibilities or commitments or schedules to meet. The freedom's terrific. I find that most of my generation want it for about a year or so. There's something they have to get out of their systems. Afterward they're ready to go back to the U.S.A. and get a regular job and marry a nice girl and breed some healthy children." He smiled. "I guess that's what I'll be doing."

I paid the bill and crossed the road to the presbytery of St.-Séverin to see Father David, the young American priest who had been helping to give out the soup. His room was on the fourth floor and his bicycle was on the landing outside it. He had a divan for a bed and two toy woolly dogs on it, one yellow and one brown. He was wearing a dark-gray sports shirt and black shoes and trousers. What remained of his hair was red.

"I came here," said Father David, "because St.-Séverin likes to have an American priest, and because it's just about the most exciting parish in Europe. They made a call for priests who were interested in working together, and now there are eleven of us. We think of it less as a parish than as a community.

"The beatniks are certainly a problem. There are a few Americans among them now, and more will be coming over with the good weather. The U.S. and U.K. beatniks are the worst of all. It has something to do with the old Puritan strains. The life has quite a giddy effect on them. The Swedes and Danes are much more intelligent about the whole thing.

"Before I got here I had the notion that most of these people were runaways. I was quite surprised to find that many of them have been kicked out of their homes. I know a Jewish girl who became converted to Catholicism and her family didn't want to have any more to do with her. Quite a lot of the kids come from decent families; some of them suddenly decided to pull out right in the middle of college.

"Girls are a special problem. Some come as *au pair* girls with French families. They find that the job's not what it's advertised to be—it's slavery, really, and no American girl likes being treated as a servant. So they quit and start looking for a job; but jobs are practically nonexistent here. Some go on the sidewalks selling *The New York Times*. That's a real drifty sort of life, because the people who sell the concessions give the best lots to the girls they're interested in. So some of the girls can't get jobs and drift into the beatnik life, and some get pregnant. Pregnancy has its own problems. Often when an American girl has a child by a French father, the father will make his name known, and if he does that, under French law the girl has no official rights to the child at all. A child born to an American citizen is automatically an American citizen. Okay. But how does she get the child to America?

"One of the most interesting things I've discovered here is that French Puritanism is quite as rampant as Anglo-American Puritanism, though it takes a different form. There's a terrific sense of guilt and self-involvement here. Some people are quite obsessed about their guilt. They *think* and *think* and *think* about it, in a way the American never does. They have an inability to escape the consequences of their own logic. Listening to Frenchmen and Americans in the confessional here is like listening to two different cultures. The Frenchman tells you that he's absolutely lost and that nothing can save him. The American generally has one specific problem. I guess he's not used to thinking—that's the other side of our naïveté."

✪

THERE ARE half a million American soldiers stationed in Europe, most of them in Germany. I went to see some at Frummingen, near Stuttgart, the headquarters of the Eighth Cavalry Division. At Stuttgart airport in the evening, I was met by a tiny, neat colonel with a round face and spectacles and the general appearance of a sparrow. He took me downstairs to wait for my luggage, and after we had waited fifteen minutes and no luggage had come, we found we should have been waiting upstairs. During the next few days things like that were to happen with the colonel all the time.

We got into a big Army station wagon driven by a very silent young soldier from California. The colonel said that Frummingen was in Baden-Württemberg, an area originally inhabited by the Swabians. It was a town of about fifty thousand people, famous for making toys. "But I'll be giving you a full press information kit tomorrow." We cleared the airport and swung onto the autobahn. It was dark, but on either side you could see trees. "This is real nice country," said the colonel. "To me Germany is just one big beautiful park. The Germans are real clean people. They're cleaner than we are."

We passed through Frummingen without seeing a soul ("the Germans," said the colonel, "are real early-bedders") and went up the hill on the other side. The colonel said the base was in two parts; the *Kaserne,* or main compound, where the offices were and most of the soldiers lived, and the area outside. I was staying outside, in what the colonel called the V.I.P. suite of the bachelor officers' quarters.

We drew up outside a barracklike building and went into a darkened hall, where the colonel shouted for the janitor. Nobody came. So the colonel went down to the basement, and the California driver and I stood uneasily in the dark, not seeing each other or saying anything. Then the colonel and the janitor appeared and led the way to the V.I.P. suite. This consisted of bedroom, sitting room and bathroom, and was a fairly modest affair. The atmosphere was stifling, and I asked the janitor to turn off the heating. The California soldier put down my luggage, and the colonel said why didn't we go over to the officers' club for a nightcap?

The bar of the officers' club was like any bar on Main Street, U.S.A. —too dark for seeing properly and too noisy for hearing. There were three people there: an aging redheaded barmaid from (the colonel said) Czechoslovakia, and two officers in civilian clothes. The barmaid was called Pat, and the two officers Klodzinski and Castile. Lieutenant Castile was from the American embassy at Helsinki, doing two weeks' reserve training. Klodzinski, whose face was the color of dough, was a regular. His family originally came from Scotland, where they were called MacLeod; they had emigrated to Poland after the rising of 1745. Pat said a party of German teachers from the town had been there that evening as guests of the teachers at the base. "The Germans like coming here and having drinks and cigarettes at Army prices," said the colonel, "but there's not too much fraternization, as I guess you've already been told. We go our way and they go theirs." We had a couple of drinks and then the colonel said he would send his car for me at nine-thirty in the morning; later we would pay a call on Frummingen's Lord Mayor.

In the V.I.P. suite I found that the janitor's efforts to turn off the heating had been in vain. The place was like Death Valley in midsummer. I tried to open a window, but the windows were sealed. There was a refrigerator in the bedroom, and I thought that I would at least have a cool drink; but the ice compartment had frozen up. I undressed and went into the bathroom to wash; but there was no soap or towel and no means of getting either. All that was left was to lie down, hot and unwashed, on the bed and read—which I would have done if there had been a bulb in the table light.

Next morning, after a small sleep, I went to the officers' club for breakfast. I waited for service a quarter of an hour, then poked my head through the kitchen door. There was a waiter in there reading a comic. I ordered coffee and scrambled eggs. He brought the coffee right away and the scrambled eggs after a further quarter of an hour, by which time the coffee was cold. There wasn't time to ask for fresh, as I had to be back in time for the colonel's car.

But the car didn't come. I waited an hour, and then a huge man, all of seven feet tall, arrived. He said he was Sergeant Cogswell and worked in the colonel's office. His uniform was bright with crazy insignia. He was very sorry the arrangements had broken down, but an emergency field exercise had been ordered at 5 A.M., and the colonel had had to take part in it. If the colonel didn't return soon, he, Sergeant Cogswell, would take me to the Lord Mayor.

Hardly had Sergeant Cogswell left when the colonel arrived. For a moment I didn't recognize him. He looked like a bit player in *The Longest Day*. He was wearing battle dress and a tin hat and a pack which was practically crushing him. He seemed tinier than ever. "When they blow this goddam whistle," he said, "you have to scramble. It *would* happen the day you arrive. Gee, I'm sorry." I was beginning to like the colonel.

He went away to change, and a little later he and I and a woman interpreter called Frau Fahle drove down to the town to see the Lord Mayor. The colonel pointed out things of interest on the way. "Back in the States we call these houses gingerbread houses, or sometimes Hansel-and-Gretel houses," he said. When we passed a church he said, "On Sundays you hear all the church bells ringing. They typify Germany."

The Lord Mayor, a baldish lawyer, received us in a big, airy room in which hung a large picture of the local mountain, the Habenstaufen. He was careful not to say anything that would offend the colonel. He said that after the war there was a good deal of friction between Germans and Americans. Many houses were commandeered for American troops, and many trees were cut down in the forests by the Americans. "We Germans have a special relationship with our forests," he said, "and each tree cut down wounded everyone in the city." One reason the situation today was different was that Germans and Americans were inclined to keep to themselves. Some Germans were almost unaware of the existence of the base; to others it had been part of the landscape as long as they could remember. I asked if the American soldiers created any problems with drunkenness and girls, and the Lord Mayor said no. "The only recent cause of friction has been the flying of helicopters over the graveyard during funerals. But now we shall tell the American general when there is a funeral, and he will order the helicopters to stay away until it is over." I asked if the townspeople would really like to see the Americans go, and he said, "To be honest, we would prefer to have German troops." He added that it was older people mostly who resented the Americans; the younger ones wanted to get to know them.

I went on to see the editor of the local newspaper, who said that most of the townspeople were glad of the presence of the Americans. "They give a feeling of safety and security. If they weren't here, nobody would be sure how much they would come to Germany's support in a crisis." About German-American relationships he said, "A lot of people say 'Why doesn't the GI get to know the townspeople more?' But why should he? The lives of soldiers in any army are always very much on the surface. They're just not interested in the people of the countries where they're billeted. Those who criticize American soldiers for keeping to themselves don't realize what a huge mental effort it requires to jump the barrier into another world. It's quite beyond most of them."

On the way back in the car Frau Fahle agreed. "Even if they wanted it," she said, "the soldiers are not here long enough to learn the language and make real use of it. Eighteen months, two years, and they're gone. Also, you must remember, they have much to do in the army, much to learn, and when the day is over they are tired and want to relax with their friends." The colonel said, "I'll tell you another thing. German girls don't seek out GI's like they used to. A lot of these boys come over here thinking they're going to have a ball. Their fathers or uncles were here in the old days after the war, when you could buy anything you wanted, like a girl or a cigarette case, for a pack of Luckies. But that's over. The German economy's booming, the young men have money in their pockets, and the German girls would rather go out with them."

✪

THE COLONEL took me to lunch in a restaurant on the Habenstaufen, and we looked down on the green Swabian countryside dotted with hummocky hills, like ant heaps. We ate thin slices of veal and drank a dry, local wine. "I don't know of too many people who don't like the

Germans," said the colonel. "Nobody gripes about them except maybe for bad driving manners. The average American admires their thoroughness, their good citizenship, their sense of beauty, and the way they keep their country clean—we have litterbugs and they don't. I would think the Americans were more like the Germans than any other people."

The colonel said that he had arranged for me to take tea that afternoon with a typical Frummingen family. He couldn't come himself, though he would fetch me later. Sergeant Cogswell would drive me there and a Sergeant Day from his office would do the interpreting. Sergeant Day had just married a Frummingen girl, and he had invited us to have a drink later that evening at their apartment in the town. "Sergeant Day speaks German like a real native," said the colonel. I was really touched by the thought he had given to my program.

Sergeant Cogswell lumbered into the V.I.P. suite at four o'clock and said he had orders to pick up a lady called Frau Stauss and take her to the tea party with us. I asked who she was, and Sergeant Cogswell said, a local writer. We must have spent an hour looking for Frau Stauss's house, with Sergeant Cogswell bellowing instructions from the back and the California driver silently obeying them. That driver was the most taciturn man I've met; even when Cogswell's instructions landed us in a cul-de-sac or a one-way street, as they frequently did, he made no comment, but shifted into neutral and waited for Cogswell to take another look at the map. When we found Frau Stauss's house, a neighbor told us she had left half an hour before.

We had more difficulties finding the place for tea, and arrived there at a quarter to six instead of half past four. This was the apartment of a government official called Herr Mäder. He wasn't there, but we were welcomed by Frau Mäder, a large, comfortable woman in her fifties, who, far from being annoyed at our lateness, seemed overjoyed that we had come at all. With her were two doe-eyed daughters in their teens, Stella and Andrea. Also sitting hungrily at the table were Frau Stauss and Sergeant Day. He had buck teeth and looked about sixteen. The table was heavy with plum cake and marmalade cake and apple strudel and bowls of cream. I murmured to Sergeant Day that they had really put themselves out to entertain me, and he said that in Germany a writer was held in high esteem.

I had understood that the object of the party was for me to ask questions about relations between the town and the base; but for Frau Stauss it was an opportunity to ask questions about a writer's life. She asked many questions and when she was through, she gave me a book of her poems. They were printed in heavy Gothic type, and I didn't understand a word. She had also brought along a play she had just finished, and would I give an opinion on that? I said that as I knew no German, my opinion would be worthless. She threw me a strange, hostile look, as though to say that this was no excuse at all.

I asked about the Americans, and Andrea said, "It is so sad we cannot fraternize more with them. They are so lonely, these boys, and very good-looking, some of them. But my parents are very strict and won't let me go to the base for dances. It is unfair." Andrea spoke excellent English, but had to repeat this in German for her mother. Frau Mäder said prostitutes went to the base, all soldiers drank, and what was wrong with German boys, anyway? Frau Stauss nodded heavily. Andrea said, "Mother is so old-fashioned. She thinks all soldiers are fiends who want to rape and murder. There's nothing wrong with German boys, but most of those I know are so *dull*." Sergeant Day said, rather boldly, "If you got to know the GI's up at the base I think you'd find them pretty dull, too." Andrea, not to be outsmarted, said, "Well, I'm sure they are dull in a different way."

By six-forty there still was no sign of the colonel; so, heavy with apple strudel and cream, we tottered down to the street. We found the colonel about fifty yards away, peering up an alleyway in search of the apartment; he said he'd been looking for it for half an hour.

The colonel and I got into his Volkswagen. "How did you make out there?" said the colonel. "I'm sorry I didn't show up." I said fine, Day's interpreting had been a great help. "He's an interesting boy, that," said the colonel. "When he first came I didn't know what to do with him. He just didn't fit into anything, and I was thinking of transferring him. But he slogged away with his German, and then he got married to this girl we're going to see—which, incidentally, is a story in itself—and the two things completely transformed him."

The colonel said he had fixed for us to drop by for five minutes at the house of the Chief of Staff. This was like about a million other American houses, with the drapes drawn and the coffee table bare and not a hair out of place or a book or magazine in sight. The Chief of Staff gave us two massive whiskies, and we stayed with him forty minutes.

We had intended to have something to eat after this, but the colonel said the Days were now expecting us and we had better go straight there. I asked where the Days lived, and the colonel said he didn't know, but we would go to where Sergeant Cogswell lived and he would tell us. We went to where the colonel *thought* Sergeant Cogswell lived, but that was a different matter. We drew up outside a gloomy barracks in which there wasn't a light showing, and the colonel disappeared inside. Presently a light came on, which lighted up the central staircase and four landings. From the Volkswagen I watched the colonel progress from floor to floor, stopping on each landing to check from a list of names that Cogswell wasn't there. Unfortunately, the colonel hadn't realized that the light was automatic, and when he reached the top landing it went out, leaving him in the dark. Alone in the Volkswagen, I laughed out loud. It was quite a time before the colonel got back.

We tried one or two more barracks and then the colonel said we should go to the officers' club and telephone somebody who would tell us where Sergeant Day lived. We passed the V.I.P. suite on the way, and parked outside it was Sergeant Day's car, containing himself and Mrs. Day and Sergeant Cogswell. They had been waiting there some time, they said, this being the rendezvous the colonel had appointed. The colonel denied strenuously having ever made such a rendezvous, and Sergeant Cogswell didn't seem disposed to argue with him. I said how-do-you-do to Mrs. Day, and Sergeant Cogswell got into the back of the Volkswagen, where his head touched the roof, and we set off in convoy for the town.

"Now that you've said hello to Mrs. Day," said the colonel, "I might as well tell you how John met her. When he'd been learning German for a while, he started walking down to the town every night —down this very road—to see if he could find someone to practice on. It wasn't easy for him, because by nature he's shy. See, he had this very puritanical upbringing—he did a year in a seminary in Chicago —and he didn't carouse around like the others. Well, this girl used to take her dog for a walk every evening, so eventually John plucked up courage and spoke to her, and they got along fine and he arranged to speak to her again the following night. After this they met regularly, and the boys used to tease poor John mercilessly. They'd say to him, 'Well, haven't you laid her yet?' and this really embarrassed him. See, he'd never laid *anyone*. When I saw the way things were going, I called him into my office and said, 'Listen, I can transfer you to Nuremberg if you like'—see, I wanted to give him an out. But he said no, he wanted to stay and go on with the girl. I told him he was young and there were millions of women in the world to meet, but he

wouldn't listen. He went ahead and got married and we all went to
the wedding and reception in the Paradise Gasthaus. The parents
weren't too keen about it to begin with, but they came round. I guess
Papa was glad to get daughter off his hands."

The car ahead turned into a sort of compound and stopped beside
a building in the middle. Sergeant Cogswell said that this was where
Day's in-laws lived, and that Day thought it would be roomier than
his apartment. We went upstairs to a long, rather bare room and were
introduced to Day's father-in-law, who was very old and fat and had
fought in both world wars, and a cousin, Ralf, in his middle forties,
and Ralf's wife. There was no sign of Day's mother-in-law, and when
I commented on this to the colonel he said, "You haven't missed a
thing. She's a real old cow. She weighs over two hundred pounds and
measures five by five." Day's wife produced a couple of bottles of
Swabian wine and some cocktail biscuits, and we all sat down. I
thought, whatever else one's views on the American Army, it was
wonderfully democratic, with the colonel and Cogswell and Day and
Day's family all mucking in together. The same sort of situation
couldn't happen in the British Army without acute self-consciousness.

I didn't do more than sip at my wine, for we hadn't eaten and I was
still a little under the influence of the massive whiskies of the Chief of
Staff. But the colonel had no such inhibitions and swigged away mer-
rily. The party was a little sticky to begin with, for it was soon clear
that Day's wife and Ralf's wife and Cogswell had been born into this
world as listeners rather than talkers. But Day made up for them,
chattering away in German and in English, interpreting freely for
one and all, endearing himself to his father-in-law, whom he called
"Papa," occasionally stroking his shoulder, pouring out wine and
handing round biscuits. He was by far the youngest person there—he
couldn't have been more than about twenty-three—and yet whatever
movement the evening possessed came from him. I remembered what
the colonel had said about his early days at the base, how useless and
lost he had been. Looking now at his frail figure, and listening to his
fluent German, I was full of admiration for what he had achieved. It
was as though the learning of the language and the marrying of the
girl had been necessary for his own development, proofs of what he
could do.

Day said that when his Army service was up he hoped to get a job
teaching at an American dependents' school in Germany. Didn't he
want to go back to America? I asked. No, since he had come to live in

Germany he didn't really like the American way of life any more; the only thing he missed was his family. He and his wife were very happy in their small flat. They bought some of their food from the commissary and some from the town. What did they eat, German or American dishes? "Oh, German mostly. German food is just wonderful."

He agreed with Frau Fahle about many GI's being too tired at the end of the day to start learning German. His own walks downtown to practice it had been very tiring. "There and back is all of three miles, and not too many GI's are prepared to consider it. The average soldier takes a taxi to the town till his money runs out and then sits in the barracks and vegetates." Ralf said that the same barriers to fraternization applied to the Germans. They too worked a long day, often until after 7 P.M., and didn't have the energy left to start learning English or entertaining Americans.

More of the Swabian wine was brought, and the colonel's glass was the first to be filled up. I wasn't too happy about the colonel—already behind the spectacles there was a glassy look to his eye. Ralf told us about his adventures in the war. He had been trained as a radio operator for the Luftwaffe, but when his training was over there were no bombers left to fly. So he was drafted into the army and was taken prisoner by the French. Of his company of 120, all but thirteen had died of starvation; the thirteen would have died, too, if the American Army hadn't suddenly shown up. The colonel said the Americans treated their prisoners best, then the British, then the French, then the Russians. "Those French concentration camps," he said, "were just as bad as the German ones. I saw those French soldiers marching those German prisoners at Casablanca, and they were kicking them on the shins. I want to tell you, I *admired* those Germans." Remembering all the brutish things the Germans had done in the war, I said angrily, "You wouldn't say that if they had occupied your country for five years." The colonel fixed an unsteady eye on me and said, "Now, don't get me wrong. I've got nothing against the French. They're great soldiers. And I want to say this. The British are great soldiers, too. In fact, in many ways I would say that the British Army was better than the American Army."

Around eleven we got up to go. The colonel could hardly stand, and Sergeant Cogswell and I had to help him to the car. "I'm going to drive you home," I said. He was too far gone to argue and got meekly into the front offside seat. Sergeant Cogswell got into the back, where again his head touched the roof.

"Do you know the way home, Sergeant Cogswell?" I said.

"Yes, sir."

"Good," I said, "because I don't."

I drove across the compound and out at the gate. There was a T junction at the end of the road, and Sergeant Cogswell said, "You make a left here, sir."

"A left?" I said.

"Right," said Sergeant Cogswell.

"What?" I said.

"You make a left," said Sergeant Cogswell, "and you go all the way."

So I made a left and drove for what seemed about ten miles, and the country got wilder and lonelier, and it felt as if we were nearing Berlin.

"Sergeant Cogswell," I said, "I don't believe this is the right road."

"Sir," said Sergeant Cogswell, "I don't believe it is, either."

So I stopped the car, and when I saw there was nothing in either direction I made a U turn across the road; and as I did, I became aware of the offside door opening a little, and a draft coming in, and then I heard, like a blow with a damp towel, the quick, wet slap on the German road of the American colonel's vomit. He himself didn't make a sound—a modest, self-effacing retcher. Six times he threw up, then he shut the door, wiped his mouth and fell asleep.

We got back into Frummingen, took another wrong road, went two miles the other side of the town, came back again, and finally found the barracks. As we approached the bachelor officers' quarters, Sergeant Cogswell said to the colonel, "Sir, you may recall that you and Mr. Kennedy were coming to the N.C.O.s' club as my guests, but if you feel you'd like to get some sleep, why, I'd be very happy to look after Mr. Kennedy myself." The colonel opened his eyes and, with as much authority as he could muster, said, "Okay, Sergeant Cogswell, I guess that's a pretty good idea." Then he got out.

The N.C.O.s' club was not unlike the officers' club, only darker and noisier and about twenty times bigger, with a band playing instead of a jukebox, and a crowded dance floor. "We figure we have a better time here than at the officers' club," said Sergeant Cogswell. "We have more money to spend, for one thing. Last week we had Lionel Hampton. Of course, the girls who come here are not of the highest class. That's why they come."

We went to the bar, where a sign said, "Whisky without ice will not be served." And I thought, If you tried that in Scotland you'd get lynched. Sergeant Cogswell told me that he had served nineteen years in the Army and was almost due to retire; he had already nicked himself a job as barman of a country club at Atlanta, Georgia. "I'll see all the ball games in Birmingham," he said. "The members always hire a bus and I'll set up a little bar for them in the bus and we'll all have a real good time."

We had one for the road and I said I hoped the colonel was all right. "Oh, the colonel's okay," said Cogswell. "My colonel sometimes gets a little sick when he goes to a party. I have to look after him at times like he was a little baby. And tomorrow morning, you can bet your life, he'll call me up and bawl me out for something I have or haven't done."

✪

NEXT MORNING I talked with two people the colonel had arranged for me to see. The first was white-faced Lieutenant Klodzinski, formerly MacLeod.

Klodzinski said he was twenty-four and had enlisted because he wanted to see Europe. "I've already put in for an extension. I'd say that life here is great, if you want to make the most of it. Let me give you a rundown on my week. An average week I spend one night working, one night on sports or gym, and about four nights on the economy in town, dating local girls and visiting friends and seeing the opera. Also I play golf every day after work, though at present I can only get in about four holes before it's dark. I find the local people here very willing to accommodate you if you speak only a little German. They're prepared to accept you because you've made an effort.

"I like dating German girls. I find them more mature for their age than American girls. An American girl of eighteen thinks of herself as a teen-ager, but a German girl of eighteen is a woman. Also, European girls seem to enjoy life more. There's an awful lot of American girls who just sit around worrying. American girls expect more from you, too, moneywise. Here you don't have to have a fistful of dollars. You can have a good time on two. I find if I have a couple of cigars in my pocket, I can make some great relationships, and they don't have to be expensive cigars. One thing I've found out is that many Germans think Americans drink a lot. It isn't true. An average German can drink a hell of a lot more than an average American before getting snuckered."

I thought of the colonel and nodded.

"Weekends I put about a thousand miles on the car seeing Europe. So far I've visited nine countries. How far I travel depends what time I get off, but with the autobahns and autostradas you can get a hell of a long way. I like visiting places where the GI's are not in a mass. I just mull in with the people and have a good time. Most bachelors love to sit around here and say how great they are, but they never see Europe and they don't put too much mileage on their cars. They judge Europe from the base, but they haven't got anything to form a judgment on. They just brag and drink and talk shop and say how much work they have to do—which isn't true but gives them an excuse to stay put."

"What places have you been to?"

"Recently I've been to the Munich Oktoberfest, and next week I'm going to the Konstanzer Volksfest, which is the second-biggest beer festival in Germany. Then tomorrow I'm going to the last illumination of King Ludwig's castle on Herrenchiemsee, which is an island in the largest lake in Bavaria. When I go on these trips I often take someone with me, but not just anyone. I try and get intellectual cross-stimulation. For example, I took one of the post teachers on one trip with me, and he told me that the roofs in a certain area were all red because this was the color of the local clay. Things like that. We usually wind up staying in German facilities, or if the weather's nice we take a shelter and sleeping bag and sleep out."

✪

THE OTHER man the colonel had arranged for me to see was a Negro sergeant called Mander, married to a German wife. You could tell right away he was an exceptional person. He was a tall, thin man with a well-cut uniform and a confident carriage. He'd been in the Army thirteen years and had another seven to go. He had already done two tours of duty in Germany; he kept coming back because he liked the countryside and the German people, and felt a sense of freedom which he didn't have in America.

He met his wife on a previous tour when she was walking home from a class in beauty treatment. Like Day, he had learned a little German and wanted to try it out. His wife at this time knew no English at all. After this tour he went back to the States and got himself a discharge. He returned to Germany as a tourist and married his wife with money from his savings. He reenlisted at Nuremberg without loss of seniority and was posted to Washington, D.C. For the next four years he and his wife lived in Virginia, about a mile outside Washington, and now he was back in Germany on his third tour. They had an apartment at a little place called Bingen, about thirty miles from Frummingen.

"What's it like for a colored man living in Germany?"

"Well, it's different than in the States. Most ways it's much freer. We have a color problem in the States because we have twenty million colored. Here they have no color problem because they have no coloreds. A colored guy who comes here wonders how he's going to be received. He's in a quite different world, in a white world. Many colored guys who come here remember Hitler's racism and wonder if all Germans are like that deep down. But I've never detected any ill-feeling toward me because of my color. I speak the language and I find people are surprised and pleased that I do."

"What's it like at Bingen?"

"In many ways it's great. But it is difficult to get to know people the way one does in the States. When we moved into our house in Virginia, everyone came to call. We were like one big happy family. But here they are so formal. I want to call people by their first name, it comes naturally to me, but these people call you by your second name however long they know you. We're very good friends with my landlord and his family. His wife brings us cakes and presents, and she and my wife sometimes garden together. But we're still on second-name terms, and I guess we always will be, because here it's the older person who decides when to go on to first-name terms. I call his son Kurt, because he's younger than me, and sometimes he calls me Cliff, but I can see what an effort it is for him. It's not prejudice or anything, just one of their customs. I guess it goes back centuries."

"Do you have any children?" I asked.

"No."

"Do you intend to?"

There was a slight pause and he said, "If it works out that way."

"What are you going to do when your Army time is up?"

"I know what I'd like to do, but that's not to say I'll do it. I'd like to get a job in U.S. government service right here in Germany. This is a great country."

"You'd rather live here than in the States?"

"Not for everything. But on balance, yes."

"And your wife?"

He smiled. "You must ask her."

So I went out to Bingen, to a bright modern house with a view across an orchard to a wooded hill. In the sitting room there were musical notes on the wall, a black bust of a white girl with blue eyes, a tea wagon on brass wheels, a stuffed toy tiger, plants in pots.

Helena Mander was a pretty, dark-haired girl in her early twenties, with rather a wooden, vacant face and none of her husband's intellect. She spoke good English, but with a limited vocabulary, and she kept her eyes on the floor. I asked her if she had ever had doubts about marrying a colored man, and she said no, that was what she had always wanted to do.

"And your parents?"

"They were very pleased. They like Cliff a lot."

"They didn't mind his being colored?"

"No, it didn't bother them."

"What's it like living here?"

She tugged at a handkerchief and said, "I get a little lonesome. See, I wanted to live on the post. But Cliff likes to get away from the post after work, and come out here. It's okay then, but in the daytime it gets lonesome. People here don't drop in on you like they do in the States. In the States they dropped in on us all the time."

"What do you do all day?"

"I go to the post most mornings and shop and see my friends. See, we have two cars."

"Are your friends white or colored?"

"Colored mostly. It doesn't bother me. Sometimes I think the whites don't want to be too friendly with the colored."

"You don't have any children?"

"No."

I felt I was embarrassing her, so I didn't push it. "I don't want children yet. I like to do things with Cliff and have a good time and go to parties."

"Do you think you might have children one day?"

"Could be."

"Do you think that having children that are half white and half colored could mean a lot of problems?"

"No, I don't see why." She answered as though she hadn't ever thought about it.

I said, "If you're lonesome here, and you don't want children yet, have you thought of taking a job?"

Eyes on the floor, she said, "When we lived in the States I had a job as cashier. It was good money. I could get a job at the post if I wanted. But they don't pay enough. It's not worth it."

"When your husband finishes with the Army, where would you like to live?"

For the first time she looked up, gave a hint of a smile and said, "Oh, the United States. It's much freer and friendlier than here. Everyone is so friendly. It's cheaper too."

It was a strange situation the Manders were in. He, an American, was happier living in Germany, while she, a German, was happier in America. How would they resolve it? And there was another thought which kept nagging at my mind: Did he, when he married her, think he was marrying above him? And did he think so still?

✪

I FOUND the colonel at the bar of the officers' club, sipping tomato juice, a shrunken, chastened figure. He shook my hand and smiled sweetly and said, "Gee, I'm sorry I bugged out on you last night. One of these days I'll have to learn not to drink wine after whisky on an empty stomach." The more I saw of the colonel the more I loved him.

We went in to lunch and the colonel told me about himself and his future. His home was in Pennsylvania, about seventy miles from Pittsburgh. His wife was taking a pharmacy course, which was why she hadn't joined him in Frummingen. They had no children. He had been in the Army nineteen years and could retire on pension after twenty. "But until I have done two years as lieutenant colonel, I would get only fifty percent of major's pay. So I think I'll stay on until the two years are up and then retire. After that I might teach or write—you know, specialist articles for *Male* or *Stag,* and things like that. Or I could stay on another six years and get promoted to full colonel. There are a lot of opportunities for advancement just now, and that would mean I could retire on full colonel's pay, which works out at—let's see"—he pulled out an army pocket diary and consulted the back—"around ten thousand dollars a year." He closed the book and said, "But I reckon that two more years will probably do me, provided I don't go on too many benders, and keep my temper to myself. Sergeant Cogswell will tell you I have the greatest difficulty in not blowing my top when things go wrong. I wish I could be more calm. That's a thing I admire in the British."

"You like the British?"

"Yes, I do. I admire your Army particularly. A British Army officer says to a man, 'Do this or that,' and the man salutes and goes away and does it. In our Army we have to do a lot more explaining. The soldiers don't take too easily to discipline and want to know the reason for doing a thing. Also, your people take everything much easier and enjoy your leisure more. A lot of the pressures and competitiveness of U.S. business life have begun to spill over into the Army. I work from eight to five on weekdays and often Saturdays, and parts of Sundays too. It's all quite unnecessary."

I spent the afternoon walking round the *Kaserne,* although, it being a Saturday, there wasn't much doing. The administration block was empty except for two sentries. At the end of a corridor was a lobby full of mementoes, sports trophies in a glass case, a citation from the Transatlantic Council of Boy Scouts, and blown-up photographs of previous commanding generals, who looked as identical and boring as mayors of English towns.

The corridor itself was hung with pictures illustrating the attributes and obligations that the United States Army expected of its soldiers. The first picture showed a GI advancing with fixed bayonet and blood-thirsty expression, and beneath was the caption "I am an American fighting man." The next showed the same man lying on his tummy, cutting barbed wire; the caption here was, "I will make every effort to escape." A third picture showed him being interrogated by the enemy, and this said, "I will give only my name, rank, and serial number and date of birth. I owe this to God, Home, Country." Finally, he was shown battling against impossible odds with a rather bomb-happy expression on his face. "I will never surrender of my own free will," said the caption. "I will trust in my God and the United States of America." For a country whose churches were unestablished, the emphasis on God was surprising.

I left the administration block and walked down Sadowski Street, the main street of the base, with trees on either side and the sun filtering down through the branches. There were a few soldiers about and I thought how ridiculously overloaded they were with badges and ribbons and insignia of rank—compensation, perhaps, for the dullness of the life. Halfway down Sadowski Street was a sign which said that Sergeant Sadowski's tank had been hit and set on fire in an action at Valhey, France, in 1944: all the crew evacuated except the bowgunner, and Sergeant Sadowski went back to save him "thru' withering cross-fire" and was killed. But his action inspired the rest of the force to attack with such ferocity that they took their objective. Pieri Avenue was named after another such hero: at one corner its original German name, Boeldestrasse, was still up.

The enlisted men's club was near here, and I went in. Although it was a warm, sunny afternoon, the place was crowded with soldiers shouting and drinking beer and playing the jukebox and fruit machines. In the lobby was a notice which said, "This Week's Special. Direct from Nashville. Grand Ole Opry and RCA Star, the Great Hank Locklin." There was a picture of Hank in a fancy jacket designed with flowers; a nice contrast to the American fighting man. Next to it, another notice said, "Today's Menu. Saulsbury steak, french fries, peas, 65 cents." Opposite was a third notice: "Regulations for Women's Dress. No halters, toreador pants, pedal pushers, blue jeans, shorts of any length."

The Special Services club up the road was quieter. There were a lot of Negroes in there, playing billiards and reading in the library and developing films in the Photo Club. There were advertisements for pottery classes and pinochle lessons, tours of Germany and Europe, and an offer by the American Express Company: "Jet Home for Christmas for Thirty Dollars Down."

Later I went back to the V.I.P. suite and lay down on the steaming bed to sleep a little before the colonel came.

✪

YOU WON'T believe the next bit.

The colonel had said at lunch that he would take me in the evening to a place called Ehsenbach to see Doc Smith and his wife, who were living on the economy. To get there by seven, we should leave at six forty-five.

The colonel showed up at six forty-five on the dot. On the way into Frummingen he said jokingly that we wouldn't get lost this time, as he had brought a map. We both forced little laughs.

We drove through Frummingen and Boll and Bad Boll, and then we were lost. "This isn't the road to Ehsenbach," said the colonel. "I guess we'll have to go back to Bad Boll and ask."

"What about the map?" I said. "Oh, the map's for when we get to Ehsenbach," said the colonel. "It's to find Doc Smith's house."

We drove back to Bad Boll and asked some people the way to Ehsenbach, but they were attending a convention and were strangers there themselves. Then a garage man showed us the road, and, believe it or not, we were soon in Ehsenbach. But then our troubles began. For the colonel's map turned out to be not a map in the generally accepted sense of the word, but a drawing which the colonel had made from Doc Smith's instructions on the telephone. We held it all ways up, but it didn't make any sense at all; it looked like a blueprint for a homemade computer. So we forgot about the map and asked people to direct us to where the Smiths lived. Most people didn't know and said so; others thought they knew and sent us in contrary directions. We arrived at Doc Smith's at five past eight, or an hour and twenty minutes after starting.

Doc Smith was a pale, bearded young doctor and he had a tall, handsome, healthy-looking wife. Neither seemed too pleased at our lateness, but the colonel was full of apologies, and they soon found, as I had, that he was such a ducky little man you couldn't be angry with him for long. "I guess yours must be the only house in the street showing lights?" said the colonel, cunningly switching the conversation. "Yeah," said Doc Smith, "the Germans live in caverns."

Mrs. Smith produced coffee and biscuits, and we sat down and talked. The Smiths were great talkers; sometimes they both talked at once, which made listening difficult.

"When we first came here, a year ago," said Doc Smith, "the Germans treated us as though we didn't exist. Then I began giving them lifts into town and gradually the barriers broke down."

"They'll never completely break down," said Mrs. Smith. "They don't know how to unbend."

"Germans never invite anyone into their houses," said the doctor, "unless they are very educated and sophisticated."

"When they do," said the wife, "they take about two weeks preparing for it. And when you get there, they tell you just where to sit."

"Of course, they love to come *here* any time," said the doctor, "and drink our booze and smoke our cigarettes. We haven't had anybody refuse an invitation yet."

"One morning soon after we got here," said his wife, "I was talking in the street to a married girl who lives a few houses away, and I asked her over for coffee. 'When?' she said, and I said, 'Right now.' So she looked completely startled and said yes, she'd love to, but instead of coming, she went back to her own house, made her face up, changed her dress, and *then* came over. Next day she asked me to have coffee with her, and I went over as I was."

"Do you both speak German well?" I said.

"We get by all right now," said the doctor, "but we couldn't speak a word when we arrived. I had to put this house in order, get a shower installed, have curtains fixed up, and the wires changed in the icebox and the dryer, all in a language I didn't understand."

"Did they take advantage of you?"

"They can do. Last year I arranged with a travel agent in Frummingen for a vacation in Greece. We were booked to go on a certain steamer, but when we saw what a broken-down old tub it was, I canceled the passage. When I got back I went to the travel agent and asked for a refund. The girl thought that because I spoke in English I couldn't understand German. I heard her say to a colleague in German, 'He's an American, he can afford it,' so I said to her in German, 'No, I can't afford it,' and I got my refund."

"The Germans put up rents for Americans," said Mrs. Smith. "It's a well-known thing. Anyone will tell you about it."

"I didn't get a telephone installed till I'd been here a year," said the doctor. "This meant that every night I was on duty I had to sleep at the post. I applied for a telephone and they said there was a long waiting list. So then a German doctor moved in on the next street, and he got a telephone right away. I went to the post office and told them, and said, 'Why can't I have one?' And they said, 'Well, he had a previous number and you didn't.' "

"Didn't you take it up at the base?"

"I mentioned it to a few people, but they weren't interested. Americans don't want to offend foreigners, because they want everyone to like them. I don't give a damn about that."

"Do you like the Germans?" I said.

"I'd put it this way," said the doc, "if I was in a fight, I'd rather have them with me than against me. They don't care about anyone except themselves. But they are something. Now there are some people who are nothing. You take those Italians who work in the toy factory in the town. You could put them into a ball of wax and throw them up against the wall and they'd still be nothing. But get alone with a German and have a real, good talk and you get somewhere."

Mrs. Smith said, "When Bob first came here, he hated England and France and thought Germany was great. Didn't you, dear?"

"Don't you think Germany's a real clean country?" said the colonel. "I'd say it was cleaner than America."

"Well, it is and it isn't," said the doc. "There's a lot of hoof-and-mouth around and a lot of T.B., and for this reason I don't eat their meat or drink their milk."

"You don't eat this nice Swabian veal?" said the colonel.

"No, sir," said the doctor, "but we're not narrow or anything. We do travel around. I'd say we'd seen more of this part of Germany than most Germans who live here. We come back from a trip and hand round the pictures, and they say, 'Where's that?' "

"They're so narrow," said Mrs. Smith, "it's unbelievable."

"I think they're waiting for another Hitler," said the doc. "One night we went to dinner with a family here, and we all got a little high, and afterward, when I was asking how it was in Germany before the war, the father goes over to a big chest and pulls out this huge scrapbook and wraps it in brown paper so that no one will see, and says to me, take that home and look at it and you will see how it was in Germany before the war. So we brought it back here and opened it, and it was full of pictures of Hitler at Nuremberg rallies and launching battleships and cheering crowds and girls with roses and Goering and Goebbels with dogs and pussy-cats and all that. My guess is that there are a lot of people around here who think that what went wrong the last two times was bad luck, but next time it will be okay."

✪

THE SILENT California driver arrived at the V.I.P. suite to take me to the airport. The colonel and Sergeant Cogswell were there, too. "Goodbye Sergeant Cogswell," I said, "and please go on taking care of the colonel." Sergeant Cogswell said he would and the colonel laughed. I was really sorry to say goodbye to the colonel, and I think he was sorry, too; we had shared much together, you could almost say we had been through the same campaign. As the car was about to draw away, the colonel said, "Hell, I never did give you that press information kit, did I? I'll have to send it on."

It was a warm, sunny day, and the German countryside looked green and pleasing. But the driver was true to form, rigid in his seat, his eyes fixed on the road ahead; and the hour's journey was broken only by the following dialogue.

"How do you like it here, driver?"

"How's that, sir?"

"I said, how do you like it here?"

"I don't like it too much, sir."

"Oh? Why's that?"

"It's too cold."

At the airport I was met by a young man with a ginger crew cut who introduced himself as Army Specialist Pete Clore. He was a reporter from the Armed Forces Network, A.F.N., and wanted to interview me about Frummingen. But he seemed more interested in talking about himself. He came from Iowa, he said, and had never done any reporting or interviewing before joining the Army. "But I really go for this news side of things," he said, "and when I quit the Army I aim to get fixed up in a job with some European broadcasting station." I asked him if he spoke any languages, and he laughed nervously and said, "Well, I'm not too good with my German, I guess, and I'm not too good with my French either." His views on any subject were banal, and each banality was preceded by a kind of trumpet voluntary designed to arrest the attention. "Here's how I see the situation. [Pause.] News is about people, and people in my estimation are great. I just love getting around and meeting people. The way I look at it is this. It's a kind of education." Or, again, "Here's how I see the Germans. [Pause.] The Germans are one of the most industrious people in Europe. In fact, I would say *the* most industrious people." I expected him to add that they didn't have too much humor, and he might have done so, but his colleague handed him a mike, and he said into it, "Army Specialist Pete Clore at Municipal Airport. . . ." Why "Army Specialist"? I thought. Why not "A.F.N. reporter"? Why always this American obsession with making things seem bigger than they are? Why "ocean" instead of "sea," why "forest" instead of "wood," "mountain" instead of "hill," *why "V.I.P. suite" instead of "guest room"?* "Slug the following," said Pete. "Interview with Ludovic Kennedy, British writer, lecturer and broadcaster . . ."

Forty minutes later I flew south.

Part Four

 NEAR EAST AND
MIDDLE EAST

ATHENS
ISTANBUL
JERUSALEM
SAUDI ARABIA
IRAN

I WENT to Athens to visit the United States Sixth Fleet. First I was to call on the Commander in Chief, Vice-Admiral Ellis, whose flagship, the cruiser *Springfield,* was at anchor in the harbor. Then I was to be flown on board the aircraft carrier *Shangri-la,* steaming toward Istanbul.

The American Sixth Fleet is the last in a long line of naval squadrons which have for generations policed the Mediterranean. For nearly two hundred and fifty years this sea was dominated by British sea power and British admirals: Mahon at Minorca, Rooke at Gibraltar, Keith at Toulon, Nelson at the Nile, Sidney Smith at Acre, de Robeck at Gallipoli, Cunningham at Matapan. But after the Second World War, with Britain no longer able to fulfill her traditional role, there was a power vacuum. This the American Sixth Fleet has since filled, its fifty ships and twenty-five thousand men ranging the whole Mediterranean from the Straits of Gibraltar to the Sea of Marmara. In older days France and Spain were the enemies. Now it is Russia, whose own ships are penetrating the Mediterranean in increasing numbers. But the job of the Sixth Fleet, both being there and being seen there, is essentially the same as its predecessors'.

In Athens I stayed at the Hilton and was given a room like any room in any Hilton anywhere. When I had drawn the curtains and shut out the Parthenon, I might have been in New York or Geneva or Mexico City. There was a stack of hotel literature in my room, including a voucher for a free drink at the Pan Bar. When I rang down and said could I have my free drink in my room, as I was leaving next day before the Pan Bar opened, they said no. Then I found a form asking for comments and suggestions on improving the hotel service, which would be forwarded to Mr. Hilton *personally*. So I wrote: "Dear Mr. Hilton: What difference does it make to you whether I have your free drink in my room or at the Pan Bar?" Then I figured how he might answer it. "Dear Mr. Kennedy: This difference, that you are more likely to have a second and third drink in the Pan Bar, and less likely in your room." But I signed it all the same.

In the morning I found a radio dial beside my bed. I flipped it on and made my first acquaintance with a broadcasting facility which was to haunt me through the Middle and Far East and which for sheer awfulness of output must be unrivaled anywhere. This was A.F.N., the American Armed Forces Network.

I forget the name of the show that I tuned in to. They had a real wise guy of a commentator called Ray. "What's the difference between a two-year-old heifer and a sixteen-year-old girl?" he said. A fall guy said he didn't know. "Well, I'll tell you," said Ray. "Fourteen years!" There was a studio audience who *laughed* at that. I imagined they had a man who put up one of those "Please laugh now" signs. "A woman was knitting and telling jokes at the same time," Ray went on; "what did they call her?" "I don't know." "You don't know? They called her a nitwit!" More laughter.

Then we had a girl who said she was a member of what sounded like the Forage Club, which I gathered was some kind of do-good organization, and it seemed she had won an important cup. "Now, who is this cup awarded by?" asked Ray, obviously knowing, and the girl went into hushed tones and said, "Ray, this cup is awarded annually by the President of the United States." The audience started clapping like mad at this, and Ray practically screamed at us, "Well, how about *that*? How about it? Isn't that just *great*?" He couldn't have got more excited if the cup had been awarded by the Holy Ghost. When the clapping died down, Ray interviewed the girl about what he called her philosophy. She said things like "One of the lessons I've learned from life, Ray, is that the most valued things are the things we share." The audience drank it all in silently, anxious to savor every moment; but they gave her what Ray asked for, a big hand at the end.

After this we had more jokes, two schmaltzy poems about God, and a hymn, and then it was time for a singer called Dick, who had appeared regularly on the show but was now leaving it, to say goodbye to Ray. Dick was almost as loathsome as Ray. "Well, Ray," he said, "I can honestly say I'll be real sorry to go. It's been real nice working with you people, you've been so nice and friendly—I know this is the right thing to say, but this group . . . well, this group—" He wanted to say they were the most wonderful group he had ever worked with, but he couldn't manage the lie. Someone in the group said quietly, "We're a great group"; and then they all laughed to hide their embarrassment, and there were more wisecracks about what a great group they were and what a great guy Dick was and how sorry Ray was and everyone else was to see him go.

There was also some very crude and nasty anti-Russian propaganda. Ray introduced a professor, who said, "We all know the difficulties the Russians have in their farming and their crops, but now it seems they're also having trouble with their fish. The sturgeon in the Sea of Azov are all dying as a result of industrial water pollution. While lectures are being given about the superiority of Communist rule, the sturgeon in the Sea of Azov are dying."

When the show was over I drew back the curtains and let in the Parthenon. Christ, I thought, this is the same air that Aristotle and Socrates breathed; they used to live round the corner. Was this the result of three thousand years of progress? My American friends never stopped telling me that American commercial television and radio were as bad as they were because of their economics, of having always to pander to the popular taste. A.F.N. was free of any such obligation, yet perversely it had chosen to copy all that was worst in the commercial system without adding anything original or beneficial of its own. Indeed, all it had added was a phony, holier-than-thou morality, which resulted in programs like this being both vulgar *and* priggish. Was this really the image of themselves that the American government and armed forces wanted to give to the world? It would seem so, for there was no attempt at simulation: the programs were beamed out for all to hear on the public airwaves of the world. It was amazing.

✪

AT A place called the Phaleron Delta landing, I was met by the Sixth
Fleet public-relations officer, a Commander Castillo, small and spectacled and sallow, and not unlike my little colonel, and we embarked
in a boat for the *Springfield*. She was a much bigger ship than most
cruisers I had seen, and as we approached I saw that on the ship's
superstructure was painted a huge map of the Mediterranean, blue
for the sea and yellow for the land. Above this was written in big
letters, "SIXTH FLEET," and below, "POWER FOR PEACE."
Commander Castillo said that the map showed the operational area
the Sixth Fleet covered, and that "Power for Peace" was its motto.
Higher up, on the side of the bridge, were huge painted medal ribbons, such as servicemen wear on their tunics. Commander Castillo
said these represented the campaigns the ship had been in during the
Second World War.

The admiral's flag lieutenant was waiting on the quarter-deck and
took us to the admiral's cabin. It was a spacious cabin, with paneled
walls on which hung another map of the Mediterranean and several
prints. The admiral was alert, dapper, clean-shaven, handsome, courteous, humorous, self-confident and modest. What American or British admiral isn't?

The admiral said he understood that I wished to study the relations
between the fleet and the peoples of the countries it visited. He was
glad of this, because it was something that occupied ninety percent of
his time and that of his staff. It was a job that never ended, because
new men were joining the fleet every week. "It's often difficult," he
said, "to convince an eighteen-year-old American boy that he's not in
his own country and can't behave as though he were; but we try like
hell. I think things *have* improved over the years. I would say we get
across to about sixty percent of the men completely and another
thirty percent almost completely, which leaves something under ten
percent that you can never get across to at all. With those we don't
waste time." He made a dramatic gesture with his arm. "We lower
the boom on them right away." I looked puzzled. "We send them
home."

"What is your biggest problem as regards relationships?" I said.

"Our biggest problem, Mr. Kennedy, is that we are now about the only navy in the world that has no alcohol on board. So when our people get ashore they are apt to drink too much too fast. Also, they're not used to wine, which in the Mediterranean is plentiful and cheap."

"Wouldn't it be a good idea if prohibition in the Navy were lifted?"

"I think that people like myself should be authorized to carry a small wine mess, so that when I entertain people who are used to wine I can offer it. The Greek royal family came to lunch when I was on the *Forrestal*, and I couldn't give them a thing. Now, Queen Frederika is a woman who likes wine with her lunch, and she made it clear that she does—dammit! I was embarrassed, I don't mind telling you. But I don't think that's sufficient reason for changing the whole system. We've been without drink too long to start it now."

"Even if it might mean less drunkenness ashore?"

"In relation to the numbers involved, it's surprising how little there is. Please don't think I'm trying to minimize it, it's something we're thinking about all the time, for one stupid incident can wipe out the good will of an entire visit. But we go to great lengths to see that the men keep out of trouble—not only with the indoctrination programs beforehand, but even after liberty has been granted. If our shore patrols see a man who obviously has had too much, they have authority to send him back on board then and there. That way we try and nip trouble in the bud."

"What ports do the sailors like visiting best?"

"Mostly the big places where they can get absorbed. Myself, I prefer small places, because it cuts down on my diplomatic activities! Cannes is delighted to see us in December but not in July, because we don't have as much money as the average tourist. The men like Barcelona, and Palma too, because of all those single British girls around."

"Are the sailors provoked by anti-Americanism?"

"I wouldn't say so. In most places anti-Americanism seems to take the form of smashing U.S.I.S. library windows. But sometimes in places like Marseilles our men are approached by Communist agents who want to make a deal with them."

"Like what?"

"Trading military secrets for money."

"What happens?"

"Generally our boys get so mad they punch them in the nose, instead of letting us know who they are. In this way we lose any advantage we might gain."

Between asking the admiral questions, I took a look round his cabin. On the paneling I noticed a Buffet reproduction and a Dufy print of Cannes, also a sad, bad picture of a gray rolling sea framed by a couple of rocks. The admiral said he loved this picture. Next to it was a picture of some Mediterranean harbor; the admiral said he didn't know where this was; it was in the cabin when he came.

There was quite a lot of greenery in the cabin, including a small tree in a red pot. "That's a good Communist cypress," said the admiral, "given to me by the mayor of Dubrovnik." Close to it was an ornate table heavily decorated with bronze. "That's a Spanish table. We cut a hole in the middle of it and put in this bronze Moroccan charcoal burner. In cold weather you fill the burner with charcoal and it keeps your feet warm. We use it as a conversation piece."

"How do you mean?"

"Well, sometimes when mayors and other dignitaries call on me, the conversation is apt to dry up. Sooner or later someone notices the table, like you did, and asks a question about it, and this gives me the opportunity to explain, and they find the whole thing very intriguing."

As we left, the admiral said, "Do you smoke?"

"No."

"Then I won't give you one of these."

I looked down and saw in his hand a cigarette lighter marked "Sixth Fleet."

✪

THE CAPTAIN of the *Springfield,* Captain Hildreth, lived on a deck above the admiral. He was good-looking, too, in a Cary Grant way. He said his wife would be arriving later to help entertain some Greeks at a community-relations lunch, and he hoped I would stay for that.

Captain Hildreth told me that the *Springfield* was based at Villefranche, though as the flagship was always on the move, they had spent only ten out of the last 117 days there. "When we get there, we send five hundred men ashore, that's half the watch, and within minutes you won't find one of them. They've gone home and changed into civilian clothes. They've *melted* into the economy."

"What's it like, living there?"

"We live in a villa ourselves," said Captain Hildreth. "We're surrounded by French people. I like it. It's great. It's a challenge." He said this as though Villefranche were a village in the African bush.

"Of course, we don't have any commissary or PX like the Army. Some of the wives were beefing about this the other day and I had to call them together and say, 'Look, girls, this isn't the U.S. We get our bread trucked down from Germany and our milk trucked down from Holland.'"

"Why don't you get French bread? It's the best in the world."

"Well, maybe it is, but the sailors don't like it. And I understand that French milk isn't considered safe for children."

"For American children?"

"Sure."

"How is your French?"

"I'm not too good with it. I like to think I speak it, but I know I don't. My wife speaks kitchen French. When she came to Villefranche, she couldn't speak a word, although she'd done three years of French in high school. I guess it must have been the wrong kind of French. She knows enough now to run a household and tell the mazook man where to put the mazook."

"Do many of your officers speak French?" I said.

"We have about sixty who speak French more or less fluently, most of them junior officers. The other day in Toulon the French cruiser *Colbert* invited fifteen officers to lunch, and I sent over fifteen perfect French speakers. The people in the *Colbert* were absolutely amazed. I think they'd detailed a lot of English speakers. They've been talking about it ever since."

"Do you have any official interpreters on board?"

"None. I have at least one officer who is fluent in the language of every country we're likely to visit."

"Including Turkish and Arabic?"

"Including Turkish and Arabic."

"To get back to Villefranche," I said, "what happens about children's education?"

"Well, a few of the children—about a dozen, I guess—go to the French schools and they learn French very rapidly. Their only problem is trying to establish an equivalency of grades when they get home. But most of the children, including ours, go to an American school in Beaulieu run by the Department of Defense. There are one hundred forty-five children there from grades one to eight."

"Do your children learn French at this school?" I asked.

"Oh, sure."

"Who teaches them, an American or French teacher?"

Captain Hildreth rubbed his hand over his chin and said, "Tell you the truth, I don't know. That's a heck of a thing! I don't know who teaches my child French." He reached for the telephone and said, "I'll ask the executive officer. He'll know." He dialed a number and spoke to the executive officer. "It seems," he said, putting down the phone, "that the French teaching used to be done on the side by a local girl who was the school secretary. But, according to the exec, we had to let this secretary go, because of the balance-of-payments position—something to do with the flow of gold—so now it seems we have an American teacher teaching French."

I thought of Mrs. Hildreth spending three years at high school learning the wrong kind of French, and I said, "That seems incredible, doesn't it, living in the middle of France and having an American teacher teach French?"

But Captain Hildreth didn't seem to think so. "Well," he said, "I guess that's the way it is."

A Negro steward approached with a tray of drinks, and I thought, Ah, a nice dry martini, and then I remembered. The steward poured out two Cokes, and Captain Hildreth and I drank each other's health.

"With all these courtesy visits you make," I said, "don't the sailors get rather bored?"

"We always have their welfare in mind. For example, before we visit a major port we contact a travel agency and they fix tours into the interior, sometimes for two or three days. If we didn't do that, some of the men who stop off at the first bar outside the dockyard gates would never get any further. We also encourage athletics. We even have a soccer team. In two years we've never won a game, but we generally lose quite respectably—five–two, that kind of thing. We get a lot of fun out of it, and so do the teams we play."

The Negro steward went out, and I said, "Do you have many colored men on board?"

"I wondered when you'd get around to asking about that," said Captain Hildreth.

"I hadn't thought of asking about it at all," I said. "It was just seeing that colored steward made me think about it."

"It's generally the first question I get asked," said Captain Hildreth. He seemed very sensitive about it. "I would guess around the national average, which is ten to eleven percent."

"Why don't you know?" I said.

"I have absolutely no documents to tell me. The only way I could find out would be to muster all the colored men on deck and count them."

"But isn't there a record of their being colored on their papers?"

"No, sir," said Captain Hildreth, "there's none. It's all part of this civil-rights thing. Not even the Navy Department knows from a man's papers whether he's white or colored. The only place it's ever marked is on the death certificate. The civil-rights people have okayed death, because you have to describe a corpse for identification purposes."

"I suppose that in their ignorance the Navy Department might appoint a ship which turned out to be one hundred percent white, or fifty percent colored?"

"I guess in theory it could," said Captain Hildreth, "but I've never known it to happen."

Captain Hildreth's wife arrived. She was a tall, pretty blonde wearing very pale lipstick and some silvery stuff on her eyelids. Captain Hildreth said she joined him in most ports to help with social commitments. He didn't get any special allowance for this, and often it turned out quite expensive.

At one we went down to the wardroom and joined twenty prominent Athenians and their wives whom the mess were entertaining to lunch. The seating had been arranged so that there was a *Springfield* officer next to each Athenian husband or wife. I sat next to one of the lieutenant commanders and a Mrs. Gollipopoulos.

For lunch we had soup, salad with an American dressing, some kind of melancholy meat, ice cream and coffee. To drink there was milk, Coke or iced water. Mrs. Gollipopoulos said, "I feel we are eating in the nursery." I said, "How do you mean?" and she said, "Not being allowed any wine. It's as though we had done something wrong and were being punished." I saw what she meant. One had this curious sense of deprivation, of being deliberately denied something that to every European peasant was as basic as water or bread. I wondered if, for all their professions of understanding, the Americans knew of the real bloody-mindedness that their policy of prohibition aroused in wine-drinking guests, and whether they would pursue it so obstinately if they did know. On this occasion certainly it was a moot point whether community relations had been improved or harmed.

"Ah, these Americans!" said Mrs. Gollipopoulos. "They do such stupid things. They had a man in the U.S.I.S. here a few years ago called Ben Jackson. He was a brilliant man. He spoke Greek fluently. He went to Greek parties, he knew all about our history and our politics and everything. And what happened? The Americans didn't like the way he was carrying on. They thought he was getting *too* interested in Greece, so they sent him somewhere like East Pakistan. How stupid can you get? And then his successor came and he was just the opposite, he couldn't speak any Greek. He learned a few phrases in his awful accent and then tried them out on you with pride. He never went to Greek parties or met Greek people. I said to his stupid wife one day, 'Why don't you get about and go to Greek parties?' and she said, 'Well, if we did that, we'd get moved like Ben Jackson to East Pakistan.' "

After the ice cream, someone banged on the table and Captain Hildreth got up and said, "Ladies and gentlemen . . . I'm particularly delighted to have the ladies here today. . . . *Springfield* only returns home every three years . . . We're very happy to visit with you and see the wonderful old monuments and ruins you have here . . . and we like your coming to visit with us, and we'd be very happy to show you something of the *Springfield* if your busy schedule permits. . . . We have arranged on the fantail a missile demonstration. . . . We have Terrier missiles which are ship-to-air missiles, and if your schedule is not too tight, why, we'd like to show them to you."

Escorted by the ship's officers, we made our way along the ship. We passed one sign which said "Officers Country" and another which said "Ladies Retiring Room" and a third which said "Herman Hubbard —Sailor of the Month."

We assembled in a group on the fantail, which was right at the stern of the ship. The missile turret was in front of us. I thought, from what Captain Hildreth had said, that we were going to see the missiles fired, but Commander Castillo said no, they were just going to show them to us. A Greek-speaking officer gave us a short lecture about them, and then the doors of the turret opened and two missiles came sliding out of their sheaths. They looked like two great randy, circumcised penises, blue on the stem and with yellow knobs. On the blue part was painted "Power for Peace," in big black letters. The missile officer moved them up and down and from side to side like a man indulging in indecent exposure, and then returned them to their sheaths and closed the door. I found it a big disappointment, and Mrs. Gollipopoulos thought it a joke. Commander Castillo must have seen the look on my face, for he gave me a blue balloon with "Power for Peace" written on it in six different Mediterranean languages. "This is a gimmick we give the children," he said. "We have kites like that, too."

I walked back to the wardroom with a bald, gentle American civilian of about sixty, whose collar was joined by a pin underneath the knot of his tie. He said he worked at the U.S.I.S. office ashore. It was he who had chosen the guests for the lunch.

"Did you once have a man there called Ben Jackson?" I asked.

"We did. We did. He was a brilliant man. Almost a genius, really."

"I hear that he went too native."

"Well, yes, he did in a way. You see, he had this absolute flair for languages. He could speak Greek like a Greek. But this did have its disadvantages. After all, the object of the U.S.I.S. is to explain the United States to foreigners, and I guess Ben Jackson got a little too identified with the other side."

"What happened to him?"

"He came and served under me in East Pakistan."

"Under you?"

"Yes, and do you know, he was speaking fluent Bengali within six months. He's really an incredible guy."

"What's he doing now?"

"As a matter of fact, he's back here in Athens. He's taking some leave. He's writing a book about some obscure Greek poet."

"What an extraordinary coincidence," I said.

"Yes, it *is* odd, isn't it. Yes."

✪

LATER THAT afternoon Commander Castillo took me to the military airport. On the way he said, "There's a little matter the executive officer is quite upset about and wants me to clear up."

I thought, What gaffe have I made?

"I understand that you were asking the Captain about who does the French teaching at the school in Villefranche, and the Captain called up Commander Hooper, and Commander Hooper said it was being done by an American teacher."

"Is Commander Hooper the executive officer?"

"Yes."

"Yes," I said, "that's what I understood him to have said."

"Well, that wasn't quite correct. The executive officer did some checking up on the matter, and now it seems that they don't have a French schedule."

"You mean no one teaches them French?"

"That's correct. I gather that in this school there has to be a very strict ratio of teachers to pupils, and they just can't afford it. Of course they have one morning's exchange a week with a local French school—our pupils go there one day and their pupils come to us another—and they pick up quite a lot of French during everyday life."

"But they don't actually get taught it?"

"No, they don't. Commander Hooper was very anxious that I should clarify the position for you. He didn't want to feel that you'd been given wrong information."

"Well, that was very good of him. Please tell him I appreciate that very much."

"I certainly will."

✪

I HAD hoped that when flying out to the *Shangri-la* I might sit next to the pilot and so see ourselves landing on the deck. But our plane had only a small cockpit for pilot and navigator, and this was sealed off from the rest by a large bulkhead. There were three passengers, and we sat in a tiny boxed-in compartment, surrounded by yellow mail-bags, and with only one small window. We wore bright-orange life-saving jackets in case we fell into the sea, and were strapped to our seats by belts over the shoulders as well as round the middle. I was told this was necessary because of the terrific pressure put on the body by the carrier's arresting gear.

The man next to me was a very young pilot who was rejoining the carrier after a week ashore. He had slightly damaged his plane while attempting to land on board and had been told on the R/T not to make a second try but to land instead on an airfield in Sicily. He was now reporting back on board. He didn't know how long it would be before his plane was repaired, but he hoped it would be soon. "Oh, boy, oh, boy," he kept saying, "it's great to be getting home. Just think, tonight I'll be sleeping in my own bunk again." He looked about twenty-two.

We waited fifteen minutes at the end of the runway, then took off and climbed to six thousand feet. We flew for about an hour, and then the "Fasten Seat Belts/No Smoking" sign came on. The young pilot leaned over and saw that I was securely strapped. He said, "When you see the carrier's wake down there, that means we're real close." I nodded. "Just before we touch down, put your head right back on the headrest—otherwise it may get thrown back."

We lost height. The sea got nearer and nearer. It changed color from blue to a greeny-white, and I realized that this must be the *Shangri-la*'s wake. The wait seemed to be interminable, and I thought, I don't want to land on this carrier after all, I've changed my mind, let's go back to Athens. Then, all at once, it seemed, the engines cut out, I saw the *Shangri-la*'s flight deck, there was a terrible roaring sound in my ears, I felt my body being crushed by a great weight and the air squeezed out of it, and then suddenly everything was very still. We had landed.

I sat for a moment where I was, getting my breath back. Someone unstrapped me, and I climbed unsteadily out. I suppose I had thought that some junior officer would meet me, but I was quite unprepared for the sight of the rear admiral commanding the carrier squadron, his chief of staff and the flag lieutenant, all standing in line to welcome me at the plane door, I shook hands with them, feeling that I was inspecting the guard.

We all trooped down to the admiral's cabin. The admiral's name was King, and the chief of staff was Captain Boyd. The admiral had a charming cabin, smaller than Vice-Admiral Ellis's, but with shiny dark paneling. Dinner was laid for four, and on the table was a bowl of marvelous orchids. I asked the admiral where they came from and he advised me to take a closer look. They were artificial.

We sat down to dinner at once. Night-flying would be going on later, and the admiral had to be on the bridge. We had a very good dinner, but conversation was sticky. I think the chief of staff and the flag lieutenant felt it not their position to say much unless asked, and the admiral himself, a shy, scholarly-looking man with a domed head and spectacles, wasn't a born conversationalist. I asked him why the *Shangri-la* was so called; a mythical place in a modern novel seemed a funny name for a warship. The admiral said that after Colonel Doolittle's famous squadron had raided Tokyo in 1942, reporters had asked President Roosevelt where the planes had come from. "Let's say they came from *Shangri-la,*" he said, not wanting, for security reasons, to say that they had come from the carrier *Wasp*. Later in the war the *Wasp* was sunk, and when a new carrier was built to replace her it was decided to name her *Shangri-la*.

After this, conversation wilted again. A glass of wine, I reflected, might have helped; and for want of something better to say, I brought the drink subject up and told the admiral what Vice-Admiral Ellis had said about giving lunch to Queen Frederika. The admiral said, "Well, I've given lunch to Queen Frederika, too, and she didn't seem to mind *at all* that there was no wine. I certainly wouldn't want to see the system changed. If ever alcohol did come back I'd like to go out of the Navy for five years and come back and see what had happened. I think a lot of people wouldn't be able to take it."

I thought, This is incredible; this man is saying that American naval officers can discipline themselves in everything except drink, that while their British, French, Italian and German counterparts can all manage not to drink to excess, they cannot.

"When I want a drink," said the admiral, "I don't just want to have one dry martini; I want to have two, maybe three martinis. I don't want to get drunk, but I just want to feel I can relax and sit back and enjoy myself. Now, you can't do that on board ship."

I remembered my wartime years in British destroyers. There were times in harbor, off duty, when we had enjoyed ourselves a lot. We had got very drunk. And there were other times, at sea, when one came down from a cold, wet Atlantic watch and was glad of a single warming glass of sherry or whisky before dinner. One had no need or wish for more. Were the United States Navy, whose fighting record in the Second World War had caught the admiration of the world, incapable of such restraint?

"We generally get on to this drink conversation," said the admiral, rather testily, "when there's nothing else to say. Generally when one has run out of other conversation, one falls back on that."

I thought, Boy, are you sensitive about the subject! Then I thought, I don't blame you, I would be myself; for to have to admit you don't carry drink on board because you can't trust yourselves to handle it is—for a people who set such store on manliness—a humiliating admission of self-defeat.

So there was a little pause, which we all rode out, and then I said, was Istanbul a port the men looked forward to, and how did it compare with other ports?

The admiral said, "I would say the men prefer the Spanish ports most of all, because it's cheaper for them, they can afford to buy things there that they can't afford in French ports, and they have a pretty good time without getting into too much trouble. Istanbul is going to be nice for them, because we shall anchor in the Strait right by the town. Also it's cheap. On the other hand, it's a very sensitive place—they have these very strong feelings about national pride."

"Like the incident of the Turkish flag?" said the chief of staff.

"I was coming to that," said the admiral. "Last year one of our liberty men went ashore in Istanbul, and he bought one of those miniature Turkish flags they sell in the souvenir shops. Later that evening, when he was in a bar and he had a few drinks, he wanted to blow his nose, so he put his hand in his pocket, found the flag and blew on that. Whether he was so drunk he mistook the flag for his handkerchief history doesn't relate. Well, this caused great offense. The barman called the police and the police arrested the fellow. He was tried and sent to prison, and he's still in prison now. He's been there nine months."

The chief of staff said, "There's another story they tell of a liberty man who went into a public toilet to relieve himself, and found in there one of those old ladies who do the cleaning, which you get in a lot of European countries. He'd never seen a woman in a men's toilet before, so he tried to shoo her out. She thought he was trying to rape her, and started screaming blue murder. I believe they straightened that one out and the man was returned to his ship. I'm not too sure."

The admiral said, "It shows the sort of thing you have to watch out for." He reached for his cap. "Like to come up on the bridge?"

☆

ON THE bridge I met the captain and the operations commander and one or two others. It was almost dark. In the blue-black sky, planes circled the carrier like wasps round a nest, waiting the order to land. Astern of us were two destroyers, ready to pick up the pilots of any planes that fell into the sea; ahead were two more destroyers and a cruiser. The admiral said the cruiser was the *Little Rock*.

One by one the planes detached themselves to make a long approach to the ship from astern. For most of the approach each plane appeared as a single light, low down in the sky and not getting any bigger; then suddenly the light blossomed into the shape of a plane, there was a crashing roar as it touched down on the deck, and within seconds one of the arresting wires had brought it to a stop. Sometimes the pilot misjudged the distance and at the last moment decided to overshoot, roaring down the length of the carrier a few feet above the deck.

When all the jets had been landed and stowed away below, another mail plane landed. You could see the difference in speed as it came trundling in. The captain said that it had been to Istanbul, where it had landed an advance shore party and liaison officers to coordinate the visit of the squadron.

The landing lights were switched off, and the captain ordered the officer on watch to turn the ship out of the wind and onto her original course. The admiral said to the operations commander, "Mr. Kennedy's one of the cheapest guests we've ever had, isn't he? There were only four radio messages about him."

The operations commander reached for the radio-message file and said, "Yes, four."

Nosy as ever, I said, "Could I see them?"

The operations commander said, "Certainly." He handed me the file.

The admiral said, "They're not classified, are they?"

The operations commander said, "Two of them are." But by this time, short of seizing the file from my hand, it was too late for them to do anything.

Three of the communications were boring messages about the time and manner of my arrival, but the fourth said this: "Mr. Kennedy is to be given the least possible information about expenditure on community relations."

I said, "I see it says I'm to be given the least possible information about expenditure on community relations."

"Oh, yes," said the admiral, "I'd forgotten that."

"Well, if it's of any help," I said, "that's not a question I'd thought of asking." I handed back the file. "But I can only assume that it's vast." I said this as a joke, not seriously at all. But nobody laughed.

At nine o'clock in the wardroom, they showed a very bad film called *Fail-safe* and the officers made rude cracks about it all the way through. Then an officer called Ensign Knott, who was small and orthodox and had been put in charge of me, said he would take me to my cabin.

My cabin was way forward, just under the flight deck on the port side, and was more depressing than the V.I.P. suite at Frummingen. It had no porthole, and the outer bulkhead curved sharply inward, being part of the bows of the ship. The whole place had been painted bright green a long time ago. Beside the built-in bunk were a tinny gray desk and a tinny gray wardrobe. A telephone on the desk appeared to be covered in dust, but on closer examination this turned out to be a fine spray of dried white paint. Inside the desk was a safe the lock of which had been broken. There was no carpet on the floor, only a scrag end of linoleum with holes in it. There was no soap in the washbasin, and the tooth glass hadn't been cleaned for an age.

As a journalist, one gets used to sleeping in all sorts of rough-and-ready places and making the best of it. But I couldn't avoid comparisons: the big hullo from the admiral on the flight deck, followed by luscious eats in his mess, and then this clapped-out, crummy old cabin. It did seem odd.

✪

NEXT MORNING I was woken at about seven by what sounded like a direct bomb hit overhead. When it happened a second time, I realized that more jets were taking off a few feet above me.

After breakfast in the wardroom, Ensign Knott came along to take me on a tour of the ship. As an ex-sailor I found everything fairly old hat: galleys and boiler rooms in an American carrier aren't much different from those in a British one. But there were one or two surprises, including a spooky moment when, passing through a hangar, I saw a sentry with a pistol beside a group of planes. I asked Ensign Knott what he was doing, and he said, "Well, those planes are armed with nuclear weapons, and we have to be extremely careful who goes near them. It's true, the bombs are not made active till they're airborne, but I guess with those things you just can't be too careful." At the end of this hangar was another sentry with a pistol, standing outside a door. Ensign Knott said the door led to the nuclear-weapons magazine, and the sentry had a list of people who were authorized to go down there. "And not only a list, but photographs of all of them, too."

As we moved about the ship I noticed that the officers had changed out of the blue uniforms they had been wearing the night before into khaki trousers and open khaki shirts. This seemed a sensible as well as attractive gear, and I wondered why the British navy had not adopted it. One or two officers wore mustaches, which looked very odd. Ensign Knott said they were allowed to grow mustaches on tours abroad, but not on duty in the States. The men working on the flight deck wore different-colored overalls, and Ensign Knott said this was for instant recognition: blue for the plane pushers, red for refueling crew, silver for firefighters, and so on.

In the pilot's briefing room a squadron commander was giving instructions to his pilots about some bombing exercise they were going to take part in. On the wall was a big blown-up photograph of three jet fighters escorting a huge bomber. The squadron commander said the bomber was Russian and had come to pry on naval exercises in the Atlantic; the fighter pilots had intercepted it at thirty thousand feet and then followed and photographed it.

I was really struck by those pilots. Some didn't look old enough to have left school, and they all had the same high spirits and boyish enthusiasm as my companion in the mail plane. After the briefing I went with the squadron commander to the flight deck to watch them take off. They clambered into their tiny cockpits like men from Mars, weighed down by rescue equipment, oxygen masks, parachute gear; they were strapped down in their little holes, and the canopies were closed over them; the planes were towed down the flight deck and placed on the catapult gear, and they were blasted into space. I said to the squadron commander that this might be his idea of an enjoyable job, but it wasn't mine. "Well," he said, "some of us would feel pretty lost if we had to sit down for a profession and put pen to paper. It depends what street you're used to walking."

Then Ensign Knott took me to the executive officer's cabin, where there was a conference in progress about arrangements for shore patrols in Istanbul. The conference consisted of the executive officer, three other commanders and four chief petty officers.

The executive officer said, "Let me put Mr. Kennedy in the picture. In every port we start off by setting up a shore patrol H.Q. in a local hall or police station, and we have a staff that stays there. This consists of an officer, a chief petty officer, a yeoman of signals, two drivers and an interpreter.

"On weekends we send two teams ashore for an early patrol at eleven hundred hours. Each team consists of a chief petty officer and ten men. At sixteen hundred, when the main body of liberty men starts coming ashore, they're relieved by four more teams. They take a map of the city with them, and divide it into four areas."

I said, "Don't the liberty men stay mainly in the downtown area?"

One of the commanders said, "You find personnel wherever you go. They tend to wander off." He made them sound like dogs.

One of the chief petty officers said, "The ones who wander off are usually all right. They're generally going somewhere, sightseeing or something. We usually find trouble in the same old places."

The executive officer said, "Our ratio is one shore patrol man to every twenty liberty men."

"That sounds high," I said.

"The other ships are sending their shore patrols too," said the executive officer, "so sometimes when the fleet's in, you'll get as many as ten chief petty officers and a hundred men all on shore patrol at the same time. But it's better to have too many than too few. If we do err, it's on the proper side."

"What are your main problems?" I said. "Drink?"

"Yes," said the executive officer, "and exchange of money."

A man called Commander Terry said, "At Catania we had a little trouble about exchange of money, and at Malta we had a lot of trouble. We found the Maltese were short-changing us."

One of the chief petty officers said, "We encourage them to take smaller bills rather than larger bills with them. That way they don't get cheated of so much."

"Can't they change their money into local currency on board?" I said.

"They can," someone said, "but too often they don't."

"How about the drunks?" I said. "What do you do with them?"

The executive officer said, "If the shore patrol finds a sailor a little drunk, they can order him back to his ship. Nothing more is said. His name is not taken and he's not punished. But if he refuses to go back, the shore patrol will give him a cancellation chit, and he's then sent back. This means his name is taken and at the next port he's not allowed to go ashore at all unless with a group or in charge of a petty officer."

Commander Terry said, "You don't put a person on a leash unless you have to. Some of these people are outstanding workers on board ship, but put them ashore and they want to turn left instead of going straight ahead."

"What happens when you get a really aggressive, out-of-control drunk?" I asked.

The chief petty officer said, "All shore patrols are armed with night sticks. We've been taught how to use these night sticks on a man's head without fracturing his skull."

The executive officer said, "We work very closely with the local police. They help our people a lot—tell them what places to expect trouble, and so on."

Commander Terry said, "That's one of the most enjoyable aspects of the job. The chief of police at Taranto and I became real good friends."

Someone else said, "Under the Status of Forces Agreement, the police of most NATO countries hand over any of our drunks they intercept to the shore patrol. Unfortunately the Turks won't accept this agreement. They arrest our people, try them *and* put them in prison."

"What places are out of bounds?"

"The houses of ill fame," said the executive commander, "and any bar or area the C.O. decides."

The chief petty officer said, "Sometimes, if there's a very well-known house of ill fame, we put two men outside it, and they tell the fellows not to go in."

Commander Terry said, "The girls in Taranto got round this in a very ingenious way. They had their own cars, or hired them, and they'd wait for the sailors in the streets. Then they'd take them off into the country, do what they had to do, and bring them back. There was nothing the shore patrol could do about it."

One of the commanders said, "A lot of them did it in the cars."

Commander Terry said, "Yes, by shifting the gear out of the way, but don't quote me on that."

"Jesus!" someone said, "that must have been uncomfortable."

✪

AT NOON Ensign Knott took me down to one of the seamen's messes for lunch. It was a help-yourself lunch. You took a molded tin platter with depressions in it for meat, vegetables, sweet, et cetera, and then filled it up with whatever you fancied. I sat between Ensign Knott and the duty officer. There were seamen all round us, but they didn't do much talking.

During lunch a couple of odd things happened. First, some men wheeled bombs past the table where we were eating. The bombs were fixed in little wheelbarrows, so the men pushing them looked like mad, surrealist gardeners. Then a small procession went by. It consisted of a marine leading, three men with closely shaven heads, and another marine bringing up the rear. Ensign Knott said the three in the middle were prisoners doing time in the brig; that was why their hair was cropped. He said they were always marched about by these marines and were now on their way back to their cells after exercise. They were not allowed to speak unless spoken to, and whenever they passed an officer they had to turn their heads to the wall. I wondered what unspeakable crimes they had committed to have to endure such humiliations. I said to Ensign Knott, "It makes one think of Dickens and the prisoners in the hulks." Ensign Knott said, "Sir?"

We finished our meal and Ensign Knott said, "Often the menu here is better than the wardroom." I said, "And sometimes perhaps worse?" Ensign Knott looked stunned and said hurriedly, "Oh, sure!"

★

After lunch about 150 officers assembled in the wardroom to hear a special briefing on Istanbul by a Lieutenant Commander Holt.

Lieutenant Commander Holt was a bright, breezy officer and he had behind them two large maps, one of Turkey, and her neighbors, the other of Istanbul itself. He referred us to a pink brochure on Istanbul which had been prepared by the public-relations office and said this would be "a good piece of gear to have on the beach with you." Then he gave a brief outline of Turkey's history. He said, "Istanbul was founded in 700 B.C. as a Greek thing, not a Turkish thing. Later the Roman Emperor Constantine made it the capital of the Roman Empire and that's how it came to be called Constantinople. As you know, Constantinople got the works. The Turks first came into the picture around 1200 A.D. I guess I'll skip the next seven hundred years. In the First World War German influence was very strong, and as a result German became the second primary language. So if any of you speak German, you ought to make out pretty well.

"Now, some of you may have seen the James Bond film *From Russia with Love,* so you'll know that this place is really on the uptake. The *Shangri-la* will be anchored here"—he pointed to the map—"which is about two blocks from the Hilton Hotel. The nice thing about Istanbul is that taxis, hotels, restaurants are all within about ten minutes of the landing stage."

He gave us a rundown on the hotels ("The Hilton has a belly dancer and a roof garden and is pretty exotic") and restaurants ("The food here is really good, better than the great Italian chow we all suffered from") and hostesses. "The hostesses in the bars work like hostesses the world over. To talk to a hostess in Istanbul you have to give her a bowl. She drinks the bowl as though she hadn't had a drink for a week. This isn't too bad, though, as it's a pretty large bowl and it takes her quite a while to get through it. I don't know what's in the bowl."

He moved on to taxis. "This is really the biggest problem in Istanbul. Unless your men are smart they can really get taken for a ride. The Turks are a lovely people, but their taxi drivers do leave something to be desired."

He read out a list of standard fares between various parts of Istanbul, and stressed that the men should either take a metered taxi or agree on a fare beforehand. "Now, one more word about taxis. If the taxi should get involved in an accident, you as the passenger are responsible, on the grounds that if it weren't for you the driver wouldn't have been there in the first place. So my advice, which I don't know if I can morally pass on to you, is that if there is an accident, throw a bunch of lire on the seat and get the hell out of there."

I thought, This man is a real old Istanbul hand.

"Lastly, let me give you some points of general advice. Look out for the young Turks. I don't mean that politically; I mean those who say they can find you a good bargain in the bazaars.

"Relations between Russia and Turkey just now are good. So strong feelings about Russia would be out of place.

"Don't fool around with cats in Turkey. They're holy. If you trip over a cat in an alley, think twice before you kick it.

"Turks are ninety-nine percent Moslems, but they don't outlaw drink. That doesn't mean you'll see a lot of Turkish drunks. You won't. And that's more than you can say about Americans.

"Another problem is shoeshine boys. They have a habit, when they're through and not sure that you're going to pay up, of pointing a razor above your Achilles tendon. Some people say, Oh, hell, I can run faster than him, and others just pay up, but my advice is, don't go near any shoeshine boys.

"Be careful about taking pictures. A lot of Moslems think that their soul as well as their picture will end up on the negative and go back to the *Shangri-la*. So don't take pictures of any Turks without permission.

"Moslem countries are very odd. If you see a couple of Turks coming down the street arm in arm or even hand in hand, it doesn't mean they're swinging. So tell your men not to laugh, or they may find themselves in a fight or even in prison.

"One last thought. There's no food provided in Turkish jails. You have to supply your own. You might remember that."

He half turned his back to show that he had finished. It had been a masterly performance; we had all hung on his words. Later, after questions, I went up and said, "You must know Istanbul pretty well?" He laughed. "Only what I've read about it. This will be my first visit."

✪

AFTER THE briefing, Ensign Knott took me to see the man in charge of community relations, the Roman Catholic chaplain, and some half a dozen sailors who were his helpers.

The chaplain said that the community-relations idea had started as an offshoot of President Kennedy's "People to People" program. Organizations in the States had donated goods of various kinds—clothing, books, toys, paint, wallpaper, household equipment—which the U.S. Navy put aboard its ships. In each port the local U.S.I.S. officer was told what goods were on board, and he made inquiries locally as to what was needed. "For example, we left ten tons of educational books in Malta the other day. They were donated by the Lions Club. The books wouldn't have been much use anywhere else in the command, because they were printed in English. The Maltese were very pleased to have them."

"We have to be careful sometimes," said Ensign Knott, "not to offend people?"

"Oh, we have to be *very* careful," said the chaplain. "When we went to Taranto last week, they specifically asked us *not* to distribute charity there, because Taranto is the home of the Italian navy. We respected their wishes."

"We have a lot of mouthwash on board," said Ensign Knott, "and we're a little chary of offering that, because it might look as though we're suggesting people have bad breath."

"But there's been a big shift recently," said the chaplain, "from *giving* things to *doing* things—things in which both we *and* the people we're helping can participate."

"Like the painting," said one of the sailors.

"Yes," said the chaplain. "In lots of places we go to, we ask the local authorities if they have any building that needs repainting, and if they do, we send along twenty or thirty volunteers and a drum of paint. Very often our people work alongside theirs."

"How about language difficulties?" I said. They all laughed. The chaplain said, "I guess we do have quite a lot of confusion." One of the sailors said, "But that's all good. If everyone understood each other, it would just be a question of 'you paint that corridor and we'll paint this one' and there wouldn't be any sense of sharing the same experience. I remember one time we were painting a school with some Italian workmen, and we had to communicate in a kind of sign language to express what we meant. Well, that was fine. That was a great thing, because it really helped bind us toward each other."

Ensign Knott said, "In Palermo we invited a whole lot of art students to come on board and have a painting contest on the flight deck. But no one had told them exactly what to paint. Some of them painted abstracts, which we hadn't expected. Others painted classified material, and we had to keep shifting them around. We had one or two of our people with art talent appointed as judges, and they brought their judges along too. But the ideas of their judges were so way out from ours that our people just climbed down and went along with them. They gave the two winning paintings to the ship."

"Do you have any plans for Istanbul?"

"Yes, we do. On most days the *Shangri-la*'s choir and band will play ashore. That's always very popular. Then there'll be the usual decorating program, a school or a hospital or whatever it is. And we're planning to hold a party on board for Turkish teen-agers. We'll take them on a tour of the ship and give them something to eat and drink and arrange a little rock and roll. These teen-agers are all being carefully chosen by the U.S.I.S. as likely to be future leaders of their country. At present they're in high school or in their first year at college. But they're all outstanding people and we want to orient them to American purposes and desires."

"So the motives of community relations," I said, "are political as well as social?"

The chaplain smiled and said, "I would say political only in the *broadest sense.*"

When Ensign Knott and I rose to go, the chaplain said, "May I see you for a moment?"

"Of course," I said, wondering what was coming.

We went into a corridor, and the chaplain said, very confidentially, "I thought you might like to know that on May 12 there are about three hundred of us going to see the Holy Father."

"I beg your pardon."

"When the ship returns to Italy, three hundred of us are going to Rome to have a special audience with the Holy Father. It's all been arranged. I can tell you everybody is quite thrilled. I thought you ought to know about it."

✪

THE PLANES took off and landed, took off and landed all day; and I marveled at the skill and stamina of the young pilots. The last landing of the day was to be at six o'clock, and I was asked if I would like to watch it from the position of the landing safety officer right aft. Normally the planes came in on a beam, but the landing safety officer was there in case the beam failed or to give last-minute instructions.

The landing safety officer worked from a little open box slung just below the port side of the flight deck, fifty to a hundred feet from the stern. We settled ourselves in there, I just behind him, our eyes level with the flight deck. There was little wind, and the evening sea was calm. One of the arresting wires lay just to our left.

The first plane came in to land. The landing safety officer picked up his telephone, but the plane came in dead on the beam. It was fascinating watching each plane fall out of the sky toward one, growing bigger with every second so that it seemed it was going to land on top of us and I ducked instinctively to avoid it. Then, with a roar and a whine, it bumped down on the flight deck, one of the arresting wires grabbed it, and, like a willful child in harness, it was brought screaming to a stop.

Once the landing safety officer told a pilot to come in a little lower, once he told one to go more to the left, and twice he said to overshoot and come in again. Apart from this, every plane landed as intended. As soon as each plane had come to a stop, it was taken below and the deck was clear for the next one. When the last plane had landed, it was suddenly, refreshingly still. The noise had been so constant all day one had forgotten what stillness was like.

The next morning I was due to be transferred to the destroyer *Dewey* for the last lap of the journey to Istanbul; so after dinner I went along to say goodbye to Captain Boyd, the admiral's chief of staff. He said, "I'm glad you came along, because I've got some papers here in connection with our indoctrination program which I think might be helpful to you. Now, you may think we are overdoing all this public-relations stuff, but we don't think so. It was Admiral George Anderson who first stressed the importance of it, and I can tell you it's paid off handsomely."

He picked up some papers from a table and said, "First two months of this year, a task force of a carrier, a cruiser and eight destroyers gave a total of 43,500 liberties. Out of that they had only sixteen shore patrol reports that required disciplinary action. Again, when another task force visited Barcelona for two weeks in February, they gave 18,500 liberties and had only five shore patrol reports. That's not bad.

"Now, here are the fleet orders for Istanbul," said Captain Boyd, picking up more papers. "It might interest you to look at them."

I read: ". . . this is an informal visit for familiarization with the port, good will and friendly relations," and there followed detailed instructions on how to behave. Some of the language was wonderfully portentous. "Naval personnel should keep away from local rallies, demonstrations, crowds, gangs and gatherings. They should not attempt to determine the nature of such congregations, but should avoid them on sight. Natural curiosity should be curbed." Again: "It is undesirable that personnel in the street should drink from anything stronger than a Coca-Cola bottle. If an alcoholic beverage is deemed necessary, it should be consumed in a bar or café."

Captain Boyd said, "Now, in addition to these orders and the briefings you've already heard, and the guide to Istanbul prepared by the public-relations office, we'll have a final conference on board the *Shangri-la* after we've dropped anchor, attended by all the executive officers of the squadron and by a liaison officer of the Turkish navy as well. There we'll go over again with a fine-tooth comb all the points we think important, and we'll finally decide what areas are to be off limits."

"That's certainly very thorough," I said.

"It's about as thorough as we can make it," said Captain Boyd. He got up. "Of course, in some ways the problem is easier than it was. The hard-living, hard-drinking sailor of the old Navy has practically disappeared. Eighty percent of the crew here have a technical rate. A lot of them want to go on tours and improve their minds. They're pretty well-educated boys." We reached the door. "On the other hand," said Captain Boyd, "a lot of them don't know how to hold their liquor, which the old-time sailors did."

I went along to say goodbye to the admiral, and I found him in his sea cabin below the bridge, wearing a pair of old blue trousers and a homely green pullover, and talking to the operations commander. The operations commander had his hands in his trouser pockets, which he wouldn't have had if he and the admiral had been in the

British navy. The admiral had a sort of heat machine strapped to his right wrist; he said the doctor had given it to him to help kill the pain of his arthritis.

The admiral said he was sorry my visit had been so short and he hoped I had got everything I wanted. I had in fact got so much, people of all ranks and ratings had given so unsparingly of their time and effort, that I found it difficult to say what I felt without appearing fulsome. "Well, thank you," said the admiral. "It's been a pleasure to have you. Now you'll enjoy yourself in the *Dewey*. She's a fine ship, and Captain Tazewell and Commander Bradley will look after you really well."

I went out onto the flight deck and stood at the guardrail overlooking the sea. On that vast runway, which had throbbed all day with the noise of jet engines, there was now no one but me. It was a calm moonlit night, and the only sound was the wash of the sea against the bows and the only movement the radar bowl on the mast turning in grave revolutions, ceaselessly combing the sky. It reminded me of nights I had spent on the bridge of destroyers in the war, when the ship had gone to sleep and one was left alone under the stars, in communion with other sea-borne watchers of the night, friends and enemies.

But now we were steaming through the heart of the Aegean, and on either side, beyond the dim shades of the escorting destroyers, I could see the outlines of the Aegean islands, where Sappho loved and Xerxes fought and Byron wrote.

But what did Admiral King and Lieutenant Commander Holt and Ensign Knott know about burning Sappho and mad, bad Byron and the rest? Very little, perhaps. And what affinity did jet fighters and community relations and indoctrination programs have with this jewel of a sea and its ancient islands? None at all.

And yet the longer I stayed on board, the more I realized that the Sixth Fleet was not acting in a vacuum, but was heir to a long and honorable Mediterranean tradition. What the American sailors were doing now, the British sailors had done for a century before them: paying courtesy calls on foreign governments, giving tea parties or barbecues to children and teen-agers, helping to redecorate schools and hospitals, sending the ship's band to play ashore, fixing football matches with local teams. One great power had taken over from another. In both cases the motive for their presence was political, as an instrument of their government's policy; but in the execution of that policy there was much that was dedicated and altruistic and humane. I remembered Dave in Colombia and how he had seemed to me to be a different version of the old British District Officer. A similar tradition was being carried on here; all that was different was the nationality and methods of those taking part.

I reached my cabin just as the ship's broadcasting system was closing down for the day. The Protestant chaplain came on and said in rich Southern tones:

"At the end of another beautiful day at sea, our heavenly Father, we thank Thee for Thy goodness, mercy and protection upon us. It's been a long, hard day, and we are tired, but the rest will refresh our bodies. Watch over those now on watch and those that will be on watch throughout the ship during the night. Amen."

✪

IN THE morning the *Dewey* came close alongside the *Shangri-la,* and they steamed on a parallel course. I was put into this great big chair, like a throne, which was fixed to one of the ship's derricks and slung out into space. The sea looked a long way below. I felt rather foolish sitting there in my old raincoat, holding a rope with one hand and my Panama hat in the other. They lowered me gently onto the *Dewey*'s deck, and the chair went back and my luggage came over in the same way.

A young officer who said his name was Lieutenant Smith took me to the bridge. It was an enclosed bridge with plenty of glass windows and central heating, not like the open-air boxes that I served in during the war. Here I met Captain Tazewell, the commander of the destroyer division, and the ship's captain, Commander Bradley. Captain Tazewell was a neat, small man with monkeylike features and the build of Eddie Cantor. Commander Bradley had a lean and handsome look. He introduced me to his executive officer, Lieutenant Commander Robinson, and to Lieutenant Commander Vishenski, the supply officer, who looked like the Michelin man, round as a rubber ball; he had been in the ship three years and was going to leave at Rhodes.

Lieutenant Smith took me round the ship, and we finished up in the Combat Information Room, where people were plotting radar and other information on a big grid. It was dark in there so that the radar operators could have a clear view of their screens. Lieutenant Smith had to go off somewhere for ten minutes, so I started talking to one of the operators. He was a radar petty officer and had steel-rimmed glasses and a peaked cap.

"When the ship gives liberty in these foreign ports," I said, "how do you spend your time?"

"In the old days the first things I used to look for were a bottle of liquor and a woman. But that was thirteen years ago, and I'm married now, so it doesn't have quite the same attraction. Now I just like going ashore with my buddies and having a few beers and something to eat and maybe getting a little drunk. And I won't say no to a woman if the right one comes along.

"In Brindisi the other day I met a pretty good woman. She had a dog and I was figuring I might get to the woman through the dog. Sweeten the dog a little and see how things worked out. I actually asked the exec for overnight liberty. I figured I might make it. The exec put two and two together. He's a pretty smart guy."

I hoped he would finish the story, tell me whether he had made the woman with the dog or not. But he said, "They're much stricter with behavior now than they ever used to be. In the old days you could get a dose of V.D. and come back and tell the doc and he'd put you right. Now if you get a dose more than once or twice a year, they'll throw you out of the Navy. All the brothels are off limits now. In the old days they not only weren't off limits, you'd probably find the skipper there as well.

"I used to be in the Pacific Fleet, and you had to be a real crazy guy to get into trouble there. In Hong Kong and Manila and Singapore you could get away with anything. But now they've gone big for this international-relations thing. They think that if there are a few drunken American sailors ashore, people will think all Americans are like that. Maybe they're right.

"I don't like going on these organized tours, and I don't go much for museums and things either. There are a lot of kids go on these tours and I don't think it right for them to see me when I'm drunk. Don't get the idea I get drunk all the time, but you build up a lot of tension in this job. You have to concentrate real hard, and when you act, you have to act quickly. Well, you need a few drinks from time to time as a release from that. I don't know any radar man in the Navy who doesn't like his drink.

"It's not like it was in the old days. In the old days I might blow all my pay in a couple of nights. Now I have to send it home so that Momma can put food on the table."

We were due to enter the Dardanelles at two o'clock, so at eleven-thirty we had an early lunch in the wardroom. The curtains had been drawn over the portholes, shutting out the light, as in an American restaurant. I have never understood this thing Americans have against natural light while eating—somebody ought to make a study of it. About twenty officers sat down, with the captain at the head and me on his right. There was a telephone at his feet, and now and then its bell sounded and he picked it up and talked to the officer or the bridge. We had a very good lunch, steaks which practically covered the plate, a green salad, and peaches and cream. Captain Tazewell had his in his cabin. The captain said he spent a lot of time in there learning Italian.

After lunch I went up to the bridge and saw that the squadron had formed single line ahead, with the *Shangri-la* leading, the *Little Rock* next, ourselves in the middle and two more destroyers astern. The captain showed me a message he had just received from the admiral which said, "Captain, you have one beautiful ship." The entrance to the Dardanelles was about five miles ahead. It was a gray, misty afternoon, but through the drizzle and haze you could see the land coming up on either side. It was green near the water's edge, but higher up it was blotted out by low cloud, as on the west coast of Scotland.

Captain Tazewell sat in a little chair on the left of the bridge, and the captain and the officer on duty stood in the middle. Now and then the officer on duty said things like "Two-third speed . . . one four two rpm . . . right ten rudder . . . steer zero three nine"— which the helmsman repeated. On the other side of the bridge Lieu-tenant Commander Vishenski had taken up position beside a micro-phone which fed into the ship's public-address system. He had *The Encyclopedia Americana* in front of him, and as we approached the narrows he began reading the entry marked "Dardanelles," for the benefit of the crew. It wasn't terrific prose in the first place, but Vi-shenski's monotonous, bored delivery killed it stone dead.

The Dardanelles! The name had been stamped on my mind as long as I could remember. The bloody campaign which the Allies had fought there against the Turks might, if it had turned out differently, have changed the course not only of the First World War, but of subsequent European history. It was one of the crucial battlefields of the twentieth century. And the names associated with it were ones to remember: Winston Churchill above all, Asquith, Fisher, Kitchener, Hamilton, de Robeck, Roger Keyes, Dunbar Nasmith, Rupert Brooke, Compton Mackenzie, to name a few. And the place that was at the center of it all, that symbolized the whole bloody futile conflict was Gallipoli. Where along this drab green coastline was it? Where were the beaches where our men had swarmed ashore in such hope, and down which, in anger and despair, they had retreated less than a year later?

Aloud, and to no one in particular, I said, "Where's Gallipoli, I wonder?"

No one responded. At length, out of politeness, Captain Tazewell said, "What was that place?" I said it again, I even spelled it, but it was clear they were hearing it for the first time. (It is possible that Vishenski might have mentioned it, but everyone had stopped listening to him long ago.) I thought, This is astonishing; surely everyone has heard of Gallipoli. Then I thought, Well, is it? Have they? What is equivalent to Gallipoli in American history? Say the *Maine* at Havana and the subsequent Spanish-American War—how many British naval officers know about that?

It was the navigating officer who finally found it on the chart. But it was spelled Gelibolu, and when it came into sight a little later, it turned out to be a small dull town of white and yellow houses with red-tiled roofs. I looked at it long and hard, searching for some point of recognition, trying to make a connection between it and the dreams of my youth. But there was no connection. Gelibolu, Gelibolu, I thought, what have you to do with my Gallipoli? Nothing at all. The false had become real and the real false: it was a surprise and a disappointment.

We went on up the strait, following in the wake of the *Little Rock* and the *Shangri-la,* obeying orders from the admiral as to course and speed. Along the green coastline white minarets began to show up, pencil thin. Two Russian merchant ships passed us going south, and dipped their flags: I knew that would please some of the boys. Then we overtook a Greek steamer called *Hermes,* carrying German tourists. Vishenski, who had finished his running commentary, looked in the encyclopedia and said, "Hermes is the Greek name for Mercury, that's the messenger of the gods."

✪

THAT NIGHT we steamed through the Sea of Marmara. I slept in the captain's day cabin, and he slept in his sea cabin near the bridge. There weren't any sheets, but it was a big improvement on the *Shangri-la*. I was woken in the morning by a pleasant young sailor who had the same sort of arrogant good looks as the late James Dean. He gave me a cup of coffee, and I asked him what he thought of Mediterranean ports. He said:

"The thing I don't like is we only meet waterfront people, and waterfront people are after your money. They short-change you. Italy is terrible that way. In Naples, if you don't look out, they'll snatch your watch from your wrist. The other difficulty is the language. You can't get to know anybody, because you can't speak to them. There were some nice-looking girls I'd have liked to meet in Italy, but in Mediterranean countries girls don't speak to strangers, especially when they can't speak the language, so what do you do?

"What I do is go on these tours. Some of them are really great. Two weeks back I went on the Malta tour. I thought, I'll probably never see this country again, so I'll take the opportunity. I had no idea it was such an interesting place. 'Course, every time we stopped to see something, some of the guys went to the nearest bar. By the time we got through they were pretty well loaded.

"I had one or two very interesting tours in Scotland. I did some time in one of the F.B.M.'s in the Holy Loch. They took us round these Scottish castles and explained why they'd been built and all that. It was real interesting. My dad's a contractor, so I had a special interest in the architectural motif—how the doors were built, that kind of thing. That really fascinates me. I always look for the architectural motif when I go round these buildings in Europe."

After breakfast I went to the bridge. It was another cold, hazy morning such as you expect in Britain or America, not on the threshold of the East. The sea was very calm. At nine we entered the Bosporus, and the mosques and minarets of Istanbul came up to port, drab and lifeless in the mist. Clustered off the end of the town were a group of fishing boats, looking like a scene from Breughel. The Blue Mosque and St. Sophia came into sight and then the fleet landing stage and behind it the Hilton Hotel.

The *Shangri-la* ordered the squadron to anchor. The other ships carried out the order smartly, but we had trouble locating our berth and went up and down, backward and forward, for half an hour. Up on the bridge everyone was very embarrassed. The captain tried to be cheerful and unconcerned, but you could see how anxious he was. Captain Tazewell sat in his chair and puffed at his pipe and said nothing; it wasn't really his business. The radar kept calling out things like "Anchorage a hundred yards south"; and the captain went to and fro across the bridge, giving orders to the wheel and engines. We could see the sailors in the other ships watching us and knew what they were thinking. I doubted whether the admiral thought we were one beautiful ship now.

At last the captain said to the signalman, "Tell *Little Rock* I'd like to drop my hook here."

The signalman said, "Affirmative, *Little Rock*."

The captain said, "Let go the anchor," and it rattled away. Someone who was watching the anchor said, "Thirteen fathoms, up and down, no strain." We started leaving the bridge, and Lieutenant Smith said to me, "Not exactly our finest hour."

In the wardroom the public-address system was playing a selection from the Beatles, and the steward was serving coffee and nuts. Now that we had come to anchor, everyone could relax for a little before starting his next job. An ensign near me said to another officer, "I talked to my mother last night." The other officer said, "Where was she?" and the ensign said, "In Stamford, Connecticut. She was surprised out of her skin. She said, 'Where are you?' and I said, 'I'm just coming into Istanbul.' "

I said, "How did you talk to your mother?" The ensign said, "On the ham radio. We do this quite a lot. Our radio people get through to the nearest ham to wherever we're calling, and he connects up with the local telephone exchange and they make it a collect call from there on, which doesn't add up to much. These hams enjoy it." I thought of the man I met in the plane from Liberia. The other officer said, "You can't be too intimate, of course. The whole world's listening to you."

Snatches from other conversations drifted across the room. "When Frank Sinatra is abroad, he can misbehave any way he likes and nobody thinks he represents anything but himself, but if an unknown young American sailor gets drunk and misbehaves, everyone says, 'Oh, that's just typical of the Americans' " . . . "I'm worried about that hurricane that just hit Indiana. My home's in Indiana and my wife was due to reach there by car yesterday. I hope she's okay." . . . "We were in Juárez, Mexico. They had the best bullfighter in Spain, and a great crowd had come from all around to see him. The bull was kind of slow to get going, so the bullfighter turned his back on the bull and faced the crowd. Well, that was it. The bull just put his head down, gored him through the thigh, lifted him up on his horn, tossed him around a few times and then dumped him down. I tell you he damn near died. . . ."

Later, the captain addressed the *Dewey*'s crew on the fantail. He warned them of the pitfalls that awaited them ashore, including the stories about those who argued with shoeshine boys or kicked cats, which I had passed on to him. And he added one or two imaginative touches of his own. "They're a tough bunch here. They're not like you or I. A Turkish ship once came in here and they found a thief on board. They requested permission to execute him. Permission was not granted. So they went to sea next day, and they were away one day, and when they came back they were one sailor short. So watch out."

I lunched in the chief petty officer's mess, and on returning to the wardroom I noticed unusual activity, people shifting the furniture about and taking the covers off the table. I asked what was happening and was told there was to be a court-martial: one of the sailors was to be tried for stealing. So I went and asked the captain if I could attend. He didn't seem very keen about it; he probably was averse to having the ship's dirty linen washed in public. But I said that in a democracy a trial was a public affair, and in the end he agreed.

It took quite a time to get the room ready. Seven chairs were placed on one side of the table for the members of the court, and three on the other side for prosecuting and defense counsel and the accused. Lawbooks and notebooks and pencils were placed on the table, and three microphones; these were connected by a wire to a huge recording machine built into a cabinet in the bulkhead. At the far end of the table sat the court reporter. His microphone was built into a thing that looked like an oxygen mask, which he held close to his face; he had to repeat into it every word that was said. This had a wire which went through a hatch into another big recording machine set up in the wardroom pantry. It was all very thorough and impressive.

When the recording machines had been tested and everything was ready, the members of the court and the prosecuting and defense counsel came in. The president was a man I hadn't met, a baby-faced lieutenant commander with crew cut and spectacles. The others were ship's officers too, and so were the two counsel. The president banged his gavel on the table and said, "There will be no smoking or drinking of cups of coffee while the court is in session. Now bring in the accused." The president seemed very nervous. I don't think he had ever presided before.

The accused came in. He was a nondescript little fellow, almost any Mom's boy. He had a small, weak face, and full lips and ears that went out a little, and soft, deep-set eyes. He wore three white stripes on his left sleeve and carried a white cap on which his name, let us say Taylor, was written in crude lettering, obviously his own.

The president read his terms of reference, prosecuting and defense counsel introduced themselves, and the court reporter and tape-recording operator were sworn in. Then the president said to the accused, "Do you appreciate that you are entitled to have enlisted men as members of this court, if you so desire?" The accused rose, whispered, "Yes, sir," and sat down.

"And do you not wish to exercise that right?"

He got up again, whispered, "No, sir," and sat down.

The president said, "When you answer questions, you may remain seated. And speak up."

The charges were read out. The first had two specifications; one was stealing a shirt belonging to Commodore Johnson, Tazewell's predecessor, the other, stealing money from a wallet. The second charge was illegally running a "slush fund," or lending out money at interest.

The accused was asked how he pleaded, and he said "Not guilty" to the first charge and "Guilty" to the second. There was a little murmur at the guilty plea, which I think had not been expected. The president said, "Do you understand that the maximum penalty for the offense for which you have pleaded guilty is dishonorable discharge, six months' imprisonment and two-thirds pay deduction?"

"Yes, sir."

"And in view of that, do you still wish to plead guilty?"

"Yes, sir."

Council for the prosecution got up and said that in view of this unexpected development, could the court recess while witnesses who would not now be required were sent away? The president banged his gavel and said, "The court will hereby recess for five minutes."

During the recess someone pulled back the curtains covering the two doors that opened onto the deck. It was a lovely sunny day, and as the ship swung in the stream one could see first the minarets and roofs on one shore and then those on the other. Several members of the court lit cigarettes. I had the feeling they were all very nervous and uncertain and would have preferred to be doing something, almost anything, else, but equally that they were ready to go to any lengths, suffer any indignity or tedium, to see that justice was done.

After the recess, the witnesses were called. The first was Lieutenant Commander Robinson, the executive officer, who told the court that after the captain had given permission for Taylor's locker to be searched, he had found a shirt in it marked J 2440. Another witness produced a laundry book showing that J 2440 was Commodore Johnson's laundry number. Lieutenant Commander Robinson also told the court how, when he was interviewing Taylor about searching his locker, Taylor had asked permission to go to the head. A burly sailor called Fallas testified how he had followed Taylor to the head and seen him leave a wallet there. This wallet was subsequently found to contain two 1,000-lire bills, one twenty-dollar bill, one five-dollar bill, and eleven one-dollar bills. Lieutenant Commander Robinson said he identified these bills as ones he had specially marked with his own initials. While this evidence was being given, I looked at Taylor. He sat very still in his chair, and kept his head down. The case against him seemed strong.

Yet, as the afternoon wore on, it was less Taylor and the squalid offenses for which he was charged that held one's interest than the amateurism of the members of the court. They were determined to follow to the letter the rules laid down in the book, to allow no point of law or procedure to go by default, to do whatever was required of them. But this clearly became more and more of a strain. They were being made to act roles for which they were in no way fitted, to play the parts of diminutive Perry Masons and say things like "Let it be written into the record . . ." and "The record may stand . . ." and "I object" and "Objection overruled"—which previously they had heard only at the films. It was too much for them; they couldn't keep it up. The president, who had to do most of the talking, got tongue-tied and kept saying things like "Does the defense counsel wish to *urgue* farther?" and "Let the record *sho sow*."

Once prosecuting counsel got so carried away that in true Perry Mason style he began pacing up and down; his foot caught in the wire from the recording gear and pulled it out of the socket; the whole trial came grinding to a halt and had to be started again. Defense counsel, a young lieutenant, was very ill at ease. He had a set list of questions of each witness, all very straightforward, and it never occurred to him to ask any supplementaries. But there was a nice moment when he was cross-examining Lieutenant Commander Robinson, his senior officer, and Lieutenant Commander Robinson said that Taylor appeared "very agitated" while his locker was being searched. "Excuse me, sir," defense counsel said, politely acknowledging the difference in rank, "but that expression of opinion is not really admissible at this stage." He turned to the president. "Request permission for witness's expression of opinion to be struck from the record." Prosecuting counsel got up and said, "I object." The president said, "Objection overruled. Permission granted. Let the record sho sow." It was like television, only better.

The ship continued swinging in the stream. They had left open the doors to the deck, and I could see the European shore through one, the Asian through the other. Looking at Istanbul's spires and minarets, and half listening to the trial behind me as, like some ancient model T, it lurched and spluttered on, the thought suddenly struck me that this was what the United States and democracy and the Sixth Fleet and Power for Peace were all about.

Not a mile from here an American sailor had been languishing in jail for nine months because he had blown his nose on a flag instead of a handkerchief; and further up the road were Russian prisons where thousands of others had been deprived of their liberty for even less. Yet here an insignificant young man, accused of a crime repugnant to all sailors—stealing from his shipmates—could be assured of an absolutely fair trial. Here, in dignity, he was being judged by men who, for all their bumbling hesitation, were fundamentally good and decent people, anxious to see justice done. Here in this alien anchorage, 13,800 miles and six months out of Norfolk, Virginia, midway between East and West and at the very gateway to the Communist world, was democratic justice in action.

Yes, I thought, looking round the court at the earnest, puzzled faces, Power for Peace isn't such a bad motto after all; for this is one thing the power is trying to preserve.

✪

I WENT ashore in one of the early evening liberty boats, and a taxi took me to the Hilton. They gave me a room overlooking the Bosporus; the squadron lay just below. When it was dark the ships were lit up by strings of electric-light bulbs running from bow to masts and from masts to stern. It was very pretty: they looked like huge golden scarabs. I had a shower and dressed, and went to the Restaurant Abdullah. It was a cozy, old-fashioned sort of place, with an Edwardian decor, bent and crumbling waiters, and plain white tablecloths.

I ordered my dinner and went to the men's room to wash. There a man was lying on the floor, and another man and a woman were attending to him. The woman had blond hair and spectacles and looked about fifty, and when I asked if I could be of any help, she said, in broad American, "It's okay, thanks, but we have the situation pretty well under control." Oh dear, I thought, here's another one who can't hold his liquor.

I went and started my dinner, and later the man who had been on the floor was brought in by the other two. He was a dark, sallow little man of about fifty-five or sixty. They sat him down on the bench against the wall at the table next to me, and in about thirty seconds he swung over sideways like a clockwork doll and ended up horizontal on the bench.

"We can't get Alan erect," said his wife. "We've been trying to get him erect, but he won't sustain it."

The other man said, in broken English, "Please allow me to take your husband to the Hilton Hotel."

"Oh, no," said the woman, "you mustn't bother yourself. We've been too much bother already."

"Well, let him rest there for a while," said the other man, "and I'll take another look at him later."

He went to a table where a woman was waiting, and sat down. The American woman said to me, "He's a Turkish heart specialist who was here by chance when Alan passed out. Wasn't that lucky. He's been darling. He had some medicines on him, and upstairs in the men's room he gave Alan a shot."

I looked at Alan's supine form and thought that it didn't seem to have done him much good.

"Alan gets like this sometimes," said the woman, "and it's just terrible. It was too cold in Japan and too hot in India, and here, I guess, the food was just too beautiful."

The waiter brought her a dish that he had been keeping hot. "We flew in from Karachi this morning," she said, "and I said to Alan, 'Alan, you wanna take it easy now,' but he was so keen on doing everything and seeing everything, because we've only got two days here, see. He would go and look at all those museums and things and, what with the food and everything, I guess it was too much."

We ate in silence, and then Alan stirred, and his wife took him by the lapels and heaved him up. He was erect now, and he managed to stay erect. The Turkish heart specialist came over and looked at his eyes and tongue and felt his pulse. "He's better now," he said. "He'll be okay, but you want to get him back to bed."

Alan opened his eyes and said to the Turkish heart specialist, sleepily, "You know, there's a lot of emotional difficulty in this. We had a lovely daughter killed in an automobile accident two years back, and ever since then I break out in these cold sweats."

The Turkish heart specialist looked at him and nodded. I wondered if he believed a word.

★

AFTER DINNER I walked through narrow crowded streets to the U.S.O., which was housed in the French club near the waterfront. This was a big building on three floors, crowded with sailors. On the top floor there was a dance going on, with a beat band from one of the ships banging away. There were quite a few girls up there with huge U.S.O. badges on their sleeves and their names written beneath. Some were dancing and some were behind a counter serving hamburgers and orange drinks; the boys outnumbered them by about five to one.

Going down to the second floor, I passed Chaplain Brown of the *Shangri-la* talking to two *Dewey* sailors.

"How are you, Mr. Kennedy, sir?" he said in his rich Southern voice.

I said I was fine.

"And did you get that prayer I sent you?"

"Yes, I did," I said, "and I'm very grateful for it."

"Well, I'm mighty glad you got that prayer," said Chaplain Brown, "because I was mighty proud that you should have wanted that prayer from me, Mr. Kennedy." He turned to the two sailors and said, "Now, don't you forget, you two go on being witnesses for the Lord, and you pray for me too in my work."

On the second floor were a ping-pong room and a souvenir stall. The souvenir stall was doing a brisk business. Chaplain Brown said it allowed the men to buy mementoes of Istanbul without getting fleeced by the Turks. There were meerschaum pipes and Turkish slippers and flags, and clay pipes and brass objects with "Istanbul" printed on them, and needlework pictures of President Kennedy, and mugs and ashtrays galore. One very drunk sailor with a mustache had put a cigarette into the end of his meerschaum pipe and was puffing away like a train.

In the ping-pong room I met one of the *Dewey*'s chief petty officers. I said I hoped he had been enjoying himself, and he said he had been to a service in the Dutch Church, which I thought an odd reply. I also met a very young sailor from the *Dewey*, about nineteen, a charming boy. He was loaded and a little sad. "What do you make of Istanbul?" I said. He swayed on his feet and said, "It's the same every place we go. They're all out to take advantage of us. They think because we're Americans we've got lots of dough. After a while it kinda gets you down."

At ten-thirty or so the U.S.O. packed up, and I made my way to where the bars and night spots were thickest. The streets here were steep and narrow and ill lighted, and there weren't many people about. Stunted, sinister Turks lurked in the lintels of doorways, promising raptures within; most wore mustaches and few had recently shaved. But the performance belied the promise. Most of the bars were silent and empty. In many of them American sailors were the only customers. They sat at small tables in groups of two and three, swilling beer, not talking, staring like dogs in a variety of uninteresting directions. Creating a row was about the last thing they looked like doing. One or two had hostesses with them, but there was little intercourse, even of the most proper kind. You got the feeling that whatever ideas the proprietors might once have had about touting for custom they had long since abandoned; that they were now only waiting for the sailors to go in order to shut up shop and retire to bed.

I went to the local police station, where the shore patrol had set up temporary headquarters. Here it was as quiet as everywhere else; no incidents or reports of incidents of any kind. Commander Marten, the shore patrol officer for the night, was about to walk around with a patrol, and he invited me to go with him.

Commander Marten was a fine, slow-moving, slow-talking sort of man, with a nice sense of humor. Sometimes when we passed American sailors, they saluted him, and he saluted back. But when they didn't salute him, he waited until the last moment before saluting *them;* then they *had* to salute back. "I try to embarrass them a little," he said. "It may be mean, but the shock of finding an officer saluting them can have the effect of sobering them up and making them take stock of themselves." After the saluting, Commander Marten would stop each man or group and say, "Now, do you know when your liberty ends?" When they said, "One o'clock, sir," as most did, he would say, "No, I guess the word didn't get around. It's twelve for nonrated men, and one for chiefs and petty officers." The men thanked him and saluted and went on; they all seemed to be as sober as bishops. Commander Marten had a wonderful way with him. Once, he saluted two junior Turkish Army officers. They were quite stunned and practically curtsied when saluting back. Commander Marten said, "That's just a bit of public relations."

We ended up at the fleet landing stage. There were a lot of sailors there waiting for their boats, and Turkish souvenir sellers trying to do business. Snatches of conversation came our way:

"Hell, that's what I keep trying to tell ya."

"It's peanuts."

"Okay. How much?"

"Fifty cents. Take it or leave it."

"That's not peanuts. That's horseshit."

Mumbles in Turkish.

"Horseshit is what I said."

We went to the main shore patrol headquarters, which was in a kiosk on the jetty. There were two officers and a dozen M.P.'s there, sitting around and smoking and drinking coffee. "What sort of a night?" asked Commander Marten, and one of the officers said, "Dead quiet. Over a thousand liberties. No shore reports, no cancellation chits, nothing."

Later Commander Castillo sent me a full report on the squadron's five-day visit: 6,051 liberties, 15 cancellation chits, one shore report. By any standards it was an amazing record.

✪

NEXT DAY I went on one of the sightseeing tours. There were about a hundred and twenty sailors from the squadron, and we went round in five buses.

It was an interesting tour: the Blue Mosque, St. Sophia, the Topkapi Palace. This last, with its stunning collection of jewels and Ming and Sèvres china, must be one of the most remarkable museums in the world; but for many of us the tour was ruined by a quartet of young, crew-cut Marines from the *Shangri-la* who had come only to blow things up. The ringleader, and the worst of them, was a horrid boy with ginger hair and piggy eyes, all of eighteen years old. When we left one room in the Topkapi to go to another, he'd say to his friends, "Okay, kids," in a loud, bored voice, as though to signify that he had had enough of that room himself. When the guide showed something of dramatic interest, such as an 800-carat uncut emerald, he would exclaim, very sarcastically, "Wow!" We came to a cradle of one of the Sultans, and he said, "Is that J. C.'s cradle? Was he born here?" And later, at the jewel-encrusted throne of Ahmed, "That's J. C.'s throne, kids. That's where he had his morning crap." His friends giggled, but nobody else said or did anything, not wanting to be the first to start a scene. But later the guide got his own back. "Could I buy that stuff?" said our friend, pointing to an exquisite chess set in hand-carved ivory. "*You* couldn't," said the guide, "because *you* couldn't afford it." His friends didn't laugh this time, but everyone else did. After this he was quieter.

In the afternoon I went to the Hilton to pack. In the lobby I ran into Alan and his wife. "How are you?" I said to Alan. "You're looking much better." Alan said, "Oh, I'm quite okay now. I was just overdoing it." He smiled. "When you saw me in that restaurant, I bet you thought I was drunk." I said, "To be honest, yes." Alan said, "That's the way it must have looked, but I wasn't. I just break out in these cold sweats. It's a heart thing."

"Of course."

"It's an emotional thing too. Two years back we lost a lovely daughter in an automobile accident . . ."

Later, I took a taxi to the airport and, at twilight in Turkey, crossed over into Asia Minor.

✪

IT WAS Easter Sunday when I landed at Jerusalem airport. The taxi driver said, "Merry Christmas, sir," and drove me to the top of the Mount of Olives, to the Intercontinental Hotel.

This was before the time of the 1967 Arab-Israeli war, and this part of Jerusalem was Jordanian territory. The doorman at the Intercontinental was dressed like no Arab I had ever seen, in a robe of many colors, and with a headdress like that of Lawrence of Arabia or one of the Hashemite kings. "Welcome," he said. All the staff at the Intercontinental said "Welcome," sometimes when they meant "Good-night."

They took me to my room, and there, outside my window, laid out in glorious Todd A-O, was Jerusalem in three colors: the milky blue of the sky, the green of the cypresses, and the biscuity beige of the buildings. It was late afternoon and the sun was already setting over the golden city, lighting up the cupola of the Moslem Dome of the Rock. Below me were the Garden of Gethsemane, the pool of Siloam, the brook Kidron; and away on the hilltop the spire of the Church of the Holy Sepulcher, scene of Christ's burial and resurrection.

I think every traveler who visits Jerusalem for the first time feels, as I did—and irrespective of his beliefs—a sense of wonder. Alone in my room, I said aloud, "Jerusalem, I'm in Jerusalem." It seemed somehow an amazing thing. We in the West have lived with Jerusalem always; it has been part of our consciousness as far back as we can remember—not as a modern town, but as an antique, almost mythical city, like Troy or Carthage. What astounds one today is to find that the antique city is still there, that little has changed in the last two thousand years. Rome is no longer the city of Caesar or Justinian, Athens no longer the city of Socrates or Aristotle; but Jerusalem, amazingly, is still the city of Christ.

I came to Jerusalem in search of American tourists, to join up with some for a day and see what they made of the sights. I did not have to look far. The corridors of the Intercontinental were thronged with elderly men wearing broad-brimmed hats and string ties. "Please take me to your leader," I said to one, and he went away and came back with Miss Harriet-Louise Patterson.

Miss Harriet-Louise Patterson was around sixty, a spry, chirpy bird, with gingery hair and spectacles and much energy and humor. She invited me to join her group the next day; it would have to be the next day, because they were leaving the day after. Tomorrow they would be visiting the Dome of the Rock, the Wailing Wall, the Stations of the Cross, the Church of the Holy Sepulcher, and the Garden of Gethsemane.

"But, oh, Mr. Kennedy," said Miss Patterson, "do, do be kind. I feel so ashamed about us Americans, we're so stupid, some of us. We go around the world and show our stupidity to everybody. Some of my group, now, they say things like 'I didn't know there was any trouble between Israel and the Arab world!' And then we expect people to love us."

Suddenly she jumped up and said, "But you must come and meet the group." This took a little time, as there were twenty-five of them and they were scattered about the hotel. There were more women than men, and they all looked pretty old. But they were friendly and welcoming and said things like "Real glad to have you come along with us." At the end, when we were in a group of four, Miss Patterson said, "Oh, how silly of me! I quite forgot to introduce you to Mrs. Hemby!" I shook hands with Mrs. Hemby, and an ancient among ancients in the group said, "Till you've met Mrs. Hemby, you haven't lived."

Miss Patterson and I went for a drink in the Seven Arches Lounge. She had tomato juice and I had a Jericho special. I asked her how she had got into the tour business, and she said that as a girl she had always been fascinated by the Bible and had majored in Biblical literature at college. Later she got a job at a department store called Higbee's in Cleveland, where she used to give lectures on Bible appreciation. "Well, Mr. Kennedy, I discovered I had this gift of talking, and lots of people used to come and listen, and the lectures were a great success. So I thought I should come here to get the authentic background picture, which I did, and one thing led to another, and I started these tours. That was many years ago now, and I've lost count of the number of tours I've taken since."

Miss Patterson said she had written several books: *How to Understand the Bible Better; Enjoy the Bible's Beauty; Around the Mediterranean with My Bible;* and *Come with Me to the Holy Land.* I asked how much of the story of Christ's life she really believed, and she said that things like the Virgin Birth, the miracles, the Resurrection, were to her quite unbelievable. "But I would never tell that to my groups. You can't take things away from people without putting something else in their place, at least not suddenly."

"Take the miracle of the loaves and fishes," I said. "What do you think happened there?"

Miss Patterson laughed. "I think the multitude brought a few sandwiches along with them. Do you find that sacrilegious?" She added, "I think Christ is inside everybody, perhaps more than most of us know. People on these tours change—I've seen it happen. What starts as a tour ends as a pilgrimage."

That night I dined at the Seven Arches Restaurant. There was a European menu and an Arabic one; I chose the European one. I waited half an hour and nothing happened. Then I called the headwaiter and said, "I ordered my dinner half an hour ago, and nothing's happened." He said, "You've only been waiting half an hour? You're lucky. Last year, if you'd been here, you'd have waited an hour and a quarter. This year is Paradise." He went away then, but later said he hoped dinner had been all right. "How many have dinner here each night?" I asked. "Tonight is full," he said; "tonight we have about two hundred and seventy." I said, "How many have the Arab dinner?" He said, "One. One person had it. The Americans and Europeans like what they know. Sometimes they ask what the Arab dinner is made of, and when I say meat and yoghurt, they go 'Ugh!' and that is that."

Miss Patterson came by with two pamphlets. I took them to my room and read them in bed. One was a list of the members of the group, the other gave their itinerary. This showed they had left New York thirteen days before and had visited Rome, Cairo, Luxor, Thebes, Beirut, Damascus, Amman, and Jerusalem. In the remaining week they were going to visit Haifa, Galilee, Tel Aviv, Athens and Corinth. The pamphlet was full of things like "This morning you will trail Moses through Moab to Madeba and Nebo. You'll thrill to the same panoramic view across the Jordan valley to Palestine that Moses saw in 1250 B.C." The total cost per person of trailing Moses, New York to Damascus and back, was $1,642.

Even more revealing was the list of tour members. This showed fifteen housewives, three physicians, and one each of dentist, insurance agent, department-store executive, engineer, retired banker, secretary and student. Their dates of birth showed that nineteen had been born in the nineteenth century, four before the First World War, and the remaining two, the secretary and the student, in 1930 and 1942; however, these two were daughters accompanying their mothers.

When I woke in the morning, I looked round for a Bible, as I thought it might be interesting to look up some of the places we were going to visit. But there wasn't a Bible anywhere. I thought of all the hotel rooms in the world where I had found Bibles crouched, lying in wait, and had put them away in a drawer. Yet here, the only hotel room where I really wanted a Bible, there wasn't one to be had.

After breakfast, we all assembled in the sunshine to wait for the limousines that were to take us to the Dome of the Rock. My fellow sightseers were a formidable lot. The men shuffled about in those old-fashioned hats and string ties, and the women had too much make-up and elaborate hair styles. They had enough cameras among them to put *Life* and *Paris-Match* out of business. Some chewed Chiclets. In a curious way they all looked alike; they had these sharp little eyes and thin lips and prim, severe faces. They were a more opulent version of Grant Wood's "American Gothic": solid, regular, taxpaying citizens; earnest, worthy, thrifty, sober; churchgoers, community-helpers, charity-givers to a woman. On this rock was America founded.

A ramshackle bus drew up beside us. Then Miss Patterson appeared with a wad of cotton wool over her ear. She said she had an infection and was full of antibiotics, and couldn't come. Everyone clucked around and sympathized. She also said that unfortunately our limousines weren't available, and we would have to go in the bus; an Arab guide called Ali would come with us. Everyone laughed, and we got in. One man said, "I think it's appropriate we're going to the Wailing Wall in this bus." I overheard another say, "We got up at three this morning and took Communion from Dr. Pauling in the Garden of Gethsemane."

The mosque of the Dome of the Rock was in the form of an octagon, with the dome rising from the center. Ali said it was here that Abraham had made his sacrifice, David had raised an altar, Solomon and later Herod had built their temples, Christ had overturned the tables of the money-changers, and Omar and later Saladin had built their mosques. At the entrance we took off our shoes and put on slippers. "You don't know who's been wearing these slippers," said one lady cautiously, "but I guess the stone floor would be too cold on the stockinged feet." It was cool inside and rather dim. In the area beneath the dome Arabs on mats prostrated themselves toward the east or read the Koran. One lady of our party plonked herself down on one of these mats and started praying, too—a nice ecumenical gesture, though the Arabs seemed a little startled.

On the way to the Wailing Wall we passed a group of Arab workmen chipping at some stones. One of our ladies said, "Such wonderful things they make, without any of the tools we have in our country. But I guess they're happy. Look, there's a lady with her face covered! And there's a man drawing water from a well! Look at that! He drinks from the jug. I guess they all drink from the same jug!" A small, mild-mannered man in the party said, "This Moslem religion makes me mad. No religion's any good unless it results in right action, and what right action does it have for them? Just look at those people! Look at the poverty! Look how far they are behind us! They want lifting up, but they won't help themselves. They make an excuse for not helping themselves by saying, 'Oh, it's God's will,' and that lets them get away with anything."

We passed some brilliant yellow acacias and then entered a long, narrow passage that led to the Wailing Wall. Here we were importuned by grubby boys who pressed round us and put out their hands and asked for *baksheesh*. "Coins?" said one man to them. "Why, I don't have any coins." One woman kept tossing her head and saying *"La! Baksheesh!"* I asked her what she was doing, and she said, "I've been taught to say *'La! Baksheesh,'* which means 'No *baksheesh!*' and toss one's head in that way. It's supposed to get rid of them." Attracted by the word *baksheesh*, the boys surrounded her, like little wasps round jam. "It seems to be having the opposite effect," I said, and the woman said, "I guess so."

The Wailing Wall was a big disappointment, just a great bare slab of masonry, like the wall in East Berlin. I found the ancient among ancients, the one who said that until you met Mrs. Hemby you hadn't lived, standing some way from it. I asked where his wife was. "Oh, she's gone to look at the wall," he said. "I guess she's wailing for her loss of independence when she married me."

Everyone took photographs of the wall, and then we walked up the Via Dolorosa to the Stations of the Cross, the landmarks along Christ's journey to his crucifixion. It is a narrow, old, rather pretty street, full of children and bustling citizens about their business. Ali gave a running commentary, delivered in a brisk shorthand, as we went along. "Here is the first Station of the Cross, where the Lord Jesus was condemned to death by Pontius Pilate. Why Pontius Pilate was coming to the Temple area? Because Pontius Pilate was afraid the

Jews would revolt against him." We moved to the next station. "Here is the Second Station of the Cross, where the Lord Jesus received the Cross." At most stations there was a little plaque in the wall, and everyone took out his camera and clicked. "Here is the Third Station of the Cross, where the Lord Jesus fell for the first time under the weight of the Cross." One saw it, felt it in one's bones, as for the first time; the pathos, the courage of this extraordinary man bearing to his execution the instrument of his own death. "Here is the Fourth Station of the Cross, where the Lord Jesus met his Mother." One saw her standing there, and again, as for the first time, thought, God, what *must* she have felt? More cameras clicked, but the group was unusually quiet. I remembered what Miss Patterson had said about the trip starting as a tour and ending as a pilgrimage. I think we all felt the drama of following in Christ's footsteps; not *exactly* here, perhaps, but certainly hereabouts; there was an unusual sense of occasion. "Here is the Fifth Station of the Cross, where Saint Simon of Cyrene helped the Lord Jesus to carry the Cross."

One woman leaned toward another. "Saint Simon of Cyrene was a Negro, did you know that?"

"*No?*"

"Yeah. An *African* Negro."

Pause.

"There weren't any *other* Negroes at that time, were there?"

"I guess not." Another pause. "He certainly didn't come from Alabamy."

"Here is the Sixth Station of the Cross, where the woman wiped the face of the Lord Jesus with a veil."

"What a beautiful, beautiful day."

"Isn't it? My, aren't we lucky to be here?"

"Here is the Seventh Station of the Cross, where the Lord Jesus fell for the second time."

It was about here that the Via Dolorosa passed through the sook, a long, covered-in bazaar, with shops of all kinds on either side. Here people pushed and jostled their way along: beefy Jordanian policemen, Greek Orthodox priests, tiny, round nuns, gaping fellow tourists; a boy carrying a sheep's head, a man holding a live fowl by its legs, another boy with bread rolls, like rubber rings, round each arm, a man in a cookshop frying strange, exotic dishes. The shops sold just about everything: rosaries and lavatory brushes and grapefruit and plastic mugs, dried fish, rubber balls, Kodak films, dark glasses, bags of grain and bottles of spice, fish from Beirut and Aqaba, bowls of black and green olives, colored eggs and feather dusters. Everywhere people shouted and chattered, and a hundred transistor radios blared out local music. One of our ladies pointed to a counter brimming with sweetmeats and said, "Is that their candy?" Ali, anxious to help, said, "Yes, you like some? I buy." Quickly the lady said, "No, *thank you*," and, to the others, "I'd rather die!" The ancient among ancients said, "If you ate that, you surely would die." An importunate Arab said, "Two dollars for color slides of the Stations of the Cross. Okay, then, lady, a dollar seventy-five."

We came out of the sook and arrived at the Church of the Holy Sepulcher, built on the alleged site of Christ's crucifixion and burial. There was not one church here, but several—Catholic, Greek Orthodox, Armenian—and the entrance gate was owned by a local Moslem. We went in through a great rococo door, and up steep stairs to Calvary. One old lady said to her husband, "I'm gonna have to go first, and you're gonna have to hold on to me." At the top were two chapels, one Greek Orthodox, one Franciscan. The Greek Orthodox one was full of oil-burning lamps and incense and ikons. The Franciscan had six plain candles with a crucifix in the middle. There was a Church of England parson sitting by the altar, reading the Bible. I thought of the Arabs I had seen reading the Koran in the Dome of the Rock, not an hour before, not a mile away. Which had found the truth?

Beyond the chapels were steps into the main body of the church, near the Stone of Unction. This was a plain stone slab, the length of a man, and was allegedly the place where Jesus was laid after being taken down from the Cross. There were Greek peasants all round it, some kneeling and praying, others kissing it. Ali said there were so many Greeks in the church because it was their Palm Sunday, and they had made special pilgrimages. They reminded me of pictures I had seen of Moslems at the Stone of the Kaaba in Mecca.

We went to the far end of the church, to the place where Jesus was believed to have been buried. A heavy stone mausoleum had been built over the top of the tomb, with an entrance so low and narrow that it could take only one person, stooped, at a time. On the walls twelve oil lamps were burning, and beneath them were portraits of the Apostles. Here a great press of people were waiting to get inside. Mostly they were women, and we, mostly women too, joined them.

We hadn't been there five minutes when a huge red-faced wall-

eyed police sergeant and two men started clearing a way for a procession. They knew nothing, this trio, of Christian behavior; they just
grabbed hold of whoever was in their way and threw them roughly
aside. The procession consisted of twelve Greek Orthodox priests,
wearing black hoods, beards, and spectacles; they were singing and
chanting with solemnity and looked like actors in a medieval Passion
play. At the rear was a huge bearded man wearing white vestments
and crown and swinging a golden incense burner. They popped into
the tomb and out again, bowed and scraped and crossed themselves,
and then disappeared, still chanting, in the direction from which they
had come.

No sooner had the crowd re-formed itself and a few more people
been allowed into the tomb than another procession, this time of
Copts, was announced, and the wall-eyed sergeant and his two men
pushed us around again. The Copts were followed by the Syrians.
While all this was going on, at the other end of the church an old
Greek archimandrite had come in and started a service. The place
was thick with old men and women, mostly Greek peasants in black,
wearing black shawls and caps. The archimandrite, who was rather a
beautiful old man, was dressed in silver. He had been placed in a sort
of wooden box about halfway up the church. But, having started the
service off, he left it to the lesser priests to carry it on. There were a
dozen or twenty of these, all wearing beards and box hats with curls
sprouting out of the back, like Elvis Presley or the Beatles. Sometimes
they walked about the church swinging incense burners, and then
two or three Jordanian police would beat the ground ahead of them
with long sticks so that the people had to move out of the way.

"Be still, and know that I am God." But there was no stillness here.
Outside Christ's tomb, incense burners were swung, torsos bowed,
mouths opened, chests crossed, batons raised, bodies pushed. Here it
was the same, with perhaps three hundred people all kneeling and
rising and genuflecting and crossing themselves, like a field of black
corn rustling in the summer wind. And over there, like bees fumb-
ling for their queen, people were still fawning and slobbering over
the Stone of Unction. What was it the little man in our party had
said about no religion being any good unless it led to right action?
Was this grinding abasement the sort of right action he had in mind?

An hour after entering the church our party was still waiting to
enter Christ's tomb. Suddenly, they had had enough; lunch and a rest
for tired feet were more important. A tomb which had gone by de-

fault for sixty or seventy years could wait another day, perhaps even another life. As they drifted away, I heard one woman consoling another: "Anyway, there's nothing to see. He's not there. He's *risen*."

I stayed on, and in time entered the tomb. It was a tiny place, little bigger than a sleeping compartment on a train. There was room for about six to stand. The only thing in there was a long marble slab, about two feet off the ground, in the shape of a bunk. This was where Christ was supposed to have been laid, but you got no feeling of it. Above were holy pictures and lamps and candles burning. An old man with a beard was holding out candles and holy water, and the people put the money for them on the marble slab.

I came out into the sunshine, and went back through the sook to the Damascus Gate to get a taxi to the hotel. I thought of all the places we had visited that morning, where Christ's presence had seemed so real, and again I felt the need for a Bible. Just outside the Damascus Gate, as if in answer to my thoughts, was a big bookstall with papers and magazines and secondhand books.

I strolled over and picked up some books at random. *Cravings,* by Jack Woodford. ("Riper than love, deeper than lust, her strange needs drove Erica to the brink"); *Maureen,* by Burton St. John ("Beautiful, dark and sultry, she kept nothing back from her wealthy white lover"); *The Twisted Ones* ("a story of strange love between beautiful women, so frankly told you will completely understand their desperate hungers"); *Sin Doll* ("The only way Cherry could get places was by going bad—and Cherry wanted to get places").

But they hadn't got a Bible, no, not anywhere there.

❂

THE GROUP lunched in the Seven Arches Restaurant, but I went along to the Demi-Tasse coffee shop, where I found Ali. The menu told me I could have a swankfurter ("a frankfurter wrapped in bacon and topped with tangy cheese"), a cheeseburger ("a hamburger topped with tangy cheese"), or an oriental-burger ("fresh ground beefsteak topped with curry sauce and chutney, a new taste sensation from the East"). I didn't fancy these and asked Ali what he'd been eating. He said sheep and rice and yoghurt, so I ordered some of that and a Jordan Valley Banana Split.

"I enjoyed your commentary very much this morning," I said, "but I wonder if I could correct you on one small thing."

"Pardon me," said Ali.

"At one moment," I said, "you referred to the Lord Jesus ascending to 'Heavens.' In English you can say either 'the Heavens' or 'Heaven,' but not just 'Heavens' on its own."

"But you say, 'for Heaven's sake,' " said Ali.

"Yes, but that really means 'for the sake of Heaven.' "

Ali smiled. "Very good. I learn. Thank you."

"How do you like the Americans?" I said.

Ali made a face. "No good!"

"Why not?"

"They tip badly. I prefer the English, the Italians, the Scandinavians, the Germans, or the French. They tip well or not at all. The Americans always give you a dollar. It's the same with the shopping. The Europeans buy something good or nothing. The Americans buy junk. They are very stupid peoples."

"People," I said.

"Not peoples?"

"No."

"Okay. People. They are very stupid people. My wife's father and my brother and all their families have gone to live in Washington. They say to me, 'Ali, why do you not come to live in Washington, too?' I can go any time I want. But I stay here."

"Why?"

"Because here I see these stupid peoples only a little part of every day. In America I would be seeing them all the times. That would be awful."

After lunch we assembled again outside. Two men in our party crossed the road and looked down at the brown, rocky fields that stretched away south of Jerusalem. One said to the other, "I can't think why the Jews and Arabs want to fight over this. You couldn't do a thing with it. It's too rocky for crops, and there's not enough grass for grazing. I guess they just like fighting each other."

Presently we walked down the Mount of Olives to the Garden of Gethsemane at the bottom. I have never really thought of Gethsemane as a garden in the formal sense so much as a field where wildflowers grew. But whatever its character in former days, there's no disputing it's a garden now. There are crisscross gravel paths, and neat, trim borders with rows of pansies and daisies and roses and pinks. Except for eight ancient olives, you might be in Surrey or Massachusetts. I think that of all the tourist attractions in Jerusalem, the Garden of Gethsemane was the only one to fail utterly to convey the presence of Christ. For one thing, it was loud with the chatter of visitors; for another, it was impossible, surveying those trim ranks of domesticated flowers, to imagine the long night of the agony, the lonely figure wrestling with his conscience on the hill, the disciples sleeping below. So I gave it up, and went and sat in the sunshine on a low wall, and eavesdropped on the pilgrims passing by.

"Hi."

"Well, hi!"

"American Express this way."

"Did you get a shot of the Blessed Virgin's tomb? Oh, it's fabulous. I liked it better than Bethlehem."

"Hi."

"Carol was sick yesterday, so we've had to stay over a day."

"Honey, how can I ever thank you for bringing us here. It's been the most wonderful, beautiful, moving experience."

"I want you to know that that Bufferin did wonders."

"Say, I believe you have the same camera as I have. Can you tell me how to set the flash?"

"My first daughter's name is Charlene. I shouldn't say this, but she has just the sweetest disposition in the world."

"That's real olive wood. If you can't smell it, lick it."

"Hi."

"She's with her niece and sister, so she's all right."

"Have you tried their butterscotch? It's real good."

"If you don't come now, Mr. Johnson, we're going to lose you. There's a whole lot of people coming up the hill."

✪

LATER, BACK at the hotel, I talked to the Intercontinental's manager, Mr. Richard Squier. A diploma on the wall said he was a Bachelor of Science from Cornell University.

"One of our main problems here has been wising up to the local travel agents. There are something like forty-two of them and while some are good, most are bad. I can prove they've made an average

profit of fifty-three percent on every tour they've done. But we're getting on top of that right now.

"Another problem is that we don't have a proper lounge. We're a
group hotel primarily, and the average age of our guests is between
fifty and sixty, so we need a proper lounge. Why we don't have a
lounge, I don't know. None of the hotel directors have been out here
since we opened, so I haven't had an opportunity to ask them. But the
matter is being rectified. We've put forward definite plans for a
lounge, and they've been approved.

"The situation about Bibles is that the Jordan government won't
allow them on public display, because this is a Moslem country. But
here's what we're going to do. The Billy Graham organization is going to send us a stack of Bibles, and I'm going to keep them here
under lock and key and loan them out to the guests as and when they
demand them.

"Our only other problem right now is that some people complain
we're too far from town. So I'm thinking of having two Volkswagens
run to the Damascus Gate every half hour, and charge a small sum to
make it worthwhile.

"Do I like it here? Well, I can't say I'm *inspired*. I don't have any
circle of friends here. There just isn't anybody to inspire me."

✪

MISS PATTERSON's group was going into Israel the next morning, but
she wasn't going with them. I gathered she was going to try and get
her ear right and then go back to the States by ship.

That night in the hotel, Miss Patterson and her group took leave of
each other, and it was quite an emotional experience. "What a wonderful group you've been," said Miss Patterson, as though they were
children who'd behaved well on the school outing. "You're just a one-
in-a-million group." They looked at her in adoration, grateful, misty-
eyed. Then they repaid the compliments, pumping her hand, telling
her the tour would have been nothing without her, saying they were
real sorry to be saying goodbye but they would all meet up again real
soon. Americans, I've noticed, seem to have more need than most of
this sort of personal reassurance.

That night I dined with Miss Patterson and some of the group. At
the end of dinner they said goodbye to the headwaiter, and tipped

him. "Goodbye, goodbye," he said. "See you again next year." For
some reason, they found this hugely funny. "See us again next year,
eh?" said the ancient among ancients. "That's pretty good." After
dinner he went round telling those who had missed it, "We all said
goodbye to the headwaiter, and he said goodbye to us, and do you
know what he said then? 'See you again next year!' That's pretty
good, don't you think?"

By the way they laughed, they did think so. I didn't think it all
that funny myself.

✪

Next day I went to get a prescription from a Dr. Kalbian, who
worked in a hospital a little way down the road. Dr. Kalbian said,
"I've had two American patients I particularly remember. The first
was a banker, a man of sixty-four. I was called in to see him and found
he hadn't had anything to drink for four days and was suffering from
liquid exhaustion. So I asked why, and he said this was his first trip
abroad and he'd been told before leaving America that if you drank
any liquid at all east of Suez, you were liable to die. He'd seen other
people drinking, but he couldn't bring himself to risk it. It took me
fifteen minutes of hard persuasion to get him to take a glass of water.
He then drank something like thirteen half pints straight off.

"I had another patient, a young American tourist, and he had to be
in bed the whole time he was here. So I was sympathizing with him
and saying I was sorry he was going to miss the sights, and he just
smiled and said, 'That's okay, Doctor, I haven't got a thing to worry
about. I've got a buddy of mine down there with my camera and he's
going to take shots of all the sights for me.' And, you know, he really
meant it."

✪

I defy anyone who is not totally dull of soul to go to Jerusalem and
not feel overwhelmed by the presence of Christ, to suffer with him in
adversity, to triumph with him at the end; for he was one of the first
to unlock the secrets of the human heart, to teach us how to live and
love and die. And yet, nearness works both ways. For if being in Jeru-

salem makes one think about Christ as a man, one realizes how little one knows him as a man. There must have been times when, like the rest of us, he passed wind and water, had a frog in his throat or a fly in his eye, suffered all the ills and inconveniences that flesh is heir to. But we do not know about these; the record is selective; the authors of the Gospels have left us what they wanted to leave, what was important to them. If it had been recorded that Christ had an attack of hiccups while addressing the Pharisees, or stubbed his toe on a rock while coming down from the Sermon on the Mount, the man might have been enlarged, but the deity would have been diminished. And so, what is still worshiped today, though by increasingly fewer people, is not a man at all, but a myth, a legend—almost, I was going to say, a god.

✪

THERE IS no more striking example of how American technology has altered a country's living standards than in Saudi Arabia.

Thirty, even twenty years ago, Saudi Arabia was living in the Middle Ages. Most of the buildings in the capital of Riyadh were of dried mud, without windows or doors; the largest and fanciest, fairy-tale castles with crenelated battlements and four round towers, belonged to the dynasty of Abdul Aziz and its founder, the legendary King Ibn Saud (whose son Faisal is Saudi Arabia's king and prime minister today). The richer families owned slaves, many of them children or grandchildren of slaves brought across the Red Sea from Ethiopia and Sudan. Camel and foot were the normal means of locomotion. Because of the puritanism of the Wahabi sect which brought Ibn Saud to power, social life was austere. Women were heavily veiled outdoors, and many indoors. Alcohol was forbidden, and the penalties against it were severe. A thief was liable to have his right hand chopped off in public, and women taken in adultery were publicly stoned to death. The only foreigners welcome were fellow Moslems on their way to Mecca. You could count Westerners on the fingers of one hand.

Today in Saudi Arabia things are different. Most of Riyadh's mud houses have been pulled down, and shiny new buildings of glass and concrete are taking their place. The slaves have been freed, though most continue to serve their past owners at nominal rates. Public mutilations and executions are on the decline. The yashmak is still worn in the streets, though increasingly leather is giving way to crepe and nylon. The camel has bowed to the Cadillac. Some of Ibn Saud's sons having developed a taste for liquor on their western junketings, this is now not impossible to obtain. And the foreigners—salesmen and agents and journalists and tourists—are increasingly within the gates.

This astonishing change in Saudi Arabian affairs is due to one thing only: oil. In 1933 the Standard Oil Company of California was granted a concession to prospect for oil in the eastern province of Saudi Arabia. The following year a small party of geologists pitched their tents near the town of Dammam and started drilling. In 1938 they struck oil in commercial quantities. Today, just thirty years later, the operations of Aramco (Arabian-American Oil Company) are spread over 1,000 square miles. At its headquarters at Dhahran, at the production center at Abqaiq, at the refinery at Ras Tanura and in smaller outlying establishments, over thirteen hundred Americans and ten thousand Saudi Arabs live and work. The countryside has been transformed. The community of al-Khobar, in 1939 a collection of mud huts, is now a town of 23,000 people. The capital investment of Aramco is over a billion dollars, and the company exports over two million barrels of oil daily. More than half the value of every barrel exported is paid in royalties and taxes to the Saudi Arabian government. Put another way, eighty percent of the income of the Saudi government comes from oil, and nearly ninety percent of its oil income comes from Aramco. That is the measure of its dependence.

I spent a week at the company's headquarters at Dhahran, and of all the American ghettos I visited it was one of the strangest. Around the township the lone and level sands stretch far away, the great desert where only wandering Bedouins live in their black tents, and only the black vultures fly. But behind the palisades lies a world more American than America, ordered, hygienic, and secure. In the big, cool administration building Americans and Saudis work together behind shuttered panes and pad down corridors as bare and antiseptic as those of any Stateside hospital. And in the evening when the Saudis go home in the company's buses, the American executives and secretaries walk home along trim American-style streets and avenues to trim one-story American-style houses, where, behind dainty formal hedges, bougainvillaea, oleander, tamarisk and acacia bloom, and sprinklers dampen the burnt lawns. For visitors there is a company guesthouse with foam-rubber mattresses in air-conditioned bedrooms, drinking fountains in the corridors and prints on the walls. All this, in architectural terms, is in the Southwestern tradition of American town planning.

Americans at Aramco make salaries between thirty and forty percent higher than their equivalents in the States, and they may retire at one-third salary after fifteen years' service. This is the compensation the company pays for the remoteness and artificiality of the life. For it is not only artificial in that it bears no relation to the Arabian way of life that exists all round it, but it also bears little relation to the American way of life it is said to represent. The essence of small-town American life is government by democracy, but government by Aramco is that of a benevolent dictatorship. Americans are much attached to the free-enterprise system of which Aramco is a shining example; but to live as an Aramco employee is to be a citizen of a superbly well-organized welfare state. What the company doesn't hand out free, like telephone and medical services, it offers at deflated prices, like food and rent and utilities. "Big Brother looks after you" might well be Aramco's motto. Even the make-up of the community is artificial, for there are no old people, no young adults, and, except in holiday time, no teen-agers above the age of fourteen. Employees retire at sixty, if not before, executives are not sent to Saudi Arabia until their late twenties, and the company's school does not teach beyond the ninth grade.

For many at Aramco time hangs heavy, and all kinds of leisure activities have been devised; there are tennis courts, a swimming pool, a hobby farm, a cinema, riding stables, a golf course, and the company's own television station. This broadcasts programs in Arabic, and these include news and adult education, as well as Westerns and old movies; an Aramco censor (the wife of one of the executives) snips out scenes of kissing, drinking and belly-dancing. An English sound track can be picked up by turning down the volume on the television set and tuning in to a wave length on the local radio station. On two other wave lengths, jazz and classical music are played nonstop throughout the day.

Women at Dhahran, mainly wives of executives but some bachelorette secretaries too, have special problems as regards leisure. My sponsor at Dhahran, a delicious owl-faced man in his fifties called Jack, said, "Some of the women here used to go nuts. Some still do. Houseboys do the housework, gardeners do the garden, children go to school, and they have nothing. So this becomes quite a trial. There's a lot of activity, quite low-key, and, of course, you can get drunk, which a few do." Some of the women's low-key activities are collecting shells and shards, having morning bridge or canasta parties, meeting at the Women's Club, buying and selling at the secondhand shop. But, as one executive said to me, "Many of the wives here don't have the cultural background to deal with their free time. So they fill it up aimlessly, with a lot of nonsense. With some women this is natural, with others it is not." One of their worst frustrations is not being allowed to drive cars outside the base; if they want to ride or play golf or go shopping in al-Khobar, they must hire a taxi. Rarely does a wife break this rule; for if she is caught, her husband will be sent to prison.

With two major exceptions Moslem law does not apply in the base itself. "This is a lawless community," said Jack. "If anyone does something he shouldn't, we don't tell the Saudis, we just ship him home. You could get away with a murder here, I guess, so long as they didn't find the body." The exceptions are that liquor and churches are forbidden.

The Americans have got round these two laws quite artfully. There are three priests at the base, Catholic, Episcopalian and Methodist. They all wear mufti. The company provides them with a house and transport, but they are paid by their own parishioners. They have converted rooms in their houses into small chapels. They are not allowed to advertise times of services publicly, but send circulars through the mail instead.

Circumventing the liquor laws requires more ingenuity. New arrivals at Aramco buy an outgoing family's liquor still; in this they brew a white substitute for gin, and a brown one for whisky. "Brown and Schweppes" and "white and tonic" are the standard drinks for visitors to any executive home. They don't taste bad. The stills cost thirty-five dollars each, and there's an explanatory booklet called "The Blue Flame," prepared by the safety engineer's department. "The materials," said Jack, "are sugar, yeast and water. You let the mixture stand for fourteen days and then you take the run. A run averages about three hours to every gallon of liquor, and it generally runs about four times. We call watching the run 'baby-sitting.' One or two people have been crazy enough to go to the movies instead of baby-sitting and have had their houses burn down. The proof goes up to around a hundred and ninety on the last run, and you cut that in two to get the drinking stuff. It costs about forty cents a quart, which makes it the cheapest drinking liquor in the world."

Among themselves the American employees are on easy, Christian-name terms; in such an enclosed order any other arrangement would be impossible. With the Saudis, relationships are less happy. It is to the Americans that the Saudis owe the revolutionary changes in their whole way of life. Saudis whose families dwelt in mud huts and lived from hand to mouth are now employed in every sort of Aramco activity from skilled engineer to hospital orderly. One sees them all over the base, spotless in white shirts and trousers, a vivid contrast to the average bedraggled Arab. Aramco has educated them, trained them, housed them, and generally fitted them for loftier things. And yet, when the day's work is over and the final whistle blows, most Saudis go home to Aramco-built houses outside the base and the Americans to theirs within it. Some senior Saudis—those who have become more American than their employers and whose only dream is to sail westward and leave old Arabia far behind—would like to live in the base, too; but Aramco has deliberately pursued a policy of encouraging them to remain in, and become leaders of, their own community. Some schizophrenia is the result; like the Indians in the days of the British raj, many Saudis lead an uneasy double life, uncertain where their true loyalties lie. The liquor laws increase the difficulties of social intercourse. As Jack said, "Americans don't ask a Saudi to a party unless they know him terribly well, and no Saudi is going to drink at a party where there are other Saudis, unless he knows them terribly well. So on the whole the Saudis miss out on the parties."

✪

ON MY second day Jack took me on a conducted tour. He was a delightful companion and made witty, pithy comments on everything we saw: there were no sacred cows for him, inside Aramco or out.

As we approached the archway at the main entrance, I read: "FASTEN SEAT BELTS, DRIVE SLOWER, LIVE LONGER." On the archway itself was written: "TAKE SAFETY HOME WITH YOU." Aramco is full of exhortations like that, though most of the inmates have long since ceased to notice them. We made a sweep past the international airport, with its Arabian-Nights reception center, built as a jet staging post between Europe and the Far East and made obsolete almost before it was completed, and passed the entrance to the port. Here was a small archway with the sign "ROYAL SAUDI NAVY." "Only navy in the world," said Jack, "that managed to sink itself by flushing the toilet." I said, "How do you mean?" and Jack said, "At the time, they only had this one launch. Some guy pulled the lever in the head and opened the seacock. The thing sank."

We came to the riding school, which consisted of twenty looseboxes in the shape of an oval, with a clubhouse in the center and a sand track between. This place too was full of exhortations: "DON'T APPROACH REAR OF HORSES"; "USE CARE WITH MATCHES AND CIGARETTES"; "RIDE WITH EITHER BRIDLE OR HACKAMORE"; "DO NOT PET OR TEASE THE HORSES." There were marvelous-looking Arab horses in the stallboxes, many snow-white. The clubhouse was empty except for a barman called Abdul, who gave us two Coca-Colas; Jack said it wouldn't get busy until the afternoon.

We went on to the golf course, which had a much nicer clubhouse with caricatures of members on the walls and trophies in a case and no exhortations at all. About a hundred goats had gathered on the first tee; there were no fairways to speak of and the greens were of oiled sand. "Golf here is a hazardous kind of a deal," said Jack. "Camels and sheep tend to eat the balls. And I'm told that at some of the tees they've had to seal up the drinking-water containers. There were complaints of the water tasting like talcum powder, and when the secretary looked into it he found that little Arab boys from al-Khobar were using them as urinals. They thought it a great game."

We drove back to the base. On the way I said, "Why does Aramco have this great big public-relations department? Apart from the Saudi government, whom do they have to impress?"

Jack said, "All big organizations have big public-relations departments as a matter of prestige, didn't you know that?" He gave a Cheshire-cat grin. "Besides, it gives us something to do. Otherwise we'd be out of a job."

I said, "The head of your department told me last night that he had to work ten and twelve hours a day and take work home with him, and that if he didn't he couldn't hold down his job."

"A lot of people here say that," said Jack. "It's partly the American hysteria about getting ahead, and partly a guilt thing. They feel guilty about the size of the salaries they're drawing, and having relatively little to do in return. There are some men here who haven't got two days' work a week. So they create a whole lot of overtime to even things out. That way their consciences are eased."

"Do you ever feel guilty?" I said.

"Oh, God, no," said Jack. "But then I don't have any huge ambitions. Very soon now I'm going back home to Oregon to live like a squire among the landed gentry."

We drove under the main archway, which said "GATEWAY TO SAFETY" in letters about ten feet high, and went to the administrative building. Here we saw Mr. Jensen, an expert on the administrative side. Mr. Jensen seemed incapable of answering the simplest question in less than five minutes, and without going down the corridor to get supporting documentation. When I asked him about housing and rents, he said, "Housing assignments are based on position plus years of service. During his time with the company a man accumulates so many points toward a more desirable type of housing. We have six main categories of housing and eighteen subsections." Thinking he was about to go into the subsections, I said quickly, "What is the average rent?" I thought Mr. Jensen would tell me whatever it was, but instead he said, "I can get that figure for you," and padded off again down the corridor. Jack said, "I guess he likes exercise."

When he had come back with the figure, I asked what the biggest problem was, apart from the artificiality of the life. Mr. Jensen said, "I would say without a doubt the problem of getting spare parts when things break down, and the further problem of buying things, especially clothes, which are the right size and style." Jack nodded and said, "This is true of almost everything outside of food." Mr. Jensen said, "For example, recently I needed a new clutch for the air-conditioning in my car. I couldn't get it here or in Bahrein or Beirut, so I had to send to the States for it. It cost a hundred dollars and was wrong when it arrived. I asked for a clutch and they sent me a pulley." Jack said, "You can multiply that experience a hundred times. I've been waiting six months now for some finishing nails." Mr. Jensen said, "Shoes are another problem, especially for children. They take three months to arrive, and then don't fit." Before we left Mr. Jensen, I asked him why people joined Aramco. "A great variety of reasons," he said, "but mainly the money and the adventure." Jack grinned and said, "We all know what the adventure is worth."

At lunchtime Jack took me to his house for a white and tonic and some sandwiches prepared by his wife, and then we set off again. In the empty streets the elegant houses and gardens baked silently in the afternoon sun. It reminded me of Bel-Air or Beverly Hills. We passed a child of five standing beside a telegraph pole and speaking into a telephone. Jack said, "That's a cute idea. We have these public telephones dotted around, and the kids call up their mothers and tell them where they are." He went on: "The kids love this place beyond description. We adults have this problem of isolation. You build up a set of friends and then they're dispersed. But with the kids it's a kind of international club, it's like a fraternity. The older ones go to school in Beirut or Europe, and then the company sends a plane to pick them up at the end of the term. That's always a wild flight."

We passed a small crescent and Jack said, "That's the street where the priests live. We call it Holy Row. When the bachelor girls lived there we called it Menopause Circle." We came to the recreation area and got out. The place was crawling with exhortations. We visited the tennis courts ("ONLY PERSONS WITH TENNIS SHOES OR SNEAKERS ARE PERMITTED ON COURTS. PERSONS WEARING OTHER TYPE SHOES MUST STAY OFF COURT SURFACES"); the bowling alleys ("USERS OF THIS FACILITY DO SO AT THEIR OWN RISK"); the cinema ("PLEASE DO NOT SPILL UNWANTED POPCORN IN THE THEATRE"); the Women's Exchange ("NO SMOKING BEYOND THIS DOOR. ALL SALES ARE FINAL"); and the Snack Bar ("B.S.A. MEETING 7:15. NO GUN. NEAT APPEARANCE"). We finished up at the swimming pool, which had so many exhortations it made you dizzy. "ENTRY FOR POOL PATRONS ONLY," it said at the entrance door, "NO DOGS ALLOWED." We went in, and saw in bold red letters: "ALL SWIMMERS MUST TAKE A SHOWER IN THE NUDE USING SOAP AND THOROUGHLY RINSING THEMSELVES BEFORE ENTERING THE POOL. ALL PERSONS WEARING BANDAGES, SUFFERING FROM COLD FEVERS, SKIN INFECTION AND INFLAMED EYES SHALL REFRAIN FROM USING THE POOL." I took a peek into the dressing room and saw a huge, hairy man thoroughly rinsing his balls and saying to a boy beside him, "Next time we'll take the tenderfoot section, John." Round the pool were more exhortations: "RESIDUAL CHLORINE IN POOL IS FOR PROTECTION OF BATHERS FROM SKIN AND OTHER POSSIBLE DISEASES ASSOCIATED WITH BATHING" and, on the inside edge of the pool, "EXPECTORATING WILL NOT BE TOLERATED EXCEPT IN THE SCUM GUTTERS." Jack smiled and said, "You'd think it would be enough to repel anyone from going in." We walked round the pool once. There were quite a few children there, full of teeth like all the Kennedys, splashing about and shouting. On the way out we passed a tiny square boy being held by his mother over a drinking fountain and taking huge draughts. He was wearing a toy

GI helmet. His mother said, "He's like a *camel*. I can't get him to stop."

We got into the car and went to the school. "So you see," said Jack, "it's not a bad life, and we're pretty well provided for." I said, "How often do you manage to get away?" Jack said, "For every month we stay here, we earn three days' vacation. So every two years we're entitled to ten weeks' vacation in the States. In addition they give us a two-week vacation every year, which most people spend in Europe."

The school was like every other building in the base, cool, bright, hygienic, with spotless linoleum flooring; I half expected to see a doctor or nurse come trundling round the corner with a patient. Classes were over for the day, but we heard the girl cheerleaders practicing for the basketball match against Ras Tanura. The group consisted of seven girls in two rows, aged about twelve or thirteen. This was their cheer:

"Is everybody ready?
    Let's go!
Have you got that spirit?
    Yeah, man!
You gonna use that spirit?
    Sure am!
Gonna get that ball?
    Sure can!
All ready?
    All right!
Go, team!
    Fight, fight!"

The team was as disciplined as the Rockettes or the Tiller girls, clapping hands at the end of each line, contorting their bodies into the strangest positions, sometimes resting on one knee, or jumping up or bending sideways. After this cheer they did another:

"S-U-C-C-E-S-S.
    That's the way to spell 'success.'
    That's no crime, that's no sin,
    That's our motto, may the best team win!"

On the way back to the guesthouse we stopped off at the commissary. Here were more exhortations: "ALWAYS ALERT, NOBODY HURT";

and "Good HOUSEKEEPING, GOOD SAFETY." I bought two pencils, and when I got back to my room I saw that on one was inscribed "Repair and prevent or neglect and repent"; and on the other, "The match you toss may cause great loss." With one of the pencils I wrote, "This must be one of the most regimented free societies ever."

Out at Half-Moon Bay on Sunday, I sat in the sea on a deck chair and watched the pale-gray and milk-white jellyfish come and go, and let the water slop over me. Next to me was a man with two bluebirds and "U. S. S. California" tattooed on his chest. He pulled at a Coca-Cola and said, "Aramco does everything for you. I would say too much. It's like going back to mother's womb. You get out of the habit of making decisions. But I like the life. With all its disadvantages I'd rather have it than life back home. Of course you have to be temperamentally suited. It's no good coming just for the money. We all do that, but you have to come for something else as well." Jack, on the other side of me, said, "I'd like to know what."

Mrs. Zinola, cool in green trousers and a green flowered blouse behind the blinds of her cool, tidy house, said, "It's certainly an easy life. If the window doesn't open, you call Housing on the phone and they come and fix it. You get on the bus and the bus is free. You go to the store and buy what's there. You don't start haggling over it, because there's only one place to buy it. And with a standard fee for utilities, you don't bother to go around switching off the lights."

At a wedding party (the wedding, forbidden in Dhahran, had taken place in nearby Bahrein), I met three wives. One was married to a Saudi; she wore glasses which made her eyes the size of billiard balls. She said, "I don't know where I belong any more. I'd like to get into some group, but I can't. We have a son of six, and he *really* doesn't know where he belongs. I feel so uneasy with people, and it makes me behave like I was a little girl of fifteen." Another, recently arrived in Dhahran, sighed and said, "We want to go and live in al-Khobar. This place is strictly for the birds." And a third, who had just completed two years, said, "You get kind of spongelike here. There's nothing to stimulate you. Have you noticed how *quiet* everything is?"

And one day I went to a lunch party and was given a drink and put on a sofa near a pretty woman who was talking on the telephone. When she rang off she looked sad, so I said sympathetically, "Problems?" She forced a little smile and said, "Well, kind of. Our little kiddie has just had an operation." I thought, How strong-willed of you not to be at the hospital, how admirable to come out to lunch. She said, "He just came out of the anesthetic, and he's still a little unsteady on his feet." I looked at her sharply and thought, Well, Christ, I should think he is, and what kind of a hospital is it that lets him try, and why aren't you over there, anyway? I said, trying to keep calm, "What's the matter with him?" She said, quietly, "My husband and I decided to have him castrated." I thought, I'm not well, I'm hearing things, women like this don't exist. Trembling, I said, "You decided to have *who* castrated?" The woman said, "Why, our little kitty, like I told you. To stop him from becoming a great, big tom."

❂

FATHER ROMAN ANENT, the Catholic priest, went in for exhortations too. "SMILE, GOD LOVES YOU," it said on the front of his door. So I smiled and pushed the bell and presently a small houseboy appeared. He took me to the dining room, where Father Roman was typing with two fingers on a table with a flowered linoleum top. Father Roman was wearing a smart gray-blue shirt tucked into well-creased gray trousers, and looked like Spencer Tracy. We smiled to show God loved us, and shook hands. There were shelves of religious books on one wall and pictures of Christ and some sheep and various popes on the other. The radio was tuned in to the classical-music wavelength.

Father Roman was drinking a white and tonic, and he offered me one. He said, reading my thoughts, "I don't make the stuff myself, but I have plenty of good friends who do." He called for his boy, "Hey, John!" and, when John appeared, gave him the order. "John takes good care of me," he said. Father Roman lit a cigarette, let the smoke out through his nostrils, and took a sip at his white and tonic. "This isn't bad stuff," he said, "but I was raised in Milwaukee in the shadow of Pabst and Schlitz, so I miss a good beer."

"How did you come to get here?" I said.

Father Roman said, "Well, I was a missionary in the jungles of Central America for thirteen years, and I had a gun on my hip for most of that time. Then I found myself leading a monastic life in a seminary in Wisconsin. My superior in Detroit got to hear that I wasn't too happy there, and when this job came up he thought it might be a challenge for me."

"How did he have a hand in it?"

"We are members of the Capuchin order, and Catholic priests in this area and right down through Ethiopia and Eritrea have always been Capuchins. This is a tradition that goes back to Richelieu and Pierre Joseph."

John appeared with my white and tonic, and Father Roman and I raised our glasses.

"How has the challenge worked out?"

"I would say pretty well. The night I moved in here, the Cairo radio broadcast that the Catholic Church was opening a cathedral in Dhahran, and mentioned my name in connection with it. They were trying to put the local people on the spot and inflame the Wahabi against me. But I'm happy to say it blew over."

"How many parishioners do you have?"

"Every Friday I have over a thousand people come here. Friday, as you know, is the Moslem day of rest, and for practical reasons the company has made it the Christian day of rest, too. Our weekend is Thursday and Friday, not Saturday and Sunday. I get around a hundred confessions every week, and in Holy Week nearly a thousand. I have two Masses every Friday and daily Mass at six o'clock and a rosary devotional every evening."

"It sounds a lot."

"It is a lot, and I have no nuns to help me. If it wasn't for the voluntary work of some of the bachelorettes, I don't know where I'd be. Also I have three hundred and six children."

"Are all your flock American?"

"Indeed not. I am a Catholic with the most Catholic flock in the world. We have many Indians here as domestic servants. Most are from Goa, which was formerly Portuguese territory, and ninety percent of them are Catholics. And we have Italians and Palestinians and Pakistanis and all sorts. A couple of weeks back we had confirmation, and the Bishop asked me about a woman called Barioli. I told him she was a Finn married to an Italian. I said, 'Bishop, that makes the fifty-first country in my flock.' "

"Where does the bishop come from?"

"Aden. He comes in a necktie—in civvies, as I call it."

"The Saudis don't mind?"

"They don't mind what we do so long as we're discreet. They know perfectly well that this is the padre's house and what goes on here. But it doesn't bother them." Father Roman lit another cigarette. "We did have one heck of a job getting some of our holy figures smuggled in, though. In the chapel we have this beautiful life-size figure of Jesus in his crib. I'll show it to you. I got a friend's daughter to bring it in. She wrapped the figure in shawls so you couldn't see the face, and cradled it in her arms, and the customs men thought it was her baby!"

"What do you think of the life here?"

"Materially speaking, I'm probably the most well-to-do missionary in the Catholic Church. On the other hand, there's always this feeling of being in a concentration camp. I find that when I take even a short trip, to Bahrein, say, it's like the lifting of a great weight. When you've been here a long time, you get moments of wanting to break out of Aramco's socialized world and do something on your own. But you can't, because outside the fence is Arabia, and you have no part in that."

We finished our drinks, and Father Roman took me to see the chapel and the confessional and Jesus in his crib. At the door he said, "Have you visited the Christian cemetery?"

"No."

"Well, ask your sponsor about it. I think it might interest you. It's the only Christian cemetery in Arabia. There's a guy called Mohlmann who runs it, and he's kind of interesting, too."

✪

AND THEN I visited the bachelor girls, who lived like birds in the wilderness, in neat little houses with never a hair out of place. They were all ages between about twenty-five and fifty, and some lived singly and some together. A few had come to Aramco a long while ago looking for husbands, and had not found them; now they had settled for Aramco's long-term benefits, sunshine and travel and a cushioned retirement, with perhaps the bottle or the Church or the occasional affair to help them along the road. I asked young and old alike why they had come and how they liked it. Most answered briefly enough. But Miranda Bugatti of the olive skin and raven hair and extravagant gesture, Miranda Bugatti who was twenty-five years old and had been at Aramco only six months, Miranda Bugatti drew a deep breath and said:

"I had this very, how do you say, cosmopolitan upbringing in San Francisco with, you know, Negroes and Mexicans and others. My brother had this, you know, creative eye for photography, and I was helping him. That's why I didn't join the Peace Corps, because they only give you about fifty dollars a month. But I never lost my interest in what you might call foreign people. I was very good friends with a Japanese housemaid in Connecticut, and this interest kept growing. And when I went to work in New York, I belonged to the Tagore Society, which helps to promote, how do you say, culture exchange like Indian dinners and music programs. And I participated in the Asia Society and I belonged to the Friends of the Middle East and I came across this Japanese poetry called haiku, which describes natural things, you know, blossom and what not, and then it also has, how do you say, philosophy, philosophical ideas. I also helped with Eastern people, you know, broadening them out. It was a kind of volunteer-type thing, and I had a Persian student and I helped him apply for college. And I was in touch with a chaplain who was associated with the Young Men's Christian Association, you know, the Y, and they looked after people in the Belgian lines, and you went to small parties, it was person-to-person like, and you taught them, you know, that 'cop' meant 'policeman.'

"So it all added up. I had this, how do you say, sensitivity to different peoples, and I wanted to travel and see them all, and then I met this man at a party, and he happened to say that Aramco had this, you know, opening. Oh, I had such great ideas of Arabic, *Rubáiyát* of Omar Khayyam and all that, and when I came here, everyone thought I was Persian or Lebanese or something, even the Saudis did. I never knew I looked like that. Last Sunday I went to a wedding at Qatif, and that was just wonderful, you know, the color and the ceremony. A lot of people, you know, Americans, don't realize what they've got here. It's like, how would you say, a personal matter. But everyone here at Aramco is so gracious and friendly. The money's wonderful. You can meet with the local people and associate with them. I feel I have a, you know, affinity with them, and they have with me.

"I don't date steady. It could be either coffee or dinner, or down to

the airport or a drive to Ras Tanura or the pool café, or sometimes I
go to the library and carry on my correspondence. I write to about
thirty people from India to, you know, Greece. I write to a German
oceanographer, a Japanese law student, a Greek officer. Once a week I
go to the hospital. I buy balloons, I take about thirty balloons down
there for the children. I meet a lot of nurses there, Indian nurses
mostly. Now, that's a whole new world. That hospital is like a, how
do you say, like a channel into the people. But when you visit, you
ought not to be too, how shall I say, artificial. If you're visiting, say, a
Jamaican, then you should be a little, you know, Jamaican.

"I remember Eleanor Roosevelt writing in a magazine and saying,
'I believe in all my travels that the American youth have the greatest
opportunity to use their vision and reach for the stars and fulfill
themselves. Then there'd be no excuse for them to say they'd love to
travel but they couldn't.' There was some wonderful thinking in this
article. It was just a little before she passed away that she wrote it. In
Woman's Day, I think it was. And my brother wrote this wonderful
poem:

> Not that you did, but you didn't
> Not that she did, but she didn't.

And in the end he just said, 'You are the losers.' It was really very
good.

"I would have liked to work in an orphanage in India, but they
have, you know, local people and can't afford Americans. I'd have
liked Catholic relief too, but I didn't want to get too, how do you say,
dedicated. I want to be both worldly and have something of myself. If
I went full time into charity work, I wouldn't accumulate enough
money to, you know, live on. Like as I say, I think the Peace Corps is
wonderful if you have a livelihood already.

"But I do love certain, you know, constants. I love the sea. I love
natives. I love Manhattan. It's good for the arts and all that. I love
children very much and, you know, people. At fourteen I could like
the *Rubáiyát;* now it might be something else. It's not in my nature
to like, how do you say, authority things. I pick up periods rather
than the whole epic from A to Z. I'm the poet-and-peasant type, not
the tower type. I don't like anything for too long. I'm not the, you
know, intellectual or aesthetic type either."

Suddenly there was silence, as when a street excavator outside one's window abruptly ceases, or one closes a door against a gale of wind. Miranda Bugatti smoothed her raven hair.

"Is that the kind of thing you want?" she said.

"That's it," I said. *"That's it exactly!"*

✪

THE HEAD of Jack's department, who was called Carl, took me to Ras Tanura for a day of lectures. Carl was giving one lecture himself, and on the way we picked up a Saudi called Hassan Ali, who was giving another.

"Do you call yourself Hassan or Ali?" said Carl when Hassan Ali had settled in.

"Mostly Hassan."

"We have three Ali Khalifas in our office," said Carl. Then he said, "One of our employees died on us yesterday."

"I know," said Hassan. "He was my friend and neighbor. I feel so bad about him."

"It was a coronary," said Carl. "Thirty-seven years old."

"He had five children, and his wife is expecting a sixth," said Hassan. "I saw him on the bus in the morning, and he seemed all right then."

"You speak very good English," said Carl.

"I went to college in Pennsylvania," said Hassan.

"This man who died," I said, "will his widow get any compensation?"

"Oh, sure," said Carl. "The company will pick up the tab on his house, and they'll also pay a lump sum so that she can buy a shop or a small business or something."

It was a long, straight road to Ras Tanura, with sand on every side and mirage all the way, so that in the far distance the road spiraled into a kind of shimmering lake, and telegraph poles and palm trees and even the silver chimneys of Ras Tanura seemed to be suspended above it, floating freely in the milk-blue sky.

At Ras Tanura it didn't need anyone to tell you, as it did at Dhahran, that the place was connected with oil. There was this complex of gleaming silver pipes, vertical and horizontal and angled, like a giant robot's intestines, and rising from it a long, thin stack crowned with a scarlet flame, which day and night burned up the waste gases. East-ward, out of the base, stretched four giant pipes, each the diameter of a steam engine's boiler, which carried the oil to the loading jetties and to the silver storage tanks squatting on the sand like cakes on a baker's tray. There was also the smell.

Carl drove us to the main dining hall, which was close to the Per-sian Gulf. We had a boring hamburger-and-fruit-pie lunch, and then came the six lectures. The best were those by Carl and Hassan. Carl talked about Aramco-Saudi relations; Hassan's talk was "Some Effects of Change among the People of the Eastern Province," and it was surprisingly sophisticated and witty. Of the other lectures, three were read by a man called Winston Trent ("You'll all remember Win-ston," said the chairman, "from when he was L.T.A. here at Ras Tanura"), but, as Winston Trent was quite unschooled in public speaking, these were even more boring than they need have been. (When I got back to Dhahran, I asked Jack what was the point of assembling people from miles around to listen to the reading of a lecture which could have been digested more profitably in bed. "Well, it's a way of filling in another day," said Jack. "It gives them all some-thing to do.")

One lecture, delivered by Trent but written by a man called Metz, was severely critical of the Saudi government: the government em-ployed 170,000 people, or one out of three potential employees, which surely was ridiculously high; nepotism was rife, corruption widespread, the civil service inefficient and the educational system an-tique. I looked at the Saudis in the audience to see how they were reacting; most looked glassy-eyed—stunned, no doubt, by sleep-giving Winston Trent. At the end of this lecture a bull-necked American got up and said, "Will the lecturer tell us when we may hope to see Saudi government agencies working eight hours a day instead of two or three?" And Trent replied, with all the primness of which only Americans are capable, "I'm glad you asked that question, because it's a sign of the real sickness that's all too prevalent in Saudi Arabia. There's a real need here for dedicated people who have a pride in their job and a sense of responsibility." My mind went back to the lady in the green hat at the Interchurch Center, and her re-marks on citizenship responsibility. She and Winston Trent would have got on well.

Walking back to the car, I asked Hassan what he had thought of this lecture. "Oh, it's all true," he said, "but the Americans are too impatient. You can't change people overnight. Besides, they make many mistakes themselves."

"What kind of mistakes?"

"Oh, it would take too long to say."

"Well, if you're doing nothing tonight, come and have dinner and tell me about them."

We drove back to Dhahran while the sun went down over the desert. After dark, Hassan came and ate with me in the dining hall. We had *Wiener Schnitzel* and waffles and coffee in hottles, which are special bottles for keeping coffee hot. And I said to Hassan, "In what way do the Americans make mistakes?"

"Basically," said Hassan, "it's that Americans outside their own country are incapable of seeing with other eyes but their own."

"Yes," I said, "I've heard that before."

"Let me give you an example," said Hassan. "They do surveys here like they do in the States, but they don't realize that a question an American would regard as completely straightforward is seen by the Saudis in a different light. They did a survey here the other day to find out what sort of household goods Saudi employees were buying. I was there for many of the interviews, and I knew that ninety percent of the answers given were false. The interviewer would ask whether a man had a radio or a food mixer or a television set, and nearly always the answer would be yes. So I'd wait behind and say, 'Why did you lie? You don't have any of those things.' And they'd say, 'You don't know what's going on.' So I'd say, 'Well, what's going on?' And they'd say, 'The Americans want to put an article in the Arab papers saying how poor and undeveloped we are.'

"The main reason a Saudi won't tell the truth in a survey is that the questions are too damn personal, that it's nobody's business but his own. But there's another reason. The Arab mind works in a different way from the American mind. I can ask a simple question like 'Are you married?' or 'How long have you lived here?' in Jidda, Riyadh, Dammam and al-Khobar, and I'll get four completely different answers. The Americans don't understand this. I tell them, but they don't understand it.

"They mean well. My God, they mean well! I think they really do try to find out how the rest of the world lives. But somehow it's beyond them. Somehow they avoid those who can tell them the truth. Instead, they listen to the reports of small people who tell them what they want to hear. The other day I took Storm Gunther down to Qatif. You know him? He's been here ten years. I took him round and showed him the employees' houses, and he had no idea, no idea at all, that they lived in houses like that.

"Let me give you another example. They used to have noonday feeding here whereby the employees could get a meal for five qrsh. You couldn't get a meal like that anywhere else. But one day the employees stopped coming to it. You see, they had not been consulted about what they wanted to eat. Oh, the company may have asked a few people, but they didn't provide a list of things available and then ask the employees to tick off what they liked."

"What else?"

"The money they waste on oil exhibits all over the country. It's fantastic what they spend, and they've no idea how much it's resented. They think they're performing a public service explaining to the Saudi about the riches under his feet. But the Saudi knows about the oil anyway, and he thinks to himself, There go the Americans boasting again!"

✪

I THOUGHT it might be useful to talk to a Saudi who was not employed by Aramco; and when I put this to Jack, he said, "We'll go and see Jaffer Sunbul's uncle. He's the mayor of Qatif." Jaffer Sunbul was a young fellow who worked in Jack's office.

Qatif is a primitive place, an oasis among the palm trees, with many mud houses still inhabited. Jaffer's uncle lived in a modern house near the center of the town, and we were shown upstairs to a big square room covered with rugs. It was nice and cool, with blue cushions on the rugs and blue curtains and blue walls. On the walls were portraits of fierce-looking Saudis, and a water color of four pointers flushing three pheasants in a cornfield, and high up in each of the four corners, an artificial tulip in a vase.

Jaffer's uncle came in, a grizzled old Arab of around sixty. He had two or three friends with him. We shook hands and sat down cross-legged on the rugs and cushions. Refreshments were brought: first coffee, then bananas, then tinned orange juice, then hot tea. We had just finished the coffee when Hassan walked in. At Ras Tanura he had been wearing a suit, but now he was in white robes. He smiled at us self-consciously and shook hands with Jaffer's uncle and sat down.

Jaffer's uncle said something, and Jaffer translated: "There is a saying in Qatif that no foreigner comes to Qatif without getting something. Either he gets rich or he gets sick."

This didn't seem to be getting us anywhere, so I said, "Ask him what he thinks of the Americans at Aramco." When his uncle had spoken, Jaffer said, "He says that when the Americans first came to the province they were very generous, but now they have become very stingy. In the early days they let anyone come to their hospitals, but now they only let the employees and their dependents come. They have built schools in many areas in the province, but they have refused to build one at Qatif."

Jack said, "I don't know about the school, but it's now company policy not to give things free. This applies as much to our own people as to the Saudis. It seems there's nothing so much resented as charity."

I said, "How have the Americans altered the life of the area?"

Jaffer's uncle said they had brought prosperity to the area and had created a whole new middle and working class. But, while they had had much influence as regards technological skills, they had had no influence as regards culture. This was not surprising, for Americans had no culture. How about the Westerns? I said. Well, said Jaffer's uncle, you could hardly call that culture. The French and the English had a great tradition of culture, and Arabic literature went back to the time of Mohammed, but America as a country didn't exist until the eighteenth century, so she couldn't be expected to have much culture.

Jack, who had been listening to all this, said, "I don't think that compared with Arabic literature, American literature does too badly."

When this was translated, there was a bit of a silence. Then Jaffer's uncle said, "My friend, what do you know of Arabic literature?"

"Only what I've read," said Jack, and gave his owl smile.

Jaffer's uncle said, "How do you like the way the defense of the Virgin Birth is handled in the Koran?"

"Done with great soundness, I would say," said Jack, "done with great sensibility."

"Have you read al-Mutanabbi?"

"I have."

"What is your impression of it?"

"My impression is that it's a book primarily concerned with manliness, courage and hospitality."

Well, I thought, that's pretty safe; surely that's what all Arabic literature is about?

"Have you read Abu-al-Ala al-Maarri?"

"Yes."

"And the Seven Golden Odes?"

"Oh, yes."

"And what about Abu Ali?"

"Funny you should mention that one," said Jack. "I was reading it in bed only last night." And he smiled.

Jack did everything so deadpan you could never tell if he was joking or not. Was his assumed knowledge of Arabic literature a gigantic bluff? I doubted it. He had not only invited the questions, but answered them confidently. And it seemed to satisfy Jaffer's uncle, for he asked no more.

Presently the meeting broke up. On the way downstairs Hassan came up to me.

"Hullo," I said, "I didn't expect to see you here."

"Listen," said Hassan, "I live here. I know these people. The mayor lies."

"What does he lie about?"

"About Aramco not building a school here. They *wanted* to build a school. Fifteen times they asked to have discussions about it, and fifteen times the mayor turned them down."

"Why?"

"Because he is like that. Because as long as there is no school, he can go on complaining about the Americans. That's why."

"Oh."

"Now you understand what I was saying to you about the Arab mind working in a completely different way?"

We reached the street. Hassan gave a quick, flushed glance and turned and walked away. Poor Hassan, I thought, in his Western suitings one day, in his Saudi robes the next, spending half his time tolerating the stupidity of his employers, the other half listening to his fellow countrymen's lies. How could he tell where his loyalties lay?

I got into the car. "That was a pretty impressive performance," I said to Jack. I wanted to test him out.

"Glad you liked it," said Jack, deadpan. "I thought it was pretty good myself."

Entering Dhahran I said, "Father Roman says I ought to see the cemetery and Mr. Mohlmann."

"Good idea," said Jack. "We'll go up there tomorrow."

✪

Mr. Mohlmann was not only the company's mortician, but in charge of sanitation and gardening too. It was in the gardening office that we found him, surrounded by hoes and rakes and flowerpots. He was a man in his middle forties with a long face and sandy hair. He looked very fit.

I asked him about his various jobs. "It was as a mortician that the company hired me," he said. "That's my primary job. But there's not too much to do in that line, so they put these other jobs onto me after I got here. I was a pharmacist's mate in the Navy, so I know something about sanitation. Gardening I didn't have much experience of, but I've picked it up okay. I have one hundred fifty-three men under me. Except for one Italian, they're all natives."

"What made you decide to come out here?"

"I used to have my own business in New York City, but the neighborhood was closing in on me. I was working a sixteen-to-seventeen-hour day, and I figured that if I went on like that, I'd soon be attending my own funeral. They advertised this job and I applied for it and was accepted. I've been here eleven years, and it's worked out fine. I have my wife with me; one of my sons is at Syracuse University and the other at high school in Lausanne, Switzerland."

"What does your job as mortician consist of?"

"Embalming mostly, for shipping bodies home. The airlines won't take them unless they're embalmed. You know about embalming?"

"No."

"You draw off all the blood and put in formaldehyde, which sets the body up nice and firm. When you've embalmed a body, you don't need refrigeration. It lasts for weeks, even months. But you have to work fast in this climate, because if you don't get the body within a day or two of death, it blows up and there's an odor, and the features are hard to set."

"Do you have anybody to help you?"

"I don't have an assistant like I would at home, because it's against

Moslem law for the Saudis to help me. Sometimes I get the Saudis asking *me* to help *them,* though. There was a Saudi air-force fellow killed recently when his plane crashed in the desert. It was three days before they found him and he was in pretty bad shape. We didn't embalm him. We just disinfected him and put him in a hermetically sealed container, so he could have a public funeral without too much of a smell.

"Then there was an Egyptian teacher at Hofuf. He'd been down a well a week, so he was in pretty bad shape, too. Real blown up with all the gases. I helped out there because they had to ship the body back to Cairo. Normally, though, I'm not supposed to touch Moslems."

"What are the main causes of death?"

"Automobile accidents and things like coronaries. We don't get many chronic diseases, because they're usually spotted in time and sent back to the States."

"How many deaths do you deal with in a year?"

"About forty, I guess. Last year it was double. We had the M.E.A. air crash with forty-eight dead, and I had to take care of that."

Mr. Mohlmann said why didn't we take a look at the embalming room, so we got into his station wagon and went up there. It was a small, squat building, like the lodge to a big house. There was an office in front, and a place at the back with a slab and a sink, and a room in between, with curtains and a thick carpet, which Mr. Mohlmann said was the reposing room.

"We can put on a pretty nice funeral here," said Mr. Mohlmann. "We even have hi-fi. Protestant, Catholic, Albert Schweitzer on the organ, whatever you want. You see those pictures on the walls. They all have a funeral theme. This is a lute player. I forget what the others are, but they're all old masters. In the office I have 'Old Man Death.' That's by an old master, too. They're reproductions, but supposed to be very good."

Behind a screen in the reposing room was a coffin. Mr. Mohlmann lifted the lid to reveal white bedding. Jack peered in and said, "Looks quite inviting." Mr. Mohlmann said, "We clothe the body and put cosmetics on it and fix it up pretty good. It looks real lifelike and natural.

"Here's another thing," said Mr. Mohlmann, going over to a table. "You can't rely on fresh flowers here, because while you can grow almost anything from October to May, not much grows after. So I ordered these artificial ferns, and people think they look pretty good."

In the office Mr. Mohlmann showed us the picture of Old Man Death. He took a bit of paper out of a drawer and said, "Actually, it's called 'The Old King,' and it's by this old master called Rouault. We have the 'Flight into Egypt' and 'Flowers,' and they're by him, too."

We went to the cemetery, which was on top of a hill. It was a big, walled, square plot, screened by rows of oleander trees. Mr. Mohlmann said there were 192 graves there, of which ninety-six were filled and ninety-six empty. The graves were all of solid concrete, as it was against Saudi law for a Christian coffin to contaminate Moslem earth. I asked Mr. Mohlmann who was buried there, and he said mostly the victims of accidents and people who had died on merchant ships. "We have quite a few babies here, too. They're in a big vault. There must be around twenty-four. They're terraced off from each other, though." We walked round the cemetery and I made a note of some of the names on the graves: "John J. O'Leary, 1901–1948"; "Clinton E. Ellesworth, 1922–1948"; "Sosama Anthony, 1930–1961"; "Carmelo Puccia, 1903–1949"; "Teng ar Mui, 1911–1955."

I asked Mr. Mohlmann who Teng ar Mui was, and he said, "A Chinaman off a merchant ship."

✪

FROM TIME to time Saudi extremists make demands that Aramco should be nationalized. What prevents these demands from provoking any response is Aramco's proclaimed policy, approved by the Saudi government, of recruiting proportionately more Saudis and fewer Americans each year, as well as continually promoting Saudis to previously American-held jobs. The long-term object of the policy is that by 1999, when the concession expires, the American executive force will have been more or less phased out and Aramco will be Saudi-run and -controlled. All that will remain then will be a peaceful changeover of ownership.

If, in the year 2000, the library at Dhahran is still in existence, it is possible this book will have found a place there; and any young Saudi executive who is curious to know what went on there in the mid-1960's may take it down from the shelf, read and wonder.

✪

AT TEHRAN airport I felt very ill, and by the time I reached the hotel I was shaking like a jelly. They showed me to a room on the third floor, and, tumbling into bed, I called for the house doctor. He came presently, a grave elderly Persian who took my temperature and surveyed my tongue and nodded. He said I had a virus and must rest, and he prescribed pills which, he said (and he was right), would turn my water bright yellow.

I had a restless night, and in the morning realized that time was going to hang heavy, for although I had several books with me, the print danced before my eyes. I stretched out a hand and turned a bedside switch. Hey presto, there was A.F.N.!

For much of the next week A.F.N. filled my days, and part of my nights too. The programs were rather more gruesome than those I had heard in Athens, but in this, I came to discover, lay their appeal. What made listening irresistible was not just the constancy of the banalities offered, but the conviction with which they were uttered. I looked forward to them in the same way, I imagine, as New Yorkers looked forward to the musical performances of that rich, dotty woman who couldn't sing a note in tune yet hired Carnegie Hall to give concerts.

In the morning there would be music programs with guest stars one had never heard, and unforgettable dialogue like this:

"And now we come to our special guest on 'Sounds of the Sixties,' and this particular time he is an old friend from down Nashville, Tennessee, way—Radio Station WSM, as a matter of fact—and we're very glad to welcome to the program today Mr. Dave Overton. Dave, welcome to 'Sounds of the Sixties.' "

"Thanks a lot, Jerry, it's very nice to be on your program, and especially nice to see you again after a good long absence from our home territory down in Nashville, Tennessee."

"Well, Dave, it has been a while, and it's very good to see you again. You know, as a special guest on 'Sounds of the Sixties,' we always ask our friends to select a particular record or perhaps a particular artist they would like, and we would like to give you that opportunity, Dave."

"Well, let me say this about the artist I would select, Jerry. Just a week or so ago, I had the distinct pleasure of meeting for the first time Mr. Al Hirt, at the International Banana Festival in Fulton, Kentucky . . ."

The International *Banana* Festival! No, I thought, this can't be true. They must be inventing it.

"He was featured there, along with the current Miss America, and I was there on an assignment. I was so impressed with the artistry of Al Hirt that anything you might pick out by Al Hirt would be just fine. Let me say, before you get into the number, though, that Al Hirt has made many appearances in Nashville, not on stage or in concerts, but he has come to Nashville to record, as you probably know, and some of his most successful albums have been cut there. I was impressed, of course, just through these albums, but, having met the man very recently, I'm doubly impressed now, so you can say I'm a real Al Hirt fan, and anything you play will be just great with me."

Was this scripted and read, I wondered, or did it come pouring out of Mr. Overton spontaneously?

"Well, Dave, one of the most unusual things we've heard in a long, long time is the recent album recorded by Al Hirt with—of all people—Arthur Fiedler and the Boston Pops Orchestra. Here's a great cut from that album. I think the folks will like this one. It's called 'The Toy Trumpet.' "

Oh, to hell with "The Toy Trumpet" and the artistry of Al Hirt and three minutes of stunning boredom. Let's get back to that dialogue.

"Well, that was a good choice, Dave. The great Al Hirt, recording with Arthur Fiedler and the Boston Pops Orchestra, and that, of course, was 'The Toy Trumpet.' Dave, we certainly appreciate your taking time to drop in on 'Sounds of the Sixties.' It's been a real pleasure talking to you again, and we hope to see you again real soon."
"Thanks very much for having me here, and I hope I'll have the opportunity to talk across the microphone with you again, Jerry. It's

good to talk with you after all of this time. We have worked together before and shared microphones together and I hope we'll have the opportunity again real soon, and my best to your listeners. Thank you."

"Thank you very much, Dave. That was our special guest on 'Sounds of the Sixties,' Mr. Dave Overton, from Radio Station WSM, Nashville, Tennessee."

Later in the day we had education. First, education of a general kind, suitable in style and content for very small children, and delivered in tones that somehow managed to combine earnestness and bonhomie with unspoken intellectual superiority.

"Let's take time out now to learn some interesting facts about the little island nation of the Dominican Republic, which claims a large number of firsts in the Western Hemisphere, including the first hospital, the first convent, the first seat of higher learning, the oldest stone fortress . . .

"The island which contains the Republic of Haiti was discovered in 1492 by Columbus. Because of its position in the Caribbean it became the center of Spanish exploration and culture and earned well its title of the Cradle of the Americas.

"Its capital, Santo Domingo, was founded in 1496 by Bartolomeo Colombo, Christopher's brother, and was for a long time the seat and center of Spanish colonial government . . .

"The Dominican Republic has been independent since 1844. Today its principal crops are sugar, cacao, coffee and tobacco. . . .

"And those are just a few of the interesting facts about a member nation of the Organization of American States, the Dominican Republic."

We were given technical education too, presented in the same cheerful, portentous way.

"This is Air Force Sergeant Bill Higginbotham reporting on new developments in aero-space research. Ever wondered why pilots and astronauts wear space suits?"

Before you could wonder whether you had wondered or not, another breezy voice had chipped in:

"This is just a capsule that allows a man to take an artificial environment with him, so that he can cope with the unfriendly environment outside this suit."

Back to hearty Higginbotham.

"So says Dick Wolf, a researcher at General Dynamic Astronautics at San Diego, California, and in addition to providing a pilot with oxygen, pressure suits provide an artificial weight on the surface of his body. At sea level, you know, the weight of the atmosphere is 14.7 p.s.i., or pounds per square inch. In most current pressure suits worn by Air Force jet pilots and astronauts the artificial weight is 3.5 p.s.i. . . ."

Then there was a program on money.

"This is 'The World of Money,' a five-minute program relating the fascinating tales of business, finance and money. Now hear, with another timely and provocative subject, Franklin Hamilton. Mr. Hamilton."

Hamilton was practically indistinguishable from Higginbotham, in fact, I sometimes wondered whether they were the same person.

"Do you tell your money where to go? Or do you merely wonder where it went? Well, one way of controlling your expenditure is by means of a device rapidly losing favor in modern America, the old-fashioned family budget. . . ."
"If you haven't bought computers and automation, the time to do it is now! They are here and they will remain. To be a continuing member of society, prepare for the age ahead. For the untrained, tomorrow can be gloomy. But for the man armed with skill and knowledge, the dawn will signal the start of the greatest adventure in the history of the world—an adventure made possible through research. Air Force Sergeant Bill Higginbotham reporting."

And so on. Once, when I was in the bathroom, peeing bright yellow, I heard a booming voice from the bedroom say:

"They lay in foothills off to the west, the outlaws, the gun-slingers, the Billy-the-Kids and worse. Most of them were varmints, but every once in a while, in one of them, there may have lived—a MAN!"

I nearly missed the pan.

We had God too, and a terrible old bore called Arthur Godfrey, who talked as though he were God, and one evening, along the same lines, this collector's gem, presented with histrionic stops full out and to the accompaniment of tinkly piano music:

"In my dream I came to a beautiful building, somehow like a bank. This bank had a brass marker on it that I was not familiar with. It said 'Time for Sale. Time for Sale.' And I saw a man, breathless and pale, painfully pull himself up the stairs like a sick man. I heard him say, 'The doctor told me I was five years too late in going to see him. I'll buy those five years now. Then he can save my life.'

"Then came another man, also older, to the clerk. He said, 'When it was too late I discovered that God had given me great capacities and endowments, and I failed to develop them. Sell me ten years so that I can be the man I would have been.'

"Then came a young man to say, 'The company has told me that starting next month I can have a big job if I'm prepared to take it. But I'm not prepared. Give me two years of time so that I'll be ready to take the job.'

"On they came, hopeless, worried, despondent, and they left smiling. Each man with a look of pleasure on his face. For he'd purchased what he so desperately needed—time.

"Then I woke from that dream, glad that I had what these men had not, what they could never buy—time. Time to do so many things. And that morning I was soon at my work. It was because a great happiness filled my heart, for I still had time."

And the piano ended, and up came the heavenly choirs singing "Till the End of Time," and burly GI's all over Persia brushed the tears from their cheeks. Oh, those were a happy, healing four days, and I was quite sorry when they were over and I was ready to face the world again.

★

I FOUND out that A.F.N. had local studios tucked away in some foothills to the north of the city, and arranged to visit them. I was welcomed by Sergeant Martin, a helpful and dedicated man, and by Captain Goldman, a thin, pale, spectacled Jew, full of nervous energy.

At the back of my mind when I was fixing this visit was the hope that I might see Higginbotham or Hamilton in the flesh, or even watch Dave and Jerry exchange sparkling dialogue. But Sergeant Martin said the station didn't originate any programs itself, it was simply a transmitting station, every show was canned in the States. They ran a television channel too, he said, though they weren't really authorized to, you had to have two thousand troops before an A.F.N. station could be authorized, and there weren't that many American troops in Iran. But they had got authorization because of other Americans there.

I asked if they had any problems, and Sergeant Martin said they had to be very careful not to offend the locals. For example, some of the shows were tailored to the days of the week, and whenever a presenter had a phrase like "on this Friday evening," they had to cut it out, because Friday was the Moslem day of rest. Again, if there was a program which mentioned Black Muslims, they cut that out, too, because of misinterpretation. Also the Iranian government had asked them not to give offense to the Russians. The other day there had been a line in a Jack Paar show, "How does a dog know if I call him a dirty Communist?" That kind of thing was always snipped out.

I asked how they got their material for news bulletins, and Captain Goldman said it was sent from Los Angeles on the military communications system three times a day. As there was a gap of thirty-six hours between the time of origin and the time of transmission, it was often very much out of date. They also had a twice-daily news roundup, the only thing they did originate themselves. "That's given us a lot of headaches, too," said Sergeant Martin, laughing. "What kind of headaches?" I said, and Captain Goldman said, "Oh, boy!"

Sergeant Martin said, "The Iranians like to play the most macabre practical jokes. Three years ago there was an earthquake here, and on the same evening, about five minutes before the end of air time, a guy

called up and said he was the Tehran police chief and the local me-
teorological office had just called him to say there would be another
quake at two in the morning, and would we put a warning out? The
duty engineer took the call and, thinking fast, gave the warning
on the last news roundup. This resulted in near-panic, with people
streaming into the countryside as fast as they could go. There was no
truth in the story at all, and as a result the station was nearly closed
down. Iranians seem to go in for this a lot. We're always getting calls
that an Iranian Airways plane has crashed and will we announce it?
Once on Iran radio someone pushed a note onto the newscaster's desk
saying that the Shah had been assassinated, and he read it out. I don't
know why, but they seem to get a big kick out of it."

❂

THE TRAIN pulled out of Tehran at one o'clock precisely. I was going
to Tabriz, four hundred miles away, on the Russian border, to see the
American consul. His name was Carleton Coon. I shared a compartment with an Iranian who wore a black coat and pepper-and-salt
trousers. His hair was parted in the middle, and he had a thin mustache. He looked like a bank clerk.

We rattled through the Tehran suburbs, and the waiter brought
lunch. First there was tomato soup with an egg in it, and then grilled
chicken and rice. I had already eaten Persian rice and found it the
best in the world, soft and dry and very sweet. We were out in the
country now; on either side was flat, sandy desert, and in the distance
a range of mountains capped with snow. It was a beautiful day with
sun and blue sky and an amazing purity of light. Twice we stopped at
tiny brick-built stations. The first was in the middle of nowhere,
with no roads leading to or from it, and no reason at all for its existence. The second was equally small; but about three miles beyond it,
across the sand, lay a walled village with a squat, gleaming mosque.
Here quite a lot of people got out.

After lunch I slept—and woke to see my companion in the act of
waxing his mustache. Our eyes met, and we both looked away, embarrassed. He went into the corridor to gossip with another Persian,
a man who hadn't shaved for days, and whose teeth were mostly gold.
Then he went down the corridor, and this other man poked his head
round the door.

"Hullo," he said. "How are you?"

"Fine," I said. "And you?"

"Very well, thank you."

I could see he wanted to improve his English, so I asked him in and he came and sat down.

"Is this your first visit to Azerbaijan?"

"Yes."

"You are a businessman, yes? You are going on business?"

"No, I'm a writer."

"A writer? You are a writer?"

"Yes. What are you?"

"I teach. I am a teacher."

"What do you teach?"

"Persian literature. My wife is a teacher, too."

"Is she? What does she teach?"

"Gymnastics."

"This other gentleman," I said, indicating the empty seat. "You know him?"

"Yes."

"What does he do?"

"He is a railway official. He works for the railway."

"Ah."

He gave a little smile and said, "You are American, yes?"

"No," I said, "I'm British. But I'm writing a book about the Americans. That is why I'm going to Tabriz. To see the American consul."

His eyes lit up. "You are writing a book about the Americans? That is very interesting. They are a fine people, yes? I have a son and a daughter who are studying in the United States."

Now it was my turn to look surprised. "Have you?"

"Yes. My son is studying engineering and my daughter business."

"That must cost you a lot of money," I said.

"Yes, that is so. That is why my wife and I both work. So we can send our children away to have a good education. That is what my country needs, to send more and more people away to the United States. To learn things, to teach us what to do."

I was hoping to find out more about how he had managed to send his children to America, but suddenly he got up. "Please, sir," he said, "I am taking up your time. I will go." And he went.

At seven-thirty, when it was growing dark, the waiter announced dinner at the other end of the train. I made my way there through several wooden carriages where women in *chadors* were nursing babies, and soldiers sat gossiping or playing cards. It was a bright, modern dining car, already full. They gave us the same soup as at lunch and a delicious *chello-kebab,* and a pot of yoghurt, and masses more rice with about two ounces of butter laid on top. Opposite me was a family in which were two small girls in identical dresses, red with green spots. One looked quite normal, but the other had huge cheeks and great bushy eyebrows and an unusually dark skin. She shoveled her food into her mouth with both hands like a demented old woman. Next to me was a policeman with his cap on, and then the railway official came in wearing a green felt hat. Headgear in Persian dining cars seemed to be *à la mode.*

When I returned to the compartment, I found the door locked. The teacher was standing outside.

"The railway official," he said, "has locked the door. Against robbers, yes?" He took out his wallet and showed me photographs of his son and his daughter, an enchantingly pretty girl of twenty-one. I showed him photographs of my wife and children.

"Your wife is beautiful," he said.

"Yes," I said. "She used to be a ballet dancer."

He seemed surprised.

"Yes. She made a film called *The Red Shoes.* It was very famous. Did you see it?"

"No. I do not often see the films."

We chatted some more, and then the railway official came back and opened the door. But he didn't stay long. An inspector arrived and bundled him out. He was followed by a man in blue dungarees, who made up three beds. Then an army officer wearing dark glasses came in, and behind him a charming Iranian of about thirty, who said he had been four years at college in Denver, Colorado. "My friend and I," he said, "are traveling second class, but we have paid the difference in order to get a good night's rest."

He told me that he was an official in local government and was going to take up a post at a small town near Tabriz. I told him what I was doing, and he said, "A great many people in Iran don't know there are Americans here. Almost as many know there are some here but they don't meet them, and the fact makes no impact. A small number, students and Communists mostly, resent them. An even smaller number realize it is better to have them with you than to be alone. There have been times in our country when we were alone and it was no good. If we have to be on a side, it is better we should be on the American side than the other."

Before turning in, I went down the corridor to the washroom. On the way I passed the teacher and the railway official chatting together. The teacher said, "I am telling my friend here what you are telling me, that your wife is a belly dancer. Like me, he finds it interesting, yes?"

✪

ONCE in the night, I woke to find the compartment flooded with moonlight. The army officer was asleep in his dark glasses, and the handsome Iranian, above him, was snoring. I looked out the window and saw that we had left the plains and were climbing through the mountains. There was a great, still pewter river running beside the track, and the bare hills beyond were bathed in a soft, amber light. It was very beautiful.

At six the waiter came in with coffee and rolls and a homemade marmalade laced with very thin strips of peel. At seven we passed Lake Riza, and at eight we steamed into Tabriz.

I was met at the station by a nice Texan called Hallmann, who said that he was the vice-consul and that the consul would be along later. I was surprised that an out-of-the-way place like Tabriz should have a vice-consul as well as a consul, but that was the State Department all over.

Mr. Hallmann drove me to his house for breakfast, and then the Coons came to fetch me. Mr. Coon was an East Coast egghead, in his fifties, I would say, Harvard educated; his wife, who had been at Radcliffe, was a bright matronly woman, quite tall, with glasses, her hair in a bun at the back. Their house was as unlike those in Aramco or Frummingen as you could imagine. It was more like an English country house, with a big sitting room opening onto a veranda and a garden, with lots of books in shelves, and other books and papers and things lying about on small tables.

The Coons had six children, three with them, and a cat called Murgatroyd and a dog called Tinker. Tinker was a cross between a setter and a Tabriz dog. "I inherited him from my predecessor," said Mr. Coon. "He's a nice dog and good with the children, but we have to watch out. Once he escaped and some local people gave him a terrible beating. If he sees anyone who reminds him of them, he's apt to turn nasty. I take him in the car a lot. He sits beside me, and the Azerbaijanis think there's nothing so ridiculous as a dog going for a ride in a car.

"To give you the background on Tabriz, there was a time when it was the first city in Iran. That was when the trade routes came through here, and the city was the gateway to the West. But now it's a blighted area. The trade routes went elsewhere, and the final kiss of death was the Russian occupation of Azerbaijan between 1941 and 1950. Then everyone who could, got out of the place and went to Tehran. That was a tough time."

Mr. Hallmann said, "We know people whose fathers were taken away in the middle of the night and never heard of again."

"As a result," said Mr. Coon, "this place hasn't grown. There's no decent restaurant, and the only tolerable hotel has just one Western john. There's no cultural life at all. The university is like a secondary school and limps along. Anyone who's any good here goes to Tehran."

"When I go to Tehran," said Mr. Hallmann, "and tell my Iranian friends I live here, they shake their heads. This is a closed society, very family-oriented, much secretiveness. There's been much treachery, many upheavals. In Tabriz no one laughs much any more."

"Though I know a French lady here," said Mrs. Coon, "who remembers Tabriz in the thirties. She says there was dancing in the hotels and sidewalk cafés, and women without *chadors*. Just think of that!"

"How many live here?" I said.

"Around three hundred thousand," said Mr. Coon, "and that includes twelve thousand Armenians. This is where the Armenians came from, before the Turks drove them out in 1915."

"This is a Turkish-speaking community," said Bill Hallmann. "Did you know that?"

"No."

"It's a brand of Turkish which I think few genuine Turks would recognize. But they don't speak Farsi at all. I know a woman here whose son is studying in Tehran. He writes to her in Farsi, and she has to get someone to translate it into Turkish. It's fantastic."

"I doubt if more than forty percent of Iranian people speak Farsi," said Mr. Coon. "About a quarter speak Turkish, a third speak Kurdish, and the Baluchi speak Baluchi. This country is an empire.

"Professionally," said Mr. Coon, "this is a very quiet post at the moment. The really interesting things are happening outside Tabriz. For example, the government is carrying out a big policy of Kurdish land reform, which could lead to Kurdish assimilation. Then there's an idea for a railroad going from Tehran right through to Turkey. This could bring back life to the region."

"If Tabriz is as blighted as you say," I said, "what is the point of having a consulate here?"

"I would say to act as a kind of listening post. To report to my government what's going on, so they can fit that information into the over-all pattern. Also, I would say, to bring a little influence to bear on events. One way or another, we have a pretty big effort in Iran, with the Peace Corps and the AID and the military missions and so on."

"How do you influence events?" I said.

"I travel around a lot. I know the governors of West and East Azerbaijan and of Kurdistan too. I go around and talk to them and they listen to what I have to say. I got back from one trip three days ago, and I am going on another the day after tomorrow. I travel in a jeep, stay in Peace Corps lodgings and hostels, live on *chello-kebab* and Pepsi-Cola and have a great time."

"What sort of social life do you have?" I asked.

Bill Hallmann laughed and said none.

"Offhand," said Mrs. Coon, "I can think of about one and a half couples with whom it would be any fun to spend an evening. We had a charming general here a short while ago, but his wife was quite illiterate."

"Doesn't it get rather boring?" I said.

"If one didn't develop an interest in history or archaeology or something," said Mrs. Coon, "one would go mad. The last consul's wife here wasn't interested in anything, and she nearly did go mad."

"We also get a lot of visitors," said Mr. Coon, "and we like that very much."

"What kind of visitors?"

"Oh, people passing through," said Mrs. Coon. "This house is like a hotel. It's inclined to be quiet in the winter, but in summer the *Wandervogel* students start trekking across from Europe."

"We're always getting a lot of professors," said Mr. Coon. "Right now we have this professor of Semitic languages. I think he's studying the dialect. The other day we had a professor of the Nestorian period. He was a real bore. When he was here we had a couple of sergeants staying from one of the military missions. God, they were a dumb pair! One of them was so dumb he didn't even play cards. They were sitting over there like two bumps on a log, and the professor went right over and bored them for two hours. Afterward one of them said to me, 'My, isn't it wonderful to have an education?' "

At lunch I met the professor of Semitic languages. He was a dark-haired man of about thirty-five with a chunky build and a face like old bark. Mr. Coon said we would be sharing a room. I never did learn his name, but I think he was the *politest* man I ever met. "Why, how do you do, Mr. Kennedy," he said. "I'm very happy indeed to know you. It certainly is a real pleasure." And he pumped my hand up and down.

In the afternoon, Bill Hallmann took the professor and me for a walk round Tabriz. It was a very dull place, a sort of mini-Moscow without the Bolshoi or the Kremlin; there wasn't a memorable building anywhere. We went to the ruins of the Blue Mosque, which hadn't been a thing of much beauty even in its day, and rooted about in the rubble. The professor picked up some pieces of chipped blue tile. "I wonder," he said. "Do you think they would mind if I were to keep one or two of these as a souvenir? I certainly wouldn't want to offend anyone's religious susceptibilities." Bill said, "Go ahead. There's plenty of it. Help yourself." The professor said he'd like to ask someone's permission, so he and Bill nosed about until they found an elderly custodian, who shrugged his shoulders and spat and walked away.

The things in the shop windows looked as though they'd been there ten years. Bill said they always dressed the prophylactics very nicely, and then we passed a butcher shop and the professor said to me, "Have you ever had to eat sheep's eyes?"

"No," I said. "I've been spared that so far."

"Sheep's testicles," said Bill, "are delicious fried for breakfast. I might have bought a pair this morning if I'd thought of it."

"There speaks a true Texan," said the professor.

We called at the local hotel, the one with the Western john, and sent a message in to Mr. Dash, the local AID man, to come to dinner at the Coons' if he was free. But Mr. Dash sent word that he was in bed with a tummy pain and had better stay where he was. Then we walked to the bazaar. On the way we saw a lot of fierce-looking men wearing colored turbans and big, baggy trousers. Bill Hallmann said they were Kurds. We passed some other men wearing red rugs, and

Bill said they were going to a public bath. "They all wear those rugs round themselves when they have a public bath. They're very modest."

The professor said, "The thing that really gets me in these Moslem countries is the men squatting down to pee and the women standing up. You know, Herodotus had something to say on that."

"There was an American Army officer here," said Bill Hallmann, "and this thing of the men squatting down to pee used to drive him crazy. For him it represented the futility and backwardness of the country. One day, right at the end of his tour of duty, he was driving along a road in the country. Suddenly he sees this man at the side of the road squatting down to pee. So he stops the car, gets out, walks over to the man, shakes him like an old rag, and shouts in his ear, *'Why don't you stand up and pee like a man?'* "

The bazaar was full of rugs of every color and size. The professor looked at them all closely, as though of a mind to buy one. "Would you mind asking that dealer," he said to Bill, "whether I might examine his carpets for a moment or two? And would he mind saying what kind of price he has in mind as a basis for bargaining for that type of carpet?" The dealer had in mind between three and five hundred dollars, which was rather more than what the professor had in mind. So he said to Bill, "How many knots are there in each carpet?"— which seemed a crazy kind of question. Bill peered down and said, "Between fifty and sixty, I guess." The professor said, "To the square inch?" and Bill said, "It's not done that way." After that, the professor kept quiet.

At dinner that night we talked about the role of the Americans in the world and that of the British before them. Bill Hallmann said that what had made the British colonialists was an excess of energy and talent which couldn't find an outlet at home; similarly the Peace Corps was harnessing energy and talent which couldn't find an outlet in the States. "We're spreading a religion, really, just as the religious fanatic used to do in the old days. Our gospel is 'Waste is wicked. It's immoral to waste one's resources.' That's what the Peace Corps and AID and everyone else is basically trying to get across."

"And do you know the paradox?" said Mr. Coon.

"What?" I said.

"This gospel is being preached by the most wasteful nation on earth."

That night the professor of Semitic languages and I lay side by side in twin beds, a table light between us, both reading. After a while I put my book on the table and lay back to sleep. The professor said, "Would it disturb you greatly if I were to continue reading a little longer?" I said, "Of course not." The professor said, "Are you quite certain about that?" Drowsily I said, "Quite." As my mind slipped away into sleep I heard the professor say, "I certainly wouldn't want to inconvenience you."

Next morning Bill Hallmann took the professor and me to visit the compound where the consulate was, and where the new offices and residence were being built. Before we left I heard Mr. Coon tell his wife that he would get a certain rifle packed.

The compound, a huge, walled property, all of twelve acres, lay on the outskirts of the town. Over the gateway flew one of those vast, absurd Stars and Stripes which Americans love to put up wherever they go, and next to it a big board which said:

CONSULATE OF THE UNITED STATES OF AMERICA
TABRIZ   IRAN
OFFICE OF FOREIGN BUILDINGS
DEPARTMENT OF STATE
UNITED STATES OF AMERICA

Edward Larrabee Barnes   Contractor
Architect A.I.A.   Mahak Company
303 East 65th Street,   Tehran
New York City

At one end were the present offices in wooden huts, and beside them a swimming pool and a tennis court, and at the other end the remains of an almond grove, where the new offices and consulate were being built. I asked Bill Hallmann what they were going to cost, and he said about a third of a million dollars. I said, "Good God!" forgetting for the moment how rich America was. Bill said, "And that's not the half of it. The consulate is going to be too big, and the residence too small. They're allowing room in the consulate to house the U.S.I.S., but the U.S.I.S. has to stay downtown for people who want to drop by and take out a book or look at some photographs. Then the residence will have only four bedrooms. Well, the Coons have six children, as you know. They'll soon be gone, but if another family comes along with six children, or even four like mine, where's every-body going to sleep?"

"Hasn't Mr. Coon complained?" I said.

"We've never stopped complaining," said Bill. "I don't know how many letters we've written to Washington. But they don't take the slightest notice."

A little before noon we walked over to Mr. Coon's office, and he said he had almost finished his morning's work, and why didn't we all have a game of tennis before lunch. Bill Hallmann had some other engagement, but an Englishwoman called Mrs. Walton was rustled up in his place, and she and I took on Mr. Coon and the professor and lost, 4–6. The professor was a model partner, always having balls ready to hand to Mr. Coon, and apologizing profusely whenever he made a bad shot.

We went back to the house for lunch, and afterward I said to Mr. Coon, "What did you do this morning?"

He looked startled. "What did I do?"

"I'm sorry," I said. "Sometimes I go too quickly. At the consulate, I mean. How did the American consul spend his morning?"

"Well," he said. He still looked surprised. "How did I spend the morning?" He laughed and felt around in his pocket. "I tell you one thing," he said, "I wouldn't want you to think I spent all morning just packing up that rifle."

For a moment I panicked. There was a defensive note in his voice, surprising in one so cosmopolitan, as though he thought I was trying to put him on the mat.

"Well, of course not," I said. "I meant, apart from that."

"Well now," he said, "let's see." He looked at the ceiling. "I wrote a classified airgram and two letters to Washington, had a talk with Tehran over the radio about this trip I'm going on, wrote a report on what Bill Hallmann was doing when I was away on the last trip, discussed with Jim Smith a new road that goes near the compound, made various telephone calls and received some, including one from the British Council representative here, who called up to say they were running a movie tomorrow and would we like to see it? How's that?"

"That's fine," I said.

"I wouldn't want you to think there's more work here than there is. I put out here about a tenth of what I used to put out in Washington at the Indian or the Cyprus desk. What takes the time there is the great machine of bureaucracy, taking in each other's washing, getting a consensus."

"Will you be sorry to leave?"

"No. This is a two-year post, and my two years are almost up. After Washington, this was wonderful. I got into the fresh air and into shape, and it was great. But after a time the novelty wears off, like with everything. Intellectually it's absolutely stultifying. No, I'll be glad to get home."

✪

THE MAITRE d'hôtel at the Hilton was a round, red-faced German, and one evening we had a drink together, and he said:

"The Germans are apt to boss, and so are the French and English, though we don't see many of them these days. The Americans are very easy to please. They only want two things, cleanliness and quickness. They always ask if the water and the salads are all right. They have this extraordinary habit of putting down their knife while eating with the fork. If I had any criticism of American guests, it would be that they automatically expect to be understood. They say they want ham and eggs sunny side up, and things like that, and they get annoyed if the waiter doesn't understand. So I train my waiters to understand these things.

"In some ways the Americans are quite humble, wanting to find out what is the right thing to do. They feel a little in awe of foreign customs. It's amazing how these old Americans travel. They bring a certain respect to things they don't understand.

"The ladies respond marvelously if you pay them a little attention. They don't seem to get that kind of attention at home. If I say to one, 'You're looking marvelous tonight, that dress really suits you,' it makes their evening, it really does. They aren't used to it.

"The Jews among them say things like 'I'm a very good friend of Mr. Hilton' or 'I'm a stockholder in the Hilton Hotel Company.' At first I thought this was true, and I went out of my way to please them. Then I came to realize it was nonsense. But of course I don't let them know that. I say, 'Why, of course you're a friend of Mr. Hilton. That's very nice for you.'

"The richer the American man or woman, the simpler they dress. At least that's what I've found. The ones who go about in those colored shirts and silly hats aren't rich at all. No, they're not good tippers. The Turks and Arabs are the best, though I would say Americans are better than most Europeans."

✪

AND THEN there was Fred. I met Fred at Kermanshah, which was south of Tabriz and on Persia's western border. There was a small American military mission there, and Fred, a captain, belonged to it. After Frummingen and the Sixth Fleet, I hadn't really intended to get embroiled with the military again. But Carleton Coon said it would be an interesting experience. He was right.

My guide to Kermanshah was a Major Searle, who picked me up at the hotel around seven in the morning. Major Searle looked like a *New Yorker* caricature of an Army officer, with dark glasses, a scrambled-egg hat, and signs and symbols all over him. On his left shoulder was a crown above a lion holding a scepter. On his right shoulder was a Red Indian head and feathers on a white ground. On his right breast was his name SEARLE in capital letters, and on his left breast a picture of a rifle on a blue ground. He said this meant having fired his rifle in combat. He smoked almost continuously and had a cough like the rumble of a turbojet.

On the way to the airport we stopped at another hotel to pick up a Colonel Smith, who was to be the new commanding officer at Kermanshah. He had just come out from Washington, and he was going to relieve Colonel Birch. Colonel Smith was a long slab of a man with a sad, droopy face. He looked a little like A. A. Milne's Eeyore.

"How did you sleep, sir?" said Major Searle politely.

"Fine until five," said Colonel Smith. "Then a fellow started unstacking a whole lot of steel pipes."

At the airport I signed a form saying that if I was killed, I wouldn't hold the United States government responsible. Then we drove out to the tarmac. Our plane was called a Beaver and our pilot Captain Vinson. Captain Vinson said they didn't know that Major Searle and I were coming, and the back seats of the plane had been filled with Colonel Smith's luggage. I looked into the plane and saw five huge black chests. Major Searle asked Colonel Smith if he would mind having them unloaded and sent on the next day. Colonel Smith said no, he guessed not, though you could see he did. While the chests were being unloaded, I asked how much they weighed, and Colonel Smith said about six hundred pounds. I asked what was in them, and Colonel Smith said, "Clothing, just clothing." When I pointed this out to Major Searle, he said, "When a guy's going somewhere for a year he needs to be pretty self-sufficient."

When all of Colonel Smith's chests had been taken out, we got into the plane, Captain Vinson and Major Searle in front, Colonel Smith and I at the back. Captain Vinson put on a thing that looked like a space helmet with "CAPT. VINSON" in white letters on the front and wires sticking out, and then we took off. It was a nice journey. We climbed to ten thousand feet and crossed a couple of mountain ranges, the top of one covered with snow. On the slopes the rocks were biscuit and beige, pink and mauve, broken by flashes of green where the soil had allowed cultivation. In the valleys we looked down on what seemed to be footprints of giant camels, perhaps a quarter of a mile apart, sometimes stretching out of sight. Major Searle said these were *quanats,* holes leading to underground water tunnels, the traditional Iranian way of irrigating the land. And sometimes, too, like drawings in the sand, we saw the contours of ancient habitations, abandoned long ago.

After about two hours' flying we landed in a green valley and taxied toward a small hut. Here we were met by a stubby gay little man in a spotted shirt, who said he was Colonel Birch. He had a green van with him, and we all got in and drove into Kermanshah.

✪

IT WAS lovely country, with mountains all round, but Kermanshah itself looked as dreary as Tabriz, shabby gray public buildings and drab yellow brick houses.

Colonel Birch took us to the street where the ten officers and eight noncommissioned men of the military mission lived in four small houses. Major Searle said the object of the mission was to show the local Iranian troops how to use the weapons America had provided.

At the main house Colonel Smith disappeared, and apart from meals I didn't see him again. When I asked Major Searle where he was, he said he was orienting himself. A young officer took me upstairs to a bedroom. It had a nice view of the garden. There were cockroaches in the handbasin and a cat under the bed.

Later I had a talk with Colonel Birch. He said they got on well with the Iranians, though in the field the language problem was often acute. "Our people always learn enough to get themselves three things—sleep, food and souvenirs. Beyond that we need interpreters."

"When you go into the field, how do you live?"

"We sleep either in their local barracks or in a hotel. If it's the barracks, we don't use their beds, because we find them pretty dirty. We take our sleeping bags along and put them on top of the beds. Their toilets are a hell of a thing. They're a kind of gymnastic. I never thought I'd get to a point where I'd find a toilet seat a luxury. We usually take halazone along for purifying the water, or a small heater. Major von Schlemmer takes his corn mash along with him and cooks it on his heater every morning. The Iranian officers stand and watch and think, 'Oh, those crazy Americans, they're nuts.' "

"How much time do you spend in the field?"

"About half in the field and half here. We keep pretty busy. We work maybe seventy to eighty hours a week. We find it's best to keep busy here. No one complains about the work."

"What do you do in your spare time?"

"I go big for this hunting, and so do several others. Here they have all sorts of hunting—ibex and wild boar and mouflon, and big rabbits and partridge and duck. The boar tastes delicious, more like veal than pork. We get up early on hunting days, often around three in the morning. Sometimes we go on our own, and sometimes we take guides and interpreters, and sometimes we meet Kurds on the hill. The Kurds just love coming with us. They won't ever take money. They love asking us into their houses. That's a helluvan experience. There's generally somebody kneading bread on the floor."

"What about the nonhunters?"

"We all have tape recorders, and a lot of the boys send their letters home by tape so the folks can hear their voices. We're supposed to get five movies a week, though some are of the Charlie Chaplin era. We had one the other day called *Underwater City*, which no one could sit through. A movie has to be pretty bad when you actually can't sit through it. We get a lot of lousy British movies too, which nobody understands. We feed terrifically well, as you'll see tonight. There's no restrictions either. We had one officer just left, and every day he ate six eggs for breakfast and six hotcakes. When he left he couldn't get into his clothes. He's got eight children, so I guess he was getting his full share for the first time."

"Do you miss anything?"

"Fresh milk. The powdered stuff is lousy. But that's not important. What really strikes you here is the way people cooperate. No one waits for an order to do something. They just do it. One of our officers wanted ice cream tonight, so he went and made it. Major von Schlemmer decided the shrubs in the garden needed fertilizing, so he bought two hundred pounds of fertilizer and sprinkled it all over. They've worked well for me. In the year I've been here there hasn't been a single disciplinary problem."

Major von Schlemmer was a long, lean monkey of a man, who did voluntary teaching at the local Iran-American society. "We had an interesting panel on the death of President Kennedy," he said. "What they really wanted to know was, did Johnson organize it so as to get the job? You see, they thought the thing was phony. They just didn't believe you could order a rifle like that through the mail. I had to show them an ad of the very same rifle that killed Kennedy to make them believe it. Then they talked the thing over and decided that their laws, where you couldn't order rifles through the mail, were maybe better."

"Are they keen to learn?"

"Oh, sure," said Major von Schlemmer, "but sometimes they try to trap me."

"How?"

"The other day they asked me what 'coon' was. So I said it was short for 'raccoon,' a scavenging animal. They said 'What else?' I said, 'Nothing else.' So they produced this dictionary which said, 'coon. . . . an American Negro.' So I told them, 'You don't want to use a word like that, it'll only get you into trouble.' Excuse my asking, but are you British?"

"Yes."

"The British aren't too well liked around here. In the war there used to be a British base near here. Now whenever there's an act of God like thunder or floods or something, they say, 'Oh, that's the British, that's British policy.' British policy means something inevitable."

Later I visited the house where the noncommissioned men were billeted, a few doors down the street. There were six of them here, including one Negro private and a white sergeant called Willis. They had a big sitting room, with *Playboy* cutouts pinned over the bar together with seventy-eight severed ties and forty-five photographs. "When a man leaves the unit," said Sergeant Willis, "we have a tie-cutting ceremony. We cut off his tie and hang it up with his photograph. You'll notice that there are more ties than photographs. That's because not everybody had photographs. Two of these ties are General Fiuzi's."

"Who's he?"

"He was the Iranian general here before the present one."

They gave me beer from the bar. I asked them how they liked Kermanshah, and they said fine; they had a good, informal relationship with the officers, they liked the hunting and fishing, and the work was out of the ordinary. "What recreations we have," said one, "we make for ourselves. A town like this don't have facilities like dance halls or bowling alleys where anybody can join in. I guess religion is still the biggest barrier. You just aren't accepted by them. You're still outside." Sergeant Willis said, "Ninety-five percent of us are married. I guess they do this deliberately because they reckon that married people are less likely to get into trouble with the locals." A sergeant up from Isfahan said his hobby was taking moving pictures of ancient monuments like Persepolis and Darius's and Xerxes' tombs. "I shoot maybe three or four thousand feet of film and then reduce it to four hundred. I pick up books about Persia, and when I send the shot list I include a summary of all the relevant facts. Then I ship it off to Castle Films. They may pay me up to a thousand dollars if they like it."

"When you move out of Tehran," someone said, "you go back anything from two hundred to two thousand years."

Sergeant Willis said, "Right! Their year now is 1344, and that's about it."

The officers were giving a dinner party that night, and the guests of honor were a Mr. Vazil-Tabori, president of the local plant of the National Iranian Oil Company, his wife, two nieces and their husbands. Mr. Vazil-Tabori was middle-aged and handsome, and everyone called him "V.T." Colonel Birch said to me, "A pity you didn't have the chance to meet V.T.'s daughter. She has flaming red hair, and hips this wide. She must be all of a hundred and seventy pounds. Her backhand at tennis is so good she'll often run across the court to take a forehand shot backhand."

We all had some strong drinks and then went down to eat. The dining room was a small room on the ground floor, with a hatch through to the kitchen and four tables with washable printed tops. There was a pair of green flowered curtains from the old British consulate, two wall vases with artificial flowers, and three old prints of cowboys. Two of the cowboys were on bucking broncos and the third, a very old cowboy, was sitting on his horse with rifle cocked, gazing into the distance. This was called "Danger at Hand."

Colonel Birch was right about the food. We had super steaks cooked on charcoal, and a banana and nut ice cream which Major Berefield had made that afternoon. The officers were a friendly lot, with one unhappy exception. This was a bullet-headed, crew-cut, hare-lipped bull of a man who came rolling in to dinner late, sat down heavily and looked vacantly around with bloodshot eyes. For a long time he said nothing, concentrating on the food. Then, when the conversation turned on how Iran was modernizing, he decided to start a row with nice Mr. V.T.

"Modernizing, hell!" he shouted across the table. "All the women around here wear the veil. You call that modernizing?"

Mr. V.T. gave a conciliatory shrug, not wanting to make an issue of it. Major von Schlemmer whispered to me, "That's Major Crippen. I guess he's had a few too many."

"Listen," said Crippen, banging the table, "all I can see of those women are two eyes. Well, that's ridiculous. They can see me, but all I can see of them are two eyes."

There was a bit of a silence, and someone said, "Steady, Bob."

"Now, listen," said Crippen, glaring at Mr. V.T., "I believe a woman is equal to a man. But do *you*? Yes or no?" He wagged a finger at Mr. V.T., who looked embarrassed and smiled. "Well, come on, come on," Crippen said. "Yes or no. It's a perfectly straight question. Let's have a straight answer."

"Of course," said Mr. V.T. quietly.

"Well, why the hell dontcha get something done about it? You're an influential guy, aren't ya?" Crippen glared round him with blood-shot eyes and back at Mr. V.T. "Your country has gotta decide which way it's going. Either ya with us or ya against us—there's no half measures. Now, those Russkies don't give a damn about health or education or the individual or anything. We do. So that's what ya gotta decide. Ya gonna go along with *us*? Or with *them*?" He pointed a finger in the general direction of the Soviet Union.

In the silence that followed, Colonel Birch said quietly, but with immense authority, "Okay, Major Crippen, let's leave it there, shall we?"

Crippen glared at Colonel Birch and for a moment I thought he was going to strike him. Then he said, in rather too loud a voice, "As you say, sir," and went out of the room.

As the door closed, everyone started chattering. "I think Crippen is getting ready for a nuthouse," said Colonel Birch. "He sat down in a chair beside me in the bar before dinner and I said to him, 'Fred's sitting there. He's just gone for a drink.' He got up, shouted, 'Goddammit!' and walked out slamming the door." Major von Schlemmer said, "He dived into the swimming pool for a bet this afternoon, with all his clothes on."

❂

IT WAS then that I met Fred. To look at, he was not unlike my Frummingen colonel, but bounding with energy. I had noticed him chattering away at another table, and now he came and sat in Crippen's empty place.

"Mr. Kennedy," he said, "I want to tell you something. When I came to England in 1940 I fell in love with my first cousin."

An officer called Mac said, "Oh, Christ, Fred, don't give us that again."

Fred ignored Mac. "She was the daughter of my mother's brother, and they all lived in this place called Bromley, Kent, and so I went to King's Cross and took a train—"

"*Charing* Cross," I said. "King's Cross goes somewhere else."

"Okay. Whatever you say. When I got to Bromley I asked the engineer where the house was, and he spoke Cockney and I couldn't understand a word." Fred gave an imitation of Cockney, which was like nothing I had ever heard. "I got there in the end, and there was my uncle's son. He welcomed me with open arms and took me down to this teahouse. We had tea in the teahouse, and then we went back and met a whole lot of people and had a swell time. It was then I met this girl, my uncle's daughter, and I'm telling you she was *beautiful*. I started to date her, and I dated her all that furlough, and the next two furloughs too. We were just nuts about each other. I wanted to marry her, and I think she wanted to marry me, too. She wasn't a

Catholic, like I am, so I wrote to the Pope for a dispensation. I never got an answer. Maybe he didn't get my letter. Well, I think I would have married her, but my mother and uncle and all the family started putting pressure on me and saying you shouldn't marry your first cousin, the children will be idiots, and she's not a Catholic. In the end I came to believe them and I didn't marry her. But I've talked to a lot of people since, and they all say there's no truth in it, about the children being idiots, so we could have got married after all."

"Did you get married to someone else?"

"Oh, sure. I've been married fifteen years, and I've got a lovely wife who's a Catholic and four lovely children. I told my wife about my cousin, and when we went to England she said to me, 'Are you going to see her?'

"I said, 'I couldn't see her even if I wanted to. She's married and got a new name and I don't know where she's living or anything.' "

"Did you want to see her?"

"I don't know. I guess so. Gee, I often wonder how it would have worked out if we had got married. Not that I don't love my wife. At least, I think I love my wife. Hell, how does anyone know how much he loves his wife? But you can't help wondering, can you? You can't help wondering how a thing might have happened if you'd acted different than you did?"

Before I could answer, there was a general move to the bar. Here we saw a lousy movie called *Paris When It Sizzles*. Fred sat beside me. When it was over he got me a drink and said, "Birth control gets to be a hell of thing when you're a Catholic. My wife was told by the doctor she shouldn't have any more children because her tubes had all gone to hell, and he persuaded her to use a diaphragm, just as an added safety to the rhythm method. As you know, the Catholics don't allow that. Well, one Saturday I said to my wife, 'Why don't we go to confession this afternoon?' and she said, 'Okay.'

Fred looked across disdainfully and turned back to me. "Well, first *I* went in to confession while she stayed with the kids. Then she went in. Afterward I said why didn't we look in at the club and have a martini and give the children a soda. When we got there, I noticed my wife was pretty blue. So I said, 'What's the matter, honey?' and she said, 'Nothing.' So I said, 'Come on, tell me.' Then she said she'd told the priest she was using the diaphragm, and the priest said it was a sin and she oughtn't to, and she was upset pretty bad. So I said, 'This priest had no right to talk to you like that, and I'm gonna go right back there and tell him what I think of him.' But my wife dissuaded me. Well, things simmered down in the end and I managed to persuade my wife to go on using the diaphragm."

Fred took a sip at his drink and gave a contented sigh. "My tour of duty is up next week," he said. "Ten days from now I'll be home with my wife. She's the only one who can stop me from talking. She wrings me out. We're gonna have four days together in New York when I get back. Her sister's gonna take care of the kids. We're gonna have a second honeymoon."

I didn't say anything, and I thought that Fred had at last run out of words. But after a bit he said dreamily, "I wonder how it would have been if I'd married my cousin. She didn't care if I was a Catholic or atheist or anything."

✪

NEXT MORNING they sent a plane with Colonel Smith's chests, and Major Searle and I rode back in it. It was another glorious day with all Iran spread below, pink and pristine. We flew lower than the day before over the *qanats* and ruins, the tents of the herdsmen and the snowy mountaintops. But I kept thinking of Fred. What other country in the world produced people who confided to perfect strangers, and within minutes of meeting them, such intimate details of their lives? And what other country produced people so racked with doubts? To the end of his life Fred would go on chewing over whether he should have married his cousin. To the end of his life it would remain a problem without an answer. And that, for Fred, was the beauty of it.

Part Five

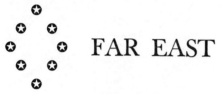 FAR EAST

INDIA
THAILAND
VIETNAM
FORMOSA
JAPAN

Two HUNDRED miles north of New Delhi, twenty-two miles north of Dehra Dun, and six thousand feet up in the Himalayas stands the fairy-tale township of Mussoorie, a hill station built by the British to escape the heat and dirt of the plains, and now a popular spa for middle-class Indians. Here all cars are banned, the only wheeled transport is the rickshaw, and the temperature, according to a sign at the entrance, varies between 63 and 75 degrees Fahrenheit.

Mussoorie is built on a long, thin fertile ridge and the cliffside immediately below it. The view either way is tremendous. To the north, across a great, empty, cavernous valley, are gigantic purple peaks, riding like ships of war the pale Himalayan sky; to the south, five thousand feet below and stretching away for perhaps fifty or sixty miles, are the burning northern plains.

Alongside the center of the ridge runs Mussoorie's main artery, the Mall, with houses above and below it; there is a handrail on the southern side to prevent people from tumbling over. Here ply the rickshaws. Each has a crew of four boys, or, to be accurate, middle-aged men. They go everywhere at the trot, spindle-legged, barefoot, their soles strips of leather, ringing little bells and chanting strange cries to shoo people out of the way.

There is a castle-in-the-clouds, storybook atmosphere about Mus-

361

soorie that lends it total enchantment. It is not merely that the things that distress one elsewhere in India—the filth, the noise, the poverty, the hopelessness—are much less evident here; it is that the place is unlike anywhere one has ever been. The height has much to do with it, and the setting, and the absence of the motorcar. One goes backward in time in Mussoorie as well as upward in space; people take on a new dimension; they seem more like characters in a costume play, less like toilers from the plains.

Toilers or actors, they are, as they stroll along the Mall, a pageant in themselves: teen-age, teddy-boy Indians in white sharkskin suits and pointed shoes with turned-up toes like those of Chinese mandarins; very old Indians with beards and button-up jackets, carrying posies; small Sikh boys on roller skates and with their hair in nets like girls; hygienic, Boy Scout policemen in khaki shirts and shorts. Nonconformists too: women in veils and Punjabi dress; tiny, tough Gurkhas from Nepal; Tibetans of all kinds—red-robed monks with shaven heads, men in felt hats and woolly stockings, women in pigtails and shawls. Two things only spoil a walk along the Mall: the Indian habits of spitting and of flushing the nose with the hand.

There is much greenery about, and after the brown of the plains it soothes the eye. Here are chestnuts and planes and pines, millions of pink-and-white daisies lighting the cliff face, stocks and pansies in the gardens. At night invisible small birds nest in the foliage of the trees, rustling and twittering like starlings. Apart from the call of the cuckoo and the cries of the rickshaw drivers, these are almost the only sounds you ever hear. Mussoorie is magically still.

And then there are the advertisements peeping from the trees— Indian copywriters murdering the English tongue. "Get a Latest Suit for Your Quick Selection and Increment," proclaim the Sewak Tailors, while the Zammar Institute urges "Controled Emaciation," a course, believe it or not, in slimming. Here, straight from the shires of England, is a local school, "Bramleigh Towers, Cambridge Academy, formerly Rockcliff"; and at Professor Banerji's dancing establishment rock 'n' roll and cha-cha-cha are dispensed at special rates to "ladies, children and mixed" ("Maximum Learning in Minimum Time"). Here is the roller-skating hall, where you can sit by the window and watch the skaters in front of you and fifty miles of India behind. At the Savoy Hotel, the crowning of the May Queen is soon to take place. And at Hakman's Hotel today there is to be a "Jam

Session, Noon to 2 P.M." Here I stop the rickshaw, unload my luggage, and go in.

✪

I HAD come to Mussoorie to catch the last two days of a three-week seminar on "American Institutions and Culture" arranged by a body called the United States Educational Foundation in India. It was being attended by thirty-five graduates from colleges and universities all over India, and five American professors. The syllabus included American politics, law, agriculture, industry and education. The "Culture" lectures were confined to literature, with such titles as "Melville's Uneasy Quest," and "Thoreau at Walden Pond." I wondered what the Indians were making of these.

The seminar was taking place in the Y.W.C.A. building, not far from the hotel. On the front was written: "Mussoorie Y.W.C.A. Home. 1902. Patroness Lady Digges LaTouche," a name no novelist would dare invent. Mrs. Jacobs, the Indian housekeeper, took me to the lecture hall and opened the door. Thirty-five youngish Indian faces looked up, and the lecture stopped. A middle-aged American in a bow tie and spectacles rose from the front and said he was Dr. Dawes, in charge of the seminar, and why didn't I take a seat? I did. The lecturer was a man of about thirty-five. At first I thought he was Indian, but when I had listened to him for a few minutes I realized he was an American Negro. His name was Dr. Garth.

He was lecturing on "America in the Sixties." Beside him was a blackboard showing a circle with six segments labeled Political, Economic, Religious, Social, Artistic, Intellectual. He was working his way through these. Dr. Garth went in for a good deal of mouthing and frowning and said earnest, obvious things. "The American family is a small nuclear affair," he said gravely, and I thought, So what? "There is evidence that the American family consists of two parents and children, and it is only rarely that other members of the family live with them." I thought, If they've only got as far as that, they haven't got anywhere at all. Dr. Garth spoke in a singsong dirge, as though delivering a sermon. "In the United States," he said, "we are sixty-six percent Protestant, twenty-six percent Catholic, and two to three percent Jewish. The remainder have little or no religious faith." I wanted to know how much faith the sixty-six percent Protestants had, but Dr. Garth had gone on to civil rights and Vietnam. "Sometimes it is necessary," he said, screwing his face into a ball, "to make the state a shield as well as a sword, to protect us from each other's evil ways. We have been criticized for not being sufficiently dynamic in internal affairs, and now we are accused of being too dynamic in external affairs." An anonymous Indian in the audience yawned loudly, and quick as anything Dr. Garth said, "In the United States we would regard that as a gross insult, but I suppose things are different here." Everybody laughed at that; it was nice to know Dr. Garth had a sense of the ridiculous.

Dr. Garth finished by reading an article by Will Durant on the grossness and vulgarity of much of American life. Then it was Dr. Dawes's turn. He was wearing a gray suit and small black boots with buckles. Dr. Dawes was a real performer; he gave of himself every time he opened his mouth. He had the American academic's supreme self-confidence, the intellectual arrogance that says, as it were, to the American businessman: We may not be making a million bucks like you, but we're cleverer than you'll ever be, and don't you forget it.

"But I must hasten on," said Dr. Dawes, a phrase with which he signaled each change of subject. "I must hasten on to our foreign policy. Our foreign policy is the containment of China, and it is for that reason alone that we are pursuing our present policy in Vietnam. We believe that if we pull out of Vietnam, Laos will go and Cambodia will go and Thailand will go, and then China will be on India's flank. So, don't kid yourselves, gentlemen, don't kid yourselves, my friends; this country is in mortal peril." He let the words sink in, then straightened himself and changed key. "Of course, I know what many of you are thinking—you are thinking that America has no right to be in Asia at all. And it's good for Americans to come here and find out what you think of them, find out that they're not the great people they thought. But there's a big debate going on in the States just now, a debate that concerns both our countries very deeply. And that debate is how much we should continue with foreign aid to countries which are hostile to American policy in Asia and which resent the American presence." He left the words dangling in mid-air, and you could see the audience pondering on their implications. Then: "But I must hasten on. . . ."

When Dr. Dawes sat down, a long, slender Indian got up. He was wearing a buttoned-up jacket, and his face was sad and beautiful.

"Yes, Mr. Pori," said Dr. Dawes.

"I want to make a comment," said Mr. Pori.

"How long will the comment take?" said Dr. Dawes, who had evidently been here before.

"It is a long comment," said Mr. Pori.

"Okay," said Dr. Dawes, "but you won't mind if we take the questions first."

So Dr. Garth and Dr. Dawes took some questions, and then Mr. Pori made his long comment.

"Countries like ours and yours," he said, "which are democracies, and countries like China, which are not, have two entirely different philosophies. Now, we believe that when there are differences they must be negotiated, and best place to negotiate is United Nations. No doubt at all that China is a great nation and therefore ought to have seat in United Nations." He sat down to a murmur of agreement and one or two claps. I wondered how Dr. Dawes could cope. He coped brilliantly.

"There are millions of people in the United States," he said, "who would agree with every word you say. And because they live in a democracy, like India but unlike China, they have perfect freedom to say it."

We broke for lunch. Dr. Dawes introduced me to his wife, to Dr. and Mrs. Oliver, and to Dr. Garth, who was a bachelor. Dr. Garth told me he was professor of sociology at a women's college at Greensboro, North Carolina, where the students were ninety-five percent Negro and the faculty forty percent white. He had been in India for a year on an exchange program at a women's college at Bangalore. Dr. Oliver was a real academic, smooth and dry, an erect, rigid sort of man with a dry, clipped voice like that of the storekeeper in a Western. He told me he was a Fulbright lecturer in American literature at a university in the Punjab, and this was his third visit to India. His resident post in the States was as head of the English department at Portland (Oregon) State College. "I guess it's good for us to get out of our little back yards and see what the great, big world looks like. Though I don't think I could ever forget where I come from—like those two Englishmen in Kinglake's *Eothen* who passed each other on camels in the desert and didn't even stop to say hello."

I also met Mrs. Jacobs's stunningly pretty daughter-in-law, Yasmin, whose husband was in the Indian Army, up in Ladakh in the cold, watching the Chinese; she had a child of four and a baby of a few months. Some of the Indians introduced themselves, showing that blend of curiosity and enthusiasm which are among the most endearing of Indian characteristics: Mr. Singh, head of the department of English at Agra Rural Institute ("You must understand, Mr. Kennedy, that not all Singhs are Sikhs"); Mr. Suresan from Andhra Loyola College; Professor Siddhanta from Serampore; Mr. Sengupta, who looked Chinese, from Calcutta; Mr. Behl from Chandigarh; Mr. Sanganker; Mr. Borgohain; Mr. Pori; and others. They all looked so young and giggled so much that it was hard to realize they were not undergraduates. They asked me what I was doing, and when I told them Mr. Singh said, "So you are a globe-trotter, eh?" and practically fell over with laughter.

I walked back to Hakman's for lunch and on the way fell in with another of the graduates, a Miss Bhatt, who was going shopping. Miss Bhatt was a serious young lady with a caste mark on her forehead and a very sober sari, and with her I had one of those dotty conversations one seems to have in India all the time.

"How has the course been?" I said.

"So-so," said Miss Bhatt.

"How's that?"

"Well, I will say this. Professors have done level best. Nobody can say they have not. But it all depends on outlook. My outlook is make seminar a much more international affair, have Pakistanis and British and Chinese and everyone. What is your university?"

"My university?"

"Yes."

"Well, I was at Oxford."

"Why is Oxford sponsoring your visit here?"

"It's not. I used to be at Oxford a long time ago."

"Then who is sponsoring your visit?"

"No one, really. I'm here on my own. I'm a writer."

Miss Bhatt looked surprised. "What are you writing?"

"A book about Americans."

"You have written chapters?"

"No, not yet. I've made a lot of notes, though."

"You are writing about professors?"

"I will do."

"How many chapters have you written?"

"Miss Bhatt, I haven't written *any* chapters yet."

We came to the Mall. "What are you thinking of modern Indian writing?" said Miss Bhatt. "Now, tell me your candid opinion." This is the sort of portmanteau question one is always being asked in India. Happily, I remembered Jack at the mayor's house at Qatif.

"Very interesting," I said, "good characterization, and some very unusual imagery."

"So!" said Miss Bhatt. "Now I go to shops, and we meet at the Nehru ceremony after lunch. Bye-bye."

✪

IN THE dining room of Hakman's Hotel, the jam session was in full swing. Trumpet, piano and drums were bashing out "It's Been a Hard Day's Night" and "Let's Twist Again" in the style of the fifties. I ate curry and rice pudding. Between mouthfuls, and earfuls, I wondered what the Nehru ceremony might be; there was nothing about it on the schedule.

Dr. Dawes told me about it when I returned to the lecture hall. This was the anniversary of Nehru's death and there was to be a special commemorative ceremony. Miss Bhatt had rigged up a kind of altar consisting of a table with a white cloth; on this was a photograph of Nehru, flanked by white lilies. At the foot of the altar incense was burning in a brass pot.

We all took our places, the graduates, the professors, Mrs. Jacobs and Yasmin, and an elderly light-colored Indian called Dr. Naik, principal of Gujarat College, the guest speaker. Miss Bhatt, at the piano, sang a wailing song, and this was followed by Dr. Naik's address. Dr. Naik wore a gray Nehru jacket and spoke of "walleys" and "wastnesses." After Dr. Naik, a man in a brown Nehru jacket got up and read extracts from Nehru's will. Then Dr. Oliver spoke about Nehru's writings, and if that wasn't enough, we had Mr. Pori. Mr. Pori fluttered his eyelids and rubbed his hands and talked nonsense. "You have heard from Dr. Naik," he said, glancing all round him, "of Mr. Nehru's interest in science [pause]. Now, Mr. Nehru was a scientist himself [pause and a look round]. By this I mean he had a scientific attitude [pause], a scientific way of looking at things [pause and another look round], a scientific cast of mind." Later he said, "Nehru's great achievement was that he immortalized rationality." I

wanted to get up and shout, "You're talking nonsense," but everyone was taking it quite seriously. Some Indians and Americans seem
to have a need for this sort of windy thing.

The ceremony had lasted an hour, and I thought this must be the
end. But it seemed that all the graduates wanted to add their widow's
mites. A bore in a dhoti spent five minutes telling us that Nehru's
death had left the world grief-stricken, and a man in a green jersey
compared Nehru to Ashoka and the Gautama Buddha. Another man
told us that Nehru's bank account at his death was half what it had
been, but without saying what it had been or where he got the information from. "That shows a great wirtue and honesty," he said,
"which is wery rare in politics."

It was left to a rather weary Dr. Dawes to conclude on a note of
realism. "One of our great difficulties in assessing Mr. Nehru," he
said, "is that our vision is blurred and not as sharp as it will be one
day. I also think it would be a disservice to Mr. Nehru to regard him
as a god or a matchless perfectionist. He didn't like people doing this
when he was alive, and we shouldn't do it now."

Everyone clapped very loudly. Conformists themselves, Indians admire the nonconformist view in others. I heard one graduate say to
another, "What Dawes is saying is true. Vision is blurred now, but
will not be later."

❂

LATER I asked Dr. Garth how an American Negro regarded the Indian scene, and he said he had been surprised to find that Indians
were what he called "dark-skinned white supremacists." He said, "I
have had some warm personal relationships while I have been here,
but this has not blinded me to the fact that Indians as a whole look
down on Negroes. You might think that a people who had been sub-
jected to racial prejudice themselves, as the Indians were under the
British, might be less inclined toward it. But this is not so. In their
conversations they make no distinction between African Negroes and
American Negroes. To them we are equally inferior. They think the
American Negro is far more downtrodden than he is, and the more
insecure of them feel this is how things should be. One man said to
me, 'In America they lynch Negroes'—not condemning the whites,

but approving of what he thought was a fact." Dr. Garth told me all this with an air of cool detachment, as though he, a trained sociologist, were somehow above the fray; yet I got the impression that this was a mask for feelings gravely shocked and wounded by the unexpected prejudices he had found.

Dr. Dawes, an historian, had spent most of his career at the Carnegie Institute of Technology. During leaves of absence he had taught history at Allahabad and Lucknow, and more recently he had come out to Delhi to help administer the Fulbright scheme. "I came because the Fulbright people asked me to. It wasn't a question of mission or dedication or the white man's burden or anything. I'd been too long in one pulpit, and I knew it."

"How has the seminar been?"

"It's the third I've organized, and the best so far. We had a hundred applications for the course, and we selected these thirty-five from colleges all over the country. They were very suspicious when they arrived. They thought they were going to have American propaganda thrown at them all the time. I think we've cleared their minds of that. Our object has not been to praise or condemn the United States, but to be as honest and self-critical as we can. Sometimes I think we've been too self-critical."

"Any disappointments?"

"Only that they didn't use the library. We brought along a library of six hundred books and they haven't touched them. The other major disappointment has been the lack of intelligent discussion. The lecture system which the British introduced has been the mortmain, the dead hand, of Indian education. These people haven't been taught how to think critically at all."

"How much is that due to the system, and how much to their own temperament?"

"I'd say a bit of both. There is one major difference between these people and ourselves, which in my view is completely unbridgeable. They are primarily interested in a state of *being*, in what life has to offer them now. We are more interested in a state of *becoming*, in what we can make of our lives in the future. We're ambitious and conscious of material rewards, and on the whole they're not."

✪

IN HAKMAN's Hotel that night, I asked to be called at 8 A.M. with tea. I was called at 6:30 A.M. with a banana. In India this sort of thing is the rule rather than the exception. The lady at the desk said, "I am very, very sorry about it. I cannot think how a thing like this came to happen. But I will do the needful and look into it. I will definitely do the needful."

✪

THE LAST lecture was called "America in the Future" and was another symposium by all three lecturers. Dr. Oliver started by telling us about population explosion and automation and living underground and farming the sea. He said he didn't know how the human mind was going to stand the incredible increase in information. The implications of automation were also staggering. "Banks and courts and places are already using automation. I think some teaching will be done by automation, too."

A graduate interrupted to say that automation would cause unemployment, and that in India, where there was mass unemployment already, this would be disastrous.

Dr. Dawes got up and said, "I welcome automation. I see no more of old men bending down under heavy burdens and women slaving their lives away in kitchens. Automation means more leisure for more people, and more jobs to make that leisure possible. I see more golf clubs and cameras being made, so that people can use them. No, I'm not frightened by automation or the population explosion, or anything else. I think that when the time comes, something else will rise up that we don't even dream of now. Our future problems are not our present ones."

Dr. Garth said he supposed he ought to talk about the Negro problem, and he did so with a great deal of mouthing and face-making and opening and closing his eyes. "We cannot expect Negroes to be more angelic than their white neighbors," he concluded. "While there are disgusting whites who bomb churches and kill civil-rights workers and all that, then there will be nasty Negroes." He turned toward Dr. Dawes. "We are all," he said, "disgustingly equal."

Dr. Dawes glanced at Dr. Garth and then at the audience. "I don't know why you look at me when you say that," he said.

Everyone laughed and clapped; this exchange had probably taught them more about the tolerance of American academic life than all the lectures of the seminar put together.

Dr. Garth said, "Dr. Dawes is an historian who knows everything about America's relationships with the outside world since 1630, and almost nothing about relationships inside the United States since 1950."

There was more laughter, and then Mr. Sengupta got up. "Do the lecturers think that America will get more popular during the coming years?"

Dr. Oliver said, "I think America's popular enough now."

They laughed again at this (they laughed at almost anything), and then Dr. Dawes said, "I think this is a very complicated problem. It goes in ups and downs, and we're in a down period now, I would say. When I was at Lucknow University a student said to me, 'You always said I could speak to you frankly. I want to tell you what's wrong with the U.S.' So I said, 'Go ahead,' and I listened avidly. 'Well,' he said, 'you shouldn't have dropped the atom bomb,' and I said, 'I couldn't agree with you more.' Then he said, 'And you adopt a very imperialist policy in Latin America.' So I said, 'That is a very superficial comment on a very complex relationship.' After that he said, 'You are a lot of greedy materialists,' and I said, 'If you mean by that that we enjoy some of the things money can buy, I plead as guilty as the rest.' Next he said he thought we were too suspicious of the Russians, which I said I thought was perfectly true, and then I asked him if there was anything else. 'Yes,' he said, 'will you help me get a scholarship to America?' "

Dr. Oliver said, "I'd like here to put in a comment of Confucius. Having everybody as friend is bad. Having nobody as friend is bad. Having the right friends is good." Everyone clapped, delighted that Dr. Oliver should be acquainted with this simple Eastern bromide.

"Two other things I'd like to say," said Dr. Oliver. "Somebody earlier mentioned the evils that can arise from nationalism. Well, I'm all for nationalism, but I want it to be cultural. With Aristotle, I want to keep nationalism but to break down national frontiers. And the other thing comes from a saying by Professor George. He once said, 'We talk about rights, civil rights, natural rights, et cetera, et cetera. But man has no rights at all except one, and that is the right to defend himself. All other rights are dependent on the permits that one group can wrest from another. The right to defend ourselves is the only right we have.' "

✪

THERE WAS an hour to fill in before lunch, so I took some of the graduates into the garden. They clustered round with grinning, cheerful faces, like urchins at an accident, all wanting to talk at once, and intoning in that curious semi-Welsh lilt which in India passes for the English tongue. They looked so very young and child-like that again I had to remind myself that these were not undergraduates but qualified teachers at Indian universities.

"What is your opinion of the seminar?" I said.

"I would say without fear of contradiction," said Mr. Singh, "that many notions have been changed."

They chorused assent. "Agreed." "Definitely." "That is what I am thinking."

"What sort of notions?" I said.

Mr. M. N. Borgohain, whose ancestors came from Thailand, said, "Well, before, I had notion that America was flowing with milk and honey. I think we were all having this notion. But now we find it is not so. America has poverty too."

"That is true," someone broke in, "but American poverty is not Indian poverty. Mrs. Barnett was telling us that in some places American children were not having enough to eat, and no shoes to go to school. Well, I agree that is bad social evil, but in India there are thousands who die every year from starvation. Now, you must agree, Mr. Kennedy, that is a worse social evil, there is really no comparison between the two."

Mr. Singh said, "This is true. We get very depressed by the poverty here. There are times when we think it can never end. But what they have done in America with natural resources gives us hope. Take that film they showed on the Tennessee Valley Authority, and what they have done with natural resources. I must say I was impressed by this. It gave encouragement. It showed what we can do."

"Agreed," said a voice from the back. "But tell me this, who is going to do the needful?"

No one answered. Perhaps there was no answer. Mr. Singh said, "Another notion changed is idea that life in the United States is very easy, and no need to work hard. We saw this isn't so, how hard people do work. This made me think of untouchables. Here untouchables are twenty-five percent of population. It is outlawed, but still goes on. You see, we feel it is dignity here to own land, but beneath dignity to work on it. This is all wrong. Americans have showed us dignity of physical labor."

Mr. Behl from Chandigarh, plump with a thin mustache, said, "I agree. I was, frankly, amazed to see Dr. Dawes carrying a heavy burden of books, which we would never carry. We would be offended if we were asked to carry a burden like that. We would not say anything, but we would be offended. 'The gospel of dirty hands' is what Nehru called it."

Mr. Suresan, who had buckteeth and curly hair, said, "I thought marriage was taken very lightly in the States, but now I find this is not so. Also I understand they are interested in peace, though prepared to use force if necessary."

Mr. Sanganker, who had a black beard and a wild eye, said, "My candid opinion is that Americans don't have firm convictions of life, and this makes men have no faith in their promises. I was thinking they were frank, but now I am thinking they are not so frank. They say they are democratic, but it is not so. They outlaw the Communist party in some states. Why? Why not let people have a free choice?"

"My opinion," said Mr. Sengupta, with the Chinese eyes, "was that President was main thing. I thought President was almost dictator. But now they have explained about checks and balances and all that, so this notion is changed. Another thing. I thought Negroes were like untouchables, just servants of the whites. But they sent this Negro lecturer who is clearly a very educated man, and it seems they have other Negroes now in key positions, so this notion is changed, too."

Mr. Pori appeared from nowhere and said, "Dr. Garth thinks all Indians have an impression the Negro is an ape. Well, I talked to him very strongly about this, and I said, 'You have got this all wrong.'"

"What about the professors?" I said. "What do you think of them?"

"They have impressed us very much," said Mr. Sengupta. "They were very self-critical. They were very candid too."

Professor Siddhanta said, "We are finding them very friendly people. When British visit our college they have a stiff-necked superiority. They are not friendly. But these Americans are friendly and informal. I am stating this as a fact. No, I am sorry, I am stating this as a fact. Another thing that surprised me was that they knew anything about India. They are knowing more about India than many of us here. Now, that is very much to their credit."

"Agreed," said several voices. But Mr. Sengupta said, "We must not form a judgment of the American people from that, because, you see, these are only a handful of intellectuals."

This started an argument among them, and while it was going on I noted a very old man walking down the garden path, carrying a basket. He was dressed in rags and had a tangle of wild white hair and looked about a hundred and ten. He sat down on the grass beneath a tree, opened the basket, pulled out a pipe and started playing. The graduates paid no attention. As the snake's head came out of the basket Mrs. Jacobs's houseboy ran past us to tell the old man to go away. Before the boy reached him the old man had started putting away his pipe. Then he closed the basket, rose wearily and moved slowly toward the gate. His legs were storklike, long and brittle. I wondered how old he was and where he would sleep and whether he had enough to eat. Then he passed through the gate and was gone.

I switched my attention to the group. Mr. Sangankar was making a long, boring speech, and Mr. Singh and his friends were having some quiet fun at his expense.

"He is being slightly mischievous."

"What does he say?"

"He is speaking English—optional."

"He is wiser than he was at the beginning. At the beginning he was not wise. He has learnt wisdom."

"Let us be serious. Now, when I am serious, I am *damn* serious." Everyone giggled.

"What's going on?" I said.

"We are doing some thinking," said Mr. Singh. "We are doing some very *loud* thinking." And they giggled again.

Mr. Sengupta said, "I wish to put this view. We cannot agree with American foreign policy." (Cries of "Agreed" and "Definitely.") "Professors did their best to defend this, but still they could not satisfy."

Professor Siddhanta said, "I would like to make this point in slightly different fashion. In Vietnam Americans are imperialists. There is no doubting this at all."

"How?" I said.

"Because," said Professor Siddhanta, "they are trying to stop Communism. You must understand, Mr. Kennedy, that to Americans Communism means something different to what it means here. To Americans it is wicked. But for Asians who are starving and dying of incorrigible diseases, it is holding out hope. What has democracy done for us? they say. Well, Communism can't be worse, and might be a jolly sight better."

"Mr. Kennedy," said a voice from the back, "here is my comment on Vietnam. How would you relish it if you lived in America and half a million Asians invaded Brazil? I am thinking you would not relish it at all."

I was thinking much the same thing when Mrs. Jacobs's houseboy rang the bell for lunch. We moved indoors.

"One other comment," said Mr. Borgohain. "Seminar had too many subjects. We should have had fewer subjects or two subjects taken at the same time, so we could have had a choice. You see, we are not all interested in same subjects."

"True," said Mr. Sengupta. "I was not benefiting from subjects I knew about, like economic. But I was benefiting from others."

Mr. Behl said, "I must tell you frankly that I was not showing much interest in sociology."

There was a chorus of sympathetic laughter. Mr. Singh said, "On this point almost all are agreed. Down with sociology is what we are saying. Down with damned sociology."

We went inside. I was about to walk up to Hakman's, when Yasmin, exquisite in a cool sari, came up. "My mother says there is plenty of food, if you would like to stay to lunch."

✪

IN THE evening there was a farewell party.

The M.C. of the party was Mr. Behl, and he asked us to sit on the floor in a circle. I sat between Yasmin, with her little daughter, and Mr. Singh. First we had ice cream and cakes, and then children's games. The first game consisted of handing round a box with slips of paper in it; you picked a slip at random and mimed whatever was written on it. Dr. Dawes's slip said, "Act like a member of the opposite sex," so he got up and minced round the room and everyone clapped like mad.

After the games, the bearers and sweepers came in, and squatted on the floor like crabs. There were fourteen of them, and as Mr. Behl called out their names they went up to collect envelopes containing money. We all clapped hard. Yasmin said to me, "One of the bearers did not come. He said he didn't have a decent coat. He only had a shabby coat and he was too ashamed to wear it. My mother said he cried."

When the last bearer had gone, Mr. Singh said, "What next?"

Mr. Behl said, "There are nine cups of ice cream left, so anyone who wants can have them. And now Miss Bhatt is going to grace us with a song."

Miss Bhatt sang a very pretty song, then Mr. Behl said, "And now magician to please come?" This was the signal for Professor Siddhanta, wearing a Kashmir shawl and dhoti. He fumbled in the folds of the shawl and produced a scrap of paper. "First, before magic," he said, "I am going to read poem." This didn't surprise me. Indians with the smallest pretense to an English education will compose and recite poems at the drop of a hat. I have never heard one which was not bizarre in the extreme, and Professor Siddhanta's was no exception:

> Feeling like composing a poem,
> Though a poet I have never been,
> When to make us appreciate Robert Frost,
> Doctor Oliver is so keen.
> If at lunchtime or dinner table,
> We eat unseen
> Jacobean curry of French bean.
> No worry if coming to Mussoorie,
> You become lean and thin,
> Be not afraid,
> The doctor will give you some medicine.

We clapped politely, and Professor Siddhanta bowed low, as though he had just given a piano recital. Then he said he would do a card trick. In the middle of the trick he panicked. "It is not going to come out," he shouted hysterically. "What shall I do?" However, he persevered and it did come out, and then he asked Mr. Borgohain to go out of the room. As Mr. Borgohain closed the door Professor Siddhanta leaned toward us conspiratorially. "Now what shall we think of? What object shall we choose?" We agreed on the wastepaper basket. "All right," shouted Professor Siddhanta, "come in, come in!" Mr. Borgohain came in.

"Is it a chair?" said Professor Siddhanta.

"No," said Mr. Borgohain. "It is not a chair."

"Is it a picture?"

"No."

"Is it a piece of clothing?"

"No."

This went on for a bit, and then Professor Siddhanta said, "Is it the wastepaper basket?"

"Yes," said Mr. Borgohain. "It is the wastepaper basket."

Everyone clapped joyfully, and Professor Siddhanta and Mr. Borgohain beamed. Mr. Behl leaned over to me and said, "I understand they agreed beforehand it would be eighth object mentioned."

We played one or two more games and then Mr. Behl proposed and Mr. Singh seconded a vote of thanks to the staff. In reply Dr. Dawes said what a happy experience the seminar had been. "I think that all of us," he said, "students and staff alike, have come to know America and India better than before. We have got to know each other. We came as strangers and we part as friends." He took some papers from an envelope. "I now wish to present certificates of participation in this seminar."

Americans have the same childlike love of certificates as Indians do of party games. These were lovingly handed round, one for everyone. Then the graduates gave the staff presents. Dr. Oliver got a Kashmiri cap and Mrs. Oliver a box, Dr. Dawes a sort of rattle and Mrs. Dawes a wooden ship, Dr. Garth a figurine of a dancing girl. Yasmin said to me, "A pity you didn't meet Dr. and Mrs. Barnett. They left before you came. Mrs. Barnett wore a sari all the time. She looked so sweet."

This should have been the end of the evening, but one graduate, a man I hadn't met, had an urge to make an impromptu speech. Indians get these urges all the time. "Let me express unreserved gratitude of all to the staff," he said. "We have read about Americans, we have heard about Americans, but seeing is believing. We have found out there are many misconceptions and misunderstandings. Americans are a great people. Indians have much to learn from America. At the same time America has much to learn from India. India must change, but not in American manner. India wants nonalignment because, having emerged bleeding from jaws of British lion, she doesn't want to be thrown into claws of Russian bear." What had started as an expression of thanks was now becoming a political speech, and people started giggling or looking bored. In England the speaker would have been shouted down, but Indians are too polite. He continued without interruption, and then finished with: "We, the teachers of India, are the arteries of India, and we hope we are making you feel the pulse of India."

There was some desultory clapping. Mr. Pori saw me writing and said, "You know, many of us were not agreeing with sentiments in that speech. Sentiments were foreign to us." Slowly the party broke up. Goodbyes were said, addresses exchanged and promises given to meet again. Dr. Dawes walked with me to the gate.

"I suppose," I said, "that the object of all this from your point of view is that these thirty-five teachers should go back to their colleges and say, 'Well, the U.S. isn't such a bad place after all'? Do you think they will?"

Dr. Dawes's answer was both realistic and nonpartisan. "I plead ignorance. Who can say? Often they say one thing to your face and another among themselves. Often they say what they think you want to hear, whether it's true or not."

"Why do they do that?"

"Insecurity, really. They're frightened of displeasing you, frightened of losing their jobs. You can't blame them. They look over their shoulders and see so many others waiting to take their place."

We reached the gates. "They talk about competition in the States," said Dr. Dawes, "but here, I think, it's keener. So many qualified people looking for so few jobs. If you don't make it as an intellectual in the States, somehow or other you can get by. But if you don't make it as an intellectual here"—he made a gesture with his hands—"why, you have only to look around you to see the kind of existence you can expect."

I looked over Dr. Dawes's shoulder to the patch of grass where the ancient snake charmer had sat and played his pipe before being so rudely hustled away.

✪

NEXT MORNING Dr. and Mrs. Oliver and I got up early, to motor to Delhi before the heat of the day. The main gate was closed, and we asked the gatekeeper to open it. He said he could not do so, as it was now after 5 A.M. and between 5 A.M. and 7 A.M. the gate had to be closed. We had a fierce argument, and eventually I persuaded him to telephone for permission to Mussoorie's chief of police. The chief of police was annoyed at being woken up, but grudgingly gave permission.

"It's incredible, isn't it," said Dr. Oliver as we drove through, "that they can carry on like that when they need all the tourist trade they can get. All that man had to do was open the gate."

"Why *do* they do it?" said Mrs. Oliver.

"It's the way they've always done things," said Dr. Oliver.

Mussoorie disappeared in the mists and we moved into the warmth of the plains. We passed through Dehra Dun and signs saying "Indian Military Academy," and "Naval Hydrographic Department," and "Air Force Accounts," et cetera. Beyond Dehra Dun we went down a wooded ravine. Here a board said "Shooting Prohibited," and we passed blue pheasants with bushy tails and proud, wild peacocks and once, rounding a corner, a monkey with two babies, one clinging to her side, the other suckling at her breast.

On the hot, dusty plain the road lay straight and empty. The Olivers told me about life at the university in the Punjab where he had been teaching. "We were the first Europeans ever to teach there," said Dr. Oliver. "There were no servants who spoke English, so we just had a sweeper, and Mrs. Oliver did the cooking. The only means of transportation was bicycle rickshaw. It was quite an adventure." Mrs. Oliver said, "When we asked at the co-op for toilet paper, they sent us to the bookshop. They didn't know what it was. But everyone was so nice and friendly."

Presently something large and red appeared on the road ahead. It was the carcass of a cow, freshly skinned. About forty vultures stood in a tight circle around it, like mourners at a wake. I wondered why they were not eating the carcass, and then saw that a pye-dog had got there first. His head was buried deep in the cow's body, and when he pulled it out it was blood red. He looked at us for a moment, chewing, then pushed his nose again into the soft flesh. As long as he stayed there, the vultures would keep their distance; but when he had had his fill and gone away to sleep, they would move in and have theirs.

"I would say," said Dr. Oliver as we edged gingerly past, "that this country still has a very long way to go."

★

IT WAS four in the morning at Palam Airport, New Delhi. A group of us were waiting by the tarmac for the round-the-world Pan Am jet to take us on to Thailand. It was almost light and very still, and the air was sharp with familiar Indian smells, the bittersweet smell of burning, and flowers and spices and dung. The sun swam gently over the horizon, sweetener of the sap in tree and testicle, precursor of another sizzling noon.

There were many Americans in our group, for this was vacation time. Some of the younger ones were chewing gum and being loud and silly. A happy businessman was being seen off by Indian friends, who had garlanded him with flowers. He didn't know that the custom in India, unlike Hawaii, is to return the garland as soon as you have put it on, and he strutted up and down like some bizarre orange peacock. "I want to tell you," he said, pumping the hands of his Indian friends, "that this has been one of the most wonderful days of my life, and I'll never forget it." Another American, bald and stout, was less tranquil. "I don't give a goddam," he shouted to an Indian by the gate. "The man told us four forty-five, and so far as I'm concerned, four forty-five it is." He glared angrily round him, and even at that hour I found it hard not to laugh. All Westerners in India have their moments like this.

Presently the plane came in and spilled out its passengers. I found a seat in the back next to a sweet, thin old Australian, who wore a kind of gray golfing cap and gold-rimmed glasses. He had a bag beside him marked "Gallipoli Veterans' Tour," and I remembered reading in the paper recently that there had been a tour of the battlefields organized for the survivors, to mark the fiftieth anniversary of the campaign.

We sat on the runway a long time. First we were delayed because a passenger called Kleinwasser had lost his briefcase. Then the captain told us on the intercom that he couldn't get clearance from traffic control. We sat in our seats and stewed. There is nothing so silent as a plane with its engines off, and when someone turned the pages of a newspaper it sounded like gunfire.

We took off at last, climbing eastward toward the rising sun, whose rays were now flooding the brown Punjabi plains. It was announced that breakfast was about to be served; and passengers who had come aboard at Frankfurt and Beirut and points beyond opened their eyes, and flexed their muscles and yawned, then teetered down the aisle to pee and shave and wash.

"What was the Gallipoli Veterans' tour like?" I said to the Gallipoli veteran.

"It was terrible. I'd never have gone if I'd known it was going to be so strenuous. Christ, they carted us about all over the place! When I say they killed us with hospitality, I'm not exaggerating. One of the fellows died on the spot, another in Istanbul, and another on the plane when it was landing at Sydney. They should never have put on a program like that. We're too old. Christ, we have to be pretty old to have taken part! I'm sixty-nine. Most of the other fellows were over seventy. I'm going back the slow way. I've been to Beirut and Tehran and Isfahan and Shiraz and Kabul and Delhi. Tomorrow I'm flying up to a place called Chung Mi."

"I went up the Dardanelles a couple of months ago," I said. "I looked for the places where the fighting was, but I didn't see them."

"You wouldn't," said the Gallipoli veteran. "None of it looks like it did. The Turks have started a big afforestation program, and they've covered up all the old trenches.

"First time I'd been back to Europe since," said the Gallipoli veteran. " 'Course, when most Australians talk of abroad, they think of Europe and the old country. But we don't belong to Europe. We belong to Asia. The old country's not going to be able to help us any more when the chips are down. If it's anyone, it'll be the Americans. That's why I'm making this trip. To see what Asia is like. To see the kind of thing we're up against, who are our friends and enemies."

He stubbed out his cigarette and said, "People can say what they like about the Americans, but when the chips are down, they're the only people who will help us."

At Bangkok airport the Gallipoli veteran and I shared a taxi into the city. On the highway we passed a big sign saying: "May is Tourist

Expenditure Survey Month—Will You Co-operate?" The Gallipoli
veteran said, "I was here in March on my way through, and that was
Tourist Expenditure Survey Month, too."

✪

GOING FROM India to Thailand is in some ways like going from South
to North America. It is a journey from a state of *being* to a state of
becoming, from poverty to affluence, darkness to light. Bangkok, like
Tokyo, is a Western-style city inhabited by Easterners. Here the taps
work, buses run, streets are cleaned, people know the way. English is
spoken almost as widely as in India and a good deal more comprehen-
sibly. Foreigners, once shunned, now have their needs catered to.
"Skin and Breast Rejuvenation," says a sign on the road to the airport. And a grocer in central Bangkok advertises: "Just arrived:
Smoked Salmon, kippers and liver sausage." *The Bangkok World* is a
better English-language newspaper than anything in India, because it
regularly takes syndicated features from the British and American
quality newspapers. In India the peasants are bent double under
crippling burdens; in Thailand they have burdens, too, but they also
have sense enough to sling them between poles.

In India two hundred years of governessy colonization has atro-
phied thought and sapped the will. This fate the Thais have happily
escaped. Where Indians are moody, mystical and just a little mad,
Thais are serene and sharp and cool as water buffaloes. They look like
dolls and speak a kind of dolls' language; hold your nose between
finger and thumb, say "Kling, klang, klong" rapidly, and you will
have an idea of how spoken Thai sounds. It is a surprise to find so
many people—doctors and taxi drivers, television technicians and
civil servants—in military uniform, but this is less indicative of authoritarian rule than of a passion for order. Theirs is a permissive
society, nor are they easily shaken. In India one flies off the handle at
least once a day: it is almost expected. In Thailand it is best to stay
calm; lose your temper with a Thai and he may laugh with joy to see
such a wonderful sight.

So many people had said to me, "If you're going to Bangkok and
want to meet an American businessman who's different, go and see
Jim Thompson: he's unlike any American businessman you've met."
"Who is Jim Thompson?" I said. "He's a kind of a legend," they said;

"he runs the Thai Silk Company, which employs three thousand people; he built it up from scratch." "He's a genius with colors," they said. "He designed the costumes for the London production of *The King and I*, and he lives in this fantastic house; it's a composite of six houses assembled from all over Thailand, and he's filled it with his own unique collection of Thai antiques. He's a man you shouldn't miss."

So I called up Jim Thompson, and he asked me to dine with him at his house on the edge of one of Bangkok's many canals, or *klongs*. From the outside it was unremarkable, little different from other Thai houses I had seen. But inside was a cool, rich world of marble and old teak and limestone Buddhas and paintings of astonishing beauty.

Jim Thompson was a surprisingly small man, in his fifties I guessed, and there was something about his firm, rather elongated face that reminded me of two very dissimilar characters—James Bond's creator, Ian Fleming, and Lawrence of Arabia. He spoke in recognizably East Coast, Ivy League accents and was dressed simply in a white silk shirt and trousers, both, I assumed, the products of his own firm.

I had thought there might be others for dinner—not necessarily a party, but the odd friend or two—and was pleased to find it was just ourselves. We sat down at a table with a smooth top and richly carved legs. Jim Thompson said that originally it had been the gaming table of King Chulalongkorn. To my left was another table with carved legs, a Chinese worship table from northern Thailand. On it were some rather quaint ornamental lions, replicas of Venetian lions made by Burmese scholars whom King Mindon Min had sent to Europe after the Napoleonic Wars. Above this table were a set of six beautiful paintings of the Incarnation of the Buddha, which had been in a temple up the river. Jim Thompson said there were another twenty paintings in the same set, and these were in other rooms in the house. I wondered how the paintings had come to leave the temple, but felt it rude to ask.

A Thai manservant brought cold soup and a beautiful white cockatoo, which he placed on the back of Jim Thompson's chair. "I got him two days after he landed from Singapore," said Jim Thompson. "I went down to the docks to get a red parrot, and I found him." I said, "He's a very handsome bird"; and Jim Thompson said, "He's forty-five years old." I wondered how he knew. "He loves Beethoven," said Jim Thompson, "and sometimes he gets carried away like we all do and starts conducting." The cockatoo sat there patiently all through dinner, sometimes cooing like a dove and sometimes leaning over Jim Thompson's shoulder to kiss his cheek. "I have a black lorikeet too," said Jim Thompson, "who's just like the blackamoor in Petrushka. He spends most of his time lying on his back and banging his head with corn-on-the-cob."

Jim Thompson said he had been born and brought up in Delaware, in a well-to-do family with a butler and servants and a French nanny. Later he went to Princeton and studied architecture. In 1939 war broke out in Europe, and in 1940, when America was still neutral, he enlisted as a private in the United States Army. "They sent us on a crazy four-week course to Plattsburgh. Winston Guest and Jock Whitney were there, too. We had a lovely time falling about in the bogs. We were all very patriotic."

I said, pointing at the things all round me, "It's difficult to imagine you as a soldier!"

"Oh, I was quite a good soldier. It's in the blood. I had a grandfather who was a general in the Civil War at the age of twenty-seven. He led the charge at Selma. He commanded the largest body of troops for a man of his age since Napoleon. His name was James H. Wilson. When he got out of the Army he built the Third Avenue El. Then he got sent to the war in Cuba, where his wife was burned up in a carriage, and from there he went to Peking to deal with the Boxers. He stayed a long time in China, and when he was an old man he used to tell me about it. It was he who first got me interested in the East."

The cockatoo made a sort of croaking noise, leaned forward and nodded its head vigorously up and down. I thought it was going to have a fit.

"I was in the Army six years," said Jim Thompson. "I got married, was made an officer, and then was posted as aide to a general. I liked the general but not the job, and I persuaded him to let me join the O.S.S. My unit was one-third British, one-third American, and one-third French, and we went into France about the time of the southern invasion. Douglas Fairbanks planned the whole thing. The only reason they let me in was that I speak French—I told you I had a French nanny—though with a perfectly horrible American accent.

"Well, then the European war ended, and they wanted to post me to Florence. But I didn't much care for that and I found I could get out of it by volunteering for special service in the East. So it was all fixed, and the day I was due to be parachuted in here, the Japanese war ended. So we flew in from Rangoon a week later. I was a major by this time, and we were billeted in the Prime Minister's Palace and lived like kings.

"Soon our embassy opened up again, and I stayed on, first as military attaché and then as political adviser. By this time I'd got to know the Siamese government very well. They insisted I stay in the Suan Kalarb Palace, that's the Rice Garden Palace, with about forty servants. I never understood how they justified this, when I was working for the United States embassy. In the end I had to move out when Herbert Hoover came over. It was the only place the Siamese government could put him."

Twice, now, Jim Thompson had used the word "Siamese," rather than "Thai," and I realized it must be deliberate. In all our conversations I never heard him speak of "Thai" or "Thailand" once.

"By now," he said, "my marriage was through, and I had got a divorce. I had no responsibilities, and I decided that rather than go back to the States and take up the architect practice, I'd see what I could find here. The prime minister knew about this and one day he said to me, 'Thompson, the tourists are coming back here, have a look at all the hotels in Bangkok, see which looks the best and fix it up.' So I decided to fix up the Oriental and make it the most beautiful hotel in Asia. I went to the States to redesign it, and Pan American was interested in putting up the money. But when I got back, I found there'd been a *coup d'état*. The old regime was out, and the new one said they didn't want any foreign capital. So then I decided to concentrate on silk."

"Why silk?" I said.

"I was in the habit of looking for silk. My wife was very fond of silk, and I used to send her silk from wherever I happened to be. The day we liberated Lyons I ran across Duchesne *père et fils,* who were both in the Resistance, and I managed to buy some silk which they'd kept hidden during the war. I was sort of silk-oriented.

"Well, when I got back from that trip to the States, I found that nobody was wearing silk any more, and therefore nobody was weaving it. They all said it was too expensive. It was never a huge trade, but people used to weave it for their own use, and for the royal family. I knew there were looms in many houses. The Chams who settled here—they're Moslems from Cambodia—were all great weavers.

"When I had decided to go ahead with the silk, I went back to the

States to settle up my affairs and sell the family estate and find agents for the weavers. I was in the States the whole of 1947. When I got back here I had a stroke of luck. There was a letter from my sister's husband, who's a lawyer, saying I was concerned in Kate Osgood's will, and did I want him to handle it? She was a rich old cousin who had just died. She had made a very curious will, leaving a fortune to be divided among fifteen people with the proviso that if any died, I was to have something. Well, most of them were younger than me, but almost immediately one of them did die, and that's how I got the money.

"It wasn't a great deal, but it was enough to get started on. I think the original stock was around twenty-five thousand dollars. I got the weavers weaving again, and I sold the silk for them on consignment. I'd send around four to five thousand dollars' worth to New York. New York paid me and I paid the weavers. To start with I picked out the things I knew would be salable, and after that I told them what I believed would sell. Up to the time of *The King and I,* I was using traditional patterns, but after that I did my own designing. Color is something that has always fascinated me. When I was studying painting for my architectural examinations I used to forget about the drawing because I wanted to get on with the coloring. I had to *discipline* myself to draw.

"At this time I was living in the Oriental Hotel, and I practically had a silk shop in my bedroom. All the guests would come rushing to my room to see what I had. Sometimes the room was knee-deep in silk. Then in 1951 I opened the shop. I never wanted to have my name on the door or anything, but the British ambassador and the American ambassador and other friends said, 'For God's sake put your name on the door. We send people to your shop and they can't find where you are.' In the end I put it up, because a Chinaman here started up a jewelry shop called 'Thompson's Gems,' and I had a lot of letters from friends congratulating me on branching into the jewelry business."

The manservant came in with an insecticide gun. He got down on the floor and started spraying my ankles. "The insects get pretty bad here in the evening," said Jim Thompson. When the manservant was through with my ankles, he did my arms and neck. Then he handed me fruit salad.

"After that we never looked back. The business just grew and grew. We've never advertised, but every time there's been publicity about us, the mail-order business has boomed. There was an article about me in *Reader's Digest,* and we had a flood of letters after that; a Finnish firm wrote, and we appointed agents in Venezuela and South Africa." He smiled. "Back in the days when I was an architect, one had to learn to hide one's light under a bushel. Now I've learned that in the business world publicity is good.

"Anyhow, the company has made money hand over fist. Every year the original stockholders get one hundred percent on their investment, and the staff get a three-month bonus at the end of the year and thirty-three and one third percent of the net profits as well. Some weavers are earning literally thousands of dollars a month. I employ about three thousand people, and I have thirty-nine agencies all over the world who write in regularly and say what they want."

"What is the business worth now?" I said.

"I simply don't know," said Jim Thompson. "I really don't. You'd have to ask Charles that. He's my partner."

"And what about the house?" I said. "Did you move straight here from the Oriental Hotel, or what?"

"I stayed in the Oriental Hotel until the middle of 1949," said Jim Thompson, "and the next year I found a perfect small house which I could rent for twenty dollars a month—by this time U.S. aid had hit Bangkok and prices everywhere had soared. I had a cook and a boy and a bed, and four chairs, a table and a desk, and I said to myself: This is all I want, I don't want any other possessions at all. Well, I lived there very happily for two years and I had a quiet life and I saw mostly Siamese people and a few Lao refugees and just a very, very few foreigners. Then in 1951 the landlord said to me, 'I'm sorry to do this to you, Mr. Thompson, but a restaurant wants to come here and has offered me a large sum, so you'll have to go. But there's a vacant lot nearby, and you used to be an architect, so why don't you build?'

"So I bought the lot and built myself a little house for four thousand dollars, and I thought I'd better get a few things to decorate the place, and that was the start of the collecting. It was a tiny house, but I did a lot of entertaining. Then about 1958 the house was getting too full for my things, and the entertaining was increasing and I thought the time had come to build myself something bigger. This was a site I had always had my eye on, as the very first looms I had are in the village opposite, on the other side of the canal. At the time this place was a builder's yard, but I found out it belonged to a man I knew, and he was willing to sell. I had a little trouble with the government, because they don't much like foreigners, but I got permission for it in the end."

We had finished dinner by now, and Jim Thompson said, "Before I tell you about how the house was built, let me show you around."

So we walked round the house, which, considering that it consisted of five houses, was much smaller than I expected. There was the dining room and a lovely, big, oblong drawing room, and Jim Thompson's study and bedroom, and a guest room and the kitchen and staff quarters, and that was about it. But in all the rooms and passages were these fantastically beautiful things: serene, smiling Buddhas of every period from 500 A.D. on; fragile paintings of scenes from the Vessantara Jataka, Burmese mats and tapestries, Chinese porcelain, painted tables, lacquer chests, glass mosaics, heads of stone and terra cotta, torsos of stucco, figures and animals in bronze. And everywhere, all round, were these glowing walls of polished golden teak, each slightly inclined inward after the Thai fashion, enveloping the treasures in a warm, protective cocoon. It was like being in a rich, exotic and brilliantly alive museum, a monument to one quiet American's stupendous individual good taste.

We sat down in the drawing room, on a sofa between the two windowless windows, and the manservant brought coffee and the white cockatoo.

"I wanted to start building in August, 1958," said Jim Thompson. "But the Brahmin astrologers wouldn't let me, and here you're wise to do what the Brahmin astrologers say. They looked at my horoscope and said I couldn't start till mid-September. So we started at twenty minutes to nine on the morning of September fifteenth.

"Of course, we weren't engaged in building, in the strict sense of the word, so much as assembling these various houses that I had seen and bought in various parts of Siam. The room we're sitting in now was part of a beautiful old house belonging to one of my weavers in the village across the canal. When I heard he was going to pull it down, I offered to buy it. The second house, which consists of the hall and dining room and stairs, came from Pak Hai in the northwest, and the connecting passages came from another house there, too. They belonged to the aunt of one of my weavers, and he told me she had gambled all her money away and was heavily in debt. So I took a trip up there. The old lady was eighty-three, four feet eight inches high, and still playing cards furiously. She said if I bought all her houses for ten thousand ticals, that would clear her debts. That's what I did. The third house is my bedroom and guest room, the pantry and kitchen come from a weaver's house across the canal, and the cook's house, which belonged to a cousin of another weaver, came from the other side of Bangkok. The old lady's houses came here by river and water, a hundred miles across Siam, and the cook's house arrived by truck at three in the morning. We had to get special police permission for it.

"The workmen assembled the houses during the winter, and the Brahmin astrologers said I could move in at nine A.M. on April third, 1959. We had a little trouble there, because the priest was basing his calculations on the assumption I had been born in Bangkok, and when I told him no, I was born in the States, he had to readjust, because of the twelve-hour time difference. However, I moved in when he said, even though the house wasn't ready. There were twenty-eight carpenters here when I moved in. Some of them liked it so much they stayed on after they had finished."

"And all the antiques," I said, "how did you get them?"

"Well, I told you I started collecting when I had that other house. It began accidentally, really. I used to go off into the country looking for looms, and sometimes I'd see or hear of something that was for sale, and I'd go and see it and if I liked it I'd buy it. After a time people got to know I was collecting, and when they heard I was in the area they'd come and see me and show me things. My biggest buy was a collection of Buddha heads that a villager up north found in a cave in the hills. They must have been there for hundreds of years. It wasn't until I got them all back here that I realized how valuable they were. Later I heard the government was interested, so I sent them a catalogue of everything I had. Then I went away on a trip, and the government sent a whole lot of people here who made notes on the heads and interviewed the servants and actually took one or two things away. Well, I was very angry when I heard this, and when I got back I changed my will, in which I'd left the house and everything in it to the Siam Society, and I made it over to a distant relative instead. Meanwhile, I open the house twice a week, on Monday and Thursday mornings. I charge visitors twenty-five tics each, and that makes a hell of a lot of money for the blind."

"Since you've been a success," I said, "do you get a lot of people pestering you?"

"They never stop. I get letters from all over the world asking me to do the nuttiest things. A widow in Miami wanted me to marry her.

Then there was this English woman who sent me a picture of four young Siamese she had met on a bicycle tour of Greece. She had invited them to go and stay with her in England, but then she found she had to go to Canada for six months and couldn't have them, and would I go and tell their parents? I couldn't understand why she didn't write their parents herself. I get a lot of begging letters too. A young man in England once wrote he had a crippled father and a crippled mother, though I don't know what that had to do with it, and he was very fond of Siamese dolls and could I send him some? A lady in Switzerland said her life was miserable and would I send her some samples? So I sent her a whole lot of samples, and I got a most grateful and wonderful reply saying that whenever she felt sad, she went and fondled the samples and it made her happy. So that was a kind of a reward."

"And here?"

"Here it's much worse, because they're right on top of you. Every week I get scores of letters from friends, and often not even friends, saying old So-and-so is about to hit Bangkok and will I look after him. In the old days I used to ask them all to dinner, because I wanted them to buy my silks." He smiled. "Now that I'm a success I have a different routine. When they call up, I ask them over to the office to see what they look like. If I like them, I ask them to dinner. If I like them a little bit, I ask them to cocktails. If I don't like them at all, I say, 'Do come and visit the house. It's open Mondays and Thursdays.' Oh, I get the most *horrible* people coming to see me. You wouldn't believe how horrible some of them are."

★

Next morning Jim Thompson was visiting his weavers in the village opposite and invited me to come with him. We met at his shop. I asked if he had a big sales staff, and he said that in addition to the local people he had two American women, two French, one Yugoslav, one German and one Dane. "One of the French ladies," he said, "is married to a Siamese diplomat, and thank God she learned the language of every country where her husband was posted. She speaks Russian, German, Spanish, Italian, Greek and about four others. We get so many people coming in who can only speak their own language."

We drove down to the *klong,* where a very small boat was waiting to take us across the filthy water to the other side. There were five of us, but the boat was so small we had to make two trips. The weavers' village stretched for perhaps a quarter of a mile down the side of the *klong* and a couple of hundred yards beyond it. The houses were all different shapes and sizes. The ground between them was marshy and filled with rotting garbage and garbage cans, especially near the *klong's* edge, and there were big teak duckboards to take us from door to door.

In some houses the looms were idle, and Jim Thompson said that either the people had made so much money that they could afford to take time off or they had finished the piecework they had been asked to do. A Siamese who was with us said that many people were not working because it was a Christian holiday. Jim Thompson laughed. "If it isn't a Christian holiday," he said, "it's sure to be a Chinese holiday. They're always having holidays." In another empty house Jim Thompson said of the owner, "I haven't seen her since she started running a restaurant."

But in many houses the looms were fully stretched. In one house I remember particularly, there were 120 looms, all owned by a family of four. "They contract out most of the work they do," said Jim Thompson, "but between them they gross between forty and fifty thousand dollars a month." I said, "A *month?*" and Jim Thompson said, "Yes"; and then I said, because it seemed so incredible, "Between forty and fifty *thousand* dollars?" and Jim Thompson said, "It sounds like a lot, I know, but they're the hardest-working family I have."

Here and in other houses I saw Jim Thompson's famous color sense in action. Beside each loom was a basket containing perhaps twelve or twenty bobbins, all of pale pastel colors, blue and green and pink and gold. He would stop and pick a bobbin from the basket, then look for others to go with it. Once or twice he got what he wanted immediately, at other times he discarded seven or eight bobbins first. His final choice never failed to be both original and harmonious.

✪

THE CONTRAST between the beauty of the silks, the cleanliness of the houses and the fastidiousness of Jim Thompson's tastes, on the one hand, and on the other the garbage that lay strewn between the houses and the stinks arising from the *klong*, has kept the memory of that morning very fresh in my mind. This was the last time on that visit I saw Jim Thompson and, though I did not know it then, the last time I was ever to see him. For Jim Thompson has disappeared. In 1967 he stayed with a friend in the Cameron Highlands of Malaysia, and one day he went for a walk and never came back. No one knows what happened, but some say he was eaten by a tiger. If so, it was a very shocking death. For so brave and gay and talented and debonair a man it was the wrong kind of death altogether.

✪

IN MOST countries the object of the United States Information Service is to project and explain the policies of the American government. But in Thailand and Laos it has a different role: to maintain the stability of the existing regimes and help them resist Communist pressures. There are several branch offices in the country, including one at Ubon, four hundred miles north of Bangkok.

The train to Ubon left Bangkok at six in the evening. It was a small wooden train with a wood-burning engine, like those in Western movies. I took a seat in the dining car next to a stolid-looking Thai with a round, pockmarked face, wearing a jungle hat the wrong way round. Opposite him was a Sikh, who wore a greasy handkerchief on his head instead of a turban. The waiter came and the Thai ordered a vast quantity of food. The Sikh picked his nails and ordered nothing.

Presently a long, scrawny Englishman sat down opposite me. His name was Davy and he was a major in the Royal Signal Corps, in some outfit attached to SEATO Command. He lived with his wife in Bangkok, but was on his way to visit a British signal post.

"What's it like living here?" I said.

"It's a bit of all right, I'd say," said Davy. "The whole thing's a swan, really. You speak the lingo?"

"No," I said.

"Don't speak it meself either," said Davy, "but I never have any trouble in making meself understood. What do you do?"

I told him.

"I've always thought I'd like to write a book meself," said Davy, "but I don't think I'd have the patience. You going to knock the Yanks?"

"No," I said. "I'm going to write what I see."

"There's an awful lot of rot talked about the Yanks," said Davy. "I work a lot with their Army officers, and I can tell you this, they've got some damned decent fellows."

The waiter put about a dozen different dishes in front of the pock-marked Thai. The Thai, still wearing his jungle hat, helped himself liberally. Then the Sikh picked up a fork and prodded at bits of food in the Thai's dishes and put them into his mouth. The Thai paid not the slightest attention.

The waiter brought us our food, and I asked Davy how he got on with Thais. He said he saw army officers mostly, and on the whole they were jolly fine chaps. He smiled and said, "They gave us a pretty rough evening last week."

"Did they?"

"Yes, they decided to push the boat out in a big way and give us this slap-up dinner. Strictly stag. After dinner they said they were going to show us a movie, so we all settled down and thought we were going to see Frank Sinatra or Julie Andrews or something. But it turned out to be a blue movie."

"What happened?"

"Well, there was this couple, a boy and a girl, and they went for a walk in the country, and then they took each other's clothes off and he poked her in a dell."

"In a what?"

"A dell. You know, a grove."

"What was it like?"

"It certainly left nothing to the imagination. Some of the close-ups were a bit sordid, I suppose, but it certainly steamed one up."

"Yes, it must have done."

"This couple thought they were alone in the dell, but it turned out there was another couple watching them. They got quite steamed up, too, and had a go themselves. Then they went down and joined the others, and there was a kind of general post."

"Really?"

"Yes, it was quite a do. And those Thai army chaps had thought of everything. When the movie was over they took us into another room, where they'd laid on a whole lot of girls. Damned nice-looking girls they were, too. Officers' daughters, somebody said." He paused.

I said, "Yes, go on."

"Well, it was damned embarrassing, I don't mind telling you. I mean, what does one do on an occasion like that, with a wife at home and everything, and yet all steamed up and not wanting to give offense?"

"What did you do?"

Davy laughed. "Ha, ha, old man," he said. "Now, that would be telling, wouldn't it?"

★

UBON WAS a pretty dismal place. There was a U.S. Air Force base quite near it, and the catarrhal rumble of the jets landing and taking off was with one all the time.

The U.S.I.S. officer was Rob Nevitt, a young man in his thirties, and he worked in an ugly Victorian building in the center of town. There were papers all over his room, an old typewriter on a roll-top desk, photographs of President Johnson and of the King and Queen of Thailand, and a ceiling fan that didn't work.

"I understand that the job of the U.S.I.S. here," I said, "is not to boost America but bolster up the Thais."

"That's right," said Rob Nevitt. "When I first came here, the number-one priority was to talk about U.S. achievements, the qualities of our President, and so on, but it didn't take us long to find out they weren't much interested in that. Nor did we have to spend time on correcting a distorted image of America, because that isn't a problem here. So the alternative was to find a significant program or quit."

"What is the significant program?"

"Communist propaganda is always saying to these people, your government doesn't do a thing for you, we could do so much more. So there's a big development plan going on, and just as important as the plan itself is telling people about it. For example, there have been several water-reclamation schemes, and this has meant having to shift people out and pay them compensation. They've been pretty upset about it. So we've gone to visit them, and sometimes the governor's gone, and we try to explain what it's all about and how they'll get more crops and benefit."

"Do they believe you?"

"Yes, but you have to work at it. It doesn't matter how many roads or dams or bridges you build, if you do it the wrong way it's no good. If you fling a hundred bucks at a man's feet, he may pick it up, but he won't thank you. But give him a nickel in the right way and he may."

"What else?"

"We go to all the villages in the area—or at least as many as we can, because there are hundreds—and we take our mobile film unit with us and tell the people what's going on. You might call it counter-Communist propaganda. We spend about twenty-four hours in each village. We usually get there about noon and set up the screen in a field. Then we go to the house of the head teacher or abbot and give them a little whisky we've brought along, and talk about the things they're thinking about, and what they need. Then we go to the house of the *Puyaibon*, or headman, and he gives us dinner. We're his guests. We offer to pay, but generally he doesn't let us. Then after dinner we have the film show. This might consist of a self-help reset-tlement film, a film on a dam already built in Thailand and how it's changed the people's lives, and then perhaps a Bureau of Reclamation film on the T.V.A."

"How often do these trips take place?" I said.

"We operate about three a month, each of seven to ten days. We have two teams of driver and projectionist, and they alternate. Sometimes I go along with them and sometimes I don't."

"You don't have any shorter trips?"

"No. Why, do you want to go on one?"

"If it's possible," I said.

Rob Nevitt thought. "There's a village forty miles north of here that we missed on the last trip. I don't see why Chousak shouldn't take you up there this afternoon. But it won't be too comfortable, and you'll have to spend the night."

✪

CHOUSAK HAD a driver called Sawaeng, and I sat beside them in the front. On the way out of Ubon we stopped at a liquor store, and I bought a bottle of whisky for the village headman. The road was very straight and empty, except for stray dogs and a few monks in orange robes. On either side of the road were *klongs* where water buffaloes wallowed, and beyond the *klongs* were wet paddy fields dotted with trees, like a waterlogged English park.

Thirty miles from Ubon we turned down a dirt road, and after ten more miles we came to the village. It was the sort of village you see in boys' picture books, with houses on stilts as protection against the monsoon rains, and pigs and dogs and little brown children everywhere running about.

Sawaeng drove to the house of the head teacher. He was out, but his wife asked us to come up the ladder and wait. We went up and found ourselves on a kind of veranda. There were several big wooden tubs, or big chatties, there, and on the wall at the back, pinned to a big board, about 150 photographs. Chousak said these were photographs of the head teacher's ex-pupils. Some were in monk's robes, some in wedding clothes, and some in academic dress.

The head teacher's wife brought a big red melon and gave us slices. She had bright red lips from chewing betel nut. There were lots of pips in the melon, and when we spat them over the edge of the veranda, hens came and gobbled them up. Across the road were a well and some coconut trees. Several women were drawing water from the well, and I saw a beautiful girl of about ten drawing a very heavy bucketful. The coconut trees had holes dug at the base of their trunks. Chousak said the villagers believed this would make the coconuts grow bigger.

We finished the melon, and the head teacher still hadn't come back, so we went down to the van. Sawaeng fixed up the loudspeaker equipment, and then Chousak drove round the village while Sawaeng announced there would be a film show at the school that evening, sponsored by the United States Information Service. We drove to the school, which was at the far end of a big grass field. We took out two long bamboo poles, a white sheet with dark-blue edging, and some guy ropes. Sawaeng and Chousak fixed the sheet to the poles and the poles to the rope, and there was our screen. About fifty children watched all this with great interest. Some of the older ones carried the smaller ones on their backs. Most were naked.

We returned to the head teacher's house and found him there. He was a small, old, birdlike man with a grizzled head and a ready smile. His wife and daughter were sitting on the veranda with mallets, breaking up two freshly killed ducks. Chousak said it was time to wash, and he gave me a loincloth and directed me to a bathhouse at the back. Here was soap, and chatties full of water. I took off my clothes and rubbed myself with soap and sluiced the water over me. Through the window space I saw a family of six in a room in the house opposite. Not one had a stitch on.

When Chousak and Sawaeng had had their baths I presented the bottle of whisky to the head teacher, and we squatted on the floor of the veranda and passed the bottle round and talked. I didn't do much talking, for only Chousak spoke English.

It was almost dark now. The fireflies began to appear, and with them came the jungle noises, birds and frogs and crickets. The women finished pounding the ducks and took them inside to cook. Other guests arrived, two merchants, the village headman, the teacher's son-in-law, the doctor. "He's not a proper doctor," said Chousak, and I took this to mean he was a witch doctor. One of the women brought a kerosene lamp and hung it from a beam on the veranda. Someone else brought a bowl of water, and the witch doctor washed his feet.

Presently dinner was ready. There were many dishes, but they all turned out to be duck: stewed duck, minced duck, fried duck, duck in bitter sauce, and duck that was almost raw. There were two kinds of rice to go with it, ordinary boiled rice and a heavier, glutinous kind which you rolled up and ate in a ball. The whisky continued going the rounds, and everyone, particularly Chousak, did a lot of talking. After the meal, the head teacher opened a tall tin marked "Superfine Crackers," pulled out tobacco and rolled a cigarette.

At seven-thirty Sawaeng went off to the school to set up his projector, but there was no budging Chousak. The whisky had taken hold and he harangued the party as though at a political meeting. The cinema show was billed to start at eight, so at eight-twenty I told Chousak I thought it time to be getting along. He agreed politely, but continued to hold forth in a loud voice as we went down the ladder and all the way to the school.

We had five films all together, and they lasted till eleven-thirty. (Chousak slept from beginning to end; he told me afterward he had seen them all about thirty times before.) The first film was about community development and water irrigation, and the next was a very old film showing the visit of the King and Queen of Thailand to America and their meeting President Eisenhower and Dag Hammarskjöld. Next was a cartoon about community development and the efforts of villagers to build themselves a bridge; the audience loved this and laughed and clapped. Then we had a film in color called *Air Boon Choo* which showed the United States Air Force repelling an imaginary invasion of Thailand, with plenty of noise and napalm. We finished with *Women in the Northeast,* which showed the various professions open to women, in particular, nursing. As propaganda all the films were pretty crude, and for a Westerner their entertainment value was nil. But how were the villagers reacting? On one level they clearly loved it. This was an event, a happening, as unusual as the birth of triplets, as magical as a lighter or a watch. But how much of the message was getting through—that community development led to an improved standard of living, that with Uncle Sam's Air Force in the wide blue yonder, you could sleep easier at night?

The villagers got up and *kling-klang-klong*ed their way into the dark. Chousak woke up and helped Sawaeng to dismantle the projector and screen and put them into the van. Then Chousak and I walked back to the head teacher's house, through the still, starry night, the friendly fireflies all round us, the crickets paving our way. I said to Chousak, "What were you telling them about so forcefully at supper, and on the way to the school?" Chousak said, "I was telling them about ways of improving the crops and how the U.S.I.S. can help village life generally, and about fertilizers and rice growing and building roads." I thought, Whatever you were telling them, my friend, it certainly wasn't that.

I slept alone that night on a mattress placed on the floor of a little room at the end of the veranda. Chousak and Sawaeng had put their mattresses on the floor outside. (Was this a compliment or an insult?) In the morning we drove round the village in the van, and Chousak and Sawaeng nailed Community Development posters to trees and buildings, and distributed literature to anyone they met. If they had been Communists they couldn't have been more thorough. At noon we left for Ubon.

✪

IN THE evening Rob Nevitt took me to the station. There was a crowd on the platform, as the adviser to the Patriarch was traveling on the train, and the governor of the province and about fifty saffron monks had come to see him off. The adviser was a great giggler. He giggled at the governor, he giggled at a soldier who came to get his blessing, and when the train moved off and the fifty saffron monks clasped their hands and bowed to him, he giggled most of all.

Still giggling, he went to his compartment, next to mine. On the other side of me was a Seventh-day Adventist, accompanied by a monkey on a chain.

✪

THE NIGHT before I left Thailand I was having a drink in the hotel bar. There were several United States Air Force officers staying in the hotel, and I got into conversation with one, an Indiana major. He was a rugged, slow-speaking sort of man with a grizzled crew cut and a face like a Christmas pudding. He was on leave from a combat mission base—not Ubon apparently, but some other air base up in the north. We had several drinks together, and he asked me if I had visited any of Bangkok's massage establishments. I said I hadn't, though I'd heard of them.

"You know what the girls do there?"

"No."

"They start out with a regular massage, and they end up massaging you all over. Get me?"

"Yes."

"It's pretty goddam terrific. I guess if you were to tell it to the folks back home, they just wouldn't believe you."

I thought of my journey to Ubon, and I said, "I met an English major in the train the other day, and he'd been to a party with some Thai officers and seen a blue movie."

"Is that right?"

"Yes. Blue movies are quite a thing here, apparently. He said it was very good."

"What was the deal?"

"Well, there was this couple doing it in the open air, in a wood or somewhere, and then another couple came along and joined them."

"Kind of a group grope?"

"You could say so."

We ordered another round and the major said, "You ever seen a blue movie?"

"I saw one in Casablanca," I said. "Or it may have been Tangier. I forget."

"I saw one in Cicero, Illinois," said the major, "and it was pretty goddam lousy. How was yours?"

"The film was very scratched," I said, "but it was quite interesting. There was this Frenchman who looked like Tarzan, and his colored girl friend. Later they were joined by a blonde."

"What kind of a deal was that?" said the major.

"Well," I said, "think of almost every event and permutation you can, and they made it."

"Oh, *boy!*" said the major. He shook his head and breathed heavily, thinking of his own particular thing.

The bar was almost empty, and the major and I decided to get a taxi and have more drinks elsewhere. We were both very joyous by now and exceedingly happy to have one another's company. Outside the hotel the taxi touts were hanging about, and one went off to get a taxi. His friend, overhearing the major and me discussing where to go, sidled up and said, "What you want, fellas? You want nice girls? You like blue film, see good fuck?"

This helpful inquiry struck a responsive chord in the major and me. "Now wait a minute!" said the major, "I believe you have something there," and I said, "That sounds a very interesting idea." Exactly what happened after that I don't recall, but my impression is that the major, the tout and I came to an agreement over a blue film. Presently the taxi arrived, and we all three got into it and set off.

We didn't say much in the taxi, and it occurred to me that the tout might be taking us somewhere to be summarily beaten and robbed. On reflection, or as much as I could muster, I thought it unlikely. The major said, "Whaddya say we'll see that movie the guy in the train was telling you about?" I said, "I was thinking that myself." "I sure hope we do," said the major, "that sounded like a great picture." We turned down a lane and stopped outside a modern villa set in its own garden. A dog barked several times. We got out. The tout said something to the taxi driver in Thai and to us, "The taxi will wait. Okay?" Then we went through the gate and up to the front door, and the tout knocked three times.

Presently the door was opened by a short, good-looking Thai of about twenty-five. He had a firm, square, fleshy face, and he was wearing a sort of loose white robe. He led us into an austere sitting room with several bamboo chairs and a plain teak table. We shook hands and sat down. There was an uncomfortable silence, and then the Thai said, very slowly, "You like beer?" I nodded and the major said, "That'll be just great."

The Thai went into another room and came back with two large bottles of beer and several glasses. He had hardly put these on the table when a woman came in. Like the man, she was wearing a white robe, but she was older, about thirty or thirty-five. She had a rather sad, kindly face, without any make-up at all, and she might have passed for a teller in a bank or a games mistress at a girls' school. We got up and shook hands with her. The Thai handed round the beer, and the major said, "Skol!"; the rest of us raised our glasses, and then there was another long silence. The Thai looked at the major, gave a big smile to show white, even teeth and said, giving equal weight to all four words, "You like see fuck?" The major, not batting an eyelid, said, "Oh, sure, that's why we're here," and the silence descended again.

The Thai said something to the tout, and the tout said to us, "You have the money. He wants the money." I looked at the Thai and he nodded and smiled. The major and I paid up, and the Thai gave the tout his cut. We were about to embark on another of those silences when the major indicated he had had enough. "Okay, kids," he said, getting up unsteadily, "let's go see the home movies."

We all got up except the tout, and, holding our glasses, the major and I followed the Thai and the woman into the next room. I wondered vaguely why the woman was coming and assumed they were a husband-and-wife partnership who operated the movie equipment together. When we entered the next room, I looked round for a screen or projector, but could see neither. However, in the middle of the room was a bare bed with a sheet on it, like an operating table. "Hold on!" I said to the major. "This isn't a movie, this is the real thing."

"Well," said the major, "for Christ's sake!"

The Thai indicated two small chairs by the wall, and the major and I sat down. Unselfconsciously the man and the woman unfastened their robes and let them fall to the floor. Then with quick movements, like athletes giving a well-rehearsed display of P.T., they jumped onto the bed. At first the man lay on his back while the woman, squatting on her heels between his legs, gently brought him to the boil. Then, as though by signal, they changed places. They did this with grace and precision, like two acrobats. Then the man put his weight on his elbows, and the major said, "Oh, boy!"

They did it in silence, and in silence the major and I watched them, sitting on our little chairs, goggle-eyed, clutching our glasses of beer. Once the major tried to say, "All the way with L.B.J.," echoing a folk phrase of the times, but it sounded all wrong even to him, and he let it die on the air. Somehow the event was asexual, highly stylized, almost a ballet. Above the waist the two had no contact at all. The man kept his eyes on the floor, giving the impression his mind was elsewhere, which it may have been; but she, with her kindly, games-mistress face, looked at him all the time. I wondered if they were married, and whether to each other or others. If not, was their relationship only a professional one? Did they live as well as work here, and who had suggested the idea in the first place?

In time they reached, or appeared to reach, a climax. Afterward, the man lay quietly for a little, then jumped off the bed and disappeared through a small door. A moment later we heard the sound of a shower being turned on. Then the woman got down, put on her white robe and spread out five fingers.

"He come five times today," she said, smiling. "Five. You get?"

"What's she saying?" said the major.

"She says that's the fifth time he's come today."

"You mean they gave four shows before this one?"

"I suppose so."

"Jesus!" said the major. "I don't make it five times a *week*. Five times a *month* is more what I shoot. These people are like animals."

"I don't think it's true," I said.

"You don't think what's true?" said the major.

"That he's made it five times today."

"Listen," said the major slowly. "You don't know what these people are like. I'm telling you they're like animals. If they want to do it ten, fifteen times a day, that's how much they'll do it. They're not like us."

The man came out of the shower and the woman went into it.

"Okay?" said the man.

"Okay," I said.

"Listen, lover boy," said the major. "My friend here says you don't never make it, you just pretend to. Well, I've been telling him that's a load of horseshit, you can fuck all night if you want to, and all day too, just like the darkies do. Now, ain't that right?"

The man, uncomprehending, nodded politely and smiled.

"There," said the major triumphantly. "What I tell you?"

The woman came back from her shower, and we went back to the other room, where the tout was sipping beer and reading the paper. He must have gone through this routine a hundred times. "Okay?" he said, and we said yes, okay. The man appeared with another bottle of beer and invited us to sit down. I didn't want to offend him, but I felt I couldn't stand another of those silences, so I said, "Thanks very much, but we have to be getting along." The major took the same view.

We shook hands all round, as though we had just been to a jolly vicarage tea party, and the man and the woman smiled pleasantly. They really were an extremely nice couple. "Come again," said the man. "Always welcome!" And the major said, "Oh, sure."

The taxi was waiting in the lane, and the tout got in the front and the major and I in the back. We didn't say anything for a long while. Then in the darkness the major said with feeling, "Christ, how can people *live* like that? What does it do to their self-*respect?*" I didn't say anything, for the American Puritan conscience at bay is a formidable thing. But the major went on worrying at it, he couldn't wipe it from his mind. "How can they *do* it?" he said. "How can they let themselves get so *degraded?*"

So then I said, "Well, how about the audience?"

There was a bit of a pause and then the major said, "Come again?"

"Without an audience," I said, "they're not even in business."

"Oh, sure."

"Well," I said, "where in the degradation stakes does that leave us?"

And this time he didn't answer.

✪

FROM A thousand feet up, the houses and streets seemed like houses and streets in any Asian country, the fields like those in Thailand or Cambodia. Yet one looked at them with a new eye, expecting them somehow to be different. For this was Saigon, a town like no place else in the world.

At the airport, opposite the rows of helicopters and parked military planes, were trim lawns and bushes, a gay green awning, and tiny exquisite air hostesses in white and peacock blue. One hadn't expected that. A taxi took me into the town, and on the way we passed a sign that said, "General Pershing Sports Ground. For Recreation and Athletics." We drove down a wide avenue shaded by tall trees as in Provence and with Provençal villas behind them, and then came to the main square, all still and sleepy in the Sunday sun. Here was the Caravelle Hotel with its melon-cold lobby and concealed amplifiers relaying the *Emperor Concerto*. Sitting alone beside the big plate-glass window in the lobby was a figure that looked familiar. It was Emlyn Williams, the actor, come to Saigon to give his rendering of Dickens reading from his own works. I hadn't expected that either.

I registered at the desk and was given my key and a booklet called *Saigon Round-Up*. Then I was shown upstairs to an airy room with a vast double bed and mirrors. I lay down and opened *Saigon Round-Up*. The opening article was called "How Good Is Your English?" and was a review of the Gowers edition of Fowler's *Modern English Usage*. The next article was called "Vietnamese Politeness and Impoliteness," and it said, "When people refer to you as *ong ay* or *ong do*, then you may be really proud of yourself. The equivalent for a female would be *ba do* or *ba ay*." There was a section on where to eat in Saigon and another on where to shop, and then came "Racing Program—Probable Runners at Phu Tho" and a list of horses with names like Ncog Xuan, Dam Do and Thanh Phung. Finally there was the sightseeing section. "At Bien Hoa, only twenty miles from Saigon, is the pottery where visitors can also observe rural life, rubber plantations, etc." I reflected that if they had been there three weeks before, they could also have observed a brilliant attack by the Vietcong on the airfield, in which many military planes were destroyed and several American servicemen were killed and wounded. "At Thu-

Dau-Mot, also only twenty miles from the capital, lacquerwork will be under way in many painstaking stages." I put down the booklet, concluding that the man who wrote it must be either mad or a practical joker, and went to sleep.

In the evening Emlyn Williams and I dined in the hotel's roof-top restaurant, which looked out over the surrounding country. There were a clean white cloth and a bowl of fresh flowers on every table. I asked the waiter where the Vietcong were, and he pointed at the country and said, "There. All round. Everywhere." I had crabmeat soup and a filet mignon, Emlyn had consommé and a sole Colbert, and we shared a bottle of *rosé*. There were sounds of merriment coming from an adjoining room; the waiter said that the German ambassador was giving a large dinner party.

In the middle of dinner a large bald middle-aged American came into the dining room with a little Vietnamese boy of about seven. He introduced himself as the father of the actor Rip Torn, who had worked with Emlyn in New York; he too was called Rip Torn, and he was working with AID. "I'm hoping to get this little fellow rehabilitated," he said, pointing to the little boy. "I found him on the street. He has no father or mother and I'm hoping to get him into a Catholic orphanage." I said, would the boy care for a Coca-Cola or something, and Rip Torn, Sr., said, "No, we just had a soda downstairs." Then they went.

After dinner, Emlyn and I went for a walk along Tu Do Street, the main street of Saigon. The bars had opened up and some of the shops too, and the streets were full of people strolling and laughing as though they hadn't a care in the world. Beside the tiny, delicate Vietnamese, the American soldiery, in slouch hats and waterproof trousers tucked into the tops of their boots, looked huge and repellent, like pink giants from beyond the seas. A man approached us with a big folio, which I thought must be views of Saigon. But they turned out to be dirty pictures, jumbo-size. A sign in a car salesroom said, "DRIVE AWAY YOUR OWN CADILLAC," and another, in a travel agent's office, "A HOLIDAY IN EUROPE FOR YOU—FIVE DIFFERENT WAYS OF GETTING THERE."

At the end of Tu Do Street was the river. It was very still there and very beautiful. The lights from the big ships flickered on the water, and on the quayside a couple were sitting on a rush mat holding hands and drinking a bottle of red wine: below, on the rocks, a man was urinating. Then I heard Emlyn say, "Look at this!" I turned and saw him standing by one of those miniature golf courses, complete with slopes and curves and little tunnels. We might have been in Bognor Regis or Margate, Atlantic City or Disneyland.

We walked home. The Americans were beginning to spill out of the bars, and the little barefoot orphaned boys were doing a brisk trade selling the drunker ones toy hats. I was told later that this was a nightly occurrence. I slept well that night in my air-conditioned room, and when I came down in the morning there was a note from Emlyn at the desk, together with a clipping. The note said, "More hot news from war-scarred city," and the clipping, from the *Saigon Daily Times,* said, "Peter Rabbit Author Dies in Massachusetts, Age 91."

A little later a contact at the American embassy telephoned. "Sorry I didn't call you yesterday," he said. "How are you making out in Saigon?"

"Fine," I said, "but it's not quite what I expected."

✪

THE DAILY press briefings took place in a theater in the U.S.I.S. building, which was not far from my hotel. They were attended by about eighty correspondents who, I was informed, represented some half of the Saigon press corps; the other half were in their offices filing stories or out on assignment in the field. Most were in civilian clothes like myself, but one or two were in battle dress. The proceedings were conducted by two men, Colonel Lou Breault of "MacV," or Military Assistance Command, Vietnam (the name for the American forces in Vietnam), and Harold Kaplan, a civilian. Colonel Breault had been an Army briefing officer for fifteen years (he had done the same job in Korea) and couldn't be faulted. Harold Kaplan was a warmer, brighter character, who looked like a distinguished professor and was always puffing at a long cigar.

These briefings had an Alice-in-Wonderland quality and were memorable for the amount of noninformation that was fed to correspondents. Like this from Mr. Kaplan: "At eight-fifty A.M. on June eleventh, there'll be a ceremony at the railroad sheds at which eighteen trucks and fifteen diesel engines will be handed over under U.S.O.M. There'll be a train ride to the railway sheds for those who want to go along." Another time he said, "The ambassador and the Prime Minister met at three-thirty this afternoon." A small man at the back said,

"What did they discuss, Harold?" And Mr. Kaplan said, "They discussed the whole range of their common interests, Bob." It was like that all the way. Another day he said, "Congressman Otis G. Pike and three other members of the Armed Forces Subcommittee of the House are arriving Monday. Anyone want further details on that?" No one did. And one day he brought along not one but three colossally boring admirals to tell us about Vietcong fishing boats. In their natty naval suitings they looked like a close-harmony trio about to break into song.

Some of the correspondents asked quite offensive questions, and in the forefront was one Joe Fried, of the New York *Daily News,* a small, tough, tenacious Jew. One day Mr. Kaplan said that the ground-breaking ceremony at the site of the new American embassy had taken place that morning. "Why didn't we get to know of it earlier?" said Joe Fried. "Security, Harold?" Mr. Kaplan said, "Well, the Prime Minister was there and the ambassador was there, and you know we have a habit of announcing things like this at short notice." Joe Fried said, "And you also have a habit of cooking things up at short notice, too, Harold." Mr. Kaplan didn't take any offense and smiled and said, "Joe, your daily remarks get more and more complimentary." Joe was a stickler for detail. "Where was that ambush, Lou?" he said. Lou said "Tien-Bong-Luc." "Spell it, Lou," said Joe; and Lou did. "Is that where the other ambush was?" said Joe. "No, Joe," said Lou, "that was Nang-Tien-Phouc," and he spelled that too. "Thanks, Lou," said Joe.

Joe had been in Vietnam almost two years and had become an institution. His colleagues said he filed five hundred words every day and tried to make each story an exclusive. He was on his own, so he couldn't spend much time in the field, for fear of missing something in Saigon. Once he wrote a good story about events near Da Nang, and to date-line it Da Nang he flew there, filed the story, and flew back.

Every correspondent had a story about Joe and his questions. One of them told me how a certain general was giving a briefing and, in answer to a question of Joe's, said, "You got it all wrong, Joe"; and Joe said, "Okay, General, you go fix it up and tell me what's right." Another time Barry Zorthian, the head of the U.S.I.S. in Saigon, was giving a press conference in which, in Joe's view, he spent rather too long thanking people for coming. "Okay, Barry, baby," said Joe at length, "let's finish the commercials and make a start on the war."

One day after the briefing I went and asked Joe why he was so aggressive. He talked very fast and looked at the floor. "I'm not that aggressive," he said, "but those midgets sometimes forget we're not here to write the administration's view of things, but our own, yes? So you have to watch them. You have to watch whether they're being on the level with you or not, yes? They're inclined not to be, not for any sinister motive, but because obviously if you're in that position there's a temptation to give good news rather than bad. Their sins are those of omission, yes? They don't lie to you, but they have a tendency to leave out anything that doesn't fit in with the optimistic picture they want to paint, yes? That's what happened in General Harkins's time. For months we were getting this distorted picture, and if it hadn't been for some of the correspondents, we'd have gone on getting it, yes? What it amounts to is a conspiracy of silence."

Next day I put the point to Barry Zorthian.

"There's been a long record here," he said, "of hostility between the press and the government. It all goes back to Harkins's time, when the press felt they were being deliberately misled, though Harkins himself didn't think he was misleading them. You may say he was blind, and maybe he was.

"Now a lot of that hostility has been removed, but there's no doubt that traces of it remain. For one thing, the needs of the press aren't the same as the needs of the government. So you have to draw a line somewhere. The big question is, Where? Another thing that confuses the situation is that this war is incredibly complicated to explain. The U.S. public expects a nice, neat front line which they can see on a map, and a regular scoreboard every day. But it's not like that, as you know. The war is everywhere and nowhere, and estimations as to enemy casualties are often sheer guesswork. I think the American press here is doing as good a job as it can, and there are very few angles left unreported. But despite the number of correspondents here, despite the enormous scope and volume of the coverage, I doubt if anyone in the United States is getting a meaningful picture of what's going on."

✪

THE AMERICAN correspondents in Saigon inhabited a world quite different from that of the military, almost antipathetic to, yet largely dependent on, it. With over a hundred and fifty of them there, the competition was fierce; yet there was cooperation too, those on the dailies often doubling up with those on the weeklies, American newsmen sharing information with newsmen from other countries. Another of their difficulties, because of the sheer distance from the States, was not knowing what their colleagues were writing. One evening in the Caravelle bar, I heard this snatch of conversation:

"Did you file a piece on Pleiku?"

"No, there wasn't any story in it."

"Well, that's what I thought, but New York wanted me to do a follow-up on that Reuters story."

"But the Reuters story wasn't true. Pleiku has *not* been captured by the V.C. It just isn't true."

"Sure it isn't true. But how do you get New York to believe that?"

So there they all were, reporters all, but each with his own status symbol, Assistant Editor, Senior Editor, Assistant Chief of Bureau, after the great American fashion. All took their jobs seriously, and some took themselves seriously as well. This attitude sometimes spilled over into their writings, so that wit of any kind, the ability to see a situation in perspective, was always at something of a premium. Art Buchwald could be witty, because that was his job; but sprinkle a little wit into your own writing and there was always the danger the folks in New York would think you were pulling their legs.

Joe Fried said, "It's a picnic here now compared to what it used to be when they had censorship, yes? In those days the censors tore the hell out of everything. Give them a radio tape which differed from your script by so much as an 'and' and you were in danger of losing the lot. So people used to look for homing pigeons, yes? Or go out to the airport to solicit passengers to take their stuff to the States, yes?"

"Isn't it very tiring, being on your own and filing every day?"

"I guess it's tiring for all of us. This is the most demanding post in the world; most newsmen here work seven days a week, yes? There's so many aspects to cover, and as a single man you can only cover one aspect at a time, yes? Also, the Vietnamese love rumors, they love fantasies, yes? So you have to spend a lot of time checking and double-checking your sources, because here the fantastic can often be the real.

"Ideally, I don't spend as much time out in the country as I should. In the Diem days I'd spend as much as three days a week in the field, yes? But now I have to centralize myself. Also I think you get more of a rounded picture when you can talk to other people and collect your thoughts in a way you can't do out in Googooville. My paper gets the U.P., A.P., and Reuters wires, so my job's to augment, not duplicate."

❂

AND THEN I went along to the Associated Press, in a building opposite the U.S.I.S., to see Mal (for Malcolm) Browne, the chief of the bureau. I had met him earlier in the hotel, a lanky, blond New Yorker; he looked twenty-five and was thirty-four, and he had a Vietnamese wife. When he first came to Saigon he had been on his own: now he had fifteen people working under him.

Mal Browne's office lay on the other side of a room where a half dozen reporters, including one Negro man, were clacking away on large typewriters. On the tables were big photographs of the war, and oil lamps for when the electricity failed. On the wall were two clocks, one at Saigon time, one at G.M.T.

Mal Browne was sitting at a desk, reading copy.

"What goes on," I said.

"For a start," said Mal Browne, "the telephone's blown." He lifted the receiver, and there was a noise such as the engineers make when you forget to put it back on the cradle.

"What else?"

"There's been this battle at Dong Xoai."

"I know. What happened?"

"The V.C. attacked it two days ago. Then the A.R.V.N.* and the Air Force counterattacked, and now half the people are dead or wounded and the place is pretty well flattened. I was there yesterday and got back last night, and Horst Faas—you met him?"

"No."

* The Army of the Republic of Vietnam, or South Vietnamese Forces.

"He's a German. One of our best people. He got back this morning."

"Have you sent a lot of copy?"

He smiled. "Not enough for New York. So they've been sending me rude cables and I've been sending rude cables back."

"Could I see them?"

He pulled a cable from a pile of papers on the desk.

"That's my second," he said. "The first was politer."

I took it and read:

There are no U.S. installations in Dong Xoai. Since it has been bombed flat, it makes no difference who holds it. In any case Vietcong now largely driven out town and compound area except for skirmishing. Point of all this is that Associated is only organization that has covered this battle directly, with Faas only newsman in town. By now our superiority in coverage ought to be pretty obvious by comparison. I suggest leave us alone when we are doing best we can. Browne.

"They never let up," said Mal Browne. "They keep the pressure on you all the time. They have to."

We went into the main room and I met a photographer called Jim Pickerell, who had recently been shot through the leg. "He's a freelance," said Mal Browne, "and therefore wealthier than all of us." Jim Pickerell laughed and said, "Oh, yeah?" Mal Browne said, "We have another photographer in the hospital with two bullets in his arm." A man at the next desk said, "That story about the A.R.V.N. claim of seven hundred V.C. dead. Shall I lead on that?" Mal Browne said, "Well, it's only an A.R.V.N. claim." I said, "I suppose, this being a wire service, nobody's stories are signed?" Mal Browne said, "They are if they contain opinion as well as fact." We reached the other side of the room and Mal said, "Peter Arnett's not here. He's gone to Bangkok with his wife for a short vacation. As a matter of policy, we try to get people out of here every three months."

Beyond the main room was a little room in which was a teletype machine and a Vietnamese, in spectacles and with three gold teeth, tinkering with it. "We just had this installed," said Mal Browne. "It came yesterday. Normally the news goes by commercial cable to Tokyo—which takes about two hours—and from there it goes instantaneously to New York. But with this we'll be able to reach New York direct."

The machine started chattering and I read: "Now is the time for all good men to come to the aid of the party." Mal Browne said, "That's New York testing. At present they're getting through to us, though we're not getting through to them."

One of the white reporters was standing behind us, and he shouted at the Negro man, "Boy, are we going to clean up U.P.I. now!" He clapped his hands with joy. "Are we going to clean up those bastards!" Mal Browne said, "See what I mean about the competition?"

We went back to his desk for a cup of coffee, and I said, "What's the important thing about this great army of newsmen here?"

"I would say the important thing," said Mal Browne, "is that they tend to become part of the news. With a couple of hundred correspondents around, people will do things I doubt they would do otherwise. For instance, I doubt that those Buddhist monks would have burned themselves to death if they had known there wouldn't be any newsmen or cameramen around to record it. I think this is true in a lesser way of other political events. Even the V.C. bomb attacks in the city. Everyone knows that any unusual event here will be immediately and massively reported. The newsmen not only report the news, they sometimes create it."

"Do you think the presence of so many American correspondents here can be justified?"

"If you mean do I think they give value for money, that if they were cut by half the American public would be starved for news about the war, the answer is no. But as the Army effort has escalated, the press has done the same. Every paper wants its own man here. That's the way things go. Most news here has little value. It's like police reporting. You have to check the usual sources every hour or so, and this has to go on night and day, which is enough to drive a man nuts. It's the same in the field, where one battle is much the same as another. The *real* news here is looking for the key that may unlock the door to what's going to happen. Will the United States go on escalating? Are they going to bomb Hanoi and send the troops north? If they do, will China come in? At present I see nothing but stalemate."

I said, "Tell me one more thing. I've seen about as much of Saigon as I want. Where else do you advise me to go?"

"If MacV can fix you up," said Mal Browne, "I think I'd go to Da Nang. It's the big air base up in the north. And if you're after newsmen, there's a small party of them living there. We have a guy by the name of Wheeler you might like to meet. He goes out on A.R.V.N. patrols and all that, and turns in some really gutsy stuff."

On the way out we passed an empty desk. Some photographs on it caught my eye, an agonized Vietnamese mother holding the dead body of her baby, an old woman with blood pouring down her face, three men bound hand and foot, village huts in flames. "That's what Faas brought back from Dong Xoai," said Mal Browne. "And here's the piece he filed." He gave me three typed quarto pages, and I read them with a mounting sense of horror. They and the pictures made the events at Dong Xoai come alive for the first time. In Faas's spare, lucid prose it was all there: the sudden attack from the jungle, the killings, the hostages; then the counterattack, the jets coming in low with bombs and napalm, the helicopters bringing the A.R.V.N. to continue the battle, horror mounting on horror until at the end there was nothing left of Dong Xoai but scorched earth and scarred bodies and women weeping for their sons who were not. And I thought, For the New York evening papers that story will get two paragraphs at most and maybe just one of those pictures at about a quarter its size. And for the man in the subway it will be a story little different from the story he read last week or last month. It'll take him twenty seconds to read; and in terms of human misery and suffering it will not, and by its nature cannot, make any impact at all.

✪

THE FLIGHT to Da Nang left from the military side of Saigon airport. The Embarkation Room was full of people, American troops mostly, some waiting to go to other parts of the country, others to go to Japan or the States. There were one or two civilians like myself, three Vietnamese nuns, and a dozen South Vietnamese soldiers dressed in spotted black-and-green camouflage, like leopards. The Americans had on a variety of hats: forage caps about four inches high, which made the smaller soldiers look ridiculous, peaked caps, red and green berets, slouch hats with struts as in ancient biplanes. Some wore dark glasses, smoked cigars, drank Coca-Cola, others read *Stars and Stripes,* pornographic paperbacks and the adolescent fantasies of Mr.

Ian Fleming. On their tunics were their names: "RAKEBRANK, MAIDAN, COLON, TRUSCOTT, CORTEZ, HUFF, WALTOS, KRASS, CLINGBEIL . . ."

At last they called our flight, and we got into a bus and drove out to the plane. This was a great, fat insect called a One-Two-Three. There was a ramp down at the rear of the plane so that vehicles could drive in, and we walked into its belly that way. It was like no other plane I had been in. The seating facilities were, from nose to tail, two rows of bucket seats along the sides, facing inward, and two more rows back to back down the center. At the forward end was a big steel bulkhead, and a ladder running up to the cockpit, way above our heads. Running the length of the ceiling was a maze of pipes and wires, as in a boiler room or small factory. A crewman was in charge of the rear end of the plane, and when we were all in he pulled up the ramp and closed the rear doors. This man was a sergeant, and he had a pistol and a knife and a bandoleer of ammunition.

We took off, banging and rattling along the runway like a gypsy caravan full of pots and kettles, and climbed slowly upward. The racket of the engines was terrific. It must have been about a minute after we took off, and as we were about to go through the cloud base, that the plane gave a sideways lurch and dived downward with engines screaming and the whole thing shaking like a jelly. I looked out the window in time to see a helicopter flash by a few feet above the port wing. About a hundred feet from the ground the pilot straightened out and headed back toward the clouds.

This time we got through and came out on a great snowy, velvety plateau with a blue sky above and visibility unlimited. The order came to unfasten our seat belts, and most of the troops then fell asleep, though a few pulled out cigarettes and comics. Most of the soldiers looked big and strong, a rebuttal of charges about soft American living. One beefy sergeant was clutching a tiny Vietnamese doll. There was a vast Negro called Kennedy and another by the name of Sawyer who wore a big circular insignia on his right breast. Round the edge was written, "Tropospheric Scatter Communications" and in the center, "Vietnam—Hang Loose with the Deuce. 362."

There was an old copy of *Life* under my seat, and I opened it. One of the stories was about Vietnam, about a Captain Gillespie and a successful patrol he had made with some Montagnards, or mountain men. The reporter, Lee Hall, wrote of what happened when they got back to camp.

Under tents made from camouflaged parachute cloth, the captain and his team partook of a traditional *montagnard* "sacrifice"—a ritual enacted whenever an event of great significance has taken place.

A half-naked priest, bright in his ceremonial shirt, squatted between the heads of two newly killed water buffalo—their hacked off tails placed above their eyes. Taking blood from the animals the priest mixed it with rice wine from nine earthen jugs placed in a row. His honored American guests drank of the strong rancid liquid through long, curving, wooden straws. The priest ended the sacrifice by giving simple brass bracelets, signifying the *montagnards'* acceptance of the Americans as brothers.

I thought, If I've read one story about Americans abroad being initiated into strange tribal rites and accepted as blood brothers, I've read a hundred; they are the American foreign correspondent's standard cliché. And yet obviously such stories fulfill a deep American need, the aching need to be accepted. Acceptance is to be had in the communion of blood and wine and water intermingling, in the sacramental sacrifice of beasts. It is to be had in a return to a state of innocence and grace, to the time before the Fall, before Bethlehem, the Industrial Revolution, Hiroshima, the color war, Vietnam; a return to a world where men were naked and simple and therefore brothers, where napalm and Kleenex, Musak and liquid oxygen, French letters and the fertility pill had not yet come to confuse the passing scenes.

We landed at Pleiku, the place which Reuters had wrongly reported as captured, exchanged some passengers, then took off for Da Nang. We sighted it forty minutes later. We flew once over the runway, then turned in a very tight circle to land; the man next to me shouted that this was to avoid the V.C., who sometimes took potshots.

At the base I was met by a Negro sergeant in a jeep who had orders to take me to the press quarters. On the way out we passed about twenty South Vietnamese walking wounded, some with crutches or with arms in plaster casts, others with bandages on hands and heads. They were waiting for a plane to take them to Saigon, and they sat there patient and resigned, like baffled cattle. This was their country and their war. Because of them the Americans were here. Yet people went to and fro past them, hardly sparing them a glance, almost as if they weren't there. For most, I suppose, it was old hat; but I was seeing it for the first time.

✪

THE PRESS quarters were the Riverside Hotel, put up by the French for tourism, a one-story, three-sided affair built on the banks of the river. The Negro sergeant took me to an office at the back and handed me over to a white sergeant. This sergeant gave me a form to fill in. He said that the hotel had been commandeered for the press only recently; before that it had been a great place for prostitutes. Then he took a key from the hook and led me to my room. There were about twenty rooms, and they all opened onto a central courtyard, like looseboxes for horses; some were marked "A.P.," "U.P.," "CBS News," et cetera, to indicate permanent residence. Most rooms had big double beds and mosquito netting and austerity French furniture.

I asked where everyone was, and I was told up at the base or out on assignment; they usually got back around five. I had a drink and an omelet in a bar on the other side of the courtyard, and then the Negro sergeant returned to take me on a tour of the base.

This was more interesting than I had expected. There was a dirt road all the way along the perimeter fence, and we drove slowly along it. The fence was heavily guarded with sentries in watchtowers, marines in bunkers, coils of barbed wire and areas marked "Keep Away. Mined." Two big radar bowls went round and round. The sergeant said that, only two weeks before, the V.C. had crept right up to the fence at night and mortared the field. They destroyed half a dozen planes and killed quite a few servicemen. "We have patrols out there now all the time, and I guess they've pushed the V.C. back. See that hill?"

"Yes."

"There's V.C. all round the base of that hill, and we have a camp on top."

"Why don't the V.C. capture the top?"

"They'd like to. They've tried many times. But it's too steep." He handed me a pair of glasses and I looked at the green trees that covered the hill and in my mind's eye saw the Americans living precariously at the top and the V.C. milling around below.

"Whoever has the top of that hill," said the sergeant, "has a real good advantage. They can see a long ways all round, can see most everything that's going on."

The air was never empty and never still. The jets screamed down the runway, bounced into the air, took off and landed all the time. The sergeant said they were going to, or coming back from, bombing missions in the north. The helicopters were active, too, buzzing about in groups like swarms of flies. At one end the field was thick with parked planes, transports and One-Two-Threes, jet fighters and helicopters, bombers loaded with rockets and napalm. In one corner I counted fifty fighters, packed as closely as herrings. Jesus, I thought, *America is rich.* An M.P. jeep going at about five miles an hour and flashing a red light came toward us. Behind it was an open truck stacked high with huge bombs. On one of the bombs lay a little Vietnamese soldier, fast asleep.

Back at the Riverside Hotel, there was still time to fill in before the others returned. Across the road from the main gate I had observed a kind of miniature park, a big mound dotted with small trees, with a low stone wall all round and a long, shallow flight of steps in the middle. Where did they lead to? I crossed the road and walked up the steps. At the top more steps fell away to a little hollow in which was a courtyard fringed by frangipani. Beyond the courtyard was a low, three-sided building without doors or windows, full of stone statuary. As I approached, I saw it was a museum full of stone statues cemented to their plinths to prevent people from taking them away. But it was no ordinary museum. It harbored the cream of Vietnam's sculptural past, treasures that even Jim Thompson in Bangkok might have envied. There were things from the seventh century and tenth century and thirteenth century, from the Cham period and the Chinese period and the period of the Chinese wars. There were statues of Vishnu and Lakshmi and Siva dancing, of fantastic Chinese elephants and lions, of giant lingams reaching for the sky, and circular rows of exquisite disembodied breasts. To add to this windfall, I seemed to have the place to myself. I wandered from object to object in a kind of dream, stunned by the unexpectedness of it all. I had come to Vietnam because of its savage, cruel war; and yet in the heart of it I had found this harbor of beauty and peace.

Indeed, so bemused was I that on entering the last of the museum's three sides I didn't see there was someone there until I was almost on him. He was a civilian, a quiet American by the name of Carrier,

working for the Rand Corporation. We looked at the remaining statues together, and a bond grew between us, like birds in the wilderness. He was an interesting man, and I was intrigued as to what he
did.

"My job," he said, "is to interview Vietcong prisoners and try to
evaluate their motivation in fighting."

"What would you say their motivation is?"

"Basically, to get a better deal for themselves. The history of the
Vietnamese villager is a history of neglect, and the history of every
Saigon government is a history of corruption."

"I've heard it said that the villagers don't really care which side
wins, all they want is a quiet life."

"At the moment they want a quiet life in that they want to be sure
the protection they're getting, whether it's South Vietnamese or Vietcong, is strong enough. But if by a quiet life is meant going on living
as they always have done, it's simply not true. These people have
been disillusioned by broken promises, first by the French, then by
their own people. They believe the Vietcong represent a regime that
really will do something to improve their standard of living."

"What do they think of the Americans?"

"They think we're here for our own good, and that's true whatever
way you care to interpret it. They think we're here to prop up a
corrupt regime, and that's true, too. No one has any idea of the extent
of the corruption of South Vietnamese officials. They say we have no
business here and they want us out. And they're terrified of our Negroes."

"Why?"

"Because when the French Foreign Legion were here, they had
these huge Senegalese native troops who frequently used to rape their
tiny women."

"What do you say to the prisoners when you first see them?"

"I have a girl interpreter and she sees them first, softens them up,
you know, the old theory. Then I come in and tell them I'm a long-
hair, I'm making a study of revolutions. The prisoners say, 'I am like
a fish on a cutting board. I don't care what you do with me.' They
expect to be killed and are surprised when they're not."

"They expect the same kind of atrocities they themselves sometimes inflict?"

"Yes and no. The reason they disembowel and decapitate is ancestor worship. When someone is cut up, he's not whole and therefore unworthy to meet his ancestors."

"Are you staying at the press hotel?" I said.

"No, I never stay with MacV. I'd like to, but I have to think of the morale of my interpreters. I stay in Vietnamese hotels with them."

"What's that like?"

"It's noisy. They stay up till all hours. The one I'm staying in now has bedroom walls which don't reach the ceiling—they're kind of partitioned. Next to me is a room shared by three Chinamen and a girl. They have the girl in turn. It's quite a racket. By the time they're through it's damn near morning."

I said, "You're an American, but you don't seem to me to be part of what one might call the American effort here, the American establishment."

"I'm not."

"No. Well, what do you think of it?"

He thought a bit and said, "Forgive me if I don't say anything too obvious. But there are two things I ought to say. First, how many Americans here or at home know anything about Vietnamese history? And if you don't know Vietnamese history, you don't know anything about this country or the people who live in it. The Vietnamese have a very strong sense of their own identity. They were occupied by the Chinese for a thousand years—how many Americans know that?— and they still kept their identity. Whether they're from the north or south, they loathe the Chinese and always have. But most Americans think the Chinese are only waiting to come down and help them."

"And the other thing?"

"You hear a lot of criticism about the American soldiers here, how ignorant and uneducated they are, and so on. It's perfectly true, but what people don't realize is that basically they're peasants. Peasants are traditionally thought of as being rural. Well, we live in an urban society, so we have *urban* peasants. But they're peasants just the same."

We walked through the courtyard, past the sweet-smelling frangipani trees, and down the steps to the road. At the bottom Mr. Carrier went on toward the town, and I crossed over to the hotel. Most of the correspondents had returned and were sitting drinking on a terrace outside the bar. I introduced myself. They represented the world's press: U.P., A.P., *Life*, NBC, *Paris-Match*, CBS, Reuters. They were all experts in their field, men trained to inquire, to observe, to record; some had been in Da Nang for months. Yet when there was a lull in the conversation and I mentioned the museum across the road and the treasures in it, they all looked blank. None of them had been there; none had even heard of it.

✪

THE CORRESPONDENTS were a mixed lot. There was Hal Boyle of A.P., a gray man in his fifties, who had won the Pulitzer Prize in 1945 for his coverage of the European war, and who told me that correspondents in this war were taking more calculated risks than he or his colleagues had ever done. There was gentle, elderly Mr. Brodie, my roommate, a war artist, whose pictures I never saw. There were two Frenchmen from *Paris-Match,* and a German and a Swiss. There was a blond reporter called Chelminski from *Life,* who had white powder on his face for a skin rash and was reading a huge book called *Humiliation: La Guerre d'Indo-Chine.* There was an Englishman working for Reuters by the name of Bruce Robson, who didn't like the Americans and told me they had tried to put an end to the French food in the bar and have hamburgers and hot dogs instead. ("We soon put a stop to that.") And then there was John Wheeler, whom Mal Browne had told me about. Wheeler would have stood out in any company. He had cropped black hair, graying at the edges, and wore olive-green battle dress. He was not only good-looking in a Cary Grant sort of way, but tough-looking too, tough inside, a man of authority, a very gentle man.

Someone said, "In about two minutes from now a half-assed colonel will show up to give us a briefing. He knows nothing about anything. Right?" There were murmurs of approval and someone said, "He's just a *beautiful* guy." He arrived soon after, a cocky, nervous little fellow, like a blown-up ball, who strutted toward us in shorts and sandals, with a junior officer at his heels. The correspondents gathered round in a way that was almost menacing. "Everyone here?" said the colonel. "Bruce Robson isn't," said someone. Someone else shouted across the courtyard, "Bruce! The colonel's here! Leave go of your cock, pick up your boots and git here."

The colonel read out a boring communiqué about jets from Da Nang strafing a Vietcong post; it was non-news all the way. The colonel looked round, expecting some kind of reaction. But the correspondents had nothing to say. In that silence you could touch the hostility between them. Eventually the colonel said, ingratiatingly, "I guess this communiqué will need a little editing by you people." If the colonel himself hadn't recognized that the communiqué was beyond editing, there was no use telling him. "It's just a beautiful piece of Air Force officialese, isn't it?" said Wheeler. The colonel said, weakly, "I guess so."

Then the colonel read another communiqué, this time from the Army, and the correspondents kept interrupting to ask for clarification or to suggest that the facts were wrong. Once the colonel said plaintively, "Well, I'm only trying to help out." Toward the end of the communiqué Wheeler said, "You're wrong on all three sets of facts there," and turned to me and said, "See what I mean?"

The contempt the correspondents had for the colonel was quite embarrassing. I thought of Breault back in Saigon. Breault was a model briefer. He had been in the game long enough to know the ground rules: be accurate in your facts and keep your distance; the correspondents mightn't like you, but at least you'd have their respect. The trouble with this colonel was that he had never had to deal with the press before. Trying to be authoritative, he sounded patronizing; trying to be friendly, he became sycophantic. He didn't know where he was.

Finally the colonel read out, "A marine was killed by a sniper this morning in an area approximately eight miles southeast of Da Nang."

Wheeler said, "Are you sure about that map reference?"

The colonel turned to his junior, and back to us, and said, "Yes."

"In that case," said Wheeler, "I'm going to file a story that you've assumed a much wider tactical area of responsibility than hitherto."

"No," said the colonel doggedly. "The T.A.O.R.'s the same."

"It isn't," said Wheeler. "You come and look at the map."

So we went into the office and looked at the map. Wheeler laid off a position eight miles southeast of Da Nang and said, "Now, you've never assumed responsibility for *that* area before, so I'm going to go ahead and file this story."

"Now, wait a minute," said the colonel, clearly on the run. "Let me go back and check that out, and have someone send down confirmation."

"Okay, Colonel," said Wheeler. "But don't be too long."

The colonel and his aide scuttered off into the darkness and drove away. Later that evening a message came through that the communiqué should have read "south*west*."

☆

THAT NIGHT and the next day I sat with Wheeler in the bar and listened while he talked. The first time we went there, the two Frenchmen and the Vietnamese barman were playing the fruit machines. Wheeler said, "It's funny how we Americans corrupt people wherever we go."

We sat down at one of the tables. Wheeler said he was thirty-four and married; his wife was living in Kuala Lumpur, where he had a temporary home. He was born in El Paso and raised at La Junta, where his father was a publisher of newspapers. "He did all the publishing and my mother did the news work. They both tried to persuade me mightily not to get involved in it. At least they succeeded in regard to the managerial side."

"Did you become a reporter right away?"

"No. I went into the Air Force. I figured it might be an interesting experience. I aimed to play it very safe and go into Public Information and get out after maybe four years. But I got caught up with flying, for maybe the same reason I go into the field here, which is not wanting to go through life as a bystander. I became a crew member—navigator, radar operator and bombardier—in a B-47 in Strategic Air Command. My plane was a cell leader. We carried nuclear weapons and I knew exactly where we had to drop them."

"In Russia?"

"In Russia."

"How did you feel about that?"

He paused and said, "They showed us photographs of our target. I got to know the place quite well. This may sound crazy to you, but I almost got to like it. And I knew that if ever I did have to drop my bombs, I would be killing thousands and thousands of children." He paused again. "All the time I was in that bomber, I had these terrible stomach pains. I went to the doctor and he gave me different kinds of medicine, but none of them did any good. Then, after five and a half years in the Air Force, I pulled out. The day I walked through the gates the stomach pains went, and I haven't had them since."

"What did you do after leaving the Air Force?"

"I joined a small newspaper in San Francisco. At that time I didn't think I'd be much good as a reporter, and all I wanted was a small hole to hide myself in. I covered all the routine city stuff—everything. Then I met the head of the A.P. bureau there, and he said why didn't I go and see him, and that's how it started."

"You joined them?"

"Yes. I told this man I wanted to travel, so a week after I joined them I started French lessons. I worked in the office by day and took the French lessons at night."

"And then they sent you here?"

"Right."

"Did you volunteer to come and live in Da Nang, or did they send you?"

"I asked to come. I don't think you get any concept of the war sitting in Saigon. I think the high command down there lies to us about what's going on, mostly by omission. Also I think it's a mistake to write copy by talking with people instead of going and getting your own impressions. Of course, this is the dilemma the reporter always faces. Because if you do spend all your time getting your own impressions, you may miss something important that somebody's said."

"I understand you spend most of your time going out with Vietnamese patrols?"

"That's right. I just got back from one today."

"Why do you do that?"

"Because that's where the action is. Where the stories and pictures are."

"You take pictures too?"

"Yes. It's not part of my contract, and A.P. doesn't pay me for them, but I find it helps me emotionally. It gives me something to do."

"Do you write in the field, or when you get back?"

"When I get back. What I try to do is put flesh on a story. When I read that a truck was driving down a road and two people got killed, it takes me back to my police-reporting days. That's just the bare fact. It's got no flesh on it. I like to put flesh on my stories."

"How long are you away at a time?"

"Three or four days. Sometimes longer."

"How do you get along with the Vietnamese?"

"All right. I speak about as much French as they do. We get by."

"How about food?"

"Well, I take along several cans of sardines, and I hand this over to the general pool. See, they make a mush of sardines and rice every morning and evening, and this entitles me to draw from it. I don't care for C rations. The Vietnamese march for an hour, then cook for twenty minutes, then march for an hour again. People who see this for the first time think they're crazy, but it does mean that when they stop at noon the rice is ready."

"What happens on these patrols? What sort of things do you see?"

He rubbed his big hands against his chest and said, "All kinds of things. Some quite rough."

"Like what?"

"We went into a village last week which was known to be sheltering Vietcong. I couldn't have told which from which, but this Vietnamese patrol I was with, they smell them out like a dog. They took thirty prisoners. They shot three of them on the spot, and the other twenty-seven when they got back to camp."

"What did you think about that?"

"I was too busy taking pictures to think anything. I got a shot of the colonel as he was going to shoot the prisoners, with the clouds in the background. I got a wide-angle shot of the prisoners with their hands tied behind their backs. Then I got a shot of the patrol marching by and looking at the corpses. They were pretty good pictures."

I said, "There was a picture in the *Saigon Post* a few days ago of two V.C. lying in a ditch with their hands bound. One was being shot by a Vietnamese officer, the other had lifted his head to watch, knowing his turn was about to come."

"That was the story," said Wheeler. "I took those pictures."

"Christ!" I said, quietly, and then, "I suppose you get used to it?"

"You *have* to get used to it, or you wouldn't be any good. When I go out with these patrols I know I'm going to see things that are unpleasant and I have to prepare for it. One time there was a big battle and when it was over, we went and looked at the battlefield. The Vietcong had cut open the stomachs of the wounded and emasculated them, and that wasn't very nice. And then there were the dead, and they had every expression on their faces you could think of. Some were really peaceful, what I would call natural battlefield deaths, with their arms folded on their chests. Others had their faces frozen with horror and terror. And then there was a man with half his head shot away. I glanced at it and then I had to look away. I guess I just couldn't take it."

"Do you find you get callous about these things?"

"Yes, in a way. The first six weeks here I was really upset by what I saw, and I wrote long letters to my wife. I got over it, but she didn't know what was happening, she thought I was coming apart at the seams. This country is a country of such violence that one has to accept all these horrible things as the norm. But they're not what I'd ever want to regard as the norm outside of here."

"Do you often feel afraid?"

"I get frightened and I get stimulated, often at the same time. The fear stimulates me. I've been here four months now and I know the bad areas. When I hear the patrol is going into a bad area, I say to myself, Well, do I go or don't I? I don't have to go. But I go. When we land with the helicopters on a paddy field, that can be very stimulating. You never know what you're going to find. You forget about everything except taking pictures." He said, "This thing about being afraid?"

"Yes."

"Almost the first patrol I went out on was hit very hard by mortar fire and machine guns. I'd never heard gunfire before. They had a U.S. adviser along with them, and he got wounded, so I took it on myself to get him out. I'd heard that the Vietnamese sometimes offer up Americans to get themselves off the hook. I put him into a personnel carrier and got him away and then we all started walking out. I was in the rear, and I kept thinking to myself, the V.C. are *bound* to catch up, and if they do, they don't make any differentiation between soldiers and journalists. I couldn't bring myself to look over my shoulder. I don't say I was in a panic, but I was pretty agitated. And when the column went into a house to eat, I thought, My God, let's keep moving! In fact we were safe, but I didn't know it."

I remembered something Mal Browne had told me, and I said, "You got a public commendation for getting that officer out, I believe?"

"That's right," said Wheeler, and then, not wanting to stay on the subject, "And he gave me his submachine gun. It was a Swedish gun." He added, "I could have used it."

"But you didn't?"

"No. I never use a gun. I never take one with me."

"You feel you're a noncombatant?"

He smiled his tough, gentle smile and said, "I just don't want to hurt anybody. I feel basically that the Vietcong are fighting for what they believe in, and that's their affair, not mine."

We talked about the war in general, and I asked him what he thought of the other correspondents. "I don't wish to knock the opposition," he said, "but one thing that working in the city hall taught me was accuracy. I was responsible directly to the publisher, and if ever I got the facts wrong, there was hell to pay. I fear that some of my colleagues here are inclined to guess. One of them filed a story the other day about a battle in which he claimed five hundred and sixty were killed and wounded. There just weren't that number of people on both sides."

"How long are you going to go on with this?" I said.

"These patrols?"

"Yes."

"I hope to take a vacation in August with my wife, and then come back here for, say, another year."

"In the field?"

"If that's where the action is."

"And after?"

"Well, initially my wife was stronger about foreign service than I was, but now she's discovered she's more of a Midwesterner than she thought. So we've made an agreement whereby I go on reporting the foreign news for another four or five years, by which time I hope I'll have made enough of a reputation to get something good back home." He smiled. "In any case, my legs won't stand another fifteen years of this kind of thing."

★

THE NEXT day I got up early to catch the plane back to Saigon. In the bar the wife of the barman gave me coffee, freshly baked rolls and cherry jam. Bruce Robson, the Reuters man, came in and I asked him what he thought of the Americans. "Some of their officers annoy me," he said. "They have absolutely no confidence in themselves. You ask a British officer a question, and if he doesn't know the answer, he'll say, 'I don't know, you'd best go and see So-and-so.' But these people hem and haw and half tell you and half don't, and seem terrified someone is watching them. They just don't know how to say no. And they have absolutely no style. In the British Army you can tell the difference between officers and men. But with these people, when they're not wearing badges of rank, there's really no means of telling.

"Another thing that annoys me is the way their radio station spends half its time encouraging its listeners to believe they really are American. They have a program about, say, Morse, who invented the Morse code, and they end up saying, 'This is part of your American heritage.' They really are unsure of themselves."

On the way out I knocked at John Wheeler's door to say goodbye. But he had already left on another patrol.

✪

BEFORE I left Saigon, I went to a party at the British embassy, in honor of Emlyn Williams. There I met some South Vietnamese journalists and asked them what they thought of the American press. One said, "Two years ago they wrote we must have democracy. Now they write we must keep dictatorship. Please, why?"

✪

TAIWAN IS an attractive island, with its lakes and hills and food and girls, and you would never guess that except for Holland it has the highest population density in the world. Taipei, the capital, is less agreeable. For the first fifty years of this century it was occupied by the industrious Japanese, and they made of it a gray, drab industrial city.

In a big gloomy building I found the American Medical Research Unit. Its staff was twelve medical officers of the United States Navy, twelve enlisted men and three hundred Chinese civilians. Its head was a doctor called Captain Phillips, who was fifty-nine and wore khaki trousers and an open shirt, and had cropped gray hair like a field of fertilized stubble. Captain Phillips smoked sixty cigarettes a day, and when I taxed him on this, as one who ought to know better, he justified it on the grounds that Taiwan was free of other irritants like smog which they had in London and Los Angeles.

Captain Phillips gave me lunch in the unit's canteen, broth and hamburgers, and told me that the unit had operated in Guam during the war but had been disbanded after it. The American Navy had one other Medical Research Unit, in Cairo, and he had been in charge of that from 1945 to 1950. After a spell in Washington he had come here in 1955 to reactivate this unit. His wife was counselor at the United States embassy and he had six children, half of whom spoke Chinese. He had liked Cairo, because there was plenty to do there, you couldn't help getting interested in archaeology, you'd go out to the Pyramids and have a picnic and dig around and find a bit of pottery you knew must be thousands of years old. But here the Japanese had stopped all crafts; here at first there was nothing.

"What kind of research are you doing?" I said.

"Our mission," said Captain Phillips, "is acute infectious diseases of the Far East—trachoma, cholera, et cetera."

"But why is the U.S. Navy doing this? They don't suffer from these diseases. They're inoculated against them."

"No, but they sail the seven seas and go to countries which do suffer from them."

"So it's mainly for humanitarian reasons?"

"It's like this," said Captain Phillips. "There are approximately five million people in the world suffering from trachoma. They live in countries which don't have the know-how to provide a cure. We do have the know-how, and therefore we have a duty, a conscience if you like, to utilize it. In addition, a man who has trachoma can maybe see enough to till a paddy field, but not enough to work on an assembly line. So some developing nations are being held back from becoming industrialized. Trying to find a cure for trachoma is one of the ways they can be helped to help themselves, and in the long run that's good for all of us."

"What's your own specialty?"

"Cholera, because it's such a fascinating disease." He took a big inhalation of smoke and said, "With cholera a person can lose half his own body weight in twenty-four hours, through diarrhea. When cholera breaks out in a country that hasn't had it for twenty years, most doctors there have never seen a case and they're scared stiff. In February 1964 we got word at nine A.M. of a cholera outbreak in Saigon. It was a Sunday morning. We got together a team of five, and ten thousand pounds of saline solution. I called up Japan and they told me to call Okinawa, which I did. I got a colonel out of church, and he sent a plane down, and we were in Saigon at ten that night, and went straight to work. When we arrived the mortality rate was thirty percent. A week later we had it down to three percent, and it stayed there until the epidemic was over."

"What sort of cholera research do you do here?"

"One of the things we're working on is the relationship between cholera and rice, as they affect the body. A child on an average rice diet who gets hit by cholera isn't likely to survive. However, by proper fertilization and selection you can increase the protein content of the rice and produce a strain that'll help the body to resist cholera. We've been cooperating with the International Rice Research Institute in the Philippines. They've sent us rice with different protein contents, and we've been studying the effects of this on rabbits. We've challenged pregnant bunnies with a cholera vibrio to see how resistant they were in relation to the type of rice they were eating. Those on the low protein content all aborted before the end of their pregnancies, and those on the high content didn't. So we learned something from that. The next thing is to see how these different strains react on humans."

After lunch Captain Phillips handed me over to a warrant officer called Chief Pancratz, who took me round the various laboratories and departments. I met Dr. Jenkins, who was doing research into rickettsial diseases, scrub typhus, and hemorrhagic fever, and was also involved in some huge bird-catching program organized from the Philippines: between one and two million migratory birds were caught each year in the Far East and then examined minutely to see if they, or the insects on them, were carriers of infectious diseases.

Dr. Fresh, a lieutenant commander, was working on the incidence of carcinoma in the nasopharynx, which the Chinese had more than any other people. One of his problems was getting human tissue. "I get it mostly from the Chinese Navy and the American Hospital. The trouble with the Chinese Navy is that it consists mostly of young men, and they don't often die." Dr. Wood, a lieutenant, j.g., who was doing his compulsory military service in the unit, was working on parasitology, isolating microfilariae from the local monkey and putting them in mosquito-cell cultures and seeing what happened. This was part of a research program into a disease called filariasis, which was caused by the bite of an insect that had bitten an infected monkey.

We met one or two other dedicated medical men, who told me about the gunya virus and the dengue virus and bee encephalitis, and then Chief Pancratz said, would I like to visit the zoo, the whole of the top floor was occupied by animals, which they used for experiments, and the man in charge was Captain Favero. So we went upstairs and met Captain Favero, who was an Army, not a Navy, captain, and when I asked why, he said the Navy didn't have a veterinary corps. In Captain Favero's office was a stuffed white rabbit in a glass case. I asked what it was doing there, and Captain Favero said, "That was a rabbit we were trying to artificially inseminate, but it didn't take. So we stuffed her."

I asked Captain Favero how many animals he had, and he said approximately 12,000 mice, 1,200 rats, 600 hamsters, 300 monkeys, 300 guinea pigs, and 150 rabbits. "We also have chickens, geese, full-grown swine, hogs, dogs, cats, and occasionally snakes. They have no rules about vivisection in Taiwan, so we follow the code of practice we use in the States. We breed most of our animals here. Monkeys we buy locally for about five dollars each. We get them from the aborigines who live in the mountains. We get quarterly returns from all the departments here as to their needs, and we aim to keep them supplied with what they want. Mice have a suckling period of three weeks, and so are easy to manipulate. Rabbits have a longer suckling period and so are less easy."

"Why do you have so many different kinds of animal?" I said.

"Different animals for different things," said Captain Favero. "For instance, they've discovered in the space program that the spinal column of a bear is nearer to that of a man than to that of a monkey. Also that the respiratory tract of a pig is very like a man's. And the Taiwan monkey is more susceptible to trachoma virus than the common laboratory monkey."

Captain Favero asked me if I had time to look round, and Chief Pancratz said, "We have plenty of time, sir. Captain Phillips wants Mr. Kennedy to see everything." We visited the breeding colony first and looked at the animals through glass portholes in the doors. Only the monkeys reciprocated our glance, putting their heads on one side and staring at us from their cages with little, childlike faces.

"Monkeys are strange creatures," said Captain Favero. "They get excited over all sorts of things, and they get especially excited when you look at them."

We went on to the experimental section, and here we were allowed into the rooms. We saw rabbits with red eyes, munching carrots, and guinea pigs and hamsters and mice. We saw a swan, a pig, and a goose.

We saw a cat in a very small cage, looking miserable. "Right now that cat is undergoing experimentation," said Captain Favero. "That's why he's in that small cage." We saw a rabbit in an even smaller cage, with his head sticking out and eating a carrot. "This rabbit," said Captain Favero, "has had part of his bowel removed and the two ends joined up. He has a tube inside him to analyze the secretions there, and eventually he'll be infected with cholera to see how the secretions change. We'll also be able to study the formation of the various antibodies on the wall of his stomach."

"Why's he in such a small cage?" I said. "He can't even move."

"We don't want him to move," said Captain Favero. "If he moved, the tube would probably fall out, and that would ruin the experiment."

Going down the stairs, Chief Pancratz pointed out the window to a pond that lay in the grounds. "We raise our own frogs in that pond," he said. "From tadpoles."

"What do you use them for?" I said.

"We use them for their skins. The underbelly of the frog has an electric potential. We put a needle through the frog's spinal cord, and then we pull the skin off him; the skin is potentially alive. We put the skin between two plastic blocks and then tighten it up so it's sealed. Then we put our test solutions in and read off the results on a recorder."

If that wasn't exactly what Chief Pancratz said, it was certainly the gist of it. I was wondering what happened to the frogs subsequently, when we reached the operating theater. There was a Negro man in there whom Chief Pancratz introduced as Chief Grant, and a Chinese girl whom Chief Grant introduced as Miss Lucy Jean. When I said that wasn't a very Chinese name, she said her real name was Chien, but Jean was easier for the Americans. Chief Pancratz asked Chief Grant what was cooking, and Chief Grant said only the routine monkey tests, and gestured to the other side of the room. Chief Pancratz said he was sure Mr. Kennedy would like to see that, and we walked over.

What I saw was something that I would have preferred not to see, and that I am sure I will never forget. Lying on his back on a small table was an ordinary gray monkey with a big bushy tail and closed eyes. His arms were stretched behind his head, and his legs were similarly splayed, each at right angles to the other; hands and feet were tied to posts at each corner of the table so that he looked crucified, about to be stretched on the rack. Chief Grant said this was to keep him from moving. There was a black teat wedged in the corner of his mouth to make an airway for his breathing. The monkey lay on a long white cushion, which Chief Pancratz said was a heated pad to keep him warm; a loose sheet of plastic over the central part of his body was there for the same purpose.

At one side of the table was a row of bottles and a glass container half full of a blue liquid. This emptied into a tube which ran under the plastic sheet and into a hole which had been bored in the monkey's stomach. A few inches away another tube had been inserted into another hole, and this carried the blue liquid out of the stomach and into a glass container at the other side of the table. Lying across the middle of the monkey's stomach was a long, thin pair of forceps or a similar instrument, and this held together the monkey's skin where the cuts had been made for the holes; I assumed these were handier and easier than stitches. At the foot of the table was a smaller table, on which lay a kidney-shaped dish containing rubber gloves and surgical instruments, and beneath it a bucket full of used bandages and other waste matter.

"We'll continue with this experiment," said Chief Grant, "until the blue ceases. The blue is the means of telling us when to stop. They call it Evans blue. It's a very simple sort of dye."

"What is it all for?" I asked.

"This monkey," said Chief Grant, "is being given a mixture of sodium 22 and sodium 24 with potassium 42, which is made in a reactor and is therefore radioactive. What we're trying to find out is how much radioactive sodium is absorbed by the monkey as the solution passes through the small intestine. We give different doses to different monkeys. Eventually, when we've discovered the correct dosage, we aim to try it out on humans and see if it helps to give us a cure for cholera."

"Do you use a lot of monkeys?"

"We try to keep a good supply on hand. I would say we were now using around two a week. We have used as many as six a week, but two or three is average."

I looked at the monkey stretched unconscious on his heated pad, mercifully unaware of what had been done to him, and I said to Chief Pancratz, "What happens to the monkeys when the experiment is over?"

"Oh," said Chief Pancratz, "we *sacrifice* them. We give them an overdose of magnesium sulphate, which is a saturated solution."

Chief Pancratz said it was time we were getting back to the captain, so we said goodbye to Chief Grant and Miss Lucy Jean and set off downstairs. Chief Pancratz chattered on about this and that, but my mind was still on the monkey. He was the apex of everything I had seen in this establishment, the epitome of all those helpless creatures held rigid in their cages, tubes in their stomachs, bandages on their wounds, infected with cholera and trachoma. I had been taught, and believed it, that the cardinal sin in life was exploitation of others for one's own ends, of using people as things. This admirable precept applied to some sections of the animal world as well: domestic and farm animals were on the whole treated with consideration; there was a limit to what could be asked of circus animals; even in the pursuit of savage animals there existed some kind of relationship. The less their freedom of action was interfered with, the more they retained their dignity; the more they retained their dignity, the more we gave them our respect.

But these pathetic creatures, monkeys and rabbits and hamsters and mice, and millions like them in laboratories all over the world, had been exploited mercilessly. Cribbed, cabined and confined, they had been deprived of their freedom of action and therefore also of their dignity; they were being used wholly as things. The justification for all this, it would be said, was the great benefits they had brought to humankind; by their deaths they had saved, and would continue to save, millions of human lives. Was might, then, right; and did the end justify the means? It would seem so. But let no one pretend otherwise. Let no scientist or doctor engaged in this work kid himself that his job is not one of exploitation and expediency, nor deny that what he is doing is—however important to man—a deeply shaming thing.

And then, as Chief Pancratz and I walked down the corridor to Captain Phillips's office, I was struck by another thought. I had just come from an Asian country many of whose people the Americans had been destroying and mutilating for years with napalm and defoliation bombs, scatter pellets and toxic gases, in the name of the general good. Yet here they were engaged in more or less the opposite. In their selfless and generous way they had set up an organization of which the world knew nothing, dedicated to ridding millions of other Asians of painful and crippling diseases—including in the last analysis the very people against whom they were fighting. Could paradox go further? In Vietnam they were crucifying humans as part of the Great Crusade; in Taiwan they were crucifying monkeys.

Chief Pancratz knocked at Captain Phillips's door and we went in. "Well, hello!" said Captain Phillips through a cloud of smoke. "How did you find the tour?"

But I wasn't going to fly any ethical kites with him.

"Absorbing," I said. "Quite absorbing." And so it was.

✪

NOW I'M on the last lap home, in some clapped-out Oriental plane, sitting next to an Englishman called Froggett. Down there through the clouds is Japan. Froggett and I have been eating plastic sandwiches out of a slippery plastic bag. He is about thirty, fed up with Britain, and emigrating to Australia. Earlier he asked me if I had been to Bangkok. When I said yes, he leered and said, "That's an aptly named place."

✪

This is the Okura Hotel, Tokyo, one of the most efficient hotels in the world. On the telephone one can dial room service, laundry, porter, et cetera, direct. When you do need the operator, she is charming, anxious to know your problem and help you solve it. And, hullo, here is a radio switch. Could it be A.F.N.?

"There's an old timer for you, the 'Jazz-Me Blues.' I was jes' looking over some beautiful one-liners, and I found one that's appropriate today, since this is our wedding anniversary and my wife's birthday. Huh—Abe Burrows wrote a song title once, 'I'm so miserable without you, it's almost like having you around.' Ha, ha, ha! 'Every time I kill myself,' he says, 'I die a little.' Huh! Then, of course, there's the old classic for which he is famous: 'If you were the only girl in the world and I were the only boy, okay, but right now nothing doing.' Ha, ha, ha! Ha, ha, ha! . . .

"And I'm afraid that we have about run out of time here today at the Diplomat Hotel in Hollywood-by-the-Sea in Florida. One of the

prettiest places I've ever seen in my life, with the inland waterway behind us, and the surf in the front yard, so to speak, and even when the weather is wet and rainy and blowy, it's still beautiful—jes' lovely. Well, see you tomorrow, be the Good Lord willing."

Rum-ti-tum-tum-tum. *"You have been listening to the Arthur Godfrey Half-Hour."*

Tum-ti-tum-ti-ta-ta. *"This is the United States Armed Forces Radio and Television Service."*

✪

Here is Mr. Takichi Shigematsu, public-relations man of the Okura Hotel. We are having a drink in the Emerald Room, where a pretty Japanese girl, plump as a robin, is singing Western songs to the accompaniment of a Japanese band. I have suggested the meeting because I want to know if many Americans stay here, and why.

"Very many Americans. About forty percent Americans all the time. Forty percent Americans, forty percent Europeans, and about twenty percent Asians."

"What do the Americans do?"

"Some are business people, and some are visitors. The visitors are increasing. We are getting more and better type of client."

"Are you?"

"Yes. We have had Mr. David Rockefeller, Mr. Richard Nixon, the president of Studebaker and his lawyer, and Mr. Schuster of Simon and Schuster. In a few weeks' time we will be having the Prime Minister of Uganda and his suite, and we are just saying goodbye to the First Lady of the Philippines and her suite. Lord Home was among our guests here and so was Mr. Mikoyan—"

"Mr. Shigematsu, it's Americans I'm really interested in."

"Yes, I understand. I think Americans are happy to be here, because we have the top-class clientele of the world. For instance, we had Baron and Baroness Philippe de Rothschild from France and President Luebke from West Germany—"

"Mr. Shi—"

"And we have also had the pleasure of receiving the sister of the Shah of Iran and her entourage. And speaking of royal families, please note that this is the first time in Japanese history that their Imperial Highnesses the Emperor and Empress of Japan have visited a common hotel. The first time was as guest of the President of Mexico in return for an invitation to the palace. The second time was for a private dinner party, which unfortunately I couldn't publicize. The Crown Prince and Princess were there, and all the royal-family members. Their coming was a very rare occasion."

"Yes, I see that, but—"

"You are asking about Americans. Well, we have had the movie stars from Hollywood—so many I forget all their names. We have had Lana Turner and Suzy Parker and Charlton Heston and Peter O'Toole. And we have had Miss Canada and Miss Sweden and Miss Brazil . . ."

The names came rattling out of Mr. Shigematsu's mouth like candy balls from a jar. At last they stopped, and he asked the pretty robin who had been singing with the band to join us for a drink. She gave the waiter her order. Then she looked at me and smiled and said, "Are you strong for alcohol?" Mr. Shigematsu said, "She means, do you like drinking?" I looked at her and smiled and said, "Yes, I am and I do."

★

"You know, when it comes to judging people, the Good Book gives some mighty true advice. 'The Lord looketh on the heart.' Putting it another way, don't judge a man because of the color of his skin, or because he's shorter or taller than you are, or because he talks a different language. All of us look different to each other. What we are or what we do comes from inside. Remember the old chestnut, you can't judge a book by its cover, and that goes for people too. So get to know your neighbor the right way. Find out what really makes him tick, before you decide what kind of a guy he is. Don't forget that's how he decides what kind of a guy you are."

Rum-tum-ta-ti-ta-tum. *"You have been listening to 'Church Call.' "*

✪

JAPAN IS the first place I've been on this tour where people have stared at me for being European. It's about the last place I expected it. It happens everywhere, often right in the middle of Tokyo. It shows that despite the postwar American occupation and influx of American culture, the actual numbers of Westerners here must still be very small. This apart, the Japanese have the most marvelous manners, bowing and smiling and seemingly such a gentle, sweet people you wonder how they got up to all those terrible tricks in the war. One or two people have told me that because they are always polite and smiling and not showing any aggressive emotions, one mustn't think they haven't any; it simmers away inside, and then one day there is a big bang and out it comes. Tokyo alone has over two hundred murders a year. The children look very sweet, like clockwork toys, and they nearly all wear hats, particularly sailor hats with ribbons, even at three or four. The women are chic, too. In Vietnam women who exchange their exquisite *ao-dais* for Western dress look common and tarty, but Japanese women in Western clothes look sexy and smart.

The main shopping areas of Tokyo are full of noise and neon signs. The traffic goes very fast, but without that lack of purpose you meet in every Eastern country from Turkey on; indeed, I felt safer in Tokyo taxis than anywhere except London. Advertising covers most downtown buildings in a thick fungus and extends even to balloons in the sky. The names of some street-level establishments are in English, like "Beauty Salon," "Groceries," and "Bar"—the last sometimes adding "Japanese Only," showing that they too can operate their own color bar. Popular restaurants give a preview of their wares by putting in the window plastic replicas of their dishes, sitting on plastic plates. It is a grisly idea: fried eggs are canary yellow, sausages look like turds, casseroles like vomit and spaghetti like the intestines of very small birds. A final nauseous touch is that, because of condensation, most dishes are covered by a thin layer of dew.

❂

"Well, next we'll hear from Steve Allaymo, but first of all I want to tell you what happened in New York City. A pickpocket on a crowded New York City bus made a happy choice of a victim, in the person of a Brazilian government official who was carrying four hundred forty-one dollars in cash. The pickpocket did the job quickly and neatly, and one stop later he dismounted from the bus. And so did two pickpocket-squad detectives, who just happened to be on the very same bus. Well, they apprehended the pickpocket. The Brazilian official was called to the police station to claim his wallet, before he was even aware of the fact that it was missing. It turned out to be Brazil's Minister of Economic Affairs, who exclaimed, 'Just wonderful! You only see this stuff on television! You people in New York have the best police department in the world!'

"Uh, huh! And so it goes. Here is Steve Allaymo. . . ."

". . . Steve Allaymo, wrapping up the program for this week. The Ira Cook Show, heard Monday through Friday the same time. Hope you'll be with me next Monday. We'll have more of the best records that we can possibly get to play for you. May I leave you with this thought for the weekend:

> *"Life itself can't give you joy,*
> *Unless you really will it,*
> *Life just gives you time and space,*
> *It's up to you to fill it."*

❂

TODAY I have been lunching with little Mrs. Yuasa, whom I met with her husband, a Tokyo banker, while waiting at Tehran airport for the flight to New Delhi. Mrs. Yuasa said then, "Come and see us in Tokyo"; and she gave me a card, like any American. Actually Mrs. Yuasa is more English than American, having been to Sherborne, a leading English girls' school, and now she talks like any witty English dowager.

Mr. Yuasa was busy banking, but Mrs. Yuasa took me to the International Center, where we had a nasty Western lunch looking at a pretty Japanese garden. After lunch we went to the Meiji Gardens, first to the shrine where people clap hands and pray and toss coins into a box for ancestor worship, and then for a walk in the park. I was much stared at. Here were white-and-purple irises growing as thickly as buttercups, and a big pond full of carp with mouths like teacups, and people feeding them with popcorn from a nearby stall. The stall also sold hot dogs and hamburgers and doughnuts and cookies. "Hot dogs," said Mrs. Yuasa, laughing. "I can remember the time when one had to ask what a hot dog was. Such a ridiculous name, don't you think? And all that chewing the Americans go in for. We were taught as children never to chew, but their grownups chew all the time." I asked Mrs. Yuasa, an English-educated upper-class Japanese, what she thought of the Americans, and she said she would tell me a story. Once when she and Mr. Yuasa were touring the States, they came to Las Vegas. During the floor show they sat next to an aging American husband and wife, both a little drunk. When the nudes came on, the wife, looking at them, said to the husband, "Shut your eyes, honey, shut your eyes!" And the husband, looking at the nudes, too, said to her, "It's okay, sweetheart, you're more beautiful than any of them." What made this so funny, Mrs. Yuasa said, was that during the exchange neither husband nor wife looked at the other; they had paid good money and didn't want to lose a second of the show. The memory of it all set Mrs. Yuasa chortling again, and because laughter is infectious, I started chortling, too: Mrs. Yuasa and I chortled together, there in front of everyone, in the middle of the Meiji Gardens.

✪

"This is Walt Sheldon in Fuju, Japan. With me today is His Grace Bishop Hilary Hacker, the Bishop of Bismarck, North Dakota. We are privileged and honored to have him here at the Far East Network microphone and, Your Grace, I'm wondering why you've come all this long distance, all the way from—if it's proper to say—the Black Hills of North Dakota to the lovely hills and rice paddies of Japan. We're delighted to see you, and I wonder if you'd tell us exactly why you're here."

✪

A FEW yards down the road from the Okura Hotel is the American embassy, and I went there to call on Mr. Thayer, the press attaché. He was out of his room when I arrived, but his secretary said he would soon be back. While waiting I saw a note on his desk which read: "Mr. Oh called from the Korean Mission."

Presently Mr. Thayer came back. He was a sallow-faced, dark-haired, clean-shaven young American, of a type I was getting to know on my travels, bright as New Mexico, and fluent in Japanese. I hadn't intended to be with him more than fifteen minutes, but he was so interesting a man and seemed so happy to share his knowledge of Japan, that I stayed more than an hour.

He kicked off by telling me a little of Japanese history, how in the sixteenth century Japan was as modern as any country in Europe, but that after that they developed a policy of keeping foreigners out, with the result that by the time Europe and America had adjusted to the Industrial Revolution, Japan was still living in the Middle Ages. In the mid-nineteenth century Admiral Perry arrived with his ships to open up the country, and in 1863 the government started a policy of forced industrialization. "They sent teams of people all over the world to study what the major powers were doing, and then they modeled their own institutions and things on them. For instance, they modeled their army on the French army until the French lost the Franco-Prussian War. They didn't model anything on America then, because America wasn't a great power."

I said, "When did American influence first begin?" He said a little before the war, but a great deal after it, during the period of the American occupation.

"You could say this phase was the final end of Japanese isolation. They still copy Western things today, but much more selectively. If they see something that attracts them, they'll chew it over for a time, discard what they don't like and add something of their own. For example, Western clothing. They use Western suits for city life because they're practical, but when they go home they change into traditional dress. But it's a modified form of traditional dress. Take the *obi*—that's the thing that goes round the middle on women's kimonos. It's a real bitch to fix, it's six feet long and takes two people half an hour to make a job of it. But now they've developed an instant *obi*, with zippers and snaps, and that only takes a few minutes.

"They're also entering a period when, in some fields, the West is beginning to copy them. They're doing some very original work in TV sets and transistors and motorcycles, and also with their bullet train, which runs between here and Kyoto and averages one hundred thirty miles an hour. We've had lots of engineers over here studying that train to see if something similar couldn't be set up for the Boston–New York–Washington run. Then, in the field of architecture and design, America has been borrowing from Japan heavily. You go into some of these Japanese houses and you'll see what I mean."

I asked Mr. Thayer if there was a big American community in Japan, and he said it was the third-biggest after Korea and Taiwan, which were both former Japanese possessions. "Apart from Canada, Japan is now America's biggest trading partner. Our trade is around two billion dollars a year. We have branches of many of our businesses here, and the Japanese have set up branches of their businesses in the United States. There are a lot of young American executives here who are doing very well, finding opportunities they feel are no longer available in the States. Bill Dixon is an example that springs to mind. He used to be in the foreign service here, then left to help set up a subsidiary of Rexall's Drugs.

"In addition, there's a big cultural community of people who are here on a long-term basis, studying on grants and teaching in universities and schools, and so on. They stay here initially two or three years, then return to the States, but keep on coming back. This is one of the great centers for study on China, now that it's impossible to have access to the Chinese mainland.

"Then there are the missionary groups, who are quite numerous, those who were born here and those who've come since. There are also the expatriates who learned the language at military schools in the war, came over in the occupation, went back to American universities to get a degree in Japanese, and then came to settle here permanently. And also my own group, those who came here at the time of the Korean War, knowing nothing about Japan at all, but gradually falling in love with it.

"Finally, there are what you might call Zen sufferers. They're mostly people who can't find any niche in the American scene, and think the mysterious Orient has something to offer. But Zen is a very aesthetic, stoic religion which demands great discipline. Most students can't take it. So we have American Zen, which is something no Japanese can comprehend, and Japanese Zen, which is something much purer. The great American exponent of the latter is Ruth Sasaki, who lives in Kyoto and is the only genuine foreign-born Zen priestess."

"How about American tourists?"

"They haven't struck here in any large numbers yet, largely because of the expense of getting here, and because there's nowhere to go on to afterward, as there is in Europe. The Japanese themselves are nuts on traveling, mostly to the United States, but increasingly to the bloc countries as well. The bloc countries are still mysterious to them."

"Has religion made any impact?" I said.

"Christianity's never been a strong influence here," said Mr. Thayer. "One of the reasons for closing the country back in the sixteenth century was the quarrels of the European missionaries whose countries were fighting one another. The second-wave Christian movement came in the nineteenth century, when Japan was receptive to new ideas, and this had some success in the upper echelons of society. Many of the universities that were founded at that time were founded as Christian universities. But Christianity missed its greatest opportunity after the last war, when the Japanese had been defeated for the first time and had had their spiritual legs knocked under them. The missionaries who came at that time simply didn't have the intellectual equipment needed.

"However, I should add that the Japanese never have been a religious-minded people, as in the West. There are various sects here, and they all coexist very well. Often a Japanese will find it hard to say what religion he belongs to. He can attend Shinto, Buddhist and Christian ceremonies without any sense of conflict. Most Japanese get married with Shinto rites and buried with Buddhist ones. The bane of the missionaries is that many Japanese are quite happy to call themselves Christians if that's what is wanted.

"But if they don't have much Christianity," said Mr. Thayer, "they do have Christmas. It came in after the war. I guess the business community here got hold of a Macy's account sheet and observed the tremendous growth spiral in December. So now we have Christmas trees and holly and 'Jingle Bells' and carols and tinsel, and the National Radio puts out the *Messiah*. It was a clever move, really, because the

Japanese like giving each other presents during the year, and this has provided the perfect occasion for it."

✪

"Oh, it was blowing here today at Hollywood-by-the-Sea. It was blowing real hard about noon and raining too. But it's great now. As I sit here on the balcony of my suite at the Diplomat Hotel, I can feel a gentle—er—southeast breeze, and the palm trees are swaying in the breeze jes' a little, and the surf comes pounding in on the beach. It's pretty regular, you know; it just comes pounding in and breaks, and goes back. All this restless energy, makes you kinda think! Yessir! Looking at that surf pounding in there makes you wanna drowse. 'S kinda like sittin' and lookin' at the fire in the fireplace. You jes' wanna sit and look at that surf and drowse. . . ."

✪

DAVID JONES was Pan American's chief representative in Tokyo, and was in and out of the Okura all the time. His name sounded Welsh and he looked Welsh, too, a little dark pixie of a man. He said he was often told he looked Welsh, and a long, long time ago his ancestors lived there.

David Jones and I had lunch in the coffee shop, and he said, "I've lived here ten years. I'm an expatriate. The expatriate is the man who doesn't show up at the cocktail party. The people who go to the cocktail parties are those who feel happy when they're together, who look forward to going home. But the expatriate likes it better here. He finds something abroad that he can't find at home. You might call it recognition. As an American in America he'd be just another face in the crowd. But here he can be someone. He can be an individualist. Oh, there's a wonderful freedom living abroad! I don't mean that one has to go native or become wholly Japanese. A man can go on eating hamburgers and hot dogs and still be an expatriate.

"As an expatriate, you become more of a patriot than you ever were at home. You represent the United States, and when people attack the President they're attacking you. I'm not a nationalist—don't get me wrong—but I'm a patriot. I spent most of my early life in San Francisco, but I had to get away from it to see how beautiful it was.

"Let me give you the names of two men who I believe are real expatriates: Ray Falk of ABC, and Ernest Hobericht of U.P.I. You never see them around. They make a lot of money, but it's not that that keeps them here. You wouldn't even know Ray spoke Japanese. He doesn't until there's a crisis, and then he speaks it as though he never spoke anything else. Americans don't like people like that, because they're different. But I admire them, because they don't give a damn. They really don't give a damn.

"You get the big shot who comes here from Des Moines or some place. At home he's a big shot, but here he's nobody. So he latches onto some American who lives here, and then he feels safe and secure. And when he leaves, he says to this guy, 'When you get to Des Moines you must come and look me up, and we'll have a ball.' So a few months later this guy turns up in Des Moines and calls up the big shot's secretary, and the big shot says, 'Oh, yeah, that's the little guy who looked after me in Japan. How long's he going to be here?' And the secretary says two weeks, and the big shot says, 'Jesus!' "

I asked David Jones about American influence in Japan, and he said there were two areas where it was very pronounced. "First, the enthusiasm the Japanese have for American Western movies. I think the reason for it is the similarity between the Western and the Japanese Samurai movie. The American cowboy draws a gun faster than anyone else, and the hero of the Samurai movie wields a sword faster than anyone else. We have a name for this enthusiasm. We call it Ginza Gulch.

"The other thing I would say has transformed Japanese life has been American influence on the Japanese woman. One of the great misconceptions about the Japanese woman is that she's very docile and servantlike. In fact, in every family it's the woman who rules the roost. But with the coming of American TV and movies, the Japanese women have developed a great penchant for being recognized, for men getting up to open the door for them. They call it ladies *fasuto*, which means ladies first. This is altering the habits and way of life of many Japanese men. It's making them courteous and polite to women in a way they never were before. Women are latching onto this outside the house now, too, and wanting chivalrous attention there.

"Of course, the Japanese are great absorbers of other people's culture, and nowhere is this more evident than at a Japanese wedding. The Japanese husband dresses himself in striped trousers and morning coat, and the bride puts on a kimono. It's always a Shinto wedding. After the wedding they have Mendelssohn's 'Wedding March,' then speeches by someone who says jokingly the couple must beware of pitfalls, by the groom's friend, who says what a lad the groom has been, and by the bride, who says what a fine wife she'll make. This is followed by a Western-style banquet and Japanese entertainment. It's really something."

✪

". . . invites you to listen to the story John Birkman."
Ta-ta-ti-tum-tum-ta.
"John? John Birkman? On stage. Curtain's about to go up."
"Here, Father Peter."
"Places, everyone. John, this will be your first appearance, and when you step out from the wings, the audience will most likely applaud you, so don't try to speak until you can be heard."
"I'll remember, Father. Father, it amazes me, no matter how often we enact the story of Susannah and the Elders, the house is packed."
"I think it's because people like to see justice triumph. At the end of the first act, the wicked elders have had everything their own way, and Susannah is condemned to death. Now the audience eagerly awaits for the second act, when Daniel, the young champion, appears as she is being led away, and turns the tables. But come, it's time for the curtain. Up with it!"

✪

HAVE I succeeded in conveying to you the impression of A.F.N. that I have been trying to convey—that my activities in Japan were punctuated by it, that it haunted my daily life? Why switch it on, did you say? Because, for one thing, I am writing a book about Americans and American influence abroad. And anyway, who can resist a good accident? There are some things in life whose attraction lies in their awfulness, which fascinate as much as they repel.

✪

BILL DIXON, whom Mr. Thayer had mentioned, said to me over lunch:

"You don't want to be too hard on A.F.N. It's not for you and me. But for American servicemen who never wanted to go abroad anyway, and now that they are abroad don't want to go outside the compound, it's a great morale-booster. It makes them feel secure and happy. It also has a strong appeal to the Bible-Belt corps—hence all those religious oriented programs. When I was at the embassy we used to have long talks about A.F.N. We tried to persuade them to put on better talks and good music sometimes, but we were never able to bring any influence to bear. They said that if you tried to lift the soldiers too high, they would just switch off and reach for their funnies."

"Well," I said, "I'd like to say two things about that. First, until you've tried better stuff, you don't know what the reaction will be. Secondly, they probably think by 'better' one means Bach and Brahms and talks by George Kennan and Herman Kahn, while what *I* mean is stuff not *all* that different to what they're doing now, but better *presented*. The whole attitude of A.F.N. seems uncompromisingly authoritarian. And when they're not being holier than thou and smug and patronizing, they're dishing out slush of the most repellent kind. They're phony all through, and they haven't an original thought in their heads. They deal entirely in clichés."

Bill Dixon laughed and said, "You seem to have let them get under your skin."

"If I have," I said, "it's only because they've been chasing me from hotel to hotel all the way from Europe. I can never get away from them. For you, as an American, it isn't all that bad. The style isn't much different from what you get at home, and there is the added advantage of no commercials. But to an educated European it is horrible. I suppose what I'm really objecting to is not the thing itself— whether you have it or not is your affair—but the fact that your government has succeeded in persuading all these Eastern governments to let it go out on the public air. The American forces in Britain listen to it the same as anywhere else, but they have it piped underground. If it were sent out on a local wavelength, as it is here, there'd be an outcry. Why can't it be piped everywhere?"

After lunch, I went up to my room, lay down on the bed, and, like any old junkie, reached for the switch.

". . . the words a man uses are the maysure of his mind, or even more than his mind, the maysure of his character, his soul, what he is inside. Said the Master of mankind, 'There is nothing from without a man that entering into him can defile him. It entereth not into his heart. But the things that come out of him, those are they that defile him.' As to the practice of profanity and suggestive, offensive humor and low-minded talk which cometh out of a man, there is this further comment from a widely respected periodical. 'In the name of realism,' it says, 'our playwrights have been subjecting the country to a nauseous overdose of foul language. . . .'

"We have no right to befoul the air or water we use, and we have no more right to befoul the moral atmosphere than we have to befoul the physical atmosphere. Paul said it to the Colossians in these seven terse words, with exceeding sharpness, 'Put filthy communication out of thy mouth!' "

Rum-tum, tum-tum-tee.

"This traditional broadcast from the Mormon Tabernacle on Temple Square is brought to you by the Armed Forces Network, and originates with Radio Station KSL in Salt Lake City. Richard P. Condy conducted the Tabernacle Choir, Alexander Schreiner was at the organ, the spoken word by Richard Evans. In another seven days, at the same hour, music and the spoken word will be heard again from the Crossroads of the West. . . ."

✪

FROM TOKYO, the crossroads of the East, I took the bullet train to Kyoto. The carriages were open-plan and the seats numbered, as on airplanes, three on one side and two on the other. We averaged over 125 miles an hour, but except in the tunnels, which built up terrific pressure on the eardrums, you would never have guessed it. There was some nice scenery too: paddy fields and tea plantations and a good view of Mount Fuji. We stopped at half a dozen stations, two minutes at each, and on arriving and departing the loudspeaker played a tinkly jingle. There was only one buffet car for perhaps a thousand people, and the food and service were quite inadequate. But a dial in the buffet car showed our speed, and another gave the distance from Tokyo.

Kyoto is the ancient capital of Japan, a city of temples and gardens and flowing water, of doll shops, sweetshops, and innumerable restaurants and bars. But I went there to see two lots of Americans: Ruth Sasaki, the Zen priestess, and the Maryknoll Fathers of New York, a group of Catholic missionaries. The one had come to learn from the Japanese an Eastern religion; the others had brought a Western religion in order to teach it to the Japanese.

I visited the Maryknollers first. There had been Maryknollers in Kyoto since the turn of the century. Now there were sixty-five of them ministering to six thousand Catholic Japanese. After the war they had only three churches in Kyoto and a handful of Japanese priests; now they had eleven churches, eighteen Japanese priests, and a Japanese bishop. So some progress had been made. On the other hand, Kyoto was a city of one and a half million people, and what was six thousand among them? Less than half of one percent. On the whole it did not seem very fruitful ground.

I talked with several of the priests, Father Diffley from Brooklyn, Father McDonnell in charge of radio and publications, and Father Casey from San Francisco. They spoke much of Father Hyatt, whom they described as "the greatest missionary of all," but he was on furlough in the States. They all wore suits or informal clothes, and they referred to non-Christians as "pagans," which sounded as patronizing as "aborigines." Their ultimate aim was to convert Japan to Christianity, then sail away to seek fresh pagans elsewhere; but they agreed that this would take time, and they reckoned to be in the country for the rest of their lives.

I saw Father Diffley first. He was a gentle, soft-spoken man in his early forties and had been in Japan for thirteen years, the last seven in Kyoto. He received me in the mission center of Kyoto's poorest parish. He said that he looked after the outcasts; there were three million outcasts living in Japan, he said, in some six thousand outcast communities.

I asked who the outcasts were, and he said, "Traditionally in Japan there were four classes: the warriors, the farmers, the manufacturers, and the traders. Then a fifth class grew up, those who did the work the other classes wouldn't do—the fighting, killing, torturing, cremating, et cetera. When all the fighting was stopped in the seventeenth century by the Shogun Iyeyasu, and society became stratified, the outcasts found themselves out of a job. So they were forced to take on a variety of lowly jobs. They became street cleaners and buriers of the dead, pimps and prostitutes, nightwatchmen and servants and beggars.

"In 1871 the Emperor Meiji declared the word 'outcast' was to be abolished, and they were to be called 'new citizens' instead. But this marked them just as much as 'outcasts,' and today the discrimination against them is as bad as against the untouchables in India, or as by whites against 'coloreds' in many parts of the world. Wherever a Japanese goes, a prospective employer will say to him, 'Let me see your papers!' Now, these papers say exactly where he was born, what street in what city. So then the prospective employer will call up a friend in that city, and the friend will look up the address and say whether it's in an outcast area or not. And if it is, the employer will tell the man there's no job available, or there's only a vacancy for a floor sweeper. And when it comes to marriage, the parents of nonoutcasts will insist on seeing the papers of bride or groom. So, however hard he tries, or whatever talents he may have, it's very difficult for a man who was born an outcast to avoid dying as one."

Father Diffley said the Maryknollers wanted to show the outcasts they were interested in their problems, so six years ago they established themselves in the area. They raised money for the mission center (much of it given by pagans), formed a school there for the children to study for higher schools (study was impossible in the shacks where they lived), and started a dispensary, a credit club and a fund for the needy.

Later we went for a walk through the parish. It was a gray, shabby area of shacks and settlements built on either side of the gray, shallow river Kano, intercut by numerous local railway tracks, and under the shadow of the big viaduct that carried the bullet train from Tokyo to Osaka. Father Diffley said that when he first came to Kyoto he lived here; it had improved since then, he said, because building the bed for the bullet train had meant clearing away some of the worst shacks. He pointed out a couple of modest apartment blocks that had taken their place, but to me these only emphasized the squalor and sadness of what remained. Some of the shacks had TV aerials on them, which looked grotesque; Father Diffley said that TV sets were supplied on the installment plan, and often people couldn't keep up the payments and the sets were taken away. Several times we passed people whom Father Diffley knew, and he nodded and smiled and occasionally had a word with them, in the way priests do. "What sort of things do outcasts do today?" I said as we walked along. "They're day laborers mostly," said Father Diffley. "Road menders, park cleaners, scrap-metal collectors, vegetable dealers, sewage and slaughterhouse workers—the kind of things they've always done."

Walking down an alley between two rows of shacks, we passed a forecourt where a woman was scrubbing clothes at a pump. Father Diffley exchanged a few words with her, and then she rose and led us toward a dark passageway at the back. "We'll just say hello to her husband," said Father Diffley. "You might like to see where they live. She has three children and is almost totally blind with trachoma." There were a number of small rooms opening out on the passageway, and the woman took us to one. It measured about twelve by eight. The husband, a man with a long face and a mop of black hair, was sitting in a corner. Father Diffley said, "He's a road repairer by trade, but I guess he isn't working today. He's a Christian, too, though he doesn't take part in any Christian activities." I looked round the room. Every corner and all available wall space were filled with cupboards and drawers, leaving a tiny space in the center for living in. The place was as clean as the White House. Father Diffley, reading my thoughts, said, "The children are away at school now, but when they come home this is the living, eating and sleeping room for five people."

On the way back to the mission center I said to Father Diffley, "You've told me about the good works you do, but how about the religious side of it? How many Catholics do you have?"

"About sixty." He must have seen the surprise on my face, for he said, "When I first came, there were only thirty."

"Isn't that very disappointing, with all those people belonging to the club, and everything you've done for them?"

"It depends on your priorities," said Father Diffley. "The Japanese aren't interested in buying Christianity as a package deal, and that's not how I want to sell it to them. I regard the first priority as getting these people to lead Christian lives, to know their neighbor and love their neighbor, which are things they haven't done before. They're now beginning to lead Christian lives even if they don't know they are. Eventually we hope this will lead them to God. It's not just preaching that's important nowadays, it's witnessing and living what you believe."

I said, "In that case, could not a social worker do what you're doing just as well?"

"No. The priest here has an entry which the social worker wouldn't have. He has a status. The Japanese may be pagans, but the Catholic Church is respected."

"You hope to convert them all eventually?"

"Certainly. But it'll take time. A hundred or maybe a thousand years."

"Why do you want to convert them? If they're leading Christian lives, isn't that enough?"

"Not quite," said Father Diffley. "You see, we want to make them part of the Mystical Body of Christ. Christianity isn't just a personal thing, it's a corporate thing. The more good Christians there are in the Church, the better it is for the Church—the better it is for everybody."

✪

FATHER MCDONNELL was in charge of radio and publications. He was in his thirties, good-looking in a scholarly way, with an odd habit of speaking out of the side of his mouth. We sat and talked in a small room in a building next to Kyoto's oldest and biggest Catholic church. There was a green-baize-covered table between us, and on it was an ashtray built in the shape of a castle. The central court of the castle was for stubbing out one's cigarette, and one of the towers was a lighter.

Father McDonnell said the Maryknollers were responsible for two religious broadcasting programs which went out on 129 stations. One was called "The Smile of the Sun" and was scripted by Father Hyatt; the other was called "The Light of the Heart" and was the work of a group of five Japanese Catholic writers. "We started this project seven years ago, and at that time the Japanese weren't even interested in selling us air time. Then Father Hyatt made a deal with one station, and he gradually expanded during the next five years to over eighty stations. The Catholic writers didn't come in till much later. Father Hyatt had approached them in the first place, but they turned him down. But they were impressed by what he was doing and they came to him and said, 'Father, we know the Japanese people, it's our business to, and we think they are intelligent enough to take the logical step from goodness to God. Talk about God in the first place and everyone will switch the radio off.'

"So they wrote these scripts according to their format, and after that, requests for information about the Catholic Church soared from an average of two hundred a month to over three thousand. One of the reasons for this success was getting hold of Momoko Kochi to read the scripts. She's a famous actress with a lovely voice. She's not a Catholic, but she knew one of the writers and agreed to do it as a favor."

"How many people listen to these broadcasts?"

"We've been told they reach ten percent of the population, or about ten million people. The programs go out very early in the morning, but we understand that there are a considerable number of people listening at this hour."

"Doesn't buying the time cost you a lot?"

"We get seventy-five percent discount from most of the stations, but we still have to pay around six thousand bucks a month, which is peanuts to a commercial firm, but a lot of money for us. We raise it in different ways. We run an English school here and teach about two thousand students. We also receive money from some five hundred Japanese who aren't even Christians, and that's one of the most amazing sides to this business."

"What are these programs about? What are you trying to say?"

"I would say that we are trying to get our audience to practice the moral virtues they already know, like truth and love. We give them examples of what other Japanese have done to make the world a better place to live in. Buddhism here is no longer a vibrant force, and we tell them we have something to put in its place.

"The whole reason for our being here can be summed up in the parable of the Good Samaritan. The idea of loving one's neighbor is incomprehensible to most of them. Let me give you an example. One of our fathers found a man drunk on a streetcar platform, and his head was lying two feet into the road. The father helped the man back onto the platform, reckoning a truck would run him over if he didn't. There were several people standing by, but they had done nothing. Why? Because they didn't want to get involved, because it was none of their business. People here don't want to help their neighbor, they don't want to enlarge their relationships. Until recently a man here wouldn't dream of changing his job, of leaving his

company, because that meant starting another relationship. Fifty percent of marriages here are still arranged."

"What effect do you think your effort here is having?"

"It depends on what view you take. If you take the short-term view
and think only in terms of numbers of converts, then there isn't too
much to show for it. One of our great problems here can be summed
up in the Japanese word *Isigashii,* which means 'I'm busy.' Busy
working, busy playing, just busy. People here work far harder than in
the West. I live next to a factory and the girls there work from seven
in the morning to seven in the evening, five days a week. They don't
have much free time left over."

"Isn't this disappointing?"

"In some ways it is. We've done a lot of soul-searching as to what is
wrong in our approach. Some have said that the Church is not ready
for Japan, others that Japan is not yet ready for the Church. There
are many missionaries who think our insistence on the primary virtues, on teaching good-neighborliness and the good life, a waste of
time. 'Why don't you go out and preach the gospel,' they say, 'and
convert those who will be converted?' But that's no good in Japan.
The Japanese aren't interested in religion. They don't want to be
converted. At least, not yet."

"Will they ever be?"

"Not for a very long time. Personally, I'm working on a forty-year
plan. I've done five years and I've got thirty-five to go. I've probably
had less results in converting pagans than any priest in Japan, but I
have my eye firmly fixed on the thousand-year vision. If I thought I
was here just to make converts, I'd get out immediately. But there's a
new theology abroad today which says that if you are not a believer,
but lead a good life according to your own lights, then that's okay.
Well, I go along with that. I think a lot of Japanese are going to
heaven. In Matthew 28:19 Christ said, 'Go ye therefore, and teach all
nations,' and if that sentence were not in the Bible, I'd be back in the
States. We aim to get the Church involved in the social life of the
country, to get people to practice love and justice, truth and purity.
Then eventually a day will come when it is a Christian country, and
Japanese priests will take over from us and do a far better job than we
could ever do, and our work will be over."

❂

AND LASTLY I called on Father Casey, an egghead who had an egg head, a bald, shining brittle dome, and the air of an absent-minded professor. His parents were Irish immigrants, and his father, a self-educated man, had worked as a streetcar driver in San Francisco for forty years. Father Casey himself had got a Master's in Scripture at U.C.L.A., a doctorate in Western religion at Harvard, a doctorate in philosophy at the Collegium Angelicum in Rome, and a doctorate in Eastern religions somewhere else. He was said to know more about Indian and Chinese Buddhism than any Westerner living. He spoke French, German, Italian, Chinese, Sanskrit, Latin, Japanese, Pali, and Spanish, and he read the New Testament in the original Greek. In addition to his parochial work, he was teaching the history of Buddhism to students at Kyoto University.

Father Casey had the best parish in Kyoto, six hundred members and a brand-new church. We had arranged to meet outside the church, but he was late for the appointment, having driven his car into a ditch. He seemed none the worse for it. We went into the church, which was very beautiful and of a most unusual herringbone design, the pews at right angles to each other, the altar toward the tail. There was a marvelous golden backcloth of Christ dressed as a Roman emperor, holding a book and saying in big Japanese lettering: "I AM THE WAY, THE TRUTH, THE LIFE." Father Casey said this had been made in Germany. There were also some lovely green curtains on either side of the altar, and long, elegant lamps hanging from the ceiling, and blue walls on which were painted the Stations of the Cross. Father Casey said that the money for the church had been given by a rich parishioner, a Japanese lady who had married a Morgenthau and become a Catholic, and then come back to live in Japan after her husband's death.

Father Casey took me to the presbytery, which he shared with eleven students who were studying at Kyoto University. We went into the students' room, which was empty. "Two were Catholics when they came," said Father Casey, "and two have since become Catholics, and the rest are pagans." There were slogans on the walls which said: "LOVE IS THE BOND OF FRIENDSHIP," and "DISCOVER YOUR HIDDEN TALENTS," and "PUT YOUR HEART INTO THINGS," and there was a photograph too of Father Casey with some of the students on a walking trip. "This is part of our community relations," he said.

Father Casey's own room was lined with books, as you might have expected. I said that the Maryknollers didn't seem to be making much progress in Japan, and what was his comment on that? Then he launched into a great exposition on Catholic history, its origins and growth and triumphs and setbacks. He quoted Saint Augustine and Horace and Teilhard de Chardin and Evelyn Waugh. And then he mentioned a man called Jean Danielou, who had written a book called *Holy Pagans of the New Testament,* and the gist of this was that there were no such things as atheists, only those who didn't know what it was they worshiped. "The more I study of prehistory, the more I feel this statement is true," said Father Casey. "Subconscious discoveries have borne it out. The Doctrine of Implied Faith, as it is called, takes in people who even declare they do not believe. In fact they do believe, but they do not know it."

This was going further than any of the other Fathers had gone. It struck me forcibly as an attempt to explain away and make acceptable the harsh realities of failure. What was it people believed but did not know they believed? The existence of God? Possibly. But did they also unknowingly believe the dogma that was at the basis of Catholic faith, the Holy Trinity, the Immaculate Conception, the Communion of Saints, the Resurrection of the Body, Life Everlasting? Hardly. To these good men, works and faith were indivisible. They simply could not accept that a man could love his neighbor and lead a good life and yet not be a Christian; to allow otherwise would be a denial of all they believed in.

We talked about Eastern religions, and I asked Father Casey if they had anything to offer the West. "I think there is a future for Zen as a psychological therapy," he said, "for both Westerners and Japanese. Zen followers are very calm and peaceful people, but they don't do much to help others. They're selfish. Chardin thinks that deeper charity is necessary, and so does Toynbee. Confucianism stresses the importance of personal relationships, but what the Western ethic stresses is the relationship betwen man and something outside."

I thought, Some would say that was begging the whole question, that what one calls "something outside" is only a description of a thought process in one's own mind. And why the assumption that Zen gave psychological therapy, but Roman Catholicism didn't? If one was to compare extremes, weren't the personal relationships of a calm and peaceful Zen likely to be as socially desirable as those of a Christian fanatic?

As I was leaving I said, "There's an American woman living here who's supposed to be the only foreign-born Zen priestess in Asia."

"Oh, Ruth Sasaki," he said.

"You know her?"

"Yes I do. I like her enormously, but I think she's very insecure. I'm afraid she is made use of by too many weirdies." He paused and said, "I think she may become a Christian. There are indications that way."

✪

Ruth Sasaki lived on the other side of town, in an ancient temple area. She didn't look like one's idea of a Zen priestess at all. She was a septuagenarian with cropped gray hair and alert blue eyes and a roundish face and spectacles. She was dressed in a yellow blouse and blue coat and skirt, and wore a string of pearls and pearl earrings; on her feet she had a pair of homely black slippers.

Her house was in marked contrast to those of the Maryknoll Fathers. They lived in priestly discomfort in gloomy presbyteries little different from those in the West. She lived in an elegant Japanese house, which she had built herself, with an entrance gate and an inner gate, and small, cool rooms with rush matting on the floor and rice-paper windows, and a garden with dripping water and little trees and a temple of meditation. There lived with her five beautiful cats with collars and bells, who were fitting adornments to the general scene, and a little yapping dog called Gomba, who wasn't. With the Maryknoll Fathers there had been an atmosphere of tranquillity, as there always is among those who live quiet lives. There was the same sort of tranquillity here. It was different from that of the Maryknollers, but just how it was different, it was impossible to say.

Ruth Sasaki took me for a walk in the garden, which I would have enjoyed more if Gomba had not kept nipping my ankles; and we looked in at the temple of meditation, which was tall and bare and would have been wonderfully peaceful, I think, if Gomba, locked out, had not kept on yapping outside; and then we walked back to the house, and Ruth Sasaki took me to her study and poured me a glass of sherry and said that dinner would be ready in half an hour.

Ruth Sasaki said, "I was born in Chicago nearly seventy-three years ago, into a strictly Presbyterian family. They attempted to bring me up with a heavy sense of sin, which I resented very much, and which I think had much to do with my subsequent life. However, from the age of childhood up to about seventeen I was a very obedient and conforming child. My father was a grain broker and a very wealthy man, but before he died he lost all his money. He just couldn't believe that gasoline would ever supplant horse power. But before this he had provided very generously for my mother and my brother and myself, and we are still living on his bounty and good judgment. My father was Canadian on both sides, and my mother's father was English from Liverpool, so in some ways I feel closer to England than I do to America. We went to England every year until I was fourteen, and also to Europe, where I learned French and German and studied the piano. I just loved music and I still do."

She talked in a very practical, matter-of-fact way, but with wit and charm, her mind open to the humor of any situation.

"When I was twenty-three, I married a successful Chicago lawyer called Edward Warren Everitt. He was twenty years older than I, but he wasn't interested in music, so music went down the drain. For the next fifteen years I led a very busy life with lots of servants and entertaining and that sort of thing. We had one child, a daughter. I wasn't well after her birth, and the doctor gave me a book on Buddhism, which was something I hadn't thought about till then. I opened the book at random and my eye fell on the line 'In Buddhism there is only one sin, and that is ignorance,' and I was immediately converted. It was as simple as that. I was twenty-five then, and I began to read more books on Buddhism and other books on philosophy and biology and things I hadn't studied at school. Eventually I decided I wanted to read Buddhist texts, so I enrolled at the university to learn Sanskrit.

"Some time after this Mr. Everitt decided to take a long vacation, and we went to China and Japan. On the way back we put in at Kyoto for a day and I was able to meet Dr. Suzuki, who was one of the great Zen teachers. I asked him about this method of meditation and whether he thought it might do for Westerners what it had done for Asiatics. And he said I could only judge that for myself, and I must come and live here and have a teacher. I told him there was no chance of that, I had a big house to look after and a child and a husband. But when I mentioned the matter to Mr. Everitt in the ship going home,

he said, why didn't I come, as he had to return on business the following year, and I could go ahead of him.

"So, during the next eighteen months I learned Japanese from a
student at the university—there were no Japanese teachers at American universities in those days—and then my secretary and I came out
here. We lived in a house in the town, but I spent most of my time in
one of the Zen monasteries, where Dr. Suzuki had arranged for me to
study. I wasn't very welcome, as there had been a few foreigners before me and they had rather messed things up. My teacher made me
come every morning at nine and stay till six to practice meditation. I
wasn't allowed to write or read newspapers or anything. After six
weeks the monks let me come and sit in their own meditation hall. By
this time I was doing up to fifteen hours' meditation daily."

Mrs. Sasaki said she went home with Mr. Everitt at the end of that
year, but was back the following year, this time with her daughter as
well as her secretary. She again took a house in the town, but she lived
mostly in the monastery. "Then Mr. Everitt joined us and we traveled extensively throughout China. But on the way home he became
very strange, and it soon became clear his mind was going. After four
years in sanatoriums he was committed to an asylum in Hartford,
Connecticut. In January 1940 he died.

"Meanwhile, I had moved with my daughter to New York to continue my Zen meditation there. My teacher was Mr. Sasaki, who was
the founder of the first Zen institution in the United States. He was
interned as an enemy alien when war broke out, but was later re-
leased and we were married. Our marriage lasted exactly ten months
and then he died. Before he died, he asked me to come over to
Japan to find another Zen teacher to take his place in New York,
and also to finish a Buddhist text he was translating. And he wanted
me to put a headstone on his mother's grave, which he was never able
to do, and which eventually I'm going to do later this year.

"Well, I decided then that I needed to know a great deal more Zen
before tackling all the problems that would be involved in translating it. So I came back here, first in 1947 for a short visit, and then
again in 1948, and I've been here ever since. It was then that I first
began my studies with the Abbot of Daitokuji, and I studied with
him six days a week for eleven years. I used to get up at four A.M.
every day and take two trams and walk a mile to get to his private
temple. By the end of eleven years I had covered the whole course of
Zen study, and I decided I knew everything I needed for my work. I

knew enough to translate it, and I really was convinced that there was a method of meditation that would work for Westerners."

Mrs. Sasaki's Japanese housekeeper came to tell us that dinner was ready, and Mrs. Sasaki led the way into the dining room. I wondered if we would sit on the floor and was relieved to see table and chairs for three. "My housekeeper eats with me," said Mrs. Sasaki. "She doesn't speak English herself, but if you speak it slowly she will understand you." The housekeeper had cooked a very good dinner: consommé with bits of chicken in it, a fish called *tai,* which tasted like halibut, French beans and peppers and huge half-tomatoes, chunks of watermelon, and slices of orange peel soaked in water and coated with syrup and sugar. After each course I turned to the housekeeper and said slowly how good it had been. She understood, and nodded and smiled. The five cats stood round us waiting for tidbits, which Mrs. Sasaki and the housekeeper freely gave. Gomba wasn't allowed in. He sat in the garden barking. He wasn't a dog conducive to meditation, and I wondered what Mrs. Sasaki saw in him.

After dinner I said to Mrs. Sasaki, "What did you do when you had completed your eleven years?"

"The Abbot wanted me to teach, and at first I resisted him, because I didn't think I was ready for it. In the end I agreed, because the Abbot was being pestered by Westerners who wanted to learn Zen, and the object of my taking it up was to see if I could devise a way of teaching it to foreigners. So I started taking students, and for the last ten years I've had them all the time."

"Who are they?"

"Mostly they're Americans, but I've had them from Israel and Britain and Australia and France and Belgium and Austria. At present I have a Swiss painter, who's been here five years and will be here another four or five more. Then there's an Austrian woman who has been here three years and will be here indefinitely, and an ex-Navy American who's been here two years and will stay another two, and a Frenchwoman who's been here three years and is now my secretary, and a Jewish boy who soon has to go back to the States for his service in the Army. Most of them are young, but I have had ones up to sixty."

"Do they live here?"

"No, they either find their own places or live in the big temple compound at Daitokuji."

"Are there people you refuse?"

"I never take anyone who I know is a practicing Christian. Sometimes missionaries apply. I always turn them down, because I know that if they practice Zen properly, their Christianity will be destroyed. You cannot reconcile Christianity and Zen."

"What *are* the Zen practices? What is it exactly you teach them?"

"The first object is to teach them Zen meditation, or *Zazen*. This takes at least a year to master, because it involves long periods of sitting in the Indian lotus or half-lotus position, which is acutely uncomfortable if you've never done it. When a student has mastered that, he must then become really proficient in Japanese, because the next stage is instruction from *Roshi,* or Zen masters—*Roshi* means literally 'old teachers'—in *koans. Koans* are the *subjects* for meditation."

"Do many fall out?" I said.

She laughed. "All the time. Many of them have no idea what they're letting themselves in for. The majority have read Suzuki on Zen, or various European or American writers who've interpreted Suzuki, but few of these writers have ever tried to practice Zen, and none has succeeded, and a great many haven't even been here. So most books on Zen are nonsense. They give no indication at all of the practical aspects, so when students come here and are told what's expected of them it's often a big shock. I shiver every time they come. The pain of the sitting posture is considerable, and for a long time it requires a great effort of will to go through with it. Many of them can't make it and go home. Those who stay and grit their teeth suffer a great deal."

"How did you become a priest?" I said.

She laughed again, not defensively, but aware of the absurdity of the idea. "The Abbot had no room for the students to meditate at Daitokuji, so I said I would build my own hall of meditation here. There was no difficulty about that, because there used to be a temple on this site before. It was called *Ryosenan,* which means 'Dragon Spring Hermitage.' It was one of the twenty-two smaller temples which were affiliated with Daitokuji. When the meditation hall was completed, the Abbot said the whole compound must now be considered a temple again, because it was devoted to the study of Zen and because the image of Bodhisattva Manjursi was in the center of it; and where there was a temple, there had to be a priest, and who more suitable than me?"

"What did you say to that?"

"I said, 'I will not shave off my hair, and I will not take off my earrings. If you want me to be a priest it'll have to be on those terms.' And he accepted."

It was getting late now. The cats were asleep all round us, and the voice of Gomba was still. "This may sound a stupid question," I said, "but can you tell me briefly, and in words I can understand, just what Zen is?"

"How admirable of you to say you don't know," she said. "So many people come here with their half-baked ideas, thinking they know everything." She paused. "No," she said, "I couldn't. It has taken me a lifetime to understand it, and it's not something you can tell briefly. But I will give you my three books on Zen. They are as short and simple as the subject will allow, and you may learn from them the rudiments of Zen."

"You can't even give me a clue?"

"The only clue I can give you is that line I read when recovering from the birth of my daughter: 'In Buddhism there is only one sin, and that is ignorance.' Zen is learning to educate oneself. I've never stopped educating myself, and that is how I've enjoyed myself and learned to be happy. For me it has all been perfectly natural and simple, and one thing has led to another. In a sense I've had a number of lives. One becomes utterly an agent."

"Can anyone learn Zen?"

"No. This may sound like a snobbish thing to say, but it's only for the rapidly developed person."

"Do you think it has a future?"

"Not in Japan, I'm sorry to say. The younger generation simply don't want to know about it. I would hope, though, that it might still be saved for the West. Its techniques and training are among the most remarkable that man has ever devised. It would be a pity if it were completely lost. The present rash of interest in it by beatniks and hippies has done it a great disservice. If it ever does seriously take root in the West, it will have to be very freely adapted. But it could profoundly influence Western thinking."

"Would you call Zen a religion?"

"Yes. It is a religion in the profoundest sense of the word."

"What do you think of other religions?"

"I think they're mostly based on expediency. Christianity is certainly expedient. I find it an utterly unbelievable religion. I don't believe in a God who created the universe. As a child I was infuriated at being told my animals wouldn't go to heaven with me, nor the poor natives in Africa. What original sin is, I don't know to this day. We all make mistakes and pay the consequences and have to bear the burden of other people's actions. But I certainly don't believe that Jesus was the only begotten son of God. Such a belief has no validity or relevance in everyday modern life. It has no validity at all."

"Then there's no likelihood of you ever reverting to Christianity?"

"Good heavens, no! Whoever suggested that?"

"Father Casey."

She smiled delightedly. "Father Casey is a very dear and clever man," she said, "but *terribly* confused. He just doesn't know *where* he is."

On the way back to Tokyo in the bullet train I kept thinking of Ruth Sasaki and the holy fathers. The religion that the Maryknollers had brought to Japan, and to which the Japanese were showing such indifference, was one that the West itself was also largely rejecting. The religion that Ruth Sasaki was preaching to a few Westerners disillusioned with their own was one the Japanese were rejecting, and even she agreed it was unlikely to be popular in the West. Religion as a topic still fascinated; but individual theologies were everywhere in decline. Clearly the Maryknollers and the followers of Zen believed profoundly in what they were doing. Both were certain they had found the truth, and both may have done so, for truths in this area cannot be measured, only apprehended in the heart. Perhaps the Lord Buddha was right, the only sin was ignorance. After that you had to chart your own course, seek your own truth, do your own thing.

✪

THE SUNDAY before I left Tokyo, I went down to the coast to see an American called Horace Bristol. He was a retired *Fortune* and *Life* photographer, married to a Japanese, and had been living in Japan since 1947.

I boarded a local train at Shimbashi station, and found myself next to an American called Howard, who was with his Japanese wife and their two children, Arthur, four, and Juliet, two. He was a civilian working for the American Army in Korea and had met his wife while she was working at the American embassy in Tokyo. Both children looked Japanese rather than American. "We named Juliet after the character in the play," said Howard. "To me the name sums up the essence of womanhood." I glanced at Juliet, who was picking her nose. "My wife speaks to them in English most of the time," said Howard, "so they don't know too much Japanese." He smiled. "Like me."

I thought Howard and Mrs. Howard and Arthur and Juliet might be fruitful territory for the book, but as soon as Howard discovered I was a writer he hardly allowed me another word. Did I write just when I felt like it, or when the mood came on? Was it an effort to write? How many hours did I write a day? How did I think of things to write about? When he had pumped me dry in this direction, he told me of a friend of his who was always going to write a book, but never did. "He read a tremendous lot, this guy. He'd quote from books all the time, but he never got around to writing his own. I've often thought I'd like to write a book myself." I half expected him to tell me about it, like the man who meets a doctor at a cocktail party and gives the state of play of his gut, thinking the doctor will be interested. I said, what was the friend doing now, and Howard said, "He's a librarian in a mental home." He didn't bat an eyelid when he said this, so I couldn't tell whether the friend was an inmate or not.

I got off at a station called Zushi and took a taxi to Miura, which was a charming little fishing port, with some white-painted ships lying in the harbor. Here I called up Mr. Bristol, who sent another taxi. This took me to a sort of quarry at the foot of a hill, beyond which lay the sea. Horace Bristol was waiting for me. He looked in his fifties and was casually dressed in a blue shirt, gray shorts and brown boots. He had a white goatee, thin tousled hair, a tomato complexion and very blue eyes.

Horace Bristol led me up a steep path to the cliff top, where he had built a country cottage. The view was terrific. Below us, hundreds of feet it seemed, was the sea, silver and lead and streaked with marbling, and scattered over it and in it the fishing boats the size of tops, like birthday-cake ornaments set in icing sugar. There was a strong wind coming in from the sea, which made it cool, and the roar of the surf came to us dully from the rocks below. Away to the right stood Fujiyama. Ahead of us, sea and sky made a thin horizon, and beyond that the great Pacific rolled, all the way to America. Soon I would be there.

We went inside, to a comfortable low room, where you still had the view from the comfort of chairs. Mrs. Bristol came to meet me. She was in her thirties, dressed in a green silk blouse and green trousers, and without make-up. Horace called her Musako. She was very sweet. She brought in a jug of Bloody Mary, and Horace and I sat by the window and looked at the view and drank the Bloody Mary and talked.

Horace said he had been born in Whittier, California, the place where President Nixon once lived. He had studied architecture after graduating, but hadn't learned much. He said he had never learned much, not even Japanese. He had joined *Fortune* as a photographer in 1934, and *Life* later, and he had covered the war as an officer in the Navy. He came to Japan for *Fortune* in 1947. "Of course, in those days a correspondent assigned to the occupation army had it really good. He could go almost anywhere he wanted, and there was no end of stories to choose from. I was given a house and five servants, and I brought my first wife up from Australia, which was more than some did." He completed his contract with *Fortune,* then set up his own agency.

Musako brought gherkins and cocktail biscuits, and Horace said, "I started building this place in 1947. It was just a couple of rooms then, a weekend retreat. Later, with my architect knowledge, I built some more houses around here, and as time went on they rose tremendously in value. So I began renting them out, and now that's the major part of my income. I eventually handed over the agency to my son by my first marriage—he also married a Japanese girl—and now I just do two or three stories a year."

"How do you get on with your neighbors?"

"I made one big mistake," said Horace, "and I haven't entirely got over it yet. When General MacArthur was here at the time of the occupation, they made a new law whereby fishermen could purchase the fishing rights of the part of the sea where they lived. Previously these had always been in the hands of the owners. Well, the fishermen here in Miura needed six thousand dollars, which was a lot of money in those days. Some of the elders came and asked if I would lend them the money, and they would pay ten percent interest. Now, I didn't want to make money out of these people, I wanted to live among them as friends. So I told them I'd lend them the money without interest. They didn't want this, but I was firm. I told them those were my conditions and they could take it or leave it.

"Well, they went away and had a talk and came back and said they could accept my terms. They had a very good catch that year—this port is one of the world's largest centers for tuna fishing—and they returned the money after only six months. Then they wanted to give me a present. I said that was very kind of them, but I didn't want a present, didn't they have a youth organization or something they could make a donation to instead? Yes, they said, they had a youth organization, but I would have to donate the money, not they. So that was how it was done. They gave the money to me, and I gave it to the youth organization. It was a question of face. The mistake I had made was not charging the interest they had suggested, and though it was all a long time ago, some of them haven't forgiven me yet. I had committed the sin of what they call *on*, which is giving a gift or concession so big the recipient feels under an obligation. Well, I learned my lesson. I'd never make that mistake again. I don't say I'd charge ten percent, but I'd certainly charge something."

I thought it odd that even an intelligent American like this simply couldn't understand that no one likes charity, however pure the motive.

Musako gave us lunch—artichokes, cold salmon and tongue, rice and cheese and cold beer. We ate off thick, burnished plates, which Horace said had been made locally for two thousand years. On shelves in the dining recess were Japanese death masks and primitive figures and a small stone Buddha. Halfway through lunch a man arrived from Yokohama to fix the fridge. He started to take off his shoes at the door, then saw it wasn't that kind of establishment, and put them on.

After lunch we went back to the window, and I told Horace about my trip to Kyoto and Ruth Sasaki and the Maryknoll Fathers trying to get the locals to love their neighbors.

Horace said, "In Japan the family is everything and friends are nothing. A lot of Westerners never get to understand this. In the West we take our family relationships for granted. Sometimes I think we feel a greater loyalty to our friends than to our families. The Japanese don't feel obligations to friends at all."

"What would you say about American-Japanese mixed marriages?" I said. This was really what I had come to ask him.

"Ours is okay," said Horace. "At least I think it is." He looked at Musako and she smiled. "But a lot have folded."

"Why?"

"Class, mainly. Often during the occupation a lower-class American boy would fall in love with a higher-class Japanese girl. Everything was okay while they were here, but she just wasn't prepared to accept the kind of life that was waiting for her in the States."

"Have you thought of going back to the States?"

"Yes, we have. I like it here; I think this is a wonderful country. But Musako wants to go and live in New York and breathe and be herself and not have any worries."

"What are her worries?"

"They're mostly about the land on these properties I have. Land isn't clearly divided here, and there are endless disputes about boundaries, and as I don't speak good enough Japanese, Musako deals with it for me."

Musako brought coffee. She alighted beside us like a pretty green butterfly.

"Have you known each other very long?" I said.

"I guess so," said Horace. He looked at Musako and said, " 'Course, there was a time when she was frightened of me."

"Frightened?"

"Frightened of all Americans. Her mother believed the Japanese wartime propaganda, and so when the war was over and she heard the Americans were coming, she sent her daughter to Hokkaido to escape a fate worse than death."

"She didn't send me far enough," said Musako. It was almost the first thing she said.

"No," said Horace. "She lost out after all."

I said, "In your relationship with each other, are there any areas where there is complete misunderstanding?"

Horace said, "Musako, where do we misunderstand each other most?" She smiled and said nothing, and he turned back to me and said, "I guess in the matter of words. We can use the same words, but they don't always mean the same. For Musako some words have a different connotation, a different background, than for me. Then again, logic is not a Japanese strong point. They aren't logical at all. And their idea of truth is quite different from ours. A Japanese will tell a lie to spare your feelings, not realizing that when you've found out you will be much more hurt. Sometimes I get really mad at them for this. But I guess East is East and you'll never change it. I told you my son is married to a Japanese girl, and he finds the same. I accept a lot of Musako's prejudices, but the silliest ones I won't tolerate at all, will I, Musako?"

He had an odd attitude toward her, love and protectiveness and hostility mixed.

She smiled again, and I was about to ask what her silliest prejudices were, when a woman came in with a tiny, bubbly baby.

"Our daughter," said Horace proudly.

Musako took the baby from the woman. She was a sweet baby, giggly and gurgly and happy.

"How old is she?" I said.

"Nine months," said Horace. "Fourteen years younger than my eldest grandchild."

"What do you call her?"

"Autumn. She was born in the autumn, and she came in the autumn of my life."

He leaned forward to touch the baby with his finger, and for a few moments he and Musako forgot I was there. I looked at the three of them, heads together, the American man, the Japanese woman, the American-Japanese child. I took an exposure of them with my eyes, froze them on my retina, captured the conversation piece for all time. And I thought then, as I have since, this is how it could be and should be, and ultimately, if there is to be peace on earth, how it will have to be. We must be encouraged to intermingle, intermarry, interbreed; and when we have done it long enough, in perhaps a thousand or two thousand years' time, longer than the Maryknollers need to convert the pagans of Japan, we shall all be as one, variations on a theme of burnt sienna, like the Cariocas today. But right now the black panthers and white panthers and yellow panthers are with us, trembling with the knowledge of their own inadequacies, prisoners of the ghettos of their minds, vibrant with fear and hate; and, oh God, the bloodshed and degradations and horrors we shall all have to live through first!

✪

In the darkness the Pan Am Boeing taxied to the end of the runway, and the old dear beside me in the window seat got out her handkerchief and started waving to her friends in the airport building, already far out of sight. She went on waving as we whizzed down the runway and took off, over the big neon signs saying "SONY" and "MITSUBISHI" and "SANYO," and she was still waving a thousand feet over Tokyo Bay.

On my other side was a short, stubby man who looked a little like Pierre Salinger, and across the aisle was his wife. At the end of dinner he eyed me in a curious way and then said, "Excuse me, but are you not going to eat your cheese?" "No," I said, "would you like it?" "Thank you," he said, "I'm just crazy about cheese."

When he was through with the cheese, I asked where he was going. "My wife and I," he said, "have just been to Japan for a vacation, and now we're going home to Hawaii. That was one of the best vacations I ever had. The fares were pretty steep—six-twenty a round trip—but it's real cheap when you get there, provided you keep off the tourist track. We stayed a month and it only cost thirteen hundred dollars all told. I don't believe we stayed in an American-type hotel more than twice. It was strictly Japanese inns all the way. We used to get two rooms and a sitting room for as little as five dollars. The beds were on the floor, but they were real comfortable. There'd be a Japanese-style bath, an icebox with beer, fruit juice and crabmeat and anything else we wanted. It was real nice. The food was fantastic and cheap too; sometimes we'd get meals as low as a dollar. The fish was really something. One week I ate nothing but fish every meal. We went everywhere, from one end of the country to the other. We did the inland sea voyage. We went second, third, and even fourth class. We were with Japanese people nearly all the time."

"What made you go there?"

"I was there in the Army in 1951, and I made a lot of Jap friends. There was a trucking family I made real friends with, father, mother, and five sons. When I went back this trip, it was like old times. All the sons were married, so that made another five families to visit. Oh, Japan's the country, I tell you. Better than Europe. But you have to get off the beaten track, get to know your way around."

We settled down to sleep, and the big jet took us through the night, and lost us a day in the process, and then, almost before we had rubbed the sleep from our eyes, we were landing at Honolulu. I stayed a couple of days there, but I can't say I liked it. I went over to Pearl Harbor, as a former Navy man should, and thought of the time when the Japanese planes with their polite little pilots had come skimming over the hills in the early morning light, fire and thunder in their bellies. I bathed at Waikiki Beach, but there are better places. Like Blackpool and Coney Island and Ostia, the place was dreadfully overcrowded with mostly unattractive people: *lumpen* youths in sneakers, groups of spinsters in *mumus*, paterfamiliases rigid with exhaustion, and old people in sports clothes, which always gives me the creeps.

But we had a lovely trip to the States, free pineapple juice at the airport with the compliments of Hawaii, free champagne in the Boeing with the compliments of Pan Am. Across the aisle from me were three handsome teen-agers, two brothers and a sister in their late teens, on the way home from vacation; Mom and Dad sat several rows ahead. The elder brother, by the window, wrote letters, but the other two had a gay time playing cards, teasing each other, lapping up all the free champagne they could get. She was a lovely, fleshy girl with honey-colored hair and white teeth and plump breasts, like an ad for bras or camping. Sometimes her brother got so mad with her teasing, he put his arms on hers and shook her, like a child, and then they both giggled. It was odd to see two such attractive people being so intimate and happy with each other without any sexual awareness. Once Mom came clucking down the aisle to see they weren't having too much of the free champagne. "Mom, we just had one glass, I swear," the boy said. He pointed to me. "I gave my second glass to this gentleman here, didn't I, sir?" I smiled. "And Shirley, she gave her second glass to Tom, didn't you, Shirl? Honest Mom, cross my heart I'm not lying." Later Mom brought a Scrabble board and said, "Why don't you play an interesting game instead of those stupid cards?" The boy took the Scrabble board politely and, when Mom had gone, put it under the seat.

There was one person on the plane I wanted to talk to before journey's end. This was the air hostess who had served me drinks, a pretty, English-looking girl with deep-set brown eyes and a wide, generous mouth, who looked about thirty and said she had been with Pan Am seven years. Many times on my travels I had wondered about the lives of these American stewardesses abroad. What sort of existence did they have? What did they think of the passengers, how did passengers behave toward them? I made a date with her, and after lunch, while the plane was sleeping, I went down the aisle and joined her at the back.

Her name was Blanche, and she was a senior stewardess. Her family came from Czechoslovakia, her widowed mother lived in Chicago, and she herself had a flat in San Francisco, which was her present base. She spoke with more of an English than an American accent, and she was very feminine in a European way, gentle and passive.

"What about the passengers?" I said. "How do they look from your end?"

"The Japanese are the quietest," she said. "They never ask for anything. They wouldn't complain if you didn't give them a meal for two days. One time I had a Japanese faint in the aisle, and his two friends just sat there and looked at him and did nothing. So I said, 'Aren't you his friends?' and they said yes, but they never moved. You can't tell whether they're angry or happy or depressed or what. The Americans, on the other hand, make themselves heard. If they don't like something, boy, you soon hear about it. The English are that way, too."

"Are they?"

"I know you're English, and I hope you don't mind my saying this, but I believe I've had more bitter complaints from the English than from the Americans. I've been really surprised how short and snappy the English can be. I've had English people on the flight write out letters of complaint to the president of Pan Am, and then give them to me. Some of these have been so unreasonable I don't think my bosses would pay much attention to them."

"What are they about?"

"Well, one Englishman got really mad because we were having lifeboat drill at a time when he wanted to wave goodbye out of the window. That kind of thing. On the other hand, we have many English stewardesses, and I haven't met one I didn't like. They have a tremendous sense of humor and say the funniest things with a straight face. They keep me in stitches. I don't believe they're typically British. We have some German stewardesses, but they're apt to be bossy and aggressive, and the pursers don't like them. And then we have a few Scandinavian girls, and they're very reserved and quiet. I like the British the best."

"I've heard some Americans say they make better stewardesses than American girls."

"Well, Americans don't make naturally good servants anywhere— in restaurants or hotels it's the same. But it's not true about all of them. I know one American stewardess who just loves looking after passengers. She says that so long as she can make one passenger happy, that is all she wants."

"Do you ever get really rude passengers?"

"Sometimes we get passengers who are rude without meaning to be, like the Latin Americans who go 'Ps-s-st!' when they want service instead of ringing the bell. When I was on that run we used to make a joke about it and say, 'We've got another snake on board.'

"But there are others who are deliberately rude, and you can meet them on any trip. Mostly they jump at us for reasons which have nothing to do with ourselves. They've been charged excess baggage, they haven't been able to get a window seat, they've had a row with their wives, or a bad day at the office. So they take it out on us. They use anything from sarcasm to profanity. This worried me terribly when I first joined, and I often used to end up in tears, but now I take no notice. There was a new girl in tears the other day. She said a sailor had deliberately put out his foot to trip her up. I said, 'Do you think he did it *deliberately?*' I'm sure he didn't, but I couldn't convince her. I used to be like that in the beginning."

"Do passengers make passes?"

"Not nearly as much as most men seem to think. I've been asked that question more times than I've had passes made at me."

"Do they date you?"

"Sometimes. Sometimes a stewardess will go out to dinner with a passenger or a group of passengers, and I do know two girls who are notorious for making a play for passengers. A few girls have married passengers, but very few. I dated a courier steadily for a year, but I would say that ninety percent of the girls who are dating steady aren't dating with passengers."

"How about the crew?"

"There are quite a lot of affairs between stewardesses and crew. Some of the young stewardesses idolize the captains—make father figures out of them. There've been a few cases recently of captains who've been married for twenty years divorcing their wives and marrying twenty-one-year-old stewardesses. Some of the foreign girls come over looking for an American husband, and will latch onto any eligible crew member. They have a real edge on the American girls."

She went away to get a passenger a couple of aspirins, and when she came back she said, "I'll tell you a funny thing about the passengers. I go up and down the aisle perhaps thirty times on a long flight, so the passengers get far more opportunity to see what I look like than *I* do with a hundred and twenty of *them*. And yet, when my chores are over and I go into town, I find I recognize their faces more often than they remember mine. Walking down the main street in Honolulu, I'll pass people who've been my passengers and smile at them, and I can see them thinking, Who the hell is that?"

"When you have a day or two off abroad," I said, "what do you do?"

"I do a lot of sightseeing. Most girls aren't too interested in sightseeing, but I love it. Then, I've made friends with quite a few people in various cities, Americans mostly but others as well. Filipinos are very friendly and often invite stewardesses to their homes—I think they do it to impress. The Japs never ask you to anything. They're the most silent people I've ever met. I like them better than I used to, though. I think they're very sincere. I've been in Japan once or twice when they've organized anti-American processions, and there've been people yelling and screaming outside the hotel window, and we've asked the waiter what was going on, and he's said, 'Oh, nothing much, just high spirits'—to save our feelings."

"What strikes you most about other Americans abroad?"

"They get gypped—short-changed—all the time. They don't understand the language, and they can't figure out the money, and people take advantage of it. I've seen it happen often. Only the other day I saw a bus driver short-change two lots of Americans. I heard them discussing it with each other in very loud voices, but in the end they couldn't be bothered to do anything. I think Americans are inclined to make themselves noticeable when they're abroad, they don't merge into the background like other people do, and I've met foreigners who resent this. They say that Americans abroad are quite different from Americans in the States."

The voice of the captain came over the intercom, telling us that the weather at Los Angeles was good, and we'd be there in just under an hour.

I said, "You say you've been with Pan Am seven years. What made you first join?"

"Do you really want to know?"

"Yes."

"Well, I was at San Juan, Puerto Rico, with two friends on vacation. I was a secretary at the time, in Chicago. We were in the hotel lobby when a Pan Am crew came in, and then later we met two of them and they asked us if we'd like to go to a party. That seemed to me then to be just about the most glamorous thing I had ever heard of, going to a Pan Am crew party, meeting people who were flying to Rio and Buenos Aires and New York and everywhere.

"Well, one of them said to me, 'Why don't you join Pan Am?' and I thought, Why not? So when I got home I said to my mother, 'I'm going to join Pan Am.' She didn't think I was serious, but I was. I took Spanish lessons for six months, and then I applied and went before a board. They said I spoke excellent Spanish, which really wasn't true, but I don't think they knew much Spanish themselves. Then they said, did I speak any other language, and when I said yes, Czech, they were really delighted, not expecting it, and I went down to Miami and started training. And you know, about a year later I met the same crew I had met in Puerto Rico, and reminded them it was they who had made me join, and they didn't remember a thing about it."

"Seven years is a long time," I said. "Do you enjoy it as much now as when you started?"

"No, not as much. It used to have glamour in the old days, but it doesn't now. Now I go through the routine mechanically. It's a job, like any other. In many ways it's a satisfying job, and it's well paid too. Yet one isn't really doing it *for* anybody. It doesn't have a point any more."

"How about your apartment in San Francisco?"

"I quite enjoy that, but it can be a letdown when you've been with people for days. The place is empty and there's no one to greet you. You feel very much alone."

"You sound as though you'd had enough."

"I think I've had enough flying. I really do."

"What would you like instead?"

She smiled and said, "What every woman wants, I suppose. Someone to come back to. Children. Staying put."

I looked at her pretty, gentle face and thought, It's incredible that you haven't got it long before now. I said, "I hope you get it soon."

✪

THE COAST came up, brown and hazy, and the plane skimmed over the lime-green sea and landed. As we came to a stop, the younger brother across the aisle took his sister's hands in his, looked deep into her eyes and said, "Darling, you know this means goodbye"—and they both had a last giggle.

Next morning I was to fly over the Pole to London, so I went to a nearby motel. A boy showed me to my room, put down my bags, and turned on the television. Sound and picture came through, and a man in close-up said: "Have you got bad breath? Most people have bad breath."

Had I? Did they? There was no other country in the world that could greet you quite like that. Truly I was back at home plate.

ABOUT THE AUTHOR

Born in Edinburgh of Scottish parents, Ludovic Kennedy was educated at Eton and Oxford and served in the Royal Navy during World War II, mostly in destroyers. Since then he has been engaged in free-lance writing, broadcasting and journalism and is today one of Britain's best-known television commentators. In that role he has covered many worldwide assignments, including American Presidential conventions and elections. He knows the United States rather well, for in addition to his many broadcasts from this side of the Atlantic, he motored completely around the country one year in the wake of the Royal Ballet when his wife, Moira Shearer, was its leading ballerina.

One of his previous books, Ten Rillington Place, *gave rise to the setting up of a special inquiry into a celebrated murder case in which a wrongly accused man had been convicted and executed. As a result of the inquiry the Queen granted a posthumous free pardon—an absolutely unique act in British justice.*

The Kennedys have three daughters and a son and they live in the Border country of Scotland, not far from where Sir Walter Scott wrote his great works.